The Bodhisattva's Practice of Moral Virtue

Kalavinka Press
8603 39th Ave SW / Seattle, WA 98136 USA
(www.kalavinkapress.org)
Kalavinka Press is associated with the Kalavinka Dharma Association, a non-profit organized exclusively for religious educational purposes as allowed within the meaning of section 501(c)3 of the Internal Revenue Code. Kalavinka Dharma Association was founded in 1990 and gained formal approval in 2004 by the United States Internal Revenue Service as a 501(c)3 non-profit organization to which all donations are tax deductible.

To refrain from doing any manner of evil,
to respectfully perform all varieties of good,
and to purify one's own mind—
This is the teaching of all buddhas.

The Ekottara Āgama Sūtra (T02 n.125 p.551a 13–14)

A Note on the Proper Care of Dharma Materials

Traditional Buddhist cultures treat books on Dharma as sacred. Hence it is considered disrespectful to place them in a low position, to read them when lying down, or to place them where they might be damaged by food or drink.

Kalavinka Press books are printed on acid-free paper.
Cover and interior designed by Bhikshu Dharmamitra.
Printed in the United States of America

The Bodhisattva's Practice of Moral Virtue

The Brahmā's Net Sutra Bodhisattva Precepts & Nāgārjuna on the Perfection of Moral Virtue

As Translated into Chinese by Tripiṭaka Master Kumārajīva
Annotated English Translation by Bhikshu Dharmamitra

Kalavinka Press
Seattle, Washington
www.kalavinkapress.org

Edition: BPMV-SA-2024-1.0 / Kalavinka Buddhist Classics Book 16
Paperback ISBN 9781935413387 / PDF ebook ISBN 9781935413394
LCCN 2024019418 (print) | LCCN 2024019419 (ebook)

Library of Congress Cataloging-in-Publication Data

Names: Kumārajīva, -412? translator. | Dharmamitra, Bhikshu, translator. | Nāgārjuna, active 2nd century. Mahāprajñāpāramitāśāstra. Chinese. | Nāgārjuna, active 2nd century. Mahāprajñāpāramitāśāstra. English.

Title: The bodhisattva's practice of moral virtue : The Brahmā's net sutra bodhisattva precepts & Nāgārjuna on the perfection of moral virtue / as translated into Chinese by Tripiṭaka master Kumārajīva ; annotated English translation by Bhikshu Dharmamitra.

Other titles: Brahmā's net sutra bodhisattva precepts | Fan wang jing pu sa jie ben. Chinese.

Description: Seattle, Washington : Kalavinka Press, [2024] | Series: Kalavinka Buddhist classics ; book 16 | Compilation of two works; the first consists of a Chinese translation of Fan wang jing pu sa jie ben preserved in India and transmitted to China by the Indian Tripiṭaka master Kumārajīva in approximately 406 AD along with a modern English translation; the second work consists of Chinese and English versions of selections from Ārya Nāgārjuna's Mahāprajñāpāramitā Upadeśa previously published in Dharmamitra's 2009 publication entitled Nāgārjuna on the six perfections. | Includes bibliographical references. | Parallel English and Chinese text, originally translated from Sanskrit. | Summary: ""The Bodhisattva's Practice of Moral Virtue" is an English translation of two of the most important Buddhist canon textual sources for understanding the universal standards of moral conduct which reigned throughout nearly the entire history of Mahayana Buddhism in China, Korea, and Japan. Part one of "The Bodhisattva's Practice of Moral Virtue" consists of Bhikshu Dharmamitra's English translation of the Chinese-language "Brahma's Net Sutra Bodhisattva Precepts" (Taisho Tripitaka No. 1484, fascicle 2, pages 1003a15 thru 1010a23) together with a translation of the semi-monthly bodhisattva precepts recitation ceremony also drawn from the Taisho Tripitaka. Part Two consists of the same translator's English translation of Arya Nagarjuna's explanation of the Perfection of Moral Virtue (sila paramita) drawn from the Chinese translation of his Mahaprajna-paramita-upadesa or "Exegesis on the Mahaprajna-paramita Sutra," (Taisho Tripitaka No. 1509, pages 153b02 thru 164a27)"-- Provided by publisher.

Identifiers: LCCN 2024019418 (print) | LCCN 2024019419 (ebook) | ISBN 9781935413387 (paperback) | ISBN 9781935413394 (adobe pdf)

Subjects: LCSH: Buddhist monasticism and religious orders--Rules. | Buddhist precepts. | Bodhisattva stages (Mahayana Buddhism) | Buddhist ethics.

Classification: LCC BQ1100 .B63 2024 (print) | LCC BQ1100 (ebook) | DDC 294.3/444--dc23/eng/20240712

LC record available at https://lccn.loc.gov/2024019418
LC ebook record available at https://lccn.loc.gov/2024019419

Dedication

Dedicated to the memory of the selfless and marvelous life of the Venerable Dhyāna Master Hsuan Hua, the Guiyang Ch'an Patriarch and the very personification of the bodhisattva's six perfections.

Dhyāna Master Hsuan Hua

宣化禪師

1918–1995

About the Chinese Text

This translation is supplemented by inclusion of Chinese source text on verso pages in both traditional (above) and simplified (below) scripts. For the traditional character version variant readings from other canonical editions are found as an appendix in the back of each section of the book and, where I have incorporated those variants into the translation, they are usually signaled with an endnote along with my rationale for making the emendation.

For Part One, "The Brahmā's Net Sutra Bodhisattva Precepts," the traditional-character Chinese text and its variant readings are from the 2004 version of the Chinese Buddhist Electronic Text Association's digital edition of the Taisho Buddhist canon whereas the simplified-character Chinese text is from an online edition of the Qianlong Chinese Buddhist Canon, the URL for which is specified on the first page of that text.

For the Part One Supplement, "The Semimonthly Bodhisattva Precepts Recitation Ceremony," the traditional-character Chinese text is from the April, 2009 version of CBETA whereas the simplified-character Chinese text is from an online edition the URL for which is specified on the first page of that text.

For Part Two, "Nāgārjuna on the Perfection of Moral Virtue," the traditional-character Chinese text is from the 2004 version of the Chinese Buddhist Electronic Text Association's digital edition of the Taisho Buddhist canon whereas the simplified-character Chinese text is from an online edition of the Qianlong Chinese Buddhist Canon, the URL for which is specified on the first page of that text.

Those following the translation in either the traditional Chinese version or the simplified Chinese version should be aware that the punctuation originates with anonymous editors, is not traceable to original editions, and is not necessarily especially reliable, hence it is best treated as merely advisory. (In any case, accurate reading of Classical Chinese should never depend too strongly on a previous editor's punctuation.)

Outlining in This Work

With the exception of the chapter titles for Chapters 21 through 23 in Part Two, "Nagarjuna on the Perfection of Moral Virtue," all outline headings in Part Two originate with the translator. Buddhist canonical texts are often so structurally dense that they are best navigated with the aid of at least a simple outline structure such as I have supplied here.

Acknowledgments

I owe many thanks to those who collaborated with me in producing this translation, first of all my good Dharma friend, Craig Neyman, who retyped my 1973 typescript draft into a digital document suitable for revision. Also, the accuracy and readability of this translation have been greatly enhanced by many corrections, review comments, and editorial suggestions generously contributed by Feng Ling, Nicholas Weeks, and Shuyu Yang, each of whom reviewed the manuscript and made very useful suggestions that I found invaluable in improving the quality of this final translation.

Were it not for the ongoing material support provided by my late guru's Dharma Realm Buddhist Association and the serene translation studio provided by Seattle's Bodhi Dhamma Center, creation of this translation would have been much more difficult.

Additionally, it would have been impossible for me to produce this translation without the Dharma teachings and personal inspiration provided to me by my late great spiritual guide, the awesomely wise and compassionate Dhyāna Master Hsuan Hua, the Guiyang Ch'an Patriarch, Dharma teacher, and exegete.

List of Abbreviations

FZ – Fazang (法藏) – 梵網經菩薩戒本疏 (T40n1813)

PDB – Princeton Dictionary of Buddhism

ZH – Zhuhong, a.k.a. Yunqi Zhuhong (雲棲袾宏) – 梵網經心地品菩薩戒義疏發隱 (X38n0679)

ZY – Zhiyi (智顗) – 菩薩戒義疏 (T40n1811)

ZX – Zhixu, a.k.a. Ouyi Zhixu (蕅益智旭) – 佛說梵網經菩薩心地品合註 (X38n0694)

The Bodhisattva's Practice of Moral Virtue

General Table of Contents

Dedication 5

About the Chinese Text 6

Outlining in This Work 6

Acknowledgments 7

List of Abbreviations 8

General Table of Contents 9

Translator's Introduction 11

Introduction Endnotes 18

Part One: The Brahmā's Net Sutra Bodhisattva Precepts 19

- Part One Table of Contents 21
- Preface to The Brahmā's Net Sutra Bodhisattva Precepts 23
- The Brahmā's Net Sutra, Chapter Ten, Fascicle Two 27
- The 10 Major Bodhisattva Precepts 37
- The 48 Minor Bodhisattva Precepts 45
- Part One Endnotes: 99
- Part One Supplement: The Precepts Recitation Ceremony 123
- Recitation Ceremony Endnotes 133
- Part One Bibliography 135
- Part One Glossary 137
- Part One Variant Readings in Other Chinese Editions 143

Part Two: Nāgārjuna on the Perfection of Moral Virtue 153

- Part Two General Table of Contents 155
- Part Two Directory to Chapter One Subchapters 157
- Ch. 1, Subchapter 21 – Explanation of the Meaning of Śīla Pāramitā 163
- Ch. 1, Subchapter 22 – On the Details and Import of the Precepts 181
- Ch. 1, Subchapter 23 – The Meaning of the Praise of Śīla Pāramitā 253
  - Subchapter 23, Pt. 1 – Additional Precept Specifics 253
  - Subchapter 23, Pt. 2 – On the Perfection of Moral Virtue 267
- Part Two Endnotes 297
- Part Two Bibliography 301
- Part Two Glossary 303
- Part Two Variant Readings in Other Chinese Editions 313

About the Translator 321

Kalavinka Buddhist Classics' Current Title List 323

Translator's Introduction

In this most recent volume of Buddhist scripture translations published by Kalavinka Press, I present two of my translations of moral virtue texts first translated into Chinese by Tripiṭaka Master Kumārajīva in Chang'an in approximately 410 CE.

The first of the two translations comprising this volume, "The Brahmā's Net Sutra Bodhisattva Precepts," is the bodhisattva moral code that eventually came to serve to a greater or lesser degree as the common standard for bodhisattva moral virtue practice for both monastics and laity throughout the ensuing history of East Asian Buddhism in China, Korea, Vietnam, and Japan. Along with this bodhisattva precept text, I include my translation of the standard *upoṣadha* recitation ceremony that came to be used together with these bodhisattva precepts in the ceremonial setting of the monastic saṃgha's group recitations occurring on full-moon and half-moon days throughout the year.

The second of this volume's two translations, "Nāgārjuna on the Perfection of Moral Virtue," although unrelated in origin, by the nature of its content, happens to serve as a beautiful and very appropriate commentary on the principles, prescriptions, and injunctions set forth in the preceding "Brahmā's Net Sutra Bodhisattva Precepts" text in which, using lovely verses, startling analogies, and traditional Buddhist moral tales, Ārya Nāgārjuna eloquently describes the essence, principles, and details of the bodhisattva's highest practice of moral goodness, the perfection of moral virtue (*śīla pāramitā*). This latter translation consists of Chapter 1, Subchapters 21–24 of Nāgārjuna's *Exegesis on the Great Perfection of Wisdom Sutra,* Nāgārjuna's immense commentary on the 25,000-line *Mahāprajñāpāramitā Sūtra, (The Mahāprajñāpāramitā Upadeśa* [大智度論] / T25, No. 1509).

Part One: The Brahmā's Net Sutra Bodhisattva Precepts

Of the two moral virtue texts I present in this volume, the first of them, "The Brahmā's Net Sutra Bodhisattva Mind Ground Precepts Chapter" is of cardinal importance as it eventually came to be one of the most influential scriptures in the history of East Asian Buddhism, for it served to portray in great detail a model of behavior in every aspect of life for all cultivators of the bodhisattva path, whether they be monks, nuns, laymen, or laywomen. Thus, for the Chinese bodhisattva path practitioner, this text became a simple, readily understandable, and easily accessible moral virtue model to be used together with the monastics' non-Mahāyāna Four-Part Dharmaguptaka Vinaya that was translated into Chinese at about the same time in the early fifth century CE.

Of the two fascicles comprising this Bodhisattva Mind Ground Precepts Chapter, the first fascicle presents an abstruse discussion of the rarified stages of bodhisattva practice encountered by the highly advanced practitioner in progressing toward the realization of buddhahood, whereas the second fascicle is devoted to a fairly detailed description of the ten major and forty-eight minor precepts that comprise the bodhisattva moral code known throughout the history of Chinese Buddhism as "The Brahmā's Net Sutra Bodhisattva Precepts." Probably not least because the first fascicle is both nearly impossibly difficult to read and nearly impenetrably hard to fathom, the first fascicle of this text was mostly ignored in nearly all of the many commentaries written on these bodhisattva precepts by Chinese exegetes, including those written by such exegetical luminaries as Zhiyi and Fazang. Their interests in this scripture lay primarily in its bodhisattva moral code, for they could easily find more extensive and clearer articulations of the stages of the bodhisattva path in other Mahāyāna scriptures such as the Avataṃsaka Sutra or the Ten Grounds Sutra.

In this second fascicle which contains the bodhisattva precepts, the precepts are portrayed as being initially proclaimed in the Lotus Flower Dais World by Rocana Buddha, the Buddha's reward body *(saṃbhoga-kāya)* to an audience of countless transformation-body Śākyamuni buddhas from innumerably many worlds, all of whom were then charged with going back and teaching these precepts to those in their own lands who dedicate themselves to cultivating and progressing along the bodhisattva path to buddhahood.

These precepts consist of untitled but often rather long and detailed descriptions of ten major and forty-eight minor precepts. Because the scripture text does not provide titles for any of these many different sorts of precepts, it fell to commentators such as Zhiyi and Fazang to compose them for greater ease of reference in their commentarial discussions. For this translation I have chosen to insert Zhiyi's precept titles into the text in bold-face type while also providing Fazang's usually very similar titles in the endnotes for ease of comparison.

The ten major precepts which deal with major issues like killing, stealing, sexual relations, and false speech are listed first. These are inviolable, for if one were to deliberately break any of them, this would constitute a *pārājika* offense for which the penalty is expulsion from the bodhisattva *saṃgha*. Breaking any of the forty-eight minor precepts is much less serious, for if one breaks any of them, one's transgression can be easily forgiven through confession.

In his preface to Tripiṭaka Master Kumārajīva's translation of Chapter Ten of *The Brahmā's Net Sutra*, Śramaṇa Sengzhao states that this "Rocana Buddha Speaks the Bodhisattva Mind Ground Precepts Chapter" was one of more than fifty scriptures translated by Kumārajīva at Caotang Monastery in Chang'an in the first decade or so of the fifth century CE. He notes that, at that time: "Daorong and Daoying together with more than three hundred others then took the bodhisattva precepts at which time each of them recited this chapter and made it foremost in their minds. Thus the Masters and their followers then became devoted to the same meaning. They then respectfully transcribed eighty-one copies of this one chapter and circulated them throughout the realm, wishing thereby to influence the people to aspire to the realization of bodhi. Having followed the example of others in awakening to the principle, they wished that later generations would all be able to hear of this in the same way."[1]

So it was that the long history of this text's powerful influence on the history of East Asian Buddhism began. It was not long before this scripture's moral code consisting of ten major and forty-eight minor precepts was adopted as the Mahāyāna moral code for both monastics and laity[2] not only in China, but also in Korea and Japan. In China and Korea, it was adopted alongside the Dharmaguptaka Vinaya, whereas in Japan it eventually replaced the traditional monastic vinaya altogether.

As for the origin of these precepts, for the most part, faithful Buddhists believe that they were set forth by the Buddha approximately 2,500 years ago, preserved in India, and finally transmitted to China by the Indian Tripiṭaka Master Kumārajīva in approximately 406 CE in Chang'an, modern Xi'an, the capital of Shaanxi Province.

Scholars are often skeptical of this point of view and tend to be divided between those who assert that these precepts were composed in central Asia some time after the life of the Buddha, those who suggest that Kumārajīva may have composed them himself, and those who believe that they were composed by Chinese in China a few decades after Kumārajīva finished his other translation work.

Those holding the view that this text was composed in China tend to take as the strongest evidence for their opinion the references in this precept text to "filial piety," apparently supposing that filial piety was somehow an exclusively Chinese invention and concern. This stance fails to recognize the fact that even the very early Pali scriptures are full of references by the Buddha himself to the need for good Buddhist practitioners to maintain filial respect and concern for the welfare of their parents. This fact alone should make it clear that concerns about filial piety in these precepts do not constitute proof of Chinese authorship.

In any case, regardless of the actual origin of this code of bodhisattva moral precepts, its powerful and lasting effect on the history of East Asian Buddhism is undeniable. "The Brahmā's Net Sutra Bodhisattva Precepts" greatly influenced the way in which Chinese, Korean, and Japanese Buddhists came to view what constitutes the correct mode of practice for all who aspire to cultivate the bodhisattva path to buddhahood. To this day, these precepts continue to be transmitted, not only to monks and nuns in their ordination sessions, but also, depending on the country,[3] to laymen and laywomen as well.

Part One Supplement: The Bodhisattva Precepts Recitation Ceremony

As a supplement to Part One, I also include "The Semimonthly Bodhisattva Precepts Recitation Ceremony" as quoted in the commentary on this ceremony by Śramaṇa Hong Zan[4] (1611–1685) of Guangzhou's Jeweled Elephant Monastery. At the end of his introductory paragraph to his commentary on this ceremony (X38_n0696), Śramaṇa Hongzan attributes the origin of this ceremony to members of the Tiantai School at the end of the Tang Dynasty or the beginning of the Song Dynasty.[5]

This precept recitation ceremony provides a formal ritual structure for carrying out an *upoṣadha* ceremony for the bodhisattva precepts somewhat modeled on the classic *upoṣadha* ceremony prescribed for the recitation of monastic precepts such as the non-Mahāyāna Four-Part Dharmaguptaka Vinaya. Ceremonies of these sorts establish a ritual procedure for confession of transgressions, declaration of purity, and renewal of the precept holder's commitment to following whichever code of precepts is the subject of the *upoṣadha* ceremony.

Part Two: Nāgārjuna on the Perfection of Moral Virtue

The second part of this book, "Nāgārjuna on the Perfection of Moral Virtue" consists of a lengthy selection drawn from my 2009 Kalavinka Press translation entitled *Nāgārjuna on the Six Perfections* in which Nāgārjuna gives a wonderfully complete exposition of the meaning of the six *pāramitās* constituting the very core of the bodhisattva's practices leading to buddhahood. Of these six perfections consisting of giving, moral virtue, patience, vigor, *dhyāna* meditation, and world-transcending wisdom, moral virtue (also the first of the three trainings consisting of *śīla, samādhi,* and *prajñā*), is arguably the most important, for success in all the other core bodhisattva metaphysical skills is entirely dependent upon it.

This treatment of the perfection of moral virtue is a three-subchapter section from Chapter One of Ārya Nāgārjuna's immense and marvelous commentary on the 25,000-line *Mahāprajñāpāramitā Sutra,* the title of which I translate as *Exegesis on the Great Perfection of Wisdom Sutra* (*The Mahāprajñāpāramitā Upadeśa* / T25, No. 1509).

The first of these three chapters, Chapter 1, Subchapter 21, is titled "An Introductory Discussion of Moral Virtue" in which Nāgārjuna provides a general definition of "moral virtue" (*śīla*), lists eight proscribed categories of physical actions and speech, and then notes the consequences of failure to observe these precepts, after which he describes the consequences of inferior, middling, and superior observance of the precepts and then emphasizes the necessity of scrupulous precept observance, introducing similes to reinforce this point. Nāgārjuna next points out the uselessness of unprecepted ascetic practices and the irrelevance of social station to gaining the fruits of careful precept observance, after which, making use of similes, verses, and a story, he describes the character, karmic circumstances, and karmic consequences first of one who breaks the precepts and next of one who observes the precepts. He then concludes the chapter with thirty-two analogies describing the wretched state of the precept breaker.

The second of these three chapters in which Nāgārjuna presents his marvelous commentary on the perfection of moral virtue is Chapter 1, Subchapter 22, "Details and Import of the Moral Precepts," where he first defines and discusses each of the five precepts and then explains the karmic effects of each of them while also treating a range of topics related to each precept, using verses, stories, analogies, and incisive argumentation to buttress the points he makes in his eloquent description of the importance of each precept. He then discusses the specific-term practice of the eight precepts, compares the five precepts and the eight precepts, and then concludes the chapter by describing four grades of lay precept observance and how these precepts constitute the initial entryway into the eightfold right path and the eventual realization of nirvana.

The third and final chapter of Nāgārjuna's commentary on the perfection of moral virtue, Chapter 1, Subchapter 23, "Aspects of *Śīla Pāramitā*," is divided into two major parts, Part One: "Additional Precept Specifics," and Part Two: "The Perfection of Moral Virtue." In Part One, Nāgārjuna explains how precepts are able to be foremost in the eightfold path, explains what is meant by the fourth of the four grades of lay precept observance, "the superior within the superior," and then discusses the monastic precepts, the special value of the monastic precepts, the four categories of monastic precepts, the origin of the *śikṣamāṇā* postulant nun category, and the bhikshuni and bhikshu ordinations.

Chapter 1, Subchapter 23, Part Two: "The Perfection of Moral Virtue," the final and perhaps most metaphysically beautiful and profound section of Nāgārjuna's commentary on *śīla pāramitā*, is an extensive and expansive treatment of this spiritual perfection. He begins this section by defining "the perfection of moral virtue" in which one becomes indifferent even to sacrificing one's own life in order to uphold the precepts purely. Then, using analogies and stories, he holds forth at length on how moral virtue generates all six perfections including even the perfection of wisdom.

Nāgārjuna concludes his commentary on the perfection of moral virtue with a discussion of how it is that a bodhisattva's practice of moral virtue is truly perfected as *śīla pāramitā*. Here, he says: "The upholding of the moral precepts is carried out solely for the sake of all beings, for the sake of success in the Buddha Path, and for the sake of gaining all of the dharmas of buddhahood." He then states that: "Then again, if the bodhisattva's practice is based in the unfindability of either offense or non-offense, it is at this time that it qualifies as *śīla pāramitā*." Here, Nāgārjuna is referring to bodhisattva practice that has achieved the realization of the emptiness of inherent existence in all things, even in karmic offense and non-offense which, due to their ultimate inapprehensibility, have no ultimately real existence of their own. (Of course, here, Nāgārjuna is in no way denying the importance of "offense" and "non-offense" in the realm of conventional existence where, even once one has realized their metaphysical emptiness, they continue to constitute the very basis of the correct practice of moral virtue.)

Finally, after an extended discussion of the meaning of the metaphysical emptiness of both beings and phenomena and after his reiteration of the importance of the realization of emptiness to right practice of moral virtue, Nāgārjuna concludes his commentary on the perfection of moral virtue by saying: "It is for this reason that [the *Sutra*] states, "It is based on the unfindability of offense and non-offense that one should engage in perfecting *śīla pāramitā*."

In Summation

It brings me great pleasure to finally bring to print this bodhisattva precepts translation project I began over fifty years ago. My interest in producing a book on the bodhisattva's practice of moral virtue began in 1972 when, as a young monk at Gold Mountain Monastery in San Francisco, I began a first-draft translation of the Brahmā's Net Sutra Bodhisattva Precepts that I finished about two years later at the Buddhist Lecture Hall in Hong Kong. Having then set the manuscript aside, I did not return to it until recently after having translated and published many other important Mahāyāna scriptures in the intervening decades. I finally returned to this manuscript about a year and half ago at which point I spent almost a year making extensive revisions nearly amounting to a complete retranslation of this scripture. Then, having circulated the revised manuscript for critical review and having then combined it with my translations of "The Semimonthly Bodhisattva Precept Recitation Ceremony" and Ārya Nāgārjuna's wonderful commentary on *śīla pāramitā* from his *Mahāprajñāpāramitā Upadeśa*, Kalavinka Press is now finally able to bring forth this volume, *The Bodhisattva's Practice of Moral Virtue*. I hope that the reader will be able to find as much spiritual enjoyment in reading these translations as I have experienced in producing them.

Bhikshu Dharmamitra,
Seattle, March 1st, 2024

Introduction Endnotes

1 T24n1484_p0997a27–b05.

2 In order for these precepts to be a practical option for laypeople, the fourth major precept, "The Precept against Sexual Relations," has traditionally been interpreted as forbidding sexual relations only for monks and nuns. For laypeople, it was not interpreted as forbidding sexual activity altogether, but rather as allowing only strictly monogamous relations between couples living in committed relationships.

3 Beginning a few decades ago, it became a not uncommon practice for laypeople in Taiwan to instead receive a code of six major and twenty-eight minor bodhisattva precepts from Chapter Fourteen of *The Sutra on the Upāsaka Precepts* (*Upāsakaśīla Sūtra*) translated into Chinese by Dharmarakṣa in 426 CE (Taisho Volume 24, Number 1488).

4 "Commentary by the Great Bodhicitta Śramaṇa Hongzan." (冐地質多沙門弘贊注.)

5 X38n0696_p0767a14.

The Bodhisattva's Practice of Moral Virtue

Part One:

The Brahmā's Net Sutra Bodhisattva Precepts

As Translated into Chinese by Tripiṭaka Master Kumārajīva
Annotated English Translation by Bhikshu Dharmamitra

Part One: The Brahmā's Net Sutra Bodhisattva Precepts
Table of Contents

Part One: The Brahmā's Net Sutra Bodhisattva Precepts 19
Part One Table of Contents 21
Preface to The Brahmā's Net Sutra Bodhisattva Precepts 23
The Brahmā's Net Sutra, Chapter 10, Fascicle Two 27
The 10 Major Bodhisattva Precepts 37
The 48 Minor Bodhisattva Precepts 45
Part One Endnotes: 99
Part One Supplement: The Precepts Recitation Ceremony 121
The Semimonthly Bodhisattva Precepts Recitation Ceremony 123
The Recitation Ceremony List of Contents 123
Part One: Taking Refuge in and Revering the Three Jewels 125
Part Two: Instigation to Cultivation 125
Part Three: Perform the Preliminary Procedures 127
Part Four: Recite the Preface to the Precepts 127
Part Five: Questioning the Assembly 129
Part Six: The Actual Recitation of the Precept Scripture 131
Recitation Ceremony Endnotes 133
Part One Bibliography 135
Part One Glossary 137
The Brahmā's Net Bodhisattva Precepts Variant Readings 143

正體字

T24n1484_p1003a14║
1003a15║ [3] 梵網經菩薩戒序
1003a16║ 諸佛子等。合掌至心聽。我今欲說諸佛大戒
1003a17║ 序。眾集默然聽。自知有罪當懺悔。懺悔即
1003a18║ 安樂。不懺悔罪益深。無罪者默然。默然故
1003a19║ 當知眾清淨。諸大德優婆塞優婆夷等諦聽。
1003a20║ 佛滅度後於像法中。應當尊敬波羅提木
1003a21║ 叉。波羅提木叉者即是此戒。持此戒時如
1003a22║ 暗遇明如貧得寶如病得差如囚繫出獄
1003a23║ 如遠行者得歸。當知此則是眾等大師。若
1003a24║ 佛住世無異此也。怖心難生善心難發。故
1003a25║ 經云。勿輕小罪以為無殃。水滴雖微漸
1003a26║ 盈大器。剎那造罪殃墮無間。一失人身萬
1003a27║ 劫不復。壯色不停猶如奔馬。人命無常過
1003a28║ 於山水。今日雖存明亦難保。

佛说梵网经卷下

This Fascicle #2 Sutra Text Downloaded on 02/22/2024 from this site: https://www.fojingzaixian.com/qianlongdazangjing.html at this site url: https://www.fojingzaixian.com/q1211.html

(This preface, though traditionally a standard part of this sutra's text, is apparently not included in the Qianlong Zang. The following simplified Chinese version was downloaded on 02/22/2024 from:http://www.shixiu.net/dujing/fojing/lvbu/2936.html)

简体字

梵网经菩萨戒序

诸佛子等。合掌至心听。我今欲说诸佛大戒序。众集默然听。自知有罪当忏悔。忏悔即安乐。不忏悔罪益深。无罪者默然。默然故当知众清净。诸大德优婆塞优婆夷等谛听。佛灭度后于像法中。应当尊敬波罗提木叉。波罗提木叉者即是此戒。持此戒时如暗遇明如贫得宝如病得差如囚系出狱如远行者得归。当知此则是众等大师。若佛住世无异此也。怖心难生善心难发。故经云。勿轻小罪以为无殃。水滴虽微渐盈大器。刹那造罪殃堕无间。一失人身万劫不复。壮色不停犹如奔马。人命无常过于山水。今日虽存明亦难保。

Part One

The Brahmā's Net Sutra Bodhisattva Precepts

Translation by the Latter Qin Kuchean Tripiṭaka Master Kumārajīva[1]
[English Translation by Bhikshu Dharmamitra]

Preface to the Bodhisattva Precepts of the Brahmā's Net Sutra

All you sons of the Buddha, place your palms together and listen with a mind of utmost sincerity. I now wish to speak the preface to the great precepts of all buddhas. Having gathered together here, the Assembly should listen in silence. If one becomes aware that one has committed an offense one should repent, for, having repented, one then becomes peaceful and happy. If one does not repent, his offenses become increasingly grave. Those who are free of offenses may remain silent. By such silence it will be known that the members of this assembly are pure. Greatly Virtuous Ones,[2] Upāsakas, and Upāsikās,[3] listen attentively:

After the Buddha's nirvāṇa, during the Semblance Dharma Age,[4] one should revere the *prātimokṣa*.[5] The *prātimokṣa* is just these very precepts. When one upholds these precepts, it is just as when one who is in darkness encounters the light, just as when one who is poor obtains a jewel, just as when one who is sick finds a cure, just as when one who has been imprisoned emerges from prison, and just as when one who has traveled afar is then able to return home. One should realize that these [precepts] serve as the great master for all those in the Assembly, no differently than if the Buddha himself were still dwelling in the world.[6]

It is difficult to develop a mind that is fearful [of committing offenses] and it is difficult to develop a mind that is devoted to goodness. Therefore a sutra says: "Do not consider minor offenses to be insignificant, taking them to be free of misfortune, for, although drops of water are tiny, they will gradually fill up even a large vessel."[7] An offense committed in a *kṣaṇa* may bring about the misfortune of falling into the Uninterrupted [Hells].[8] Having once lost the human body, one may not regain it even after a myriad kalpas. Like the passing of a galloping horse, a strong body does not remain for long. A person's life passes more quickly[9] than the [rapidly flowing] waters of a mountain stream. Although it may remain today, it would be difficult to guarantee it will still be here tomorrow.

眾等各各一心
1003a29 勤修精進。慎勿懈怠懶惰睡眠縱意。夜即攝
1003b01 心存念三寶。莫以空過徒設疲勞後代深
1003b02 悔。眾等各各一心謹依此戒。如法修行應當
1003b03 學。
1003b04
1003b05

正體字

众等各各一心勤修精进。慎勿懈怠懒惰睡眠纵意。夜即摄心存念三宝。莫以空过徒设疲劳后代深悔。众等各各一心谨依此戒。如法修行应当学。

简体字

Members of the Assembly, each of you should single-mindedly and diligently seek to cultivate with vigor. Take care and do not become indolent or lazy or allow your mind to become uncontrolled when sleeping. At night, one should focus the mind and remain mindful of the Three Jewels.[10] One must not allow it to occur that, by letting the time go by fruitlessly, one's efforts are expended in vain so that, later on, one will be bound to experience deep regret. Members of the Assembly, you should each single-mindedly and diligently abide by these precepts. You should train in them by cultivating them in accordance with the Dharma.

正體字

1003b06 ‖ **[*]梵網經盧舍那佛說菩薩心地**
1003b07 ‖ **戒品第十卷下** /1003b08 ‖ (blank)/
1003b09 ‖ [*]後秦龜茲國三藏鳩摩羅什譯
1003b10 ‖ [4]爾時盧舍那佛。為此大眾。略開百千恒河
1003b11 ‖ 沙不可說法門中心地。如毛頭許。是過去一
1003b12 ‖ 切佛已說。未來佛當說。現在佛今說。三世菩
1003b13 ‖ 薩已學當學今學。我已百劫修行是心地。
1003b14 ‖ 號吾為盧舍那。汝諸[5]佛轉我所說。與一切
1003b15 ‖ 眾生開心地道。時蓮花臺藏世界赫赫天光
1003b16 ‖ 師子座上盧舍那佛放光光。告千花上佛。
1003b17 ‖ 持我心地法門品。而去復轉為千百億釋迦
1003b18 ‖ [6]及一切眾生。次第說我上心地法門品。汝
1003b19 ‖ 等受持讀誦一心而行。
1003b20 ‖ 爾時千花上佛千百億釋迦。從蓮花藏世界
1003b21 ‖ 赫赫師子座起。各各辭退舉身放不可思議
1003b22 ‖ 光。[7]光＋（**光**）皆化無量佛。一時以無量青黃赤白
1003b23 ‖ 花供養盧舍那佛。受持上[8]說心地法門品
1003b24 ‖ 竟。各各從此蓮花藏世界而沒。沒已入體
1003b25 ‖ 性虛空花光三昧。還本源世界閻浮提菩提
1003b26 ‖ 樹下。從體性虛空華光三昧出。

简体字

佛说梵网经卷下
菩萨心地品之下

尔时，卢舍那佛为此大众，略开百千恒河沙，不可说法门中心地，如毛头许："是过去一切佛已说，未来佛当说，现在佛今说；三世菩萨已学、当学、今学。我已百劫修行是心地，号吾为卢舍那。汝诸佛子，转我所说与一切众生，开心地道。"时，莲华台藏世界，赫赫天光师子座上，卢舍那佛放光，光告千华上佛："持我《心地法门品》而去，复转为千百亿释迦及一切众生，次第说我上《心地法门品》。汝等受持读诵，一心而行。" 尔时，千华上佛，千百亿释迦，从莲华藏世界赫赫师子座起，各各辞退，举身放不可思议光。光光皆化无量佛，一时以无量青、黄、赤、白华，供养卢舍那佛。受持上所说《心地法门品》竟，各各从此莲华藏世界而没，没已入体性虚空华光三昧，还本源世界，阎浮提菩提树下，从体性虚空华光三昧出。

Rocana Buddha Speaks the Bodhisattva Mind Ground Precepts

The Brahmā's Net Sutra, Chapter Ten, Fascicle Two

At that time, of the mind ground Dharma gateways as numerous as a hundred thousand ineffables[11] of Ganges' sands, Rocana Buddha presented for this great assembly a summary explanation of only as many as could fit on the tip of a single hair.

[He said], "These have been taught by all buddhas of the past, will be taught by all buddhas of the future, and are taught by all buddhas of the present. They have been studied, will be studied, and are now studied by the bodhisattvas of the three periods of time. I have already cultivated this mind ground for one hundred kalpas. I am called 'Rocana.' All of you buddhas should transmit what I have taught and open the path of the mind ground for all beings."

At that time, sitting in the Lotus Flower Dais World on the lion throne blazing with gloriously radiant celestial light, Rocana Buddha emanated brilliant light and thereby[12] told the thousand buddhas sitting on the lotus flower [petals], "Take up my 'Mind Ground Dharma Gateway Chapter' and then go forth and pass it on for the benefit of the hundreds of thousands of *koṭis* of Śākyamunis as well as for the benefit of all beings, doing so by sequentially explaining for them the above-taught 'Mind Ground Dharma Gateway Chapter.' You should all accept, retain, read, recite, and single-mindedly practice it."

At that time, the thousand buddhas atop the lotus flower [petals] and the hundred thousand *koṭis* of Śākyamunis all arose from their gloriously radiant lion thrones in the Lotus Flower Dais World whereupon they each took their leave and withdrew. In doing so, their entire bodies emanated inconceivable light, every ray of which[13] transformationally created countless buddhas who simultaneously made offerings to Rocana Buddha of countless blue, yellow, red, and white flowers.

After they had received and retained the above-taught "Mind Ground Dharma Gateway Chapter," each of them then disappeared from this Lotus Flower Dais World. After disappearing, they then entered "the flower light samādhi with the essential nature like empty space" and returned to their places beneath the bodhi trees on the continent of Jambudvīpa in their original worlds. They then emerged from the flower light samādhi with the essential nature like

正體字

出已方坐
1003b27 金剛千光王座。及妙光堂說十世界[9]海。復
1003b28 從座起至帝釋宮說十住。復[10]從座起至
1003b29 炎天中說十行。復從座起至第四天中說
1003c01 十迴向。復從座起至化樂天說十禪[11]定。復
1003c02 從座起至他化天說十地。復至一禪中說
1003c03 十金剛。復至二禪中說十忍。復至三禪中
1003c04 說十願。復至四禪中摩醯首羅天王宮。說
1003c05 我本源蓮花藏世界盧舍那佛所說心地法門
1003c06 品。其餘千百億釋迦亦復如是無二無別。如
1003c07 賢劫品中說。
1003c08 爾時釋迦[12]牟尼佛。從初現蓮花藏世界。東
1003c09 方來入天[13]王宮中說魔受化經已。下生南
1003c10 閻浮提迦夷羅國。母名摩耶父字白淨吾
1003c11 名悉達。七歲出家三十成道。號吾為釋迦
1003c12 牟尼佛。於寂滅道場坐金剛花光[14]王座。乃
1003c13 至摩醯首羅天王宮。[15]其中次第十住處所
1003c14 說。時佛觀諸大梵天王網羅幢因為說。無
1003c15 量世界猶如網孔。

简体字

出已，方坐金刚千光王座，及妙光堂，说十世界法门海。复从座起，至帝释宫，说十住。复从座起，至焰天中，说十行。复从座起，至第四天中，说十回向。复从座起，至化乐天，说十禅定。复从座起，至他化天，说十地。复至一禅中，说十金刚。复至二禅中，说十忍。复至三禅中，说十愿。复至四禅中，摩醯首罗天王宫，说我本源莲华藏世界，卢舍那佛所说《心地法门品》。其余千百亿释迦，亦复如是，无二无别。如《贤劫品》中说。

尔时，释迦牟尼佛，从初现莲华藏世界，东方来入天宫中，说《魔受化经》已。下生南阎浮提，迦夷罗国，母名摩耶，父字白净，吾名悉达。七岁出家，三十成道，号吾为释迦牟尼佛。于寂灭道场，坐金刚华光王座，乃至摩醯首罗天王宫，其中次第十住处所说。

时，佛观诸大梵天王，网罗幢因，为说无量世界，犹如网孔，

empty space. Having emerged from it, they then sat down on their vajra royal thrones emanating a thousand light rays and went to the Hall of Sublime Light where they expounded on the ten oceans of worlds. They next arose from their thrones and went to Indra's palace where they expounded on the ten abodes. Then they arose from their thrones and went into the Yāma Heaven where they expounded on the ten practices. They next arose from their thrones and went into the fourth heaven, [the Tuṣita Heaven],[14] where they expounded on the ten dedications. Then they arose from their thrones and went to the Nirmāṇarati Heaven where they expounded on the ten *dhyāna* absorptions. They next arose from their thrones and went to the Paranirmita-vaśavartin Heaven where they expounded on the ten grounds. Then they went to the first *dhyāna* [heavens][15] where they expounded on the ten *vajra* [minds]. They next went to the second *dhyāna* [heavens][16] where they expounded on the ten kinds of patience. Then they went to the third *dhyāna* [heavens] where they expounded on the ten vows. They next went into the fourth *dhyāna* [heavens] and then entered the palace of the Maheśvara Heaven King where they expounded on "The Mind Ground Dharma Gateway Chapter" taught by Rocana Buddha of our place of origin, the Lotus Flower Dais World. The rest of the hundred thousand *koṭis* of Śākyamunis also proceeded in this same way, with no second or different means of doing so, just as is explained in "The Bhadra Kalpa Chapter."

At that time, after first appearing in the Lotus Flower Dais World, Śākyamuni Buddha came eastward and entered the palace of the deva king. Then, having spoken *The Sutra on the Conversion of the Māras,* he descended and took birth on the southern continent of Jambudvīpa in the state of Kapilavastu where his mother was named Māyā and his father was name Śuddhodana.

"I was named Siddhārtha.[17] Seven years after leaving the home life, I attained enlightenment at the age of thirty-[five], whereupon I became known as Śākyamuni Buddha."[18]

From the time he sat on the Vajra Flower Light King's throne in the quiescent site of enlightenment until he reached the palace of the deva king, Maheśvara, there were ten dwelling places in which [these teachings] were sequentially expounded.

At that time, having observed the curtain net canopies of the Mahābrahma deva king, the Buddha said, "The countless worlds are comparable to the openings in those curtain net canopies. Each

正體字

一一世界各各不同別異
1003c16 無量。佛教門亦復如是。吾今來此世界八千
1003c17 返。為此娑婆世界坐金剛[16]花光王座。乃至
1003c18 摩醯首羅天王宮。為是中一切大眾略開心
1003c19 地[17]法門[18]品竟。復從天王宮下至閻浮提
1003c20 菩提樹下。為此地上一切眾生凡夫癡闇之
1003c21 人。說我本盧舍那佛心地中初發心中常所
1003c22 誦一戒光明。金剛寶戒是一切佛本源。一切
1003c23 菩薩本源。佛性種子。一切眾生皆有佛性。一
1003c24 切意識色心是情是心皆入佛性戒中。當當
1003c25 常有因故。[19]有當當常住法身。如是十波羅
1003c26 提木叉。出於世界。是法戒是三世一切眾生
1003c27 頂戴受持。吾今當為此大眾重說十無盡
1003c28 藏戒品。是一切眾生戒本源自性清淨。
1003c29 我今盧舍那　方坐蓮花臺
1004a01 周匝千花上　復現千釋迦
1004a02 一花百億國　一國一釋迦
1004a03 各坐菩提樹　一時成佛道
1004a04 如是千百億　盧舍那本身
1004a05 千百億釋迦　各接微塵眾

简体字

一一世界，各各不同，别异无量，佛教门亦复如是：“吾今来此世界八千返，为此娑婆世界，坐金刚华光王座，乃至摩醯首罗天王宫，为是中一切大众，略开心地法门竟。复从天王宫，下至阎浮菩提树下，为此地上一切众生、凡夫、痴闇之人，说我本卢舍那佛心地中，初发心中，常所诵一戒，光明金刚宝戒。是一切佛本源，一切菩萨本源，佛性种子。一切众生皆有佛性，一切意、识、色、心，是情是心，皆入佛性戒中。当当常有因故，当当常住法身。如是十波罗提木叉，出于世界，是法戒，是三世一切众生顶戴受持。吾今当为此大众，重说十无尽藏戒品，是一切众生戒本源，自性清净。

“我今卢舍那，方坐莲华台，
周匝千华上，复现千释迦。
一华百亿国，一国一释迦，
各坐菩提树，一时成佛道。
如是千百亿，卢舍那本身，
千百亿释迦，各接微尘众，

and every one of the worlds are different and their variations are innumerable. The gateways into the Buddha's teaching are also just like this. I have now returned to this world eight thousand times during which, for the sake of the Sahā World, I have sat on the Vajra Flower Light King's throne [and in each of the other places], up to and including in the palace of the deva king, Maheśvara. There, after having finished presenting a summary explanation of 'The Mind Ground Dharma Gateway Chapter' for the sake of all the great assemblies in each of these places, I again descended from the palace of the deva king to the bodhi tree on the continent of Jambudvīpa where, for the benefit of all the beings and common people of this world benighted by the darkness of delusion, I taught this foremost [code of] moral precepts[19] always recited by our Rocana Buddha when, on the mind ground, he first brought forth the resolve [to attain bodhi]."

"These radiant vajra jewel precepts are the original source of all buddhas, the original source of all bodhisattvas, and the seed of the buddha nature. All beings possess the buddha nature. All those possessed of mind consciousness, who have form and mind, and who possess these sentiments and this mind—they all enter into the precepts of the buddha nature. Because they definitely[20] possess the cause, they definitely always abide in the Dharma body. In this way, the ten *prātimokṣa* precepts came forth into the world. These Dharma precepts are reverently received and upheld by all beings of the three periods of time. Now, for the sake of this Great Assembly, I shall once again speak "The Ten Inexhaustible Treasury Precepts Chapter." They are the precepts of all beings and the purity of their original self nature.

Now I, Rocana,
sit here upon this lotus flower dais,
as, surrounding me on a thousand flower [petals],
there also appear a thousand Śākyamunis.

For each flower [petal] there are a hundred *koṭis* of lands
and in each there is a Śākyamuni.
Each of them sits beneath a bodhi tree
where, at the same time, they all attain buddhahood.

In this way, there are a hundred thousand *koṭis* in all
for whom Rocana is their original body.
Of the hundred thousand *koṭis* of Śākyamunis,
each is associated with a congregation as numerous as motes of dust.

正體字

1004a06 俱來至我所　聽我誦佛戒
1004a07 甘露門[1]則開　是時千百億
1004a08 還至本道場　各坐菩提樹
1004a09 誦我本師戒　十重四十八
1004a10 戒如明日月　亦如瓔珞珠
1004a11 微塵菩薩眾　由是成正覺
1004a12 是盧舍那誦　我亦如是誦
1004a13 汝新學菩薩　頂戴受持戒
1004a14 受持是戒已　轉授諸眾生
1004a15 諦聽我正誦　佛法中戒藏
1004a16 波羅提木叉　大眾心諦信
1004a17 汝是當成佛　我是已成佛
1004a18 常作如是信　戒品已具足
1004a19 一切有心者　皆應攝佛戒
1004a20 眾生受佛戒　即入諸佛位
1004a21 位同大覺已　真是諸佛子
1004a22 大眾皆恭敬　至心聽我誦
1004a23 爾時釋迦牟尼佛。初坐菩提樹下成無上
1004a24 覺初結菩薩波羅提木叉。孝順父母師僧三
1004a25 寶孝順至道之法孝名為戒亦名制止。[2]佛

简体字

俱来至我所，听我诵佛戒。
甘露门则开，是时千百亿，
还至本道场，各坐菩提树，
诵我本师戒，十重四十八，
戒如明日月，亦如璎珞珠。
微尘菩萨众，由是成正觉。
是卢舍那诵，我亦如是诵！
汝新学菩萨，顶戴受持戒，
受持是戒已，转授诸众生。
谛听我正诵，佛法中戒藏，
波罗提木叉，大众心谛信。
汝是当成佛，我是已成佛，
常作如是信，戒品已具足。
一切有心者，皆应摄佛戒，
众生受佛戒，即入诸佛位，
位同大觉已，真是诸佛子！
大众皆恭敬，至心听我诵！”

尔时，释迦牟尼佛，初坐菩提树下成无上觉，初结菩萨波罗提木叉，孝顺父母、师僧三宝，孝顺至道之法。孝名为戒，亦名制止。

They have all come to where I am
to hear me recite the Buddha's precepts.

When then the gateway of *amṛta*[21] opens,
at this time, those hundred thousand *koṭis* [of Śākyamunis]
return to their original sites of enlightenment
where each sits beneath a bodhi tree
and recites "the precepts of [Rocana Buddha], our[22] original teacher,"
the ten major and the forty-eight minor precepts.

These precepts are like the bright sun and moon
and are also like the jewels on a necklace.
The bodhisattvas of this congregation, as numerous as motes of dust,
because of these, attain right enlightenment.
These are recited by Rocana
and I, too, also recite them in this way.[23]

You bodhisattvas who are still early in your training
should receive and uphold these precepts with utmost reverence.
Having received and upheld these precepts,
you should transmit them on to all beings.

Listen attentively as I rightly recite
the precept treasury within the Buddha's Dharma,
the *prātimokṣa* precepts.
O Great Assembly, in your minds should truly believe
that you will attain buddhahood in the future
[just as] I am one who has already attained buddhahood.

If one always maintains faith such as this,
then all the types of precepts are as if already perfected.[24]
All those possessed of mind
should take on the Buddha's precepts.

If beings receive the Buddha's precepts,
they will then enter the station of all buddhas.
When one's station equals that of the Greatly Enlightened One,
then one truly becomes a son of all buddhas.

All those in the Great Assembly should become reverential
and, with earnest minds, listen to my recitation."

At that time, after Śākyamuni Buddha had first sat beneath the bodhi tree and realized the unsurpassed enlightenment, he first established the bodhisattva *prātimokṣa,* [thereby also encouraging] filial respect for parents, teachers among the Saṃgha,[25] and the Three Jewels. Filial respect is a dharma of the ultimate path. Filial respect is synonymous with moral virtue and it also refers to restraint.

正體字

1004a26 即口放無量光明。是時百萬億大眾諸菩薩。
1004a27 十八梵天六欲天子十六大國王。合掌至心
1004a28 聽佛誦一切[3]佛大[4]乘戒。[5]佛告諸菩薩言。
1004a29 我今半月半月。自誦諸佛法戒。汝等。一切發
1004b01 心菩薩亦[6]誦。乃至十發趣十長養十金剛十
1004b02 地諸菩薩亦誦。是故戒光從口出。有緣非
1004b03 無因故。光光非青黃赤白黑。非色非心。
1004b04 非有非[7]無。[8]非因果法。是諸佛之本源[9]菩
1004b05 [10]薩之根本。是大眾諸佛子之根本。是[11]故大
1004b06 眾諸佛子應受持應讀誦[12]善學。佛子諦聽。
1004b07 若受佛戒者。國王王子百官宰相。比丘比丘
1004b08 尼。十八梵天六欲天[13]子。庶民黃門婬男婬女
1004b09 奴婢。八部鬼神金剛神畜生乃至變化人。但
1004b10 解法師語。盡受得戒。皆名第一清淨者。
1004b11 佛告諸佛子言。有十重波羅提木叉。若受
1004b12 菩薩戒不誦此戒者。非菩薩非佛種子。
1004b13 我亦如是誦。一切菩薩已學。一切菩薩當學
1004b14 一切菩薩今學。[14]已略說菩薩波羅提木叉相
1004b15 貌。

简体字

佛即口放无量光明。是时，百万亿大众、诸菩萨、十八梵天、六欲天子、十六大国王，合掌至心，听佛诵一切诸佛大乘戒。

佛告诸菩萨言：“我今半月半月，自诵诸佛法戒。汝等一切发心菩萨亦诵，乃至十发趣、十长养、十金刚、十地诸菩萨亦诵。是故戒光从口出，有缘非无因故。光光非青黄赤白黑，非色非心，非有非无，非因果法。是诸佛之本源，行菩萨道之根本，是大众诸佛子之根本。是故大众诸佛子，应受持，应读诵，应善学。

“佛子谛听！若受佛戒者，国王、王子、百宫、宰相、比丘、比丘尼、十八梵天、六欲天子、庶民、黄门、淫男、淫女、奴婢、八部鬼神、金刚神、畜生，乃至变化人，但解法师语，尽受得戒，皆名第一清净者。”

佛告诸佛子言：“有十重波罗提木叉，若受菩萨戒，不诵此戒者，非菩萨，非佛种子。我亦如是诵，一切菩萨已学，一切菩萨当学，一切菩萨今学。我已略说菩萨波罗提木叉相貌，

The Buddha then emanated countless rays of light from his mouth. At this time, the hundred myriads of *koṭis* of beings in the Great Assembly including the bodhisattvas, the devas of the eighteen brahma heavens,[26] the *devaputras* of the six desire realm heavens, and the kings of the sixteen great countries all placed their palms together and listened with single-minded attention to the Buddha's recitation of the Great Vehicle precepts of all buddhas.

The Buddha told the bodhisattvas: "Now, every half month, I myself recite the Dharma precepts of all buddhas. All of you bodhisattvas at the stage of initial resolve should also recite them and so too, all the bodhisattvas up to and including those at the ten initiatory stages, the ten stages of development, the ten vajra stages, and the ten grounds should also recite them. Therefore this precept light comes forth from my mouth. This is based on conditions and does not occur without a cause. These rays of light are neither blue, yellow, red, white, nor black. They are neither form nor thought, they are neither existent nor nonexistent, and they are not a dharma of cause and effect. They are the original source of all buddhas, the origin of the bodhisattvas, and the origin of all the sons of the Buddha in the Great Assembly. Therefore, all the sons of the Buddha in this assembly should receive and uphold these precepts, should read them, recite them, and study them well.

"Sons of the Buddha, listen attentively. If one is to receive the Buddha's precepts, whether one is a king, a prince, one of the many officials, a prime minister, a bhikshu, a bhikshuni, a deva of the eighteen brahma heavens, a *devaputra* of the six desire realm heavens, one of the common people, a eunuch, a male prostitute, a female prostitute, a slave, one of the eight types of ghosts and spiritual beings, a vajra spirit, an animal, or a transformationally manifested person, if one simply understands the Dharma master's words, one will fully receive and acquire the precepts. All such beings will henceforth be known as possessed of the foremost purity."

The Buddha then told all those sons of the Buddha: "There are ten major *prātimokṣa* precepts. If anyone who has received the bodhisattva precepts fails to recite these precepts, he is not a bodhisattva and is not one possessed of the seed of buddhahood. I too recite these precepts in this way. All bodhisattvas have studied them in the past, all bodhisattvas will study them in the future, and all bodhisattvas now study them in the present. I have now already briefly described the character of the bodhisattva *prātimokṣa* precepts.

正體字

[15]是事應當學敬心奉持。
1004b16 佛[16]言。

[1. The Precept against Killing. (ZY: "第一殺戒." / FZ: "殺戒第一.")**]**

佛子。若自殺教人殺方[17]便讚歎殺
1004b17 見作隨喜。乃至呪殺。殺[18]因殺緣殺法殺業。
1004b18 乃至一切有命者不得故殺。是菩薩應起
1004b19 常住慈悲心孝順心。方便救護[19]一切眾生。而
1004b20 [20]自恣心快意殺生[21]者。是菩薩波羅夷罪。

[2. The Precept against Stealing. (ZY: "第二盜戒." / FZ: "盜戒第二.")**]**

1004b21 若佛子。自盜教人盜方便[22]盜[23]盜因盜緣盜
1004b22 法盜業[24]呪盜乃至鬼神有[25]主劫賊物。一切
1004b23 財物一針一草不得故盜。而菩薩[26]應生佛
1004b24 性孝[27]順慈悲心。常助一切人生福生樂。而
1004b25 反更盜人[28]財物[＊]者。是菩薩波羅夷罪。

[3. The Precept against Sexual Relations. (ZY: "第三婬戒." / FZ: "婬戒第三.")**]**

1004b26 若佛子。自婬教人婬。乃至一切女人不得
1004b27 故婬。婬因[29]婬緣婬法婬業。乃至畜生女諸天
1004b28 鬼神女。及非道行婬。

简体字

应当学，敬心奉持。

佛言："佛子，若自杀，教人杀，方便杀，赞叹杀，见作随喜，乃至咒杀，杀因、杀缘、杀法、杀业，乃至一切有命者，不得故杀。是菩萨，应起常住慈悲心、孝顺心，方便救护一切求生。而反恣心快意杀生者，是菩萨波罗夷罪。

"若佛子，自盗，教人盗，方便盗，咒盗，盗因、盗缘、盗法、盗业，乃至鬼神有主物，劫贼物，一切财物，一针一草，不得故盗。而菩萨应生佛性孝顺心、慈悲心，常助一切人生福生乐。而反更盗人财物者，是菩萨波罗夷罪。

"若佛子，自淫，教人淫，乃至一切女人，不得故淫，淫因、淫缘、淫法、淫业，乃至畜生女，诸天鬼神女，及非道行淫。

You should study these matters and uphold them with a respectful mind."

The Buddha said:

The Ten Major Bodhisattva Precepts

1. The Precept against Killing.[27]

Sons of the Buddha, [it is an offense] if one personally kills, if one encourages others to kill, if one adopts expedient means to kill, if one praises killing, if one accords with and delights in seeing others engage in killing, and so forth up to and including if one uses mantras to kill, if one involves oneself in the causes of killing, the conditions of killing, the methods of killing, or the karma of killing. One must not deliberately kill any living being. This bodhisattva should bring forth a constantly abiding mind of loving-kindness and compassion and a mind imbued with filial respect[28] with which he uses skillful means to rescue and protect all beings. Hence, [especially] if, [on the contrary][29] one proceeds with a personally unrestrained mind to delight in killing beings, this constitutes a bodhisattva *pārājika* offense.

2. The Precept against Stealing.[30]

[It is an offense] if a son of the Buddha steals himself, if he encourages others to steal, if he adopts expedient means to steal, if he involves himself in the causes of stealing, the conditions of stealing, the methods of stealing, the karma of stealing, or if he uses mantras to steal. One must not deliberately steal even the possessions of ghosts or spirits, the possessions of thieves, or any valuables at all, even if they be merely a needle or a blade of grass. Thus a bodhisattva should bring forth the mind of the buddha nature, the mind of filial respect, and the mind of loving-kindness and compassion with which he always helps everyone to produce merit and bliss. Hence [especially] if, on the contrary, one steals a person's valuables, this constitutes a bodhisattva *pārājika* offense.

3. The Precept against Sexual Relations.[31]

[It is an offense] if a son of the Buddha engages in sexual relations himself or if he encourages others to engage in sexual relations. He must not deliberately engage in sexual relations with any woman, nor may he involve himself in the causes of sexual relations, the conditions of sexual relations, the methods of sexual relations, or the karma of sexual relations. This prohibition extends to sexual relations with female animals, goddesses, female ghosts or spirits, and sexual relations 'contrary to the path.'[32] Thus a bodhisattva

正體字

而菩薩應生孝順心。
1004b29 ‖ 救度一切眾生。淨法與人。而反更起一切
1004c01 ‖ 人婬不擇畜生乃至母女姊妹六親行婬
1004c02 ‖ 無慈悲心[＊]者。是菩薩波羅夷罪。

[4. The Precept against False Speech. (“第四妄語戒.” / FZ: “妄語戒第四.”)**]**

1004c03 ‖ 若佛子。自妄語教人妄語方便妄語。妄語
1004c04 ‖ 因[30]妄語緣妄語法妄語業。乃至不見言見。
1004c05 ‖ 見言不見。身心妄語。而菩薩常生正語[31]正
1004c06 ‖ 見。亦生一切眾生正語正見。而反更起一切
1004c07 ‖ 眾生邪語邪見[32]邪業[＊]者。是菩薩波羅夷罪。

[5. The Precept against Dealing in Intoxicants. (ZY: 第五酤酒戒. / FZ: 酤酒戒第五.)**]**

1004c08 ‖ 若佛子。自酤酒教人酤酒。酤酒因[33]酤酒緣酤
1004c09 ‖ 酒法酤酒業。一切酒不得酤。是酒起罪因
1004c10 ‖ 緣。而菩薩應生一切眾生明達之慧。而反更
1004c11 ‖ 生[34]一切眾生顛倒[35]之心[＊]者。是菩薩波羅
1004c12 ‖ 夷罪。

[6. The Precept against Discussing Transgressions Committed by Members of the Four Assemblies. (ZY: “第六說四眾過戒.” / “說過戒第六.”)**]**

1004c13 ‖ 若佛[36]子。自說出家在家菩薩比丘比丘尼罪
1004c14 ‖ 過。教人說罪過。罪過因

简体字

而菩萨应生孝顺心，救度一切众生，净法与人。而反更起一切人淫，不择畜生，乃至母女姊妹六亲行淫，无慈悲心者，是菩萨波罗夷罪。

“若佛子，自妄语，教人妄语，方便妄语，妄语因、妄语缘、妄语法、妄语业，乃至不见言见，见言不见，身心妄语。而菩萨常生正语、正见，亦生一切众生正语、正见。而反更起一切众生邪语、邪见、邪业者，是菩萨波罗夷罪。

“若佛子，自酤酒，教人酤洒，酤酒因、酤酒缘、酤酒法、酤酒业，一切酒不得酤，是酒起罪因缘。而菩萨应生一切众生明达之慧。而反更生一切众生颠倒之心者，是菩萨波罗夷罪。

“若佛子，口自说出家、在家菩萨、比丘、比丘尼罪过，教人说罪过，罪过因、

should bring forth a mind of filial respect, liberate all beings,[33] and provide people with the dharmas of purity. Hence [especially] if, on the contrary, he leads everyone into sexual relations, not even restricting himself from engaging in sexual relations with animals and so forth, up to and including engaging in sexual relations with his mother, his daughters, his sisters, or his other relatives, thus behaving toward them without any thoughts of kindness or compassion, this is a bodhisattva *pārājika* offense.

4. The Precept against False Speech.[34]

[It is an offense] if a son of the Buddha engages in false speech himself, if he encourages others to engage in false speech, if he uses expedient means to engage in false speech, if he involves himself in the causes of false speech, the conditions of false speech, the methods of false speech, or the karma of false speech, and so forth, up to and including if he says that he has seen what he has not seen, if he says that he has not seen what he has seen, or if he engages in false speech with body or mind. Thus a bodhisattva always brings forth right speech and right views and also leads all beings to bring forth right speech and right views. Hence [especially] if, on the contrary, he leads all beings to engage in wrong speech, wrong views, and wrong actions, this is a bodhisattva *pārājika* offense.

5. The Precept against Dealing in Intoxicants.[35]

[It is an offense] if a son of the Buddha deals in intoxicants himself, encourages others to deal in intoxicants, or involves himself in the causes of dealing in intoxicants, the conditions of dealing in intoxicants, the methods of dealing in intoxicants, or the karma of dealing in intoxicants. One must not deal in any kind of intoxicants. These intoxicants are causes and conditions for the arising of karmic offenses. This being so, the bodhisattva should [instead] lead all beings to develop clear penetrating wisdom. Hence [especially] if, on the contrary, [by dealing in intoxicants], he leads all beings to develop minds beset by the inverted [views], this is a bodhisattva *pārājika* offense.

6. The Precept against Discussing Transgressions Committed by Members of the Four Assemblies.[36]

[It is an offense] if a son of the Buddha discusses the transgressions of monastic bodhisattvas, lay bodhisattvas, bhikshus, or bhikshunis, if he encourages others to speak of their transgressions, or if he involves himself in the causes [of speaking] of their transgressions,

正體字

[37]罪過緣罪過法罪
1004c15 過業。而菩薩聞外道惡人及二乘惡人說佛
1004c16 法中非法非律。常生[38]悲心教化是惡人輩。
1004c17 令生大乘善信。而菩薩反更自說佛法中罪
1004c18 過[*]者。是菩薩波羅夷罪。

[7. The Precept against Praising Oneself and Disparaging Others. (ZY: "第七自讚毀他戒." / FZ: "自讚毀他戒第七.")**]**

1004c19 若佛[*]子。自讚毀他亦教人自讚毀他。毀他
1004c20 因[39]毀他緣毀他法毀他業。而菩薩[40]應代一
1004c21 切眾生受加毀辱。惡事自向己好事與他
1004c22 人。若自揚己德隱他人好事。令他人受毀
1004c23 者。是菩薩波羅夷罪。

[8. The Precept against Acting Miserly and Insulting Others. (ZY: "第八慳惜加毀戒." / FZ: "故慳戒第八.")**]**

1004c24 若佛子。自慳教人慳。慳因[41]慳緣慳法慳業。
1004c25 而菩薩見一切貧窮人來乞者。隨前人所須
1005a01 一切給與。而菩薩[1]以惡心瞋心。乃至不施
1005a02 一錢一針一草。有求法者。不為說一句一
1005a03 偈一微塵許法。而反更罵辱[*]者。是菩薩波羅
1005a04 夷罪。

简体字

罪过缘、罪过法、罪过业。而菩萨闻外道、恶人，及二乘恶人，说佛法中非法非律，常生慈心，教化是恶人辈，令生大乘善信。而菩萨反更自说佛法中罪过者，是菩萨波罗夷罪。

"若佛子，口自赞毁他，亦教人自赞毁他，毁他因、毁他缘、毁他法、毁他业。而菩萨应代一切众生受加毁辱，恶事自向己，好事与他人。若自扬己德，隐他人好事，令他人受毁者，是菩萨波罗夷罪。

"若佛子，自悭，教人悭，悭因、悭缘、悭法、悭业。而菩萨见一切贫穷人来乞者，随前人所须，一切给与。而菩萨以恶心、瞋心，乃至不施一钱一针一草；有求法者，不为说一句、一偈、一微尘许法；而反更骂辱者，是菩萨波罗夷罪。

the conditions [of speaking] of their transgressions, the methods [of speaking] of their transgressions, or the karma [of speaking] of their transgressions. This being so, whenever a bodhisattva hears evil-minded non-Buddhists or evil-minded followers of the Two Vehicles[37] speak of [behavior] within the Dharma of the Buddha that is contrary to the Dharma or contrary to the moral codes, he should always bring forth a mind of compassion with which to instruct these types of evil-minded people and cause them to develop sincere faith in the Great Vehicle. Hence [especially] if, on the contrary, a bodhisattva personally speaks of those within the Buddha Dharma who have committed transgressions, this is a bodhisattva *pārājika* offense.

7. The Precept against Praising Oneself and Disparaging Others.[38]

[It is an offense] if a son of the Buddha praises himself and disparages others, encourages others to praise themselves and disparage others, or involves himself in the causes of disparaging others, the conditions of disparaging others, the methods of disparaging others, or the karma of disparaging others. Thus a bodhisattva should substitute for all other beings by undergoing the disparagement and insults which might otherwise be inflicted on them. He should take on unfortunate circumstances for himself and see to it that good circumstances are bestowed on others. Hence, [especially] if he advertises his own virtues and conceals the good works of others and thereby causes others to be disparaged, this is a bodhisattva *pārājika* offense.

8. The Precept against Acting Miserly and Insulting Others.[39]

[It is an offense] if a son of the Buddha acts in a miserly manner himself, if he encourages others to be miserly, or if he involves himself in the causes of miserliness, the conditions of miserliness, the methods of miserliness, or the karma of miserliness. This being so, whenever a bodhisattva sees any poverty-stricken person come and plead for assistance, in accordance with whatever the person before him needs, he should provide him with all of it.

Thus, if due to having a mind affected by what is unwholesome or a mind affected by hatred, a bodhisattva does not give him even a penny, a needle, or a blade of grass, or if he refuses to speak even so much as a sentence, a verse, or a dust mote's measure of Dharma for one who seeks Dharma, and [especially] if he instead scolds and humiliates such a person, this is a bodhisattva *pārājika* offense.

[9. The Precept against Acting with a Hateful Mind and Refusing to Accept Apologies. (ZY: "第九瞋心不受悔戒." / FZ: "瞋戒第九.")]

1005a05 若佛子。自瞋教人瞋。瞋因[2]瞋緣瞋法瞋業。
1005a06 而菩薩應生一切眾生中善根無諍之事。常
1005a07 生[3][+慈]悲心。而反更於一切眾生中。乃至於非
1005a08 眾生中。以惡口罵辱加以手打。及以刀[4]杖
1005a09 意猶不息。前人求悔善言懺謝。猶瞋不解
1005a10 [*]者。是菩薩波羅夷罪。

正體字

[10. The Precept against Slander of the Three Jewels. (ZY: "第十謗三寶戒." [亦云 "謗菩薩法戒," 或云 "邪見邪說戒."] / FZ: "謗三寶戒第十.")]

1005a11 若佛子。自謗三寶教人謗三寶。謗因[5]謗緣
1005a12 謗法謗業。而菩薩見外道及以惡人一言謗
1005a13 佛音聲。如三百鉾刺心。況口自謗不生信
1005a14 心孝順心。而反更助惡人邪見人謗[*]者。是
1005a15 菩薩波羅夷罪。
1005a16 善學諸[6]仁者。是菩薩十波羅提木叉。應當
1005a17 學。於中不應一一犯如微塵許。何況具足
1005a18 犯十戒。若有犯者不得現身發菩提心。亦
1005a19 失國王位轉輪王位。亦失比丘比丘尼位。亦
1005a20 失十發趣十長養十金剛十地佛性常住妙
1005a21 果。一切皆[7]失墮三惡道中。二劫三劫不聞
1005a22 父母三寶名字。

简体字

"若佛子，自瞋，教人瞋，瞋因、瞋缘、瞋法、瞋业。而菩萨应生一切众生中善根无诤之事，常生慈悲心、孝顺心。而反更于一切众生中，乃至于非众生中，以恶口骂辱，加以手打，及以刀杖，意犹不息；前人求悔，善言忏谢，犹瞋不解者，是菩萨波罗夷罪。

"若佛子，自谤三宝，教人谤三宝，谤因、谤缘、谤法、谤业。而菩萨见外道及以恶人，一言谤佛音声，如三百鉾刺心，况口自谤！不生信心、孝顺心，而反更助恶人、邪见人谤者，是菩萨波罗夷罪。

"善学诸仁者！是菩萨十波罗提木叉，应当学，于中不应一一犯如微尘许，何况具足犯十戒！若有犯者，不得现身发菩提心，亦失国王位、转轮王位，亦失比丘、比丘尼位，亦失十发趣、十长养、十金刚、十地。佛性常住妙果，一切皆失。堕三恶道中，二劫、三劫，不闻父母三宝名字。

9. The Precept against Acting with a Hateful Mind and Refusing to Accept Apologies.[40]

[It is an offense] if a son of the Buddha becomes hateful, encourages others to become hateful, or involves himself in the causes of hatred, the conditions of hatred, the methods of hatred, or the karma of hatred. Thus a bodhisattva should create circumstances between all beings which conduce to roots of goodness and an absence of contentiousness and he should always bring forth a mind of [kindness and] compassion [and a mind of filial respect].[41] Hence [especially] if, on the contrary, in dealing with any sentient or insentient beings, he scolds and insults them with harsh speech or attacks them with his fists, a knife, or a cane, and even then his mind does not desist, or if, even when the person before him seeks forgiveness and sincerely repents, he continues to be hateful and does not let go of it, this is a bodhisattva *pārājika* offense.

10. The Precept against Slander of the Three Jewels.[42]

[It is an offense] if a son of the Buddha slanders the Three Jewels himself, if he encourages others to slander the Three Jewels, or if he involves himself in the causes of slandering them, the conditions of slandering them, the methods of slandering them, or the karma of slandering them. Thus, whenever a bodhisattva hears the sound of even a single word of a non-Buddhist's or evil-minded person's slander of the Buddha, it is as if three hundred spears were piercing his heart. How then could he possibly utter such slander himself and thus fail to maintain a faithful mind and a mind of filial respect? Hence, [especially] if, on the contrary, he were to assist evil-minded persons or persons with wrong views in slandering [the Three Jewels], this is a bodhisattva *pārājika* offense.

Virtuous students of the path, you should train in these ten bodhisattva *prātimokṣa* precepts and you should not violate any one of them to even the slightest extent, how much the less should you completely violate all ten of these precepts. Whoever violates them [to such a degree] will remain unable to resolve to attain bodhi in his present life. They will also lose any position as the king of a country or as a wheel-turning king. They will also lose any position as a bhikshu or bhikshuni and will also lose any position among the ten initiatory stages, the ten developmental stages, the ten vajra stages, the ten grounds, or the eternally dwelling sublime fruition of the buddha nature. They will lose all of them and they will fall into the three wretched destinies after which, for two or three kalpas, they will not even hear the names of their parents or

正體字

以是不應一一犯。汝等一
1005a23 切諸菩薩今學當學已學。[8]如是十戒應當
1005a24 學敬心奉持。八萬威儀品當廣明。
1005a25 佛告諸菩薩言。已說十波羅提木叉竟。四
1005a26 十八輕今當說。

[1. The Precept against Disrespecting Teachers and [Dharma] Friends. (ZY: "第一不敬師友戒." / FZ: "輕慢師長戒第一.")**]**

1005a27 [9]佛言。若佛子。欲受國王位時。受轉輪王
1005a28 位時。百官受位時。應先受菩薩戒。一切鬼
1005a29 神救護王身百官之身。諸佛歡喜。既得戒
1005b01 已。生孝順心恭敬心。見上座[10]和上[11]阿闍
1005b02 梨[12]大(+德）同學同見同行者。[13]應起承迎禮拜問
1005b03 訊。而菩薩反生憍心[14]慢心癡[15]心(+瞋心）。不起承迎
1005b04 禮拜。一一不如法供養。以自賣身國城男女
1005b05 七寶百物而供給之。若不爾者。犯輕垢罪。

[2. The Precept against Consuming Intoxicants. (ZY: "第二飲酒戒." / FZ: "飲酒戒第二.")**]**

1005b06 若佛子。故飲酒而生酒過失無量。若自身手
1005b07 過酒器與人飲酒者。

简体字

以是不应一一犯。

"汝等一切诸菩萨，今学，当学，已学。如是十戒，应当学，散心奉持。《八万威仪品》当广明。"

佛告诸菩萨言："已说十波罗提木叉竟，四十八轻今当说。"

"若佛子，欲受国王位时，受转轮王位时，百官受位时，应先受菩萨戒。一切鬼神救护王身、百官之身，诸佛欢喜。既得戒已，生孝顺心、恭敬心，见上座、和尚、阿阇黎、大德、同学、同见、同行者，应起承迎，礼拜问讯。而菩萨反生憍心、慢心、痴心、瞋心，不起承迎礼拜，一一不如法供养。以自卖身、国城、男女、七宝、百物而供给之，若不尔者，犯轻垢罪。

"若佛子，故饮酒，而酒生过失无量。若自身手过酒器，与人饮酒者，

of the Three Jewels. For these reasons, one should not violate any one of them.

You bodhisattvas all train in these ten precepts now, will train in them in the future, and have trained in them in the past. These ten precepts should be studied and upheld respectfully. They will be extensively explained in "The Eighty Thousand [Rules of the] Awesome Deportment Chapter."

The Buddha then told the bodhisattvas, "Now that the ten *prātimokṣa* precepts have been set forth, I shall now explain the forty-eight minor precepts."

The Buddha said:

The Forty-Eight Minor Bodhisattva Precepts

1. The Precept against Disrespecting Teachers and [Dharma] Friends.[43]

If a son of the Buddha is about to ascend to the position of the king of a country or is about to take on the position of a wheel-turning king or one of the hundred officials, he should first take the bodhisattva precepts. Then all the ghosts and spirits will protect that king or official and the buddhas will be pleased. After having received the precepts, he should bring forth a mind of filial respect and a mind of reverence such that, whenever he sees a senior member of the Saṃgha,[44] an *upādhyāya*,[45] an *ācārya*,[46] a greatly virtuous fellow student,[47] one holding the same views,[48] or one who cultivates the same practices, he should rise, welcome him, bow down in reverence to him, and then half bow to him [with joined palms]. Thus if, on the contrary, [on meeting such persons], a bodhisattva gives rise to a mind of arrogance, a mind of pride, a foolish mind, or a hateful mind,[49] and hence does not rise, welcome them, and bow in reverence to them, but rather, in each and every case, he fails to make offerings to them in accordance with Dharma by [being willing if necessary to] personally borrow to do so through pledging as security himself, his country, his city, his sons or daughters, the seven precious things, or the hundred kinds of valuables—if he fails to do so, he thereby commits a minor defiling offense.

2. The Precept against Consuming Intoxicants.[50]

If a son of the Buddha deliberately consumes intoxicants, he thereby gives rise to the countless faults associated with intoxicants. If, with his own hand, he passes a bottle of wine and gives it to another person so that he may drink the wine, he may have no

正體字

五百世無手。何況自
1005b08 ‖ 飲。不得教一切人飲。及一切眾生飲酒。況
1005b09 ‖ 自飲[16]酒。若故自飲教人飲[＊]者。犯輕垢罪。

[3. The Precept against Eating Meat. (ZY: "第三食肉戒." / FZ: "食肉戒第三.")**]**

1005b10 ‖ 若佛子。故食肉一切肉不得[17]食。（+夫食肉者）斷大慈悲
1005b11 ‖ [18](+佛)性種子。一切眾生見而捨去。是故一切菩薩
1005b12 ‖ 不得食一切眾生肉。食肉得無量罪。若故
1005b13 ‖ 食者。犯輕垢罪。

[4. The Precept against Eating the Five Kinds of Pungent Plants. (ZY: "第四食五辛戒." / FZ: "食五辛戒第四.")**]**

1005b14 ‖ 若佛子。不得食五辛。大蒜革葱[19]慈葱蘭葱
1005b15 ‖ 興蕖。是五種一切食中不得食。[20]若故食者。
1005b16 ‖ 犯輕垢罪。

[5. The Precept against Failure to Teach Repentance of Offenses. (ZY: "第五不教悔罪戒." / FZ: "不舉教懺戒品第五.")**]**

1005b17 ‖ 若佛子。見一切眾生犯八戒五戒十戒。毀
1005b18 ‖ 禁七逆八難一切犯戒罪。應教懺悔。而菩薩
1005b19 ‖ 不教懺悔[21]共住同僧利養。而共布薩同一
1005b20 ‖ 眾住說戒。而不舉其罪[22]教悔過者。犯輕
1005b21 ‖ 垢罪。

[6. The Precept against Failure to Make Offerings and Request the Dharma. (ZY: "第六不供給請法戒." / FZ: "不敬請法戒第六.")**]**

1005b22 ‖ 若佛子。見大乘法師大乘同學同見

简体字

五百世无手，何况自饮？亦不得教一切人饮，及一切众生饮酒，况自饮酒？一切酒不得饮，若故自饮，教人饮者，犯轻垢罪。

"若佛子，故食肉，一切众生肉不得食。夫食肉者，断大慈悲佛性种子，一切众生见而舍去。是故一切菩萨，不得食一切众生肉。食肉得无量罪！若故食者，犯轻垢罪。

"若佛子，不得食五辛：大蒜、茖葱、慈葱、兰葱、兴渠。是五种，一切食中不得食。若故食者，犯轻垢罪。

"若佛子，见一切众生犯八戒、五戒、十戒、毁禁、七逆、八难，一切犯戒罪，应教忏悔。而菩萨不教忏悔，同住，同僧利养，而共布萨，同一众住说戒，而不举其罪，不教悔过者，犯轻垢罪。

"若佛子，见大乘法师、大乘同学、同见、

hands for five hundred lifetimes. How much the worse would that [retribution] be if he were to drink it himself. One must not encourage any person or any other being to drink intoxicants. How much the less should one drink intoxicants himself. If one deliberately drinks them himself or encourages others to drink them, he thereby commits a minor defiling offense.

3. The Precept against Eating Meat.[51]

[It is an offense] if a son of the Buddha deliberately eats meat. One must not deliberately eat any kind of meat. Eating meat cuts off the great kindness and compassion and the seed of the buddha nature.[52] Any being who sees him will then depart. Therefore all bodhisattvas must not eat the flesh of any being. If one eats meat, he acquires countless karmic offenses. If one deliberately eats it, he thereby commits a minor defiling offense.

4. The Precept against Eating the Five Kinds of Pungent Plants.[53]

A son of the Buddha must not eat the five kinds of pungent plants,[54] namely: garlic; green onions; scallions; alpine leeks;[55] and asafoetida. These five kinds must not be eaten as an ingredient in any food. If one deliberately eats them, he thereby commits a minor defiling offense.[56]

5. The Precept against Failure to Teach Repentance of Offenses.[57]

If a son of the Buddha sees any beings transgress against the eight precepts, the five precepts, or the ten precepts, if he sees them violate any of the prohibitions, if he sees them commit any of the seven heinous offenses[58] [or other offenses entailing] the eight difficulties[59] [as their karmic result], or if he sees them commit any other offenses constituting transgressions of the precepts, he should instruct them to repent and reform. Thus, if a bodhisattva fails to instruct them to repent and reform even as they dwell together, share the Saṃgha's offerings, and join in the same assembly for the *upoṣadha* ceremony[60] and the speaking of the precepts—if he then still fails to bring up their offenses and instruct them to repent of their transgressions, he thereby commits a minor defiling offense.

6. The Precept against Failure to Make Offerings and Request Dharma.[61]

If a son of the Buddha sees a Great Vehicle Dharma master, a fellow Great Vehicle student, one who holds the same views, or one

正體字

同行。來
1005b23 | 入僧坊舍宅城邑。若百里千里來者。即[23]起
1005b24 | 迎來送去禮拜供養。日日三時供養。日食三
1005b25 | 兩金百味飲食床座[24]醫藥供事法師。一切所
1005b26 | 須盡給與之。常請法師三時說法。日日三
1005b27 | 時禮拜。不生瞋心患惱之心。為法滅身請
1005b28 | 法不懈。若不爾者。犯輕垢罪。

[7. The Precept against Failure to Listen to the Dharma Due to Indolence. (ZY: "第七懈怠不聽法戒." / FZ: "不聽經律戒第七.")**]**

1005b29 | 若佛子。一切處有[25]講(+法)毘尼經律。大宅舍中
1005c01 | 講法處。是新學菩薩應持經律卷至法師
1005c02 | 所聽受諮問。若山林樹下僧地房中。一切說
1005c03 | 法處悉至聽受。若不至彼聽受者。犯輕垢
1005c04 | 罪。

[8. The Precept against Turning Away from the Great and Turning toward the Small. (ZY: "第八背大向小戒." / FZ: "背正向邪戒第八.")**]**

1005c05 | 若佛子。心背大乘常住經律。言非佛說。而
1005c06 | 受持二乘聲聞外道惡見一切禁戒邪見經
1005c07 | 律者。犯輕垢罪。

[9. The Precept against Failure to Look after the Sick. (ZY: "第九不看病戒." / FZ: "不瞻病苦戒第九.")**]**

1005c08 | 若佛子。見一切疾病人。

简体字

同行来，入僧坊、舍宅、城邑，若百里、千里来者，即起迎来送去，礼拜供养。日日三时供养，日食三两金，百味饮食，床座医药，供事法师，一切所须，尽给与之。常请法师三时说法，日日三时礼拜，不生瞋心、患恼之心。为法灭身，请法不懈。若不尔者，犯轻垢罪。

"若佛子，一切处有讲法毗尼经律，大宅舍中有讲法处，是新学菩萨，应持经律卷，至法师所听受谘问。若山林树下、僧地房中，一切说法处，悉至听受。若不至彼听受谘问者，犯轻垢罪。

"若佛子，心背大乘常住经律，言非佛说，而受持二乘声闻，外道恶见，一切禁戒邪见经律者，犯轻垢罪。

"若佛子，见一切疾病人，

who cultivates the same practices who has come to enter a Saṃgha dwelling, a household, a city, or a town, having come from thirty miles or three hundred miles away,[62] he should immediately arise and welcome him when he arrives and then escort him off when he leaves, bowing in reverence and making offerings to him every day, three times each day, serving him each day the hundred flavors of food and drink worth three ounces[63] of gold while also supplying the Dharma master with bedding, meditation cushions, and medicines, completely providing him with everything he needs, always requesting the Dharma master three times to teach the Dharma, bowing to him in reverence three times[64] each day, never having hateful thoughts or troubled and afflicted thoughts, always being willing to sacrifice himself for the sake of the Dharma, and always remaining tireless in requesting the Dharma. If one fails to act in accordance with this, he thereby commits a minor defiling offense.

7. The Precept against Failure to Listen to the Dharma Due to Indolence.[65]

For a son of the Buddha, wherever there are teachings on Dharma,[66] the *vinaya*,[67] the scriptures, or the moral codes, whether they be presented in a large house or some other place for lectures on Dharma, this bodhisattva who has only recently taken up the training should take copies of the sutras or moral precept scriptures to the place where the Dharma master is abiding to listen and ask questions. Whether it be beneath a tree in the mountain forests or in a Saṃgha dwelling, he should go and listen wherever the Dharma is being taught. If he fails to go there and listen to the teachings, he thereby commits a minor defiling offense.

8. The Precept against Turning Away from the Great and Turning toward the Small.[68]

If a son of the Buddha's mind turns away from the Great Vehicle's eternally dwelling scriptures and moral codes or he says of them that they were not spoken by the Buddha, whereupon he then accepts and upholds the unwholesome views of the Two Vehicles' *śrāvaka* disciples or non-Buddhists, any of their restrictive observances, or any of their scriptures and moral codes based on wrong views, he thereby commits a minor defiling offense.

9. The Precept against Failure to Look after the Sick.[69]

If a son of the Buddha sees any person afflicted with illness, he

正體字

[26]常應供養如佛無
1005c09 異。八福田中看病福田第一福田。若父母師
1005c10 僧弟子[27]疾病。諸根不具百種病苦惱。皆[28]養
1005c11 令差。而菩薩以[29]惡心瞋恨。不至僧房中城
1005c12 邑曠野山林道路中。見病不[30]救者犯輕垢
1005c13 罪。

[10. The Precept against Collecting Weapons Used for Killing Beings. (ZY: "第十畜殺眾生具戒." / FZ: "畜諸殺具戒第十.")]

1005c14 若佛子。不得畜一切刀[＊]杖弓箭鉾斧鬪戰
1005c15 之具。及惡[31]網羅殺生之器。一切不得畜。而
1005c16 菩薩乃至殺父母尚不加報。況[32][餘＝殺]餘一切眾
1005c17 [33]生。若故畜[34]一切刀[＊]杖[＊]者。犯輕垢罪。如
1005c18 是十戒。應當學敬心奉持。下[35]六品中[36]當
1005c19 廣明。

[11. The Precept against Acting as a Country's [Military] Emissary. (ZY: "第十一國使戒." / FZ: "通國入軍戒第十一.")]

1005c20 佛言。佛子。不得為利養惡心故。通國使
1005c21 命軍陣合會。興師相伐殺無量眾生。而菩
1005c22 薩[37]不得入軍中往來。況故作國賊。若故
1005c23 作者。犯輕垢罪。

简体字

常应供养，如佛无异。八福田中，看病福田，第一福田。若父母、师僧、弟子病，诸根不具，百种病苦恼，皆供养令差。而菩萨以瞋恨心不看，乃至僧房中、城邑、旷野、山林、道路中，见病不救济者，犯轻垢罪。

"若佛子，不得畜一切刀杖、弓箭、鉾斧、斗战之具，及恶罗网杀生之器，一切不得畜。而菩萨乃至杀父母，尚不加报，况杀一切众生？不得畜杀众生具，若故畜者，犯轻垢罪。

"如是十戒应当学，敬心奉持，下《六度品》中广明。

佛言："佛子，不得为利养、恶心故，通国使命，军阵合会，兴师相伐，杀无量众生。而菩萨尚不得入军中往来，况故作国贼？若故作者，犯轻垢罪。

should always make offerings to him just the same as if and no differently than if he were the Buddha himself. Of the eight fields of merit,[70] the field of merit of looking after the sick is the foremost field of merit. If one's father, mother, Saṃgha teacher, or disciple becomes so ill that their faculties are no longer completely normal or they are beset by the sufferings and afflictions of any of the hundred kinds of diseases, one should care for them all and enable them to be cured of their sickness. Thus, especially if, due to being possessed of an evil mind or hatred, a bodhisattva does not go into the Saṃgha dwelling or into the city, the villages, the wilderness, the mountain forests, or out on the roads in order to look after the sick and so does not save them, he thereby commits a minor defiling offense.

10. The Precept against Collecting Weapons Used for Killing Beings.[71]

A son of the Buddha must not collect any kinds of weapons of war such as knives, clubs, bows, arrows, spears, or battle-axes, nor may he collect instruments of wrongdoing such as nets or other equipment used for killing beings. One must not collect any of them. Thus a bodhisattva would not even seek revenge for the killing of his own father or mother, how much the less would he kill[72] any living being [for any other reason]. If he deliberately collects any knives or clubs, he thereby commits a minor defiling offense.

One should study and respectfully uphold these ten precepts. They will be extensively explained in the following six chapters.

11. The Precept against Acting as a Country's [Military] Emissary.[73]

The Buddha said:

Sons of the Buddha, one must not, acting for the sake of personal benefit or with evil intentions, transmit a country's commands to bring about a confrontation of military forces to which troops will be dispatched who will then attack each other, resulting in the killing of countless beings. Thus a bodhisattva must not even come and go from the midst of the military, how much the less may he deliberately become a traitor to his country [by serving in such a role]. If he deliberately acts in this way, he thereby commits a minor defiling offense.

正體字

[12. The Precept against Carrying on [Uncompassionate Kinds of] Trade. (ZY: "第十二販賣戒." / FZ: "傷慈販賣戒第十二.")]

1005c24 | 若佛子。故販賣良人奴婢六畜。市易棺材板
1005c25 | 木盛死之具。尚[38]不[39]自作況教人作。[40]若故
1006a01 | 作者。犯輕垢罪。

[13. The Precept against Slandering Others. (ZY: "第十三謗毀戒." / FZ: "無根謗人戒第十三.")]

1006a02 | 若佛子。以惡心故無事謗他良人善人法師
1006a03 | 師僧國王貴人。言犯七逆十重。[1]於父母兄
1006a04 | 弟六親中。應生孝順心慈悲心。而反更加
1006a05 | 於逆害墮不如意處[*]者。犯輕垢罪。

[14. The Precept against Starting [Destructive] Fires. (ZY: "第十四放火燒戒." / FZ: "放火損燒戒.")]

1006a06 | 若佛子。以惡心故放大火。燒山林[2]曠野。
1006a07 | 四月乃至九月。放火若燒他人家屋宅城邑
1006a08 | 僧房田木及鬼神官物。一切有主物不得故
1006a09 | 燒。若故燒者。犯輕垢罪。

[15. The Precept against Deviant Teachings. (ZY: "第十五僻教戒." / FZ: "法化違宗戒第十五.")]

1006a10 | 若佛子。自佛弟子及外道[3]人。六親一切善
1006a11 | 知識。應一一教[4]受持大乘經律。[5]應教解
1006a12 | 義理。使發菩提心十[6]發心十長養心

简体字

"若佛子，故贩卖良人、奴婢、六畜，市易棺材板木盛死之具，尚不应自作，况教人作？若故自作，教人作者，犯轻垢罪。

"若佛子，以恶心故，无事谤他良人、善人、法师、师僧、国王、贵人，言犯七逆十重。父母兄弟六亲中，应生孝顺心、慈悲心。而反更加于逆害，堕不如意处者，犯轻垢罪。

"若佛子，以恶心故，放大火烧山林旷野，四月乃至九月放火，若烧他人家屋宅、城邑、僧房、田木及鬼神、官物。一切有主物，不得故烧。若故烧者，犯轻垢罪。

"若佛子，自佛弟子，及外道恶人，六亲，一切善知识，应一一教受特大乘经律，教解义理，使发菩提心。十发趣心、十长养心、

12. The Precept against Carrying on [Uncompassionate Kinds of] Trade.[74]

[It is an offense] if a son of the Buddha deliberately traffics in good people, male or female slaves, or the six kinds of domestic animals,[75] and so, too, if he trades in coffins, in the wooden boards for making them, or in other products intended to contain [the bodies of] the dead. He should not even do so himself, how much the less should he encourage others to do so. If he deliberately does so, he thereby commits a minor defiling offense.

13. The Precept against Slandering Others.[76]

[It is an offense] if a son of the Buddha, because of evil intentions, proceeds with no basis to slander other good people, virtuous people, Dharma masters, teachers among the Saṃgha, the king, or members of the nobility, saying of them that they have committed one of the seven heinous offenses or have violated the ten major precepts. One should bring forth a mind of filial respect and a mind of kindness and compassion toward [all beings by which he regards them just as he would][77] his own father, mother, elder and younger brothers, and the rest of the six close relatives.[78] If one instead inflicts contrary sorts of harm on them and thus causes them to fall into undesirable circumstances, he thereby commits a minor defiling offense.

14. The Precept against Starting [Destructive] Fires.[79]

[It is an offense] if a son of the Buddha with bad intentions deliberately starts a great blaze by which he burns mountain forests or the wilderness, starts fires between the fourth and ninth lunar months,[80] or burns other people's houses or dwellings, cities, villages, Saṃgha residences, fields, groves, or the possessions of ghosts, spirits, or officials. One must not deliberately burn anything that belongs to anyone.[81] If one deliberately burns them, he thereby commits a minor defiling offense.

15. The Precept against Deviant Teachings.[82]

A son of the Buddha should teach [everyone] from the disciples of the Buddha to the non-Buddhists and [everyone] from one's six close relatives to all of one's good spiritual friends, teaching each and every one of them to accept and uphold the Great Vehicle scriptures and moral codes. One should teach them to understand their principles and induce them to bring forth the resolve to realize bodhi. Whether it be the ten initiatory minds, then ten devel-

正體字

十金
1006a13 剛心。[7]三十心中一一解其次第法用。而菩
1006a14 薩以惡心瞋心。橫教[8]他二乘聲聞經律外
1006a15 道邪見論等。犯輕垢罪。

[16. The Precept against Teaching in a Perverse Manner for Personal Benefit. (ZY: "第十六為利倒說戒." / FZ: "惜法規利戒第十六.")**]**

1006a16 若佛子。應好心先學大乘威儀經律。廣開解
1006a17 義味。見後新學菩薩有[9]從百里千里來求
1006a18 大乘經律。應如法為說一切苦行。若燒身
1006a19 燒臂燒指。若不燒身臂指供養諸佛非
1006a20 出家菩薩。乃至餓[10]虎狼師[11]子一切餓鬼。悉
1006a21 應捨身肉手足而供養之。[12]後一一次第為
1006a22 說正法。使心開意解。而菩薩為利養[13]故應
1006a23 答不答。倒說經律文字無前無後謗三
1006a24 寶說[*]者。犯輕垢罪。

[17. The Precept against Begging in Reliance on the Powerful. (ZY: "第十七恃勢乞求戒." / FZ: "依官強乞戒第十七.")**]**

1006a25 若佛子。自為飲食錢[14]物利養名譽故。親近
1006a26 國王王子大臣百官。恃作形勢。乞索打拍牽
1006a27 挽。橫取錢[*]物一切求利。名為惡求多求。
1006a28 教他人求。

简体字

十金刚心，于三十心中，一一解其次第法用。而菩萨以恶心、瞋心，横教二乘声闻经律，外道邪见论等，犯轻垢罪。

“若佛子，应好心先学大乘威仪经律，广开解义味。见后新学菩萨，有从百里千里来求大乘经律，应如法为说一切苦行，若烧身、烧臂、烧指。若不烧身、臂、指供养诸佛，非出家菩萨，乃至饿虎、狼、狮子、一切饿鬼，悉应舍身肉手足而供养之。然后一一次第为说正法，使心开意解。而菩萨为利养故，为名闻故，应答不答，倒说经律文字，无前无后，谤三宝说者，犯轻垢罪。

“若佛子，自为饮食、钱财、利养、名誉故，亲近国王、王子、大臣、百官，恃作形势，乞索打拍牵挽，横取钱财。一切求利，名为恶求、多求，教他人求，

opmental minds, or the ten vajra minds, [one should teach them] to understand the sequence and Dharma function of the contents of each and every one of them. Hence if, due to having a mind affected by what is unwholesome or a mind affected by hatred, a bodhisattva perversely teaches them the Two Vehicles' *śrāvaka* scriptures and moral codes or the non-Buddhists' wrong views, treatises, and such, he thereby commits a minor defiling offense.

16. The Precept against Teaching in a Perverse Manner for Personal Benefit.[83]

A son of the Buddha, proceeding with good intentions, should first train in the Great Vehicle's awesome deportment, scriptures, and moral codes and extensively open up and understand their meaning and flavor. Thereafter, whenever he sees bodhisattvas who have come along after him and who are new to their studies who may have come from thirty or three hundred miles away seeking Great Vehicle scriptures and moral codes, he should explain for their sakes and in accordance with Dharma all of the austere practices, whether this be the burning of one's body, the burning of one's arm, or the burning of one's finger. [He should explain to them that], if one is not willing to burn his body, arm, or finger as an offering to the buddhas, he is not a [true] monastic bodhisattva and, furthermore, he should even be willing to sacrifice the flesh of his body, hands, and feet as offerings to starving tigers, wolves, lions, or hungry ghosts.[84] Afterward, he should explain right Dharma for them, point by point, in correct sequence, thereby enabling their minds to develop a reasoned understanding of it. Thus if a bodhisattva, for the sake of gaining personal benefit or offerings, does not respond when he should respond, if he explains the scriptures and moral codes in a perverse manner, if he explains passages out of context, or if he speaks in a way that slanders the Three Jewels, he thereby commits a minor defiling offense.

17. The Precept against Begging in Reliance on the Powerful.[85]

If a son of the Buddha, for the sake of food and drink, wealth, benefit, or fame draws near to kings, princes, great government ministers, or the many types of officials in order to rely upon the power of such relationships to make coercive demands of others and forcibly seize their wealth or property, all such means of seeking personal benefit constitute evil and excessive means of seeking [one's own benefit]. [If he pursues his own benefit in such ways] or encourages others to pursue their own benefit in such ways, be-

正體字

都無慈心無孝順心[*]者。犯輕
1006a29 垢罪。

[18. The Precept against Serving as a Teacher with Insufficient Understanding. (ZY: "第十八無解作師戒." / FZ: "無知為師戒第十八.")**]**

1006b01 若佛子。[15]學誦戒[16]者。日夜六時持菩薩戒。
1006b02 解其義理佛性之性。而菩薩不解一句一
1006b03 [17]偈戒律因緣。詐言能解者。即為自欺誑亦
1006b04 欺誑他人。一一不解一切[18]法。而為他人作
1006b05 師[19]授戒者。犯輕垢罪。

[19. The Precept against Divisive Speech. (ZY: "第十九兩舌戒." / FZ: "鬪謗欺賢戒第十九.")**]**

1006b06 若佛子。以惡心故。見持戒比丘手捉香爐
1006b07 行菩薩行。而鬪搆兩頭謗欺賢人無惡不
1006b08 造。[20]若故作者。犯輕垢罪。

[20. The Precept against Failure to Practice the Liberation of Beings. (ZY: "第二十不行放救戒." / FZ: "不能救生戒第二十.")**]**

1006b09 若佛子。以慈心故行放生[21]業[+應作是念]。一切男子是
1006b10 我父。一切女人是我母。我生生無不從之
1006b11 受生。故六道眾生皆是我父母。而殺而食者。
1006b12 即殺我父母亦殺我故身。一切地水是我先
1006b13 身。一切火風是我本體。故常行放[22]生。生生
1006b14 受生[23]

简体字

都无慈悯心，无孝顺心者，犯轻垢罪。

"若佛子，应学十二部经，诵戒，日日六时持菩萨戒，解其义理佛性之性。而菩萨不解一句一偈，及戒律因缘，诈言能解者，即为自欺诳，亦欺诳他人。一一不解，一切法不知，而为他人作师授戒者，犯轻垢罪。

"若佛子，以恶心故，见持戒比丘，手捉香炉，行菩萨行，而鬬遘两头，谤欺贤人，无恶不造者，犯轻垢罪。

"若佛子，以慈心故，行放生业，应作是念：'一切男子是我父，一切女人是我母。我生生无不从之受生，故六道众生皆是我父母，而杀而食者，即杀我父母，亦杀我故身。一切地水是我先身，一切火风是我本体，故当行放生业。生生受生，

cause these actions are all devoid of a mind of loving kindness or a mind of filial respect, he thereby commits a minor defiling offense.

18. The Precept against Serving as a Teacher with Insufficient Understanding.[86]

If a son of the Buddha is training in and reciting the precepts, he should uphold the bodhisattva precepts in the six periods of the day and night and develop an understanding of their meaning, their principles, and the nature of the buddha nature. This being so, if a bodhisattva does not understand so much as a single sentence or a single verse of the causes and conditions of the moral codes and yet he falsely claims to be able to explain them, this amounts to deceiving himself while also deceiving others. Thus, if in each and every instance he fails to understand any of these dharmas and yet he serves for others as a Dharma teacher in the transmitting of the precepts, he thereby commits a minor defiling offense.

19. The Precept against Divisive Speech.[87]

If a son of the Buddha motivated by evil intentions sees precept-holding bhikshus, censers in hand, practicing the bodhisattva practices, and then proceeds to provoke hostility between two of them by slandering and deceiving such virtuous persons, [saying of one to the other], "There is no evil he will not do"—if he deliberately does this, he thereby commits a minor defiling offense.

20. The Precept against Failure to Practice the Liberation of Beings.[88]

If a son of the Buddha motivated by loving kindness practices the karmic deed of liberating beings, he should reflect in this manner,[89] "All male beings are my fathers [from earlier lifetimes] and all female beings are my mothers [from earlier lifetimes]. During the course of my previous rebirths, there are none of them from whom I have not been born. Therefore all beings of the six paths of rebirth are my fathers and mothers. Thus, whenever anyone kills and eats any of them, they are just killing my own fathers and mothers while also killing my former bodies, for all elemental earth and water have composed my bodies from earlier lifetimes and all elemental fire and wind have served as my fundamental essence."

Therefore one should always practice the liberation of life and, in life after life, wherever one takes birth, [to accord with] the eter-

正體字

常住之法。教人放生。若見世人殺畜
1006b15 生時。應方便救護解其苦難。常教化講說
1006b16 菩薩戒救度眾生。若父母兄弟死亡之日。
1006b17 [24]應請法師講菩薩戒[25]經[+律]福資[26]亡者。得
1006b18 見諸佛生人天上。若不爾者犯輕垢罪。如
1006b19 是十戒應當學敬心奉持。如滅罪品中[27]廣
1006b20 明一一戒[28]相。

[21. The Precept against Taking Revenge with Hatred or Blows. (ZY: "第二十一瞋打報仇戒." / FZ: "無慈忍酬怨戒第二十一.")]

1006b21 佛言。佛子。不得以瞋報瞋以打報打。若殺
1006b22 父母兄弟六親不得加報。若國主為他人
1006b23 殺者。亦不得加報。殺生報生不順孝道。
1006b24 尚不畜奴婢打拍罵辱。日日起三業口罪
1006b25 無量。況故作七逆之罪。而出家菩薩無[29]慈
1006b26 報[30]讎。乃至六親[31]中故[32]報者。犯輕垢罪。

[22. The Precept against Failure to Request Dharma Due to Arrogance or Pride. (ZY: "第二十二憍慢不請法戒." / FZ: "慢人輕法戒第二十二.")]

1006b27 若佛子。[33]初始出家未有所解。而自恃聰明
1006b28 有智。或[34]恃高貴年宿。或恃大姓高門

简体字

常住之法，教人放生。' 若见世人杀畜生时，应方便救护，解其苦难。常教化讲说菩萨戒，救度众生。若父母兄弟死亡之日，应请法师讲菩萨戒经律，福资亡者，得见诸佛，生人天上。若不尔者，犯轻垢罪。

"如是十戒，应当学，敬心奉持。《灭罪品》中，广明一一戒相。"

佛言："佛子，不得以瞋报瞋，以打报打。若杀父母兄弟六亲，不得加报；若国主为他人杀者，亦不得加报。杀生报生，不顺孝道。尚不畜奴婢打拍骂辱，日日起三业，口罪无量，况故作七逆之罪？而出家菩萨，无慈心报仇，乃至六亲中，故作报者，犯轻垢罪。

"若佛子，初始出家，未有所解，而自恃聪明有智，或恃高贵年宿，或恃大姓、高门、

nally abiding Dharma, one should also teach others to liberate beings. Thus if one sees some worldly person about to kill beings, one should devise a skillful means to rescue them, protect them, and liberate them from their suffering and difficulty.

Furthermore, one should always teach and explain the bodhisattva precepts in order to rescue and liberate beings. On the day that one's mother, father, elder brother, or younger brother dies, one should invite a Dharma master to lecture on the Bodhisattva Precepts Scripture's moral code[90] to generate merit for the benefit of the deceased so that they may be able to see the Buddhas and attain rebirth among humans and devas. If one fails to do this, one thereby commits a minor defiling offense.

The bodhisattva should study and respectfully uphold the aforementioned ten precepts in accordance with the expansive explanation of every aspect of the precepts found in "The Extinguishing Offenses Chapter."

The Buddha said:

21. The Precept against Taking Revenge with Hatred or Blows.[91]

A son of the Buddha must not repay hatred with hatred and must not repay blows with blows. Even if someone kills one's father, mother, elder brother, younger brother, or other close relatives,[92] one still must not take revenge. And even if the ruler of one's country is murdered by others, one must not take revenge then, either. Killing one being to revenge the murder of another being is contrary to the path of filial respect. One must not even keep slaves or menials whom one might strike, slap, scold, or insult, for to do so ensures the daily creation of the three kinds of bad karma along with countless verbal karmic offenses. How much the less may one deliberately commit any of the seven heinous offenses. Thus, if a monastic bodhisattva[93] acts without kindness and then deliberately takes revenge on others, even if it is for harm done to his own close relatives, he thereby commits a minor defiling offense.

22. The Precept against Failure to Request Dharma Due to Arrogance or Pride.[94]

It may be that a son of the Buddha who has only recently left the home life and still does not have much that he understands personally relies on his own intelligence and possession of knowledge, or perhaps he relies on his upper class origins or seniority in age, or perhaps he relies on his great family name, aristocratic back-

大解

1006b29 大[35] 福。大富。饒財七寶。以此憍慢而不諮受先學
1006c01 法師經律。其法師者。或小姓年少卑門貧[36]窮
1006c02 諸根不具。而實有德一切經律盡解。而新學
1006c03 菩薩不得觀法師種姓。而不來諮受法師
1006c04 第一義諦者。犯輕垢罪。

[23. The Precept against Arrogance and Speaking [the Dharma] in a Distorted Manner. (ZY: "第二十三憍慢僻說戒." / FZ: "經新求學戒第二十三.")]

正體字

1006c05 若佛子。佛滅度後。欲[37]~~心~~[以]好心受菩薩戒
1006c06 時。於佛菩薩形像前自誓受戒。當七日佛
1006c07 前懺悔。得見好相便得戒。若不得好[38]相。
1006c08 [39]應二七三七乃至一年。要得好相。得好相
1006c09 已。便得佛菩薩形像前受戒。若不得好相。
1006c10 雖佛像前受。戒不得戒。若現前先受菩薩
1006c11 戒法師前受戒時。不須要見好相[40]何以
1006c12 故。[41]以是法師師師相授故。不須好相。是以
1006c13 法師前受戒即得戒。以[42]生[+至]重心故便得戒。

简体字

大解，大富饶财七宝，以此憍慢，而不谘受先学法师经律。其法师者，或小姓、年少、卑门、贫穷、下贱，诸根不具，而实有德，一切经律尽解。而新学菩萨，不得观法师种姓，而不来谘受法师第一义谛者，犯轻垢罪。

"若佛子，佛灭度后，欲以好心受菩萨戒时，于佛菩萨形像前，自誓受戒。当七日佛前忏悔，得见好相，便得戒。若不得好相时，应二七、三七，乃至一年，要得好相。得好相已，使得佛菩萨形像前受戒。若不得好相，虽佛像前受戒，不得戒。若现前先受菩萨戒法师前受戒时，不须要见好相。何以故？是法师，师师相授，故不须好相。是以法师前受戒时，即得戒；以生至重心故，便得戒。

ground, prodigious understanding, great merit, great wealth,[95] or possession of bounteous riches, including the seven precious things. Then, because of this arrogance and pride, he may refuse to seek out and receive teachings on the sutras and moral codes from Dharma masters who began their training before him, [refusing to do so because] those Dharma masters may have lesser family names, may be younger in years, may be of inferior social station, may be poor, or may be physically disabled, [refusing to approach them] even though [those Dharma masters] are truly virtuous and possessed of an exhaustive understanding of all the sutras and moral codes. Therefore a bodhisattva new to the training must not judge Dharma masters on the basis of their family background. Thus if he refuses to come to a Dharma master to seek out and receive teachings on the ultimate truth, he thereby commits a minor defiling offense.

23. The Precept against Arrogance and Speaking [the Dharma] in a Distorted Manner.[96]

Sons of the Buddha, after the Buddha's nirvāṇa, whenever there is a person who, with good intentions,[97] wishes to receive the bodhisattva precepts, he should go before the images of the Buddha and the bodhisattvas and make a vow to take the precepts. Then he should practice repentance before an image of the Buddha for seven days. If he succeeds in seeing auspicious signs,[98] he then succeeds in acquiring the precepts. If he does not see auspicious signs,[99] he should continue to [to practice repentance] for two weeks, three weeks, or even up to a year. It is necessary to see auspicious signs. After one has seen auspicious signs, one has then succeeded in receiving the precepts before the images of the Buddha and the bodhisattvas. If one does not succeed in seeing auspicious signs, even though [one has sought] to receive the precepts before the image of the Buddha, one has not yet acquired the precepts.

However, when one receives the precepts directly from a Dharma master who has previously received the bodhisattva precepts himself, it is not necessary that one see auspicious signs. Why not? Because this Dharma master has already received the precepts as personally conferred from master to master, it is not necessary to first see auspicious signs. Therefore, when receiving the precepts in the presence of a Dharma master, one immediately receives the precepts. It is because one brings forth an ultimately sincere mind[100] that one then acquires the precepts.

正體字

1006c14 若千里內無能授戒師。得佛菩薩形像[43]前[+自誓]
1006c15 受戒而要見好相。若法師自倚解經律大
1006c16 乘學戒。與國王太子百官以為善友。而新
1006c17 學菩薩來問若經義律義。輕心惡心慢心。不
1006c18 一一好答問者。犯輕垢罪。

[24. The Precept against Failure to Practice and Train in the Buddha's Precepts. (ZY: "第二十四不習學佛戒." / FZ: "背正向邪戒第二十四.")]

1006c19 若佛子。有佛經律大乘[44][-~~王~~]法正見正性正法
1006c20 身而不能勤學修[45]習而捨七寶。反學邪
1006c21 見二乘外道俗典。阿毘曇雜論[46]書記。是斷
1006c22 佛性障道因緣。非行菩薩道。[47]若故作者。
1006c23 犯輕垢罪。

[25. The Precept against Failure to Skillfully Maintain Harmony in the Saṃgha. (ZY: "第二十五不善和眾戒." / FZ: "為主失儀戒第二十五.")]

1006c24 若佛子。佛[48]滅[+度]後。為說法主為僧[49]房主[50]教
1006c25 化主坐禪主行來主。應生慈心善和鬪[51]訟。
1007a01 善守三寶物莫無度用如自己有。而反亂
1007a02 眾鬪諍恣心用三寶物[＊]者。犯輕垢罪。

简体字

若千里内无能授戒师，得佛菩萨形像前自誓受戒，而要见好相。若法师自倚解经律、大乘学戒，与国王、太子、百官，以为善友；而新学菩萨来问，若经义律义，轻心、恶心、慢心，不一一好答问者，犯轻垢罪。

“若佛子，有佛、经、律、大乘法，正见、正性、正法身，而不能勤学修习；而舍七宝，反学邪见、二乘、外道、俗典，阿毘昙、杂论、一切书记，是断佛性障道因缘，非行菩萨道者。若故作者，犯轻垢罪。

“若佛子，佛灭度后，为说法主，为行法主，为僧房主，为教化主、坐禅主、行来主，应生慈心，善和斗诤；善守三宝物，莫无度用，如自己有。而反乱众鬬诤，恣心用三宝物者，犯轻垢罪。

If there is no master able to transmit the precepts within three hundred miles,[101] then, before the images of the Buddha and the bodhisattvas, one may make a personal vow[102] to take the precepts. Then it will be necessary to see auspicious signs.

If a Dharma master personally relies on his understanding of sutras, moral codes, and his Great Vehicle training in the precepts as well as on his position as the good spiritual friend of kings, princes, and the various government officials, doing so in such a way that, when bodhisattvas new to the training come and inquire about the meaning of the sutras or the moral codes, he treats them with a slighting, offensive, or arrogant attitude and fails to answer well every one of their questions, he thereby commits a minor defiling offense.

24. The Precept against Failure to Practice and Train in the Buddha's Precepts.[103]

If a son of the Buddha already has the Buddha, the sutras, the moral codes, the Dharma of the Great Vehicle,[104] right views, the right nature, and the right Dharma body, and yet he is unable to diligently study, cultivate, and practice them so that he then abandons these seven precious things and instead studies the wrong views found in [the writings of followers of] the Two Vehicles or the non-Buddhist traditions, in worldly texts, in the various *abhidharma* treatises, or in other such writings and records, these are the causes and conditions for cutting off the buddha nature and obstructing progress on the path. This is not the practice of the bodhisattva path. If one deliberately does this, he thereby commits a minor defiling offense.

25. The Precept against Failure to Skillfully Maintain Harmony in the Saṃgha.[105]

If after the Buddha's nirvāṇa a son of the Buddha serves as a Dharma lecturing host, as the head of a Saṃgha dwelling, as a [Dharma] teaching host, as the head of a *dhyāna* meditation facility, or as a guest prefect, he should bring forth a mind of loving kindness and skillfully establish harmony whenever disputes arise while also skillfully safeguarding the possessions of the Three Jewels, never using them immoderately as if they were one's own possessions. Thus if, on the contrary, one aggravates disputes within the Saṃgha or uses property of the Three Jewels in a careless manner, one thereby commits a minor defiling offense.

正體字

[26. The Precept against Accepting Offerings Solely for Oneself. (ZY: "獨受利養戒." / FZ: "待賓乖式戒第二十六.")**]**

1007a03 若佛子。先[1]在僧[*]房中住。[2]後見客菩薩比
1007a04 丘來入僧[*]房舍宅城[3]邑國王宅舍中。乃至
1007a05 夏坐安居處及大會中。先住僧應迎來送
1007a06 去。飲食供養房舍臥具。繩[4]床[+木床]事事給與。若
1007a07 無物應賣自身及[*]以男[5]女（＋身應割自身肉賣）供給所須悉
1007a08 [6]以與之。若有[7]檀越來請眾僧。客僧有利
1007a09 養分。僧[*]房主應次第差客僧受請。而先住
1007a10 僧獨受[8]請不差客[9]僧。僧[*]房主得無量罪。
1007a11 畜生無異非沙門非釋種[10]姓。[11]若故作者。
1007a12 犯輕垢罪。

[27. The Precept against Accepting Discriminatory Invitations. (ZY: "第二十七受別請戒." / FZ: "受別請戒第二十七.")**]**

1007a13 若佛子。一切不得受別請利養入己。而此
1007a14 利養屬十方僧。而別受請即取十方僧物
1007a15 入己。八福[12]田[+中]諸佛聖人一一師僧父母病人
1007a16 物自己用故。犯輕垢罪。

简体字

"若佛子，先在僧坊中住，若见客菩萨比丘，来入僧坊、舍宅、城邑，若国王宅舍中，乃至夏坐安居处，及大会中，先住僧应迎来送去，饮食供养，房舍、卧具、绳床、木床，事事给与。若无物，应卖自身，及男女身，应割自身肉卖，供给所需，悉以与之。若有檀越来请众僧，客僧有利养分，僧坊主应次第差客僧受请。而先住僧独受请，而不差客僧者，僧坊主得无量罪，畜生无异，非沙门，非释种姓，犯轻垢罪。

"若佛子，一切不得受别请利养入己，而此利养属十方僧，而别受请，即是取十方僧物入己。八福田中，诸佛、圣人、一一师僧、父母、病人物，自己用故，犯轻垢罪。

26. The Precept against Accepting Offerings Solely for Oneself.[106]

If a son of the Buddha who has previously established residence in a Saṃgha dwelling later sees a guest bodhisattva bhikshu come and enter the Saṃgha dwelling, a guest house or residence, a city or town, a residence provided by the king, or any other place up to and including a residence for the summer retreat or a Great Assembly, this previously established Saṃgha member should welcome that guest Saṃgha member when he comes, escort him off when he leaves, and provide him with offerings of food and drink, a residence, bedding, sitting mats, a rope-net bed or a wooden bed,[107] and all of the other essentials. If he has nothing to offer him, he should be willing to pledge himself or his male or female attendants as security or should even be willing to cut off and sell his own flesh[108] in order to obtain the means to supply the guest Saṃgha member with whatever he needs.

If a *dānapati*[109] comes and extends an invitation [to receive offerings] to the community of Saṃgha members, the guest Saṃgha member deserves to receive a share of any offerings that he provides. The head of the Saṃgha dwelling should send the guest Saṃgha member in response to invitations in accordance with his position in the sequential order. Thus if he allows the previously established Saṃgha members to accept the invitation solely for themselves and does not send along the guest Saṃgha member, the head of the Saṃgha dwelling thereby incurs a measureless amount of karmic offenses. He is no different from an animal, he is not a *śramaṇa*,[110] and he is not a member of the lineage of Śākyamuni Buddha. If one deliberately does this, he thereby commits a minor defiling offense.

27. The Precept against Accepting Discriminatory Invitations.[111]

If one is a son of the Buddha, he must not in any case accept a discriminatory invitation or offering for himself alone, for this offering belongs to the Saṃgha of the ten directions. Thus to accept discriminatory invitations is just to take the property of the Saṃgha of the ten directions for oneself. Because one diverts to one's own use the possessions of those in[112] the eight fields of merit[113] including those of the buddhas, the *āryas*,[114] each and every one of one's [monastic] teachers, the Saṃgha, one's father, one's mother, and the sick, one thereby commits a minor defiling offense.

正體字

[28. The Precept against Extending Discriminatory Invitations to Members of the Saṃgha. (ZY: "第二十八別請僧戒." / FZ: "故別請僧戒第二十八.")]

1007a17 | 若佛子。有出家菩薩在家菩薩及一切檀越。
1007a18 | 請僧福田求願之時。應入僧[＊]房問知事
1007a19 | 人。今[13]欲[+請僧求願知事報言]次第請者即得十方賢聖僧而世
1007a20 | 人別請五百羅漢菩薩僧。不如僧次一凡夫
1007a21 | 僧。若別請僧者。是外道法。七佛無別請法。
1007a22 | 不順孝道。若故別請僧者。犯輕垢罪。

[29. The Precept against Living by a Wrong Livelihood. (ZY: "第二十九邪命自活戒." / FZ: "惡伎損生戒第二十九.")]

1007a23 | 若佛子。以惡心故為利養[14]故。販賣男女
1007a24 | 色。自手作食自磨自舂。占相男女。解夢吉
1007a25 | 凶。是男是女。呪術工巧調鷹方法。和[15]合百
1007a26 | 種毒藥千種毒藥蛇毒生金[16]銀(＋毒)蠱毒。都無
1007a27 | [17]慈心。[18]若故作者。犯輕垢罪。

[30. The Precept against Not Respecting the Right Time. (ZY: "第三十不敬好時戒." / FZ: "違禁行非戒.")]

1007a28 | 若佛子。以惡心[＊]故自身[19]謗三寶。詐現親
1007a29 | 附。口便說空

简体字

"若佛子，有出家菩萨、在家菩萨，及一切檀越，请僧福田求愿之时，应入僧坊问知事人，今欲请僧求愿。知事报言，次第请者，即得十方贤圣僧。而世人别请五百罗汉、菩萨僧，不如僧次一凡夫僧。若别请僧者，是外道法，七佛无别请法，不顺孝道。若故别请僧者，犯轻垢罪。

"若佛子，以恶心故，为利养贩卖男女色，自手作食，自磨自舂，占相男女，解梦吉凶，是男是女，咒术工巧，调鹰方法，和合百种毒药、千种毒药、蛇毒、生金银毒、蛊毒，都无慈愍心，无孝顺心。若故作者，犯轻垢罪。

"若佛子，以恶心故，自身谤三宝，诈现亲附，口便说空，

28. The Precept against Extending Discriminatory Invitations to the Saṃgha.[115]

Whenever a son of the Buddha is in the circumstance of a monastic bodhisattva, a lay bodhisattva, or any other *dānapati* who is extending an invitation to the Saṃgha as a field of merit, thus seeking to fulfill his wishes, he should enter the Saṃgha dwelling and inquire of one of the stewards, saying, "I now wish [to issue an invitation to the Saṃgha to fulfill my wishes." The steward should reply, saying],[116] "If one extends an invitation in accordance with [the monastics'] proper order, he then acquires [merit] equivalent to that of making offerings to the worthies[117] and *āryas* among the Saṃgha of the ten directions, whereas, if a worldly person extends a discriminatory invitation to five hundred arhats or bodhisattvas among the Saṃgha, that would not be as good as making an offering in accordance with proper order to a single common person[118] Saṃgha member.

If one extends discriminatory invitations to members of the Saṃgha, that is a dharma of the non-Buddhists. None of the Seven Buddhas have allowed the Dharma of discriminatory invitations. It does not accord with the path of filial respect. If one deliberately extends a discriminatory invitation to members of the Saṃgha, he thereby commits a minor defiling offense.

29. The Precept against Living by a Wrong Livelihood.[119]

If, due to evil intentions or a desire for offerings, a son of the Buddha solicits male or female prostitutes, if he makes food with his own hands, hulling it himself and grinding it himself, if he serves as a physiognomist for men and women, serves as one who interprets the auspiciousness or inauspiciousness of dreams, as one who foretells the gender of unborn children, as one who practices sorcery, as a skilled craftsman, as one who trains falcons, as one who combines a hundred kinds of toxic herbs, a thousand kinds of toxic herbs, the venom of snakes, or produces "gold and silver poison"[120] or "*gu* poison,"[121] all of these practices are bereft of the mind of loving kindness. If one deliberately engages in such actions, he thereby commits a minor defiling offense.

30. The Precept against Not Respecting the Right Time.[122]

If, due to unwholesome intentions, a son of the Buddha by his own actions slanders the Three Jewels even as he deceptively appears to be closely reliant on them, if he speaks in terms of emp-

正體字

行在有中。[經理白衣。]為白衣通致男女
1007b01 交會婬[20]色縛著。於六齋日年三長齋月。作
1007b02 殺生劫盜破齋犯戒者。犯輕垢罪。[21]如是十
1007b03 戒。應當學敬心奉持。制戒品中廣解。

[31. The Precept against Failure to Practice the Rescuing and Ransoming [of Sacred Objects and Individuals When Witnessing Their Endangerment]. (ZY: "第三十一不行救贖戒." / FZ: "見厄不救戒第三十一.")]

1007b04 佛言。佛子。佛滅度後[22]於惡世中。若見外道
1007b05 一切惡人劫賊賣佛菩薩父母形像。[23]販賣
1007b06 經律。販賣比丘比丘尼亦賣發心菩薩道
1007b07 人。或為官使。與一切人作奴婢者。而菩薩
1007b08 見是事已。應[24]生[25]慈心方便救護處處教
1007b09 化。取物贖佛菩薩形像。及比丘比丘尼[26]發
1007b10 心菩薩一切經律。若不贖者。犯輕垢罪。

[32. The Precept against Harming Beings. (ZY: "第三十二損害眾生戒." / FZ: "畜作非法戒第三十二.")]

1007b11 若佛子。不得畜刀仗弓箭。販賣輕[27]秤小
1007b12 斗。因官形勢取人財物。害心繫縛破壞成
1007b13 功。長養猫狸猪狗。若故[28]作者。犯輕垢罪。

简体字

行在有中；为白衣通致男女，交会淫色，作诸缚著；于六斋日，年三长斋月，作杀生、劫盗、破斋犯戒者，犯轻垢罪。

"如是十戒，应当学，敬心奉持。《制戒品》中广明。

佛言："佛子，佛灭度后，于恶世中，若见外道、一切恶人、劫贼，卖佛菩萨、父母形像，及卖经律，贩卖比丘、比丘尼，亦卖发心菩萨道人，或为官使，与一切人作奴婢者，而菩萨见是事已，应生慈悲心，方便救护，处处教化，取物赎佛菩萨形像，及比丘、比丘尼、一切经律。若不赎者，犯轻垢罪。

"若佛子，不得畜刀杖弓箭，贩卖轻秤小斗，因官形势取人财物，害心系缚，破坏成功，长养猫狸猪狗。若故养者，犯轻垢罪。

tiness even as his actions betray involvement in existence, [if he serves as one who exerts influence on the laity],[123] if he thus serves as a go-between for men and women of the laity and thereby leads them into sensual attachment, or if he influences them in such a way that they engage in killing beings, stealing, nonobservance of the abstinence days, or otherwise breaking precepts on the six days of abstinence[124] or during the year's three long months of abstinence,[125] he thereby commits a minor defiling offense.

One should study and respectfully uphold the ten precepts as described above. They are extensively explained in "The Prohibitions Chapter."

The Buddha said:

31. The Precept against Failure to Practice the Rescuing and Ransoming [of Sacred Objects and Individuals When Witnessing Their Endangerment].[126]

Sons of the Buddha, during the evil age that follows after the Buddha has entered nirvāṇa, if one sees non-Buddhists, evil people, or thieves selling images of the Buddha, of bodhisattvas, or of one's parents, if one sees them trafficking in copies of the sutras or the moral codes, if one sees them selling bhikshus or bhikshunis, or if one sees them selling people who have resolved to pursue the bodhisattva path, perhaps selling them to become servants for officials or slaves to someone else—whenever a bodhisattva has witnessed circumstances such as these, he should bring forth a mind of loving-kindness and then use skillful means to rescue and protect them, in case after case teaching the transgressors while also acquiring the means necessary to pay the ransom to recover these buddha and bodhisattva images as well as these bhikshus, bhikshunis, bodhisattvas who have brought forth the resolve, and all editions of the sutras and moral codes. If one fails to pay the ransom for them, one thereby commits a minor defiling offense.

32. The Precept against Harming Beings.[127]

A son of the Buddha must not collect knives, clubs, or bows and arrows, must not deal in scales showing less than the actual weight or measures showing less than the actual volume, must not, backed by official power, confiscate people's wealth or possessions, must not act with injurious intentions by tying up others or destroying their successes, and must not raise cats, raccoon dogs,[128] pigs, or dogs.[129] If one deliberately does these things, he thereby commits a minor defiling offense.

正體字

[33. The Precept against Wrong Actions or Thought (ZY: "第三十三邪業覺觀戒." / FZ: "觀聽作惡戒第三十三.")]

1007b14‖ 若佛子。以惡心故觀一切男女等鬪。軍陣
1007b15‖ 兵[29]將劫賊等鬪。亦不得聽吹貝鼓角琴瑟
1007b16‖ 箏笛箜篌歌叫伎樂之聲。不[30]得摴蒱圍碁
1007b17‖ 波羅[31]賽[32]戲彈碁六博拍[33]毬擲石投[34]壺八道
1007b18‖ 行[35]城[36]爪鏡[37]蓍草楊枝鉢盂髑髏。而作卜
1007b19‖ 筮。不[38]得作盜賊使命。一一不得作。若故
1007b20‖ 作者。犯輕垢罪。

[34. The Precept against Even Briefly Abandoning the Bodhi Resolve. (ZY: "第三十四暫離菩提心戒." / FZ: "堅持守心戒第三十四.")]

1007b21‖ 若佛子。護持禁戒。行住坐臥日夜六時讀誦
1007b22‖ 是戒。猶如金剛。如帶持浮囊欲[39]度大海
1007b23‖ 如草繫比丘。常生大乘[40]善信。自知我是未
1007b24‖ 成之佛。諸佛是已成之佛。發菩提心。念念
1007b25‖ 不去心。若起一念二乘外道心者。犯輕垢 1007b26‖ 罪。

[35.The Precept against Failure to Make Vows. (ZY: "第三十五不發願戒." / FZ: "不發大願戒第三十五.")]

1007b27‖ 若佛子。常應發一切願。孝順父母師僧[41]三
1007b28‖ 寶。願得好師同學善[42][-友]知識。常教我大乘
1007b29‖ 經律。十發趣十長養十金剛十地。使我開解。
1007c01‖ 如法修行堅持佛戒。寧捨身命

简体字

"若佛子，以恶心故，观一切男女等斗，军阵兵将劫贼等斗。亦不得听吹呗、鼓角、琴、瑟、筝、笛、箜篌，歌叫妓乐之声。不得樗捕、围棋、波罗塞戏、弹棋、陆博、拍毱、掷石、投壶，牵道八道行城，爪镜、蓍草、杨枝、钵盂、髑髅而作卜筮。不得作盗贼使命。一一不得作。若故作者，犯轻垢罪。

"若佛子，护持禁戒，行住坐卧，日夜六时，读诵是戒犹如金刚；如带持浮囊，欲渡大海；如草系比丘。常生大乘善信，自知我是未成之佛，诸佛是已成之佛，发菩提心，念念不去心。若起一念二乘、外道心者，犯轻垢罪。

"若佛子，常应发一切愿；孝顺父母、师僧；愿得好师，同学、善知识，常教我大乘经律，十发趣，十长养，十金刚，十地；使我开解，如法修行；坚持佛戒，宁舍身命，

33. The Precept against Wrong Actions or Thought[130]

[it is an offense] if a son of the Buddha motivated by unwholesome intentions watches the quarreling among men and women or others or if he watches the fighting between armies, soldiers, thieves, or others. So, too, he must not listen to the blowing of conch shells, the sounds of drums, horns, zithers, zitherns, cithers, flutes, harps, singing, or other types of musical sounds. He must not play at dice, go, *prasena*,[131] chess, backgammon, ball games, billiards, darts, checkers, or other such games. He must not practice fortune telling or divination in which one uses such things as "the fingernail mirror,"[132] yarrow stalks, willow branches, bowls, or skulls. And he must not serve as an accomplice to a thief. He must not do any one of these things. If he deliberately does any of these things, he thereby commits a minor defiling offense.

34. The Precept against Even Briefly Abandoning the Bodhi Resolve.[133]

In guarding and upholding the moral precepts, while walking, standing, sitting, and lying down, and during the six periods of the day and night, as he studies and recites these precepts, a son of the Buddha should be as solid as vajra, being like one who clings to a life raft as he wishes to cross over a great sea, or like the bhikshus [who dared not move when] tied down by rushes,[134] always bringing forth wholesome faith in the Great Vehicle, personally knowing that, "I am a not-yet-realized buddha and all buddhas are already-realized buddhas," bringing forth the bodhi resolve that, even in each succeeding mind-moment, never departs from his mind. If he gives rise to even a single thought of pursuing the paths of the Two Vehicles or the non-Buddhists, he thereby commits a minor defiling offense.

35. The Precept against Failure to Make Vows.[135]

A son of the Buddha should always make all the vows, vowing to maintain filial respect toward his father, mother, teachers among the Saṃgha, and the Three Jewels, vowing to acquire good teachers, fellow students, and good spiritual guides[136] "who will always teach me the Great Vehicle sutras and moral codes, the ten stages of advancement, the ten developmental stages, the ten vajra stages, and the ten grounds, thereby enabling me to develop in understanding," [and vowing] to cultivate in accordance with the Dharma and solidly uphold the Buddha's moral precepts with such resolve that, "I would rather sacrifice my own body and life

正體字

念念不去 1007c02 ║ 心。若一切菩薩不發是願者。犯輕垢罪。

[36. The Precept against Failure to Make Resolutions. (ZY: "第三十六不發誓戒." / FZ: "不起十願戒第三十六.")**]**

1007c03 ║ 若佛子。發十大願已。持佛禁戒。作是願
1007c04 ║ 言。寧以此身投熾然猛火大坑刀山。終不
1007c05 ║ 毀犯三世諸佛經律與一切女人作不淨
1007c06 ║ 行。1007c07 ║ 復作是願。寧以熱鐵羅網千重周匝纏身。
1007c08 ║ 終不以[43]破戒之身受於信心檀越一切衣 1007c09 ║ 服。
1007c10 ║ 復作是願。寧以此口吞熱鐵丸及大流猛
1007c11 ║ 火經百千劫。終不以[＊]破戒之口食信心
1007c12 ║ 檀越百味[44]飲食。
1007c13 ║ 復作是願。寧以此身臥大猛火羅網熱鐵
1007c14 ║ 地上。終不以[＊]破戒之身受信心檀越百種 1007c15 ║ 床座。
1007c16 ║ 復作是願。寧以此身受三百鉾[45]刺經一
1007c17 ║ 劫二劫。終不以[＊]破戒之身受信心檀越百 1007c18 ║ 味醫藥。
1007c19 ║ 復作是願。寧以此身投熱鐵鑊[46]經百千
1007c20 ║ 劫。終不以[＊]破戒之身受信心檀越千種房
1007c21 ║ 舍屋宅園林田地。
1007c22 ║ 復作是願。寧以鐵[47]鎚打碎此身從頭至
1007c23 ║ 足令如微塵。終不以[48]破戒之身受信心
1007c24 ║ 檀越恭敬禮拜。
1007c25 ║ 復作是願。寧以百千熱鐵刀鉾挑其兩目。

简体字

念念不去心。若一切菩萨不发是愿者，犯轻垢罪。

"若佛子，发是十大愿已，持佛禁戒，作是愿言：宁以此身，投炽然猛火，大坑刀山，终不毁犯三世诸佛经律，与一切女人作不净行。

"复作是愿：宁以热铁罗网千重，周匝缠身，终不以此破戒之身，受信心檀越一切衣服。

"复作是愿：宁以此口吞热铁丸，及大流猛火，经百千劫，终不以此破戒之口，食于信心檀越百味饮食。

"复作是愿：宁以此身卧大流猛火，罗网热铁地上，终不以此破戒之身，受于信心檀越百种床座。

"复作是愿：宁以此身受三百鉾刺身，经一劫二劫，终不以此破戒之身，受于信心檀越百味医药。

"复作是愿：宁以此身投热铁护，经百千劫，终不以此破戒之身，受于信心檀越千种房舍、屋宅、园林、田地。

"复作是愿：宁以铁锤打碎此身，从头至足，令如微尘，终不以此破戒之身，受于信心檀越恭敬礼拜。

"复作是愿：宁以百千热铁刀鉾挑其两目，

[than transgress against them] as, in each successive mind-moment, [these vows] never leave my mind." If any bodhisattva fails to make these vows, he thereby commits a minor defiling offense.

36. The Precept against Failure to Make Resolutions.[137]

Having made these ten great vows,[138] a son of the Buddha upholds the Buddha's moral precepts and makes the following [additional] vows:

"I would rather cast this body into a fiercely blazing fire, into a great abyss, or onto a mountain of knives than ever violate the sutras and moral codes of all buddhas of the three periods of time by engaging in impure actions with any woman."

He then also makes this vow: "I would rather my body were wrapped in a thousand layers of red-hot iron netting than ever accept with a body in violation of the precepts any clothing offered by a faithful *dānapati*."

He then also makes this vow: "With this very mouth, I would rather gulp down red-hot iron pellets and an immense river of fierce flames, doing so throughout a hundred thousand kalpas, than ever eat with a mouth in violation of the precepts the hundred flavors of food and drink offered by a faithful *dānapati*."

He then also makes this vow: "With this very body, I would rather lie down on an immense hammock of red-hot iron netting or on a ground of red-hot iron than ever accept with a body in violation of the precepts any of the hundred kinds of bedding from a faithful *dānapati*."

He then also makes this vow: "With this very body, I would rather experience being [repeatedly] impaled by three hundred spears throughout one or two kalpas than ever accept with a body in violation of the precepts any of the hundred varieties of medicines offered by a faithful *dānapati*."

He then also makes this vow: "I would rather cast this body into a red-hot iron cauldron [and continue to burn there] for a hundred thousand kalpas than ever accept with a body in violation of the precepts any of the thousand types of houses, residences, gardens, groves, or fields offered by a faithful *dānapati*."

He then also makes this vow: "I would rather this body were smashed to dust from head to toe with an iron sledgehammer than ever accept with a body in violation of the precepts the respect or reverential bows of a faithful *dānapati*."

He then also makes this vow: "I would rather experience a hundred thousand red-hot iron knives and spears plucking out my

正體字

1008a01 終不以[*]破戒之心視他好色。
1008a02 復作是願。寧以百千鐵錐[1]遍[2]劖刺耳根
1008a03 經一劫二劫。終不以[*]破戒之心聽好音 1008a04 聲。
1008a05 復作是願。寧以百千刃刀割去其鼻。終不
1008a06 以[*]破戒[3]之心貪嗅諸香。
1008a07 復作是願。寧以百千刃刀割斷其舌。終不
1008a08 以[*]破戒[*]之心食人百味淨食。
1008a09 復作是願。寧以利斧斬斫其身。終不以
1008a10 [*]破戒[*]之心貪著好觸。
1008a11 復作是願。願一切眾生[4]悉得成佛。[5]而菩薩
1008a12 若不發是願者。犯輕垢罪。

[37. The Precept against Risking Danger When Traveling. (ZY: "第三十七冒難遊行戒." / FZ: "故入難處戒第三十七.")**]**

1008a13 若佛子常應二時頭陀冬夏坐禪結夏安居。
1008a14 常用楊枝澡豆三衣瓶鉢坐具錫杖香爐漉
1008a15 水囊手巾刀子火燧鑷子繩床經律佛像菩薩
1008a16 形像。而菩薩行頭陀時及遊方時。行來百
1008a17 里千里。此十八種物常隨其身。頭陀者從
1008a18 正月十五日至三月十五日。八月十五日至
1008a19 十月十五日。是二時中[6]此十八種物。常隨
1008a20 其身如鳥二翼。若布薩日新學菩薩。半月半
1008a21 月布薩誦十重四十八[7]輕戒。

简体字

终不以此破戒之心，视他好色。

“复作是愿：宁以百千铁锥，劖刺耳根，经一劫二劫，终不以此破戒之心，听好音声。

“复作是愿：宁以百千刃刀割去其鼻，终不以此破戒之心，贪嗅诸香。

“复作是愿：宁以百千刃刀割断其舌，终不以此破戒之心，食人百味净食。

“复作是愿：宁以利斧斩斫其身，终不以此破戒之心，贪著好触。 “复作是愿：愿一切众生成佛。菩萨若不发是愿者，犯轻垢罪。 “若佛子，常应二时头陀：冬夏坐禅，结夏安居。常用杨枝、澡豆、三衣、缾、鉢、坐具、锡杖、香炉、漉水囊、手巾、刀子、火燧、镊子、绳床、经、律、佛像、菩萨形像。而菩萨行头陀时，及游方时，行来百里千里，此十八种物常随其身。头陀者，从正月十五日至三月十五日，八月十五日至十月十五日。是二时中，此十八种物，常随其身，如鸟二翼。若布萨日，新学菩萨，半月半月布萨，诵十重四十八轻。

two eyes than ever gaze at the beautiful form of another with a mind in violation of the precepts."

He then also makes this vow: "I would rather experience a hundred thousand iron awls everywhere piercing and stabbing my ears throughout one or two kalpas than ever listen to beautiful sounds with a mind in violation of the precepts."

He then also makes this vow: "I would rather experience a hundred thousand sharp knives cutting off my nose than ever smell any fragrances with a mind in violation of the precepts."

He then also makes this vow: "I would rather experience a hundred thousand sharp knives cutting off my tongue than ever eat others' hundred flavors of pure food with a mind in violation of the precepts."

He then also makes this vow: "I would rather experience my body being chopped up with a sharp hatchet than ever lust after the experience of [another's] fine touch with a mind in violation of the precepts."

He then also makes this vow: "I vow that all beings will gain the realization of buddhahood."

If a bodhisattva does not make these vows, he thereby commits a minor defiling offense.

37. The Precept against Risking Danger When Traveling.[139]

A son of the Buddha should always practice the *dhūta* austerities[140] two times [each year],[141] cultivate *dhyāna* meditation in the winter and summer, and observe the summer [rains] retreat. He should always use a willow branch [toothbrush], soap, the three robes, a [water] bottle, an alms bowl, a sitting mat, a tin-headed staff,[142] a censer, a water filter, a washcloth, a knife, a fire-starting device, tweezers, a rope bed,[143] sutras, the moral codes, a buddha image, and bodhisattva images. When the bodhisattva is practicing the *dhūta* austerities and when he is traveling, whether it be for thirty miles or three hundred miles, he should always take along these eighteen things.

The *dhūta* austerities are practiced from the fifteenth day of the first lunar month to the fifteenth day of the third lunar month and from the fifteenth day of the eighth lunar month to the fifteenth day of the tenth lunar month. During these two periods, these eighteen things always accompany one's person just as closely as a bird is accompanied by its two wings.

Every half month, on the *upoṣadha* days, the bodhisattva new to the training recites these ten major and forty-eight minor precepts.

正體字

時於諸佛菩
1008a22 ‖ 薩形像[8]前。一人布薩即一人誦。若二[9]人三
1008a23 ‖ 人[10]乃至百千人亦一人誦。誦者高座。聽者下
1008a24 ‖ 坐。各各披九條七條五條袈裟。結夏安居一
1008a25 ‖ 一如法。若頭陀時莫入難處。若國難惡王。
1008a26 ‖ 土地高下草木深邃。師子虎狼水火風[11]難。
1008a27 ‖ 及以劫賊道路毒蛇。一切難處悉不得[12]入。
1008a28 ‖ [13]若頭陀行道乃至夏坐安居。是諸難處[14]悉
1008a29 ‖ 不得[15]入。[16]若故入者。犯輕垢罪。

[38. The Precept against Deviating from Proper Order of Seniority. (ZY: "第三十八乖尊卑次序戒." / FZ: "眾坐乖儀戒第三十八.")]

1008b01 ‖ 若佛子。應如法次第坐。先受戒者在前坐。
1008b02 ‖ 後受戒者在後坐不問老少比丘比丘尼貴
1008b03 ‖ 人國王王子乃至黃門奴婢。皆應先受戒者
1008b04 ‖ 在前坐。後受戒者次第而坐。莫如外道癡
1008b05 ‖ 人。若老若少無前無後。坐無次第兵奴之
1008b06 ‖ 法。我佛法中先者先坐後者後坐。而菩薩
1008b07 ‖ [17]不次第坐[*]者。犯輕垢罪。

简体字

若诵戒时，于诸佛菩萨形像前诵，一人布萨，即一人诵；若二及三人，至百千人，亦一人诵。诵者高座，听者下座，各各披九条、七条、五条袈裟。结夏安居，一一如法。若头陀时，莫入难处：若国难恶王，土地高下，草木深邃，狮子虎狼，水、火、风，劫贼道路，毒蛇，一切难处，悉不得入。若头陀行道，乃至夏坐安居，是诸难处，亦不得入。若故入者，犯轻垢罪。

"若佛子，应如法次第坐，先受戒者在前坐，后受戒者在后坐。不问老少，比丘、比丘尼，贵人、国王、王子，乃至黄门、奴婢，皆应先受戒者在前坐，后受戒者次第而坐。莫如外道痴人，若老若少，无前无后，坐无次第，如兵奴之法。我佛法中，先者先坐，后者后坐。而菩萨一一不如法次第坐者，犯轻垢罪。

At this time, when reciting while sitting before the images of the Buddhas and the Bodhisattvas, if but one person is observing the *upoṣadha*, then just one person recites the precepts. If two people, three people, or even a hundred thousand people are observing the *upoṣadha*, still, only one person recites the precepts. The reciter sits on a high seat while those who are listening sit on lower seats with everyone wearing the nine-strip, the seven-strip, and the five-strip *kāṣāya*[144] robes.

In observing the summer [rains] retreat, everything should be carried out in accordance with the Dharma. When one is practicing the *dhūta* austerities, one must not enter dangerous places. Whether it be dangerous countries, states with evil kings, precipitous terrain, dense and remote undergrowth and forests, places much inhabited by lions, tigers, or wolves, lands beset by floods, fires, or wind disasters, roads preyed upon by bandits, or places infested with poisonous snakes, one must not enter any such dangerous places. Whether one is practicing the path by observing the *dhūta* austerities or one is engaged in the summer meditation's "peaceful dwelling" [during the summer rains retreat], one must not enter any of these dangerous places. If one deliberately enters them, one thereby commits a minor defiling offense.

38. The Precept against Deviating from Proper Order of Seniority.[145]

A son of the Buddha should accord with the Dharma by sitting in the proper order according to which those who received the precepts first sit in front and those who received the precepts later sit behind them. This is the case irrespective of whether one is older or younger, a bhikshu or a bhikshuni, one of noble birth, a king, a prince, and so forth, including even if one is a eunuch or a male or female slave. In every case, it should be that those who first received the precepts sit in front and those who received the precepts later sit in order behind them.

One must not imitate the senseless followers of non-Buddhist traditions for whom, whether one is older or younger, there is no basis for determining who sits in front or behind as, after the manner of soldiers or slaves, they may sit without adhering to any particular order. In my Buddha Dharma, those who [took the precepts] first are first to take their seats whereas those who [took the precepts] later sit down after them. Hence if a bodhisattva does not [accord with the Dharma in each and every case][146] by following the correct order when sitting down, he thereby commits a minor defiling offense.

[39. The Precept against Failure to Cultivate Merit and Wisdom. (ZY: "第三十九不修福慧戒." / FZ: "應講不講戒第三十九.)]

正體字

1008b08 若佛子。常應教化一切眾生。建立僧房山
1008b09 林園田立作佛塔。冬夏安居坐禪處所。一切
1008b10 行道處。皆應立之。而菩薩應為一切眾生
1008b11 講說大乘經律。若[18]疾病國難賊難。父母兄
1008b12 弟和上阿闍梨亡滅之日。及三七[19]日乃至七
1008b13 七日。亦[20]應讀誦講說大乘經[21]律。齋會求
1008b14 福行來治生。大火[22]所燒大水[23]所[漂*寸]。黑風
1008b15 所吹船舫。江河大海羅剎之難。亦[24]應讀誦
1008b16 講說此經律。乃至一切罪報三[25]報[26]七逆八
1008b17 難。杻械枷鎖繫縛其身。多婬多瞋多愚癡
1008b18 多疾病。皆應[27]讀誦講說此經律。而新學菩
1008b19 薩若不爾者。犯輕垢罪。[28]如是九戒。應當
1008b20 學敬心奉持。梵[29]壇品當說。

[40. The Precept against Discrimination in Transmitting the Precepts. (ZY: "第四十揀擇受戒戒." / FZ: "受戒非儀戒第四十.")]

1008b21 佛言。佛子。與人受戒時。不得[30]簡擇一切
1008b22 國王王子大臣百官。

简体字

"若佛子，常应教化一切众生，建立僧房，山林园田立作佛塔。冬夏安居坐禅处所，一切行道处，皆应立之。而菩萨应为一切众生讲说大乘经律。若疾病、国难、贼难，父母、兄弟、和尚、阿阇黎亡灭之日，及三七日、四五七日，乃至七七日，亦应讲说大乘经律。一切斋会求福，行来治生，大火所烧，大水所漂，黑风所吹船舫，江河大海罗刹之难，亦读诵讲说此经律。乃至一切罪报，三恶、八难、七逆、杻械枷锁系缚其身，多淫、多瞋、多愚痴、多疾病，皆应讲此经律。而新学菩萨若不尔者，犯轻垢罪。

"如是九戒，应当学，敬心奉持。《梵坛品》当说。"

佛言："佛子与人授戒时，不得拣择。一切国王、王子、大臣、百官，

39. The Precept against Failure to Cultivate Merit and Wisdom.[147]

A son of the Buddha should always teach and transform all beings and establish Saṃgha dwellings, mountain and forest retreats, gardens, and fields. He should erect Buddha stupas and places for sitting in *dhyāna* meditation during the winter and summer retreats. He should establish every kind of place for practicing the path. Then, for the sake of all beings, the bodhisattva should provide instruction on the Great Vehicle sutras and moral codes. Whenever there is serious illness, national hardship, hardship inflicted by bandits, on the day when one's father, mother, brother, *upādhyāya*, or *ācārya* passes away, as well as for three to seven weeks after their death, then too, one should recite and provide instruction on the Great Vehicle sutras and moral codes.

On occasions when monastic feast gatherings are being held to seek merit, when there are those who are setting forth on travels or who are establishing a means of livelihood, when there are those who are threatened with being burned by immense fires, when there is the danger of being carried away by great floods, when a ship is liable to being capsized by fierce windstorms, and when in fear of the *rākṣasas*[148] on rivers, lakes, and the great ocean, then, too, one should recite and provide instruction on these sutras and moral codes.

So too, when there are those who are faced with all the kinds of retribution for karmic offenses including the three phases of karmic retribution,[149] [retribution for] the seven heinous offenses,[150] [retribution in the form of] the eight difficulties,[151] being bound by manacles, shackles, the yoke, or chains which restrain one's body, or becoming overtaken by much lust, hatred, delusion, or sickness—for all such circumstances one should recite and provide instruction on these sutras and moral codes.

Thus, if a bodhisattva new to the training does not act accordingly, he thereby commits a minor defiling offense.

One should study and respectfully uphold these nine precepts as described above. They will be explained in "The Brahmadaṇḍa[152] Chapter."

The Buddha said:

40. The Precept against Discrimination in Transmitting the Precepts.[153]

Sons of the Buddha, one must not discriminate in conferring the precepts. All kings, princes, high ministers, the hundred sorts of

正體字

比丘比丘尼信男信女
1008b23 婬男婬女。十八梵[31]天六欲天[32]子無根二根
1008b24 黃門奴婢。一切鬼神盡得受戒。應教身所
1008b25 著袈裟。皆使壞色與道相應。皆染使青黃
1008b26 赤黑紫色一切染衣。乃至臥具盡以壞色。身
1008b27 所著衣一切染色。若一切國土中國人所著
1008b28 衣服。比丘皆應與[33]其俗服有異。若欲受
1008b29 戒時[34]師應問言。[35]汝現身不作七逆罪耶。
1008c01 菩薩法師不得與七逆人現身受戒。七逆
1008c02 者。出佛身血。殺父。殺母。殺[36]和上。殺阿闍
1008c03 梨。破羯磨轉法輪僧。殺聖人。若具七[37]遮即
1008c04 [38]現身不得戒。餘一切人[39]盡得受戒。出家
1008c05 人法不向國王禮拜。不向父母禮拜。六親
1008c06 不敬。鬼神不[40]禮。但解[41]師語。有百里千里
1008c07 來求法者。而菩薩法師。以惡[42]心而不即
1008c08 與授一切眾生戒[43]者。犯輕垢罪。

[41. The precept against acting as a teacher for personal benefit. (ZY: "第四十一為利作師戒." / FZ: "無德詐師戒第四十一.")]

1008c09 若佛子。教化人起信心時。菩薩與他人
1008c10 作教[44]誡法師者。

简体字

比丘、比丘尼、信男、信女，淫男、淫女，十八梵天、六欲天子，无根、二根、黄门、奴婢，一切鬼神，尽得受戒。应教身所著袈裟，皆使坏色，与道相应。皆染使青、黄、赤、黑、紫色。一切染衣，乃至卧具，尽以坏色。身所著衣，一切染色；若一切国土中，国人所著衣服，比丘皆应与其俗服有异。若欲授戒时，应问言：'现身不作七逆罪耶？'菩萨法师不得与七逆人现身授戒。七逆者：出佛身血、杀父、杀母、杀和尚、杀阿阇黎、破羯磨转法轮信、杀圣人。若具七逆，即现身不得戒，余一切人，尽得受戒。出家人法，不向国王礼拜，不向父母礼拜，六亲不敬，鬼神不礼，但解法师语。有百里千里来求法者，而菩萨法师，以恶心、瞋心，而不即与授一切众生戒者，犯轻垢罪。

"若佛子，教化人起信心时，菩萨与他人作教诫法师者，

officials, bhikshus, bhikshunis, faithful laymen, faithful laywomen, male prostitutes, female prostitutes, any of the devas of the eighteen brahma heavens, the *devaputras* of the six desire heavens, an asexual person, a hermaphrodite, a eunuch, a male or female slave, and all sorts of ghosts and spirits may all receive the precepts.

One should instruct [those monastics who take these precepts] to dye the *kāṣāya* robes they wear so that they are all caused to become a muted color which accords with the path. They should all be dyed a color consisting of [a blend of] blue-green, yellow, red, black, and purple. All of one's dyed robes as well as one's sitting cloth and bedding should all be of this dyed color. The robes that a bhikshu wears should all be different in appearance from the clothes worn by the laypeople in any country in which he resides.

Whenever someone wishes to receive these precepts, the precept master should ask him, "Have you refrained from committing any of the seven heinous offenses in this present lifetime?" A bodhisattva Dharma master must not allow anyone to receive these precepts who has committed any of the seven heinous offenses in this present lifetime. The seven heinous offenses are: drawing the blood of a buddha; killing one's father; killing one's mother; killing one's *upādhyāya*, killing one's *ācārya*; breaking up a Dharma-wheel-turning Saṃgha proceeding; and killing an *ārya*. If one has committed any of these seven obstructive transgressions, he cannot receive these precepts in this present lifetime. Everyone else may receive these precepts.

The Dharma of the monastic Saṃgha prohibits them from bowing in reverence to kings. They do not bow in reverence to their parents, do not pay formal respects to the six types of relatives, and do not bow in reverence to ghosts or spirits.

Whenever any being who is at least able to understand the speech of the Dharma master comes seeking the Dharma, whether it be from thirty or three hundred miles away, and yet, due to having a bad attitude or [an attitude affected by hatred],[154] the bodhisattva Dharma master does not immediately transmit these "precepts of all beings" to him, he thereby commits a minor defiling offense.

41. The Precept against Acting as a Teacher for Personal Benefit.[155]

Whenever a son of the Buddha is teaching people and inspiring them to develop a faithful mind and whenever a bodhisattva is serving as a Dharma master providing instruction in the precepts,

正體字

見欲受戒人。應教請二
1008c11 師[*]和上阿闍梨。二師應問言 。汝有七遮罪
1008c12 不。若現身有七[45]遮。師不[46]應與[47]受[48]戒。
1008c13 [49]無七遮者得[50]受。若有犯[51]十戒者[52]應教
1008c14 懺悔。在佛菩薩形像前。日夜六時誦十[53]重
1008c15 四十八輕戒。[54]若到禮三世千佛得見好
1008c16 [55]相。若一七日二三七日乃至一年要見好
1008c17 相。好相者。佛來摩頂見光[56]見華種種異相。
1008c18 便得滅罪。若無好相雖懺無益。是人現身
1008c19 亦不得戒。而得[57]增受[58]戒。若犯四十八輕
1008c20 戒者。對[59]首[60]懺罪滅。不同七遮。而教[*]誡師
1008c21 於是法中一一好解。若不解大乘經律若
1008c22 輕若重是非之相。不解第一義諦。習種性
1008c23 長養[61]性[+性種性]不可壞性道種性[62]正[+法]性。其中多少
1009a01 觀行出入十禪支一切行法。一一不得此
1009a02 法中意。而菩薩為利養[*]故

简体字

见欲受戒人，应教请二师，和尚、阿闍黎二师。应问言：‘汝有七遮罪否？’若现身有七遮罪者，师不应与授戒；若无七遮者，得与授戒。 若有犯十重戒者，教忏悔。在佛菩萨形像前，日夜六时，诵十重、四十八轻戒，若到礼三世千佛，得见好相者。若一七日，二三七日，乃至一年，要见好相。好相者，佛来摩顶，见光华种种异相，便得灭罪。若无好相，虽忏无益。是人现身亦不得戒，而得增长受戒益。若犯四十八轻戒者，对首忏悔，罪便得灭；不同七遮。而教诫师，于是法中，一一好解。若不解大乘经律，若轻若重，是非之相，不解第一义谛，习种性、长养性、性种性、不可坏性、道种性、正觉性。其中多少观行出入，十禅支，一切行法，一一不得此法中意。而菩萨为利养，

if he sees anyone who wishes to receive the precepts, he should instruct him to request the assistance of two masters, an *upādhyāya* and an *ācārya*.[156] Those two masters should ask [the precept candidate], "Have you or have you not committed any of the seven obstructive offenses?"[157] If he has committed any of the seven obstructive offenses in the present lifetime, the masters should not allow him to take the precepts. However, so long as he has not committed any of the seven obstructive offenses, he may receive them.

If he has transgressed against any of the ten precepts, they should teach him to repent before the images of the Buddha and the bodhisattvas, reciting the ten major and the forty-eight minor precepts during the six periods of the day and night, taking pains to bow in reverence to the thousand buddhas of the three periods of time until he sees an auspicious sign. Whether it takes one week, two weeks, three weeks or even up to a year, it is essential that one see an auspicious sign. As for "auspicious signs," this refers to the Buddha coming and rubbing the crown of one's head, seeing light, seeing flowers, or seeing many different sorts of unusual signs. Then one succeeds in extinguishing his offenses. If there are no auspicious signs, although one has repented, it has still been without benefit. This person still does not acquire the precepts in this present lifetime. However he does increase his prospects of taking the precepts [again in the future].

If one has transgressed against any of the forty-eight minor precepts, if he repents before a superior [member of the Saṃgha], these offenses are extinguished. This circumstance is different from that of someone who has committed any of the seven obstructive offenses.

The master who provides instruction in the precepts should well understand each and every aspect of these dharmas. If he does not understand the aspects of what is right and what is wrong with regard to the Great Vehicle sutras and moral codes, whether it be with regard to those which are minor or those which are major, if he does not understand what constitutes the ultimate truth, the habitually acquired lineage,[158] the developmental nature , the intrinsic lineage,[159] the indestructible nature, the lineage of the path,[160] and the right Dharma nature[161] along with how much contemplative practice is involved in emerging from and entering them as well as all the practice dharmas of the ten "limbs" of *dhyāna*[162]—if he has not realized the meanings involved in each and every one of these dharmas and yet, for the sake of personal

正體字

為名聞故。惡
1009a03 | 求[1]多求貪利弟子。而詐現解一切經律。為
1009a04 | 供養故。是自欺詐亦欺詐他人。故與人[*]受
1009a05 | 戒者。犯輕垢罪。

[42. The Precept against Speaking the Precepts for Bad People. (ZY: "第四十二為惡人說戒." / FZ: "非處說戒戒第四十二.")]

1009a06 | 若佛子。不得為利養[2]故於未受菩薩戒
1009a07 | 者前[3]若外道惡人前說此千佛大戒。邪見
1009a08 | 人前亦不得說。除國王餘一切不得說。是
1009a09 | 惡人輩不受佛戒。名為畜生。生生不見三
1009a10 | 寶。如木石無心。名為外道邪見人輩。木頭
1009a11 | 無異。而菩薩於是惡人前說七佛教戒者。
1009a12 | 犯輕垢罪。

[43. The Precept against Accepting Gifts without a Sense of Shame. (ZY: "第四十三無慚受施戒." / FZ: "故毀禁戒戒第四十三.")]

1009a13 | 若佛子。信心出家受佛正戒。故起心毀犯聖
1009a14 | 戒者。不得受一切檀越供養。亦不得國王
1009a15 | 地上行。不得飲國王水。五千大鬼常遮其
1009a16 | 前。鬼言大賊。[4]若入房舍城邑宅中。鬼復常
1009a17 | 掃其脚跡。一切世[5]人罵言佛法中賊。一切
1009a18 | 眾生眼不欲見。犯戒之人畜生無異木頭無
1009a19 | 異。若[6][+故]毀正戒者。犯輕垢罪。

简体字

为名闻故，恶求多求，贪利弟子，而诈现解一切经律，为供养故，是自欺诈，亦欺诈他人，故与人授戒者，犯轻垢罪。

"若佛子，不得为利养故，于未受菩萨戒者前，若外道恶人前，说此千佛大戒。邪见人前，亦不得说。除国王，余一切不得说。是恶人辈，不受佛戒，名为畜生。生生不见三宝，如木石无心。名为外道邪见人辈，木头无异。而菩萨于是恶人前，说七佛教戒者，犯轻垢罪。

"若佛子，信心出家，受佛正戒。故起心毁犯圣戒者，不得受一切檀越供养。亦不得国王地上行，不得饮国王水。五千大鬼常遮其前，鬼言大贼。入房舍城邑宅中，鬼复常扫其脚迹。一切世人皆骂言：'佛法中贼！'一切众生，眼不欲见。犯戒之人，畜生无异，木头无异。若故毁正戒者，犯轻垢罪。

gain, for the sake of fame, because of unwholesome desires, excessive desires, or a desire to acquire disciples, this bodhisattva deceptively presents the appearance of understanding all the sutras and moral codes, doing so for the sake of receiving offerings, this amounts to cheating himself while also cheating others. If [under such circumstances] he then deliberately transmits the precepts to others, he thereby commits a minor defiling offense.

42. The Precept against Speaking the Precepts for Bad People.[163]

A son of the Buddha must not for the sake of personal benefit discuss these great precepts of the Thousand Buddhas in the presence of those who have not yet received the bodhisattva precepts or in the presence of evil non-Buddhists.[164] He also must not discuss them in the presence of those with wrong views and must not speak them to anyone else except for the kings of countries. These sorts of evil people will not accept the bodhisattva precepts. They are like animals who will pass through life after life without seeing the Three Jewels. They are as mindless as trees and stones. They are known as non-Buddhists and as the sorts of people with wrong views who are no different from logs of wood. Thus if a bodhisattva discusses these precepts from the teachings of the Seven Buddhas in the presence of these sorts of evil people, he thereby commits a minor defiling offense.

43. The Precept against Accepting Gifts without a Sense of Shame.[165]

A son of the Buddha who has left the home life with a faithful mind and then accepted the Buddha's orthodox precepts but then who has deliberately brought forth the intention to violate the precepts of the Āryas does not deserve to accept the offerings of any *dānapati* and also does not deserve to walk on the king's lands or drink the king's water. Five thousand huge ghosts always block his way. The ghosts call him a great thief and whenever he enters any house, city, town, or building, the ghosts again always sweep away even his very footprints. All of the common people scold him, calling him a thief within the Buddha's Dharma. Any being who lays eyes on him does not wish to see him. One who breaks the precepts is no different from an animal and no different from a log of wood. Thus if one deliberately[166] violates any of the orthodox precepts, one thereby commits a minor defiling offense.

[44. The Precept against Failure to Make Offerings to the Sutras. (ZY: "第四十四不供養經典戒." / FZ: "不敬經律戒第四十四.")]

1009a20 若佛子。常應一心受持讀誦大乘經律。剝
1009a21 皮為紙刺血為墨。以髓為水[7]析骨為筆
1009a22 書寫佛戒。木皮穀紙絹素[8]竹帛亦應悉書
1009a23 持。常以七寶無價香花一切雜寶。為箱囊
1009a24 盛經律卷若不如法供養者。犯輕垢罪。

[45. The Precept against Failure to Teach Beings (ZY: "第四十五不化眾生戒." / FZ: "不化眾生戒第四十五.")]

正體字

1009a25 若佛子。常起大悲心。若入一切城邑舍宅。
1009a26 見一切眾生。[9]應[10]當唱言。汝等眾生盡應
1009a27 受三歸十戒。若見牛馬猪羊一切畜生。應
1009a28 心念口言。汝是畜生發菩提心。而菩薩入一
1009a29 切處山林川野。皆使一切眾生發菩提心。
1009b01 是菩薩若不教化眾生[*]者。犯輕垢罪。

[46. The Precept against Speaking the Dharma in Ways That Do Not Accord with the Dharma. (ZY: "第四十六說法不如法戒." / FZ: "說法乖儀戒第四十六.")]

1009b02 若佛子。常行教化起大悲心。入檀越貴人
1009b03 家一切眾中不得立為白衣說法。[11]應白
1009b04 衣眾前高座上坐。法師比丘不得地立為四
1009b05 [12]眾說法。若說法時。法師高座香花供養。四

简体字

"若佛子，常应一心受持读诵大乘经律。剥皮为纸，刺血为墨，以髓为水，析骨为笔，书写佛戒。木皮谷纸、绢素竹帛，亦应悉书持。常以七宝，无价香华，一切杂宝为箱囊，盛经律卷。若不如法供养者，犯轻垢罪。

"若佛子，常起大悲心，若入一切城邑、舍宅，见一切众生，应唱言：'汝等众生，应尽受三归十戒。'若见牛马猪羊，一切畜生，应心念口言：'汝是畜生，发菩提心。'而菩萨入一切处，山林川野，皆使一切众生发菩提心。是菩萨若不教化众生者，犯轻垢罪。

"若佛子，常行教化起大悲心，入檀越贵人家，一切众中，不得立为白衣说法。应在白衣众前，高座上坐。法师比丘，不得地立为四众白衣说法。若说法时，法师高座，香华供养。四众听者

44. The Precept against Failure to Make Offerings to the Sutras.[167]

A son of the Buddha should always single-mindedly accept, uphold, read, and recite the Great Vehicle sutras and moral codes, [being willing even] to peel off his own skin to use as paper, to draw his own blood to use as ink, to use the liquid from his own marrow [to mix the ink], and to split his own bones to make a pen with which to write out the Buddha's precepts. They should all also be written out and preserved on tree bark, mulberry paper,[168] white silk, bamboo slats, or silk cloth and one should always use the seven precious things, priceless incense and flowers, and all kinds of various jewels to make cases and slipcovers in which to place the fascicles of the sutras and moral codes for safekeeping. If one fails to make offerings to them in accordance with the Dharma, one thereby commits a minor defiling offense.

45. The Precept against Failure to Teach Beings.[169]

A son of the Buddha should always bring forth the mind of great compassion. Whenever he enters any city, town, dwelling, or other accommodation and sees any beings, he should call out to them, saying, "All of you beings should take the Three Refuges and the ten precepts." If he sees cows, horses, pigs, sheep, or any other animals, he should think to himself and say aloud to them, "You are animals. Bring forth the resolve to attain bodhi." Thus, whenever a bodhisattva enters any place, whether it be in the mountains, the forests, along the rivers, or in the wilderness, he should encourage all beings to bring forth the resolve to attain bodhi. If this bodhisattva fails to teach and transform beings, he thereby commits a minor defiling offense.

46. The Precept against Speaking the Dharma in Ways That Do Not Accord with the Dharma.[170]

A son of the Buddha always practices the teaching and transformation of others while bringing forth the mind of great compassion. Whenever he enters the home of a *dānapati* or one of high social station and whenever he is in the midst of any group of beings, he must not stand as he speaks the Dharma for laypeople. Rather he should sit on a high seat in a superior position at the front of the group of laypeople. A Dharma master who is a bhikshu must not remain standing in a low position when speaking the Dharma for the fourfold assembly.[171] Whenever he is speaking the Dharma, the Dharma master should sit on a high seat and be presented with offerings of incense and flowers while the fourfold assembly of

正體字

1009b06 眾聽者下坐。[13]如孝順父母敬順師教。如
1009b07 事火婆羅門。其說法者若不如[14]法犯輕垢
1009b08 罪。

[47. The Precept against Imposing Restrictions That Do Not Accord with the Dharma. (ZY: "第四十七非法制限戒." / FZ: "非法立制戒第四十七.")**]**

1009b09 若佛子。皆以信心受[15]佛戒者。若國王太子
1009b10 百官四部弟子。自恃高貴破滅佛法戒律。
1009b11 明作制法制我四部弟子。不聽出家行道。
1009b12 亦復不聽造立形像佛塔經[16]律。[立統制眾安藉記僧比丘菩薩地立白衣高座廣行非法如兵奴事主而菩薩應受一切人供養而反為官走使非法非律若國王百官好心受佛戒者莫 作是]破三寶之
1009b13 罪。而故作破法者。犯輕垢罪。

[48. The Precept against Destroying the Dharma. (ZY: "第四十八破法戒." / FZ: "自壞內法戒第四十八.")**]**

1009b14 若佛子。[17]以好心出家而為名聞利養。於國
1009b15 王百官前說[18]~~七~~佛[19]戒。橫與比丘比丘尼
1009b16 [20]菩薩[+戒]弟子[21]作繫縛事。[22][+如獄囚法

简体字

下坐，如孝顺父母，敬顺师教，如事火婆罗门。其说法者，若不如法说，犯轻垢罪。

"若佛子，皆以信心受戒者。若国王、太子、百官、四部弟子，自恃高贵，破灭佛法戒律，明作制法，制我四部弟子，不听出家行道，亦复不听造立形像、佛塔、经律。立统制众，安籍记僧。菩萨比丘地立，白衣高座，广行非法，如兵奴事主。而菩萨应受一切人供养，而反为官走使，非法非律。若国王百官，好心受佛戒者，莫作是破三宝之罪。而故作破法者，犯轻垢罪。

"若佛子，以好心出家，而为名闻利养，于国王百官前说佛戒者，横与比丘、比丘尼菩萨戒弟子作系缚事，如狱囚法、

listeners sits in a lower position, respectfully complying with the Dharma master's teaching just as they would in rendering filial respect to their own parents or just as fire-worshipping brahmans [would dutifully serve their fires]. Thus, if one who is speaking the Dharma does not accord with the Dharma, he thereby commits a minor defiling offense.

47. The Precept against Imposing Restrictions That Do Not Accord with the Dharma.[172]

Sons of the Buddha all receive the Buddha's precepts because they have developed a mind of faith. Thus [it is contrary to Dharma] if a king, a prince, one of the hundred officials, or any of the fourfold assembly of disciples relies upon his own lofty and noble position to damage or destroy Buddha's Dharma or moral codes or to knowingly create regulatory laws that impose restrictions on my fourfold assembly of disciples by which they are not permitted to leave the home life and practice the path and also are not permitted to create images, erect stupas, or produce copies of the sutras or moral codes. {[So, too, it is contrary to Dharma] if he establishes regulatory means to control the assembly and register the Saṃgha, if he imposes rules requiring bhikshu bodhisattvas to remain standing in a low position even as laypeople sit on high seats, or if he extensively implements such protocols contrary to the Dharma by which [these bhikshu bodhisattvas] become like soldiers or slaves bound to serve their masters, for bodhisattvas are those who should be receiving the offerings of everyone. Thus if, on the contrary, they [are compelled to] become like subservient messengers who must obey officials, this is contrary to Dharma and contrary to the moral codes. Therefore, if the king or any of the hundred officials have received the Buddha's precepts with good intentions, they must not engage in any of these}[173] karmic offenses which serve to destroy the Three Jewels. Thus if one deliberately engages in actions contributing to the destruction of the Dharma, he thereby commits a minor defiling offense.

48. The Precept against Destroying the Dharma.[174]

If, for the sake of fame or personal benefit, a son of the Buddha who has left the homelife with good intentions then speaks the Buddha's precepts[175] in the presence of a king or any of the hundred officials in such a way that he perversely causes bhikshus, bhikshunis, or bodhisattva-precept disciples[176] to become subject to imprisonment or to rules like those appropriate for prisoners or

正體字

如兵奴之法]如師子身中蟲自
1009b17 食師子[23]肉。[+非餘外蟲如是佛子自破佛法]非外道天魔能破。若受佛戒
1009b18 者。應護佛戒如念一子。如事父[24]母。[+不可毀破.]而菩
1009b19 薩聞外道惡人以惡言謗佛戒。[25]時[=之聲]。如三
1009b20 百鉾刺心。千刀萬杖打拍其身等無有異。
1009b21 寧自入地獄[26]經[27][+於]百劫。而[28]不用一聞惡言[謗]
1009b22 破佛戒之聲。[29]而況自破佛戒。教人[30]破法
1009b23 因緣。亦無孝順之心。若故作者。犯輕垢罪。
1009b24 [*]如是九戒應當學敬心奉持。
1009b25 諸佛子。是四十八輕戒。汝等受持。過去諸菩
1009b26 薩已誦。未來諸菩薩當誦。現在諸菩薩今誦。
1009b27 [31]諸佛子[32]諦聽。此[33]十重四十八[34]輕戒。三世
1009b28 諸佛已誦當誦今誦。我今亦如是誦。汝等一
1009b29 切大眾。若國王王子百官。比丘比丘尼信男
1009c01 信女。受持菩薩戒者。應受持讀誦解說
1009c02 書寫佛性常住戒卷。流通三世一切眾生化
1009c03 化不絕。得見千佛

简体字

兵奴之法。如狮子身中虫，自食狮子肉，非余外虫；如是佛子，自破佛法，非外道天魔能破。若受佛戒者，应护佛戒，如念一子，如事父母，不可毁破。而菩萨闻外道恶人，以恶言谤佛戒之声，如三百鉾刺心，千刀万杖打拍其身，等无有异。宁自入地狱，经于百劫，而不闻一恶言，破佛戒之声！况自破佛戒，教人破法因缘，亦无孝顺之心。若故作者，犯轻垢罪。

“如是九戒，应当学，敬心奉持。

“诸佛子，是四十八轻戒，汝等受持！过去诸菩萨已诵，未来诸菩萨当诵，现在诸菩萨今诵。

“诸佛子，听十重、四十八轻戒，三世诸佛已诵、当诵、今诵，我今亦如是诵。汝等一切大众，若国王、王子、百官、比丘、比丘尼、信男、信女、受持菩萨戒者，应受持、读诵、解说、书写，佛性常住戒卷，流通三世，一切众生化化不绝，得见千佛，

rules like those appropriate for soldiers or servants,[177] he thereby becomes like a parasite in the body of a lion who himself eats the flesh of the lion [and harms it] in a way that no other parasite coming from without could ever do. A son of the Buddha such as this does more damage to the Buddha's Dharma himself[178] than even non-Buddhists or heavenly *māras* could ever inflict.

If one has received the Buddha's precepts, he should protect the Buddha's precepts just as one would be mindfully protective of one's only son or just as one would care for one's own father and mother. One cannot damage them.[179] Thus, for a bodhisattva, on hearing the sound[180] of a non-Buddhist or evil-minded person using evil speech to slander[181] the Buddha's precepts, it is just as painful to him and no different from the pain he would feel if three hundred spears were plunged into his own heart or a thousand knives or ten-thousand clubs were to strike his body. He would rather enter the hells himself and go through a hundred kalpas of suffering there than have to listen even one time to the sound of even a single word of slander intended to damage the Buddha's precepts. How much the less would he damage the Buddha's precepts himself, teach others causes and conditions that could lead to damaging the Dharma, or fail to maintain a mind of filial respect. If one deliberate engages [in any of these actions], he thereby commits a minor defiling offense.

One should study and respectfully uphold these nine precepts as described above.

Sons of the Buddha, you should receive and uphold these forty-eight minor precepts. They have been recited by all bodhisattvas of the past, will be recited by all bodhisattvas of the future, and are recited by all bodhisattvas of the present.

Sons of the Buddha, listen attentively. These ten major and forty-eight minor precepts have been recited, will be recited, and are now recited by all buddhas of the three periods of time. I now also recite them in this same way. All of you in the Great Assembly, whether you be kings, princes, any of the hundred officials, bhikshus, bhikshunis, faithful laymen, or faithful laywomen, you who uphold the bodhisattva precepts should receive, uphold, read, recite, explain, and write out these eternally dwelling precepts of the Buddha nature. Thus you should circulate them to all beings throughout the three periods of time so that [these precepts] continue to transform them repeatedly and incessantly, thereby enabling them to see the thousand buddhas and personally receive

正體字

佛佛授手。世世不墮
1009c04 ‖ 惡道八難。常生人道天中。我今在此樹下。
1009c05 ‖ 略開七佛法戒。汝[35]等[+大眾]當一心學波羅提木
1009c06 ‖ 叉歡喜奉行。如無相天王品勸學中一一
1009c07 ‖ [36]廣明。三千學[37]士時坐聽者。聞佛自誦。心心
1009c08 ‖ 頂戴喜躍受持。
1009c09 ‖ 爾時釋迦牟尼佛。說上蓮花臺藏世界盧舍
1009c10 ‖ 那佛心地法門品中十無盡戒法品竟。千百
1009c11 ‖ 億釋迦亦如是說。從摩醯首羅天王宮至
1009c12 ‖ 此道樹[38][+下]十住處說法品。為一切菩薩不可
1009c13 ‖ 說大眾受持讀誦解說其義亦如是。千百
1009c14 ‖ 億世界蓮花藏世界。微塵世界。[per Zhixu: 亦如是說]
一切佛心藏
1009c15 ‖ 地藏戒藏無量行願藏。因果佛性常住藏。[39]如[+是]
1009c16 ‖ 如一切佛說無量一切法藏竟。千百億世界
1009c17 ‖ 中。一切眾生受持歡喜奉行。若廣開心地相
1009c18 ‖ 相。如佛花光[40]王[七行]品中說。
1009c19 ‖ 明人忍慧強　　能持如是法
1009c20 ‖ 未成佛道間　　安獲五種利

简体字

佛佛授手，世世不堕恶道八难，常生人道天中。

“我今在此树下，略阴七佛法戒。汝等大众，当一心学波罗提木叉，欢喜奉行。如《无相天王品》劝学中，一一广明。”

三千学士，时坐听者，闻佛自诵，心心顶戴，喜跃受持。

尔时，释迦牟尼佛说上莲华台藏世界，卢舍那佛《心地法门品》中，十无尽戒法品竟。千百亿释迦亦如是说，从摩醯首罗天王宫，至此道树下住处说法品，为一切菩萨，不可说大众，受持读诵，解说其义亦如是。千百亿世界，莲华藏世界，微尘世界，一切佛心藏、地藏、戒藏、无量行愿藏、因果佛性常住藏。如是一切佛说，无量一切法藏竟。千百亿世界中，一切众生受持，欢喜奉行。若广开心地相相，如《佛华光王七行品》中说。

“明人忍慧强，能持如是法，
未成佛道间，安获五种利：

their transmission from each successive buddha so that they may go through life after life without ever falling into the wretched destinies or encountering the eight difficulties as they always continue to be reborn in the path of human rebirth or among the devas. Now, beneath this tree, I have concluded a general explanation of the precepts of the Dharma of the Seven Buddhas. All of you in this Great Assembly[182] should all single-mindedly study these *pratimokṣa* precepts, delight in them, and uphold them in practice in accordance with how each and every one of them is extensively explained in the exhortation section of "The Signless Heavenly King Chapter."

At that time, as the students of Dharma throughout the world system of a billion worlds[183] sat and listened to the Buddha's recitation, in each successive mind-moment they reverently and joyfully received and upheld [his teaching of the precepts].

Then, as Śākyamuni Buddha finished speaking the above chapter on the Dharma of the ten inexhaustible precepts from within "The Mind Ground Dharma Gateway Chapter" taught by Rocana Buddha in the Lotus Flower Dais World, a hundred thousand *koṭis* of Śākyamuni Buddhas also finished their simultaneous speaking of it in the same way. Proceeding from the palace of the Maheśvara Heaven King to the base of this bodhi tree, he spoke this [precept] Dharma chapter in ten places for all the bodhisattvas and the members of an ineffably large number of great assemblies who also received, retained, recited, and explained their meanings in the same way. So, too, in a hundred thousand *koṭis* of worlds, in the Lotus Dais Treasury World, and in all the worlds as numerous as motes of dust, [they also spoke in the same way][184] the mind treasury of all buddhas, the treasury of the grounds, the precept treasury, the treasury of measureless conduct and vows, and the treasury of cause and effect and the eternally abiding buddha nature. In this same way,[185] after all these buddhas spoke the measurelessly many treasuries of all dharmas, all the beings in the hundred thousand *koṭis* of worlds received, retained, and joyfully upheld them in practice. If one were to present an extensive explanation of all the characteristics of the mind ground, it would be as explained in the chapter called "The Seven Practices[186] of the Buddha Floral Brilliance King."

Those possessed of knowledge, strong in patience and wisdom,
are able to uphold dharmas such as these.
So long as they have not yet realized buddhahood,
they securely acquire five kinds of benefit:

正體字

1009c21 一者十方佛　愍念常守護
1009c22 二者命終時　正見心歡喜
1009c23 三者生生處　為[41]諸菩薩友
1009c24 四者功德聚　戒度悉成就
1009c25 五者今後世　性戒福慧滿
1010a01 此是[1]佛行處　智者善思量
1010a02 [2]計我著相者　不能[3]信是法
1010a03 滅[4]盡取證者　亦非下種處
1010a04 欲長菩提苗　光明照世間
1010a05 應當靜觀察　諸法真實相
1010a06 不生亦不滅　不常復不斷
1010a07 不一[5]亦不異　不來亦不去
1010a08 如是一心中　方便勤莊嚴
1010a09 菩薩所應作　應當次第學
1010a10 於學於無學　勿生分別想
1010a11 是名第一道　亦名摩訶衍
1010a12 一切戲論[6]~~處~~[惡]　悉[7]~~由~~[從]是處滅
1010a13 諸佛薩婆若　悉由是處出
1010a14 是故諸佛子　宜發大勇猛
1010a15 於諸佛淨戒　護持如明珠

简体字

一者十方佛，愍念常守护；
二者命终时，正见心欢喜；
三者生生处，为诸菩萨友；
四者功德聚，戒度悉成就；
五者今后世，性戒福慧满。
此是佛行处，智者善思量；
计我著相者，不能信是法；
灭尽取证者，亦非下种处。
欲长菩提苗，光明照世间，
应当静观察，诸法真实相：
不生亦不灭，不常复不断，
不一亦不异，不来亦不去。
如是一心中，方便勤庄严，
菩萨所应作，应当次第学，
于学于无学，勿生分别想，
是名第一道，亦名摩诃衍。
一切戏论处，悉由是处灭，
诸佛萨婆若，悉由是处出。
是故诸佛子，宜发大勇猛，
于诸佛净戒，护持如明珠。

First, the buddhas of the ten directions
are sympathetically mindful of them and always protect them;
Second, when their lives come to an end,
they are possessed of right view and their minds are blissful;

Third, wherever they dwell in life after life,
they become friends with all bodhisattvas;
Fourth, the collection of meritorious qualities,
the precepts, and the rest of the perfections are all fully developed;

and fifth, in the present and subsequent lives,
the precepts of the nature,[187] merit, and wisdom become fulfilled.
This is a place in which the buddhas course.
Those who are wise skillfully contemplate it.

Those who reckon the existence of self and become attached to signs
are unable to have faith in this Dharma.
For those seizing on realization of the complete cessation absorption,[188]
this is also not a place in which they plant their seeds.

As for those wishing to grow the sprouts of bodhi
so that their light may then illuminate the world,
they should in stillness contemplate
the true character of all dharmas:

It is neither produced nor destroyed,
neither eternal nor cut off,
neither singular nor differentiated,
and neither coming nor going.

In this way, within the one mind,
one diligently cultivates skillful means as adornments.
That which the bodhisattva should engage in—
It is in that which one should sequentially train.

Toward those still in training and those beyond training,
one must not bring forth discriminating perceptions.
This is what is known as the foremost path
and what is also known as the Mahāyāna.

All the evils of conceptual proliferation
are entirely extinguished from this place.[189]
The *sarvajña*[190] of all buddhas
all comes forth from this place.

Therefore all the sons of the Buddha
rightly bring forth great courageous valor
in practicing all buddhas' pure moral precepts,
guarding and upholding them like bright jewels.

正體字

1010a16 過去諸菩薩　已於是中學
1010a17 未來者當學　現在者今學
1010a18 此是佛行處　聖主所稱歎
1010a19 我已隨順說　福德無量聚
1010a20 迴[8]以施眾生　共向一切智
1010a21 願聞是法者　疾得成佛道
1010a22 [9]梵網經盧舍那佛說菩薩心地戒品第十之
1010a23 下

简体字

过去诸菩萨，已于是中学，
未来者当学，现在者今学。
此是佛行处，圣主所称叹，
我已随顺说，福德无量聚。
回以施众生，共向一切智，
愿闻是法者，疾得成佛道！”

All bodhisattvas of the past
have trained themselves in these.
Those of the future shall also train in them,
and those of the present now train in them as well.

This is the place in which the Buddhas practice
and which the Lords of the Āryas[191] praise.
From my having followed along in speaking [these moral precepts],
their arises a measureless collection of merit

which I now return and bestow on beings
that all together may progress toward all-knowledge.
May all of those who hear this Dharma
swiftly succeed in realizing buddhahood.

The End of the Brahmā's Net Sutra Bodhisattva Precepts

Part One – Bodhisattva Precepts Translation Endnotes

1. Kumārajīva lived from 344–413 CE. He is generally considered to be one of the greatest translators of Buddhist scriptures into Chinese.
2. "Greatly Virtuous Ones" is a literal translation of the Chinese (大德) which in turn translates the Sanskrit *bhadanta* which, at least in this context, is a form of address for eminent monastics.
3. "Upāsakas" and "upāsikās" are the Sanskrit designations for male (*upāsaka*) and female (*upāsikā*) lay disciples who have at least taken the Three Refuges..
4. "Semblance Dharma Age" [像法] refers to the second of the three Dharma ages: the Right Dharma Age, the Semblance Dharma Age, and the Dharma-ending Age. It is a period in which appearances (ornate temples, etc.) tend to be more and more prominent, whereas deep practice and attainment of realizations tend to be less common.
5. "*Prātimokṣa*" (波羅提木叉) is the Sanskrit word for the code of monastic precepts. As translated into Chinese (別解脫), it was considered to mean "individual liberation." The actual meaning of the Sanskrit word is "leading to liberation." Thus, just as the monastic precepts taken at the time of ordination are described as "*prātimokṣa* precepts" which lead the practitioner toward liberation, so too it is with these ten major bodhisattva precepts.
6. More literally, this says: "One should realize that these serve as the great master for all those in the congregation. If the Buddha were dwelling in the world, it would be no different from this." But this doesn't really seem to fully express the intended meaning, hence my slightly free translation intended to encourage the reader to revere these precepts just as one would revere the Buddha himself if he were still here among us.
7. This is a quote from the seventeenth chapter of the Dharmapada (法句經, 惡行品) found at T04n0210_p0565a02-03 as "莫輕小惡，以為無殃，水渧雖微，漸盈大器".
8. "Uninterrupted [Hells]" (無間[地獄]) refers to the Avīci Hells.
9. "Passes more quickly" here is more literally "is more impermanent than" (人命無常過於山水。).
10. The "Three Jewels" refers to the Buddha, the Dharma, and the Saṃgha.
11. An "ineffable" translates the Sanskrit *anabhilāpya*, an ineffably large number among the very largest of the one hundred and twenty-plus numbers described in "The *Asaṃkhyeya* Chapter" of *The Avataṃsaka Sutra*.

12. Most commentators note that Rocana is communicating here through the emanation of light.
13. In accordance with the Song, Yuan, and Ming editions as well as to accord with common sense and what the text clearly intends to mean, I emend the text here by duplicating the "light" character (光) to allow for reading this phrase as "every ray of which transformationally created countless buddhas…" (光光皆化無量佛).
14. The Tuṣita Heaven is the fourth level of heavens after, in order: the Heaven of the Four Heavenly Kings; the Trayastriṃśa Heaven; and the Yāma Heaven.
15. The first *dhyāna* heavens consist of the three levels of Brahma Heavens: the Brahma-pāriṣadya Heaven; the Brahma-purohita Heaven; and the Mahābrahma Heaven.
16. The second *dhyāna* heavens consist of the Parīttābha Heaven, the Apramāṇābha Heaven, and the Ābhasvara Heaven.
17. Somewhat oddly, here and below, the text switches back and forth between third-person and first-person narration.
18. These biographical details differ slightly from the usual received biography in which, having married young, the Buddha renounced the home life at the age of twenty-nine and became enlightened at the age of thirty-five. Hence my inclusion here of "five" in brackets as "thirty-[five]" to accord with the Buddha's biography as recorded nearly everywhere else in the Canon."
19. In interpreting the meaning of this passage, I follow Zhuhong who instructs that *yi jie* (一戒), literally "one precept(s)" is to be construed to mean "these precepts" while also stating that "these precepts are the most supreme and foremost of precepts" (一戒猶言此戒。又此戒是最上第一戒也。 / X38n0679_p0157c12).
20. I follow Zhixu who interprets this *dang-dang* (當當) as meaning "definitely, really" (的的確確), doubled for emphasis. (當當。猶言的的確確。 / X38n0694_p0643c03–4)
21. *Amṛta* means "the deathless" and is otherwise a reference to the devas' "elixir of immortality." Here it is euphemism for nirvāṇa, the idea being that careful observance of the precepts constitutes the gateway to ultimate success on the path to buddhahood and the nirvāṇa of a buddha.
22. The "our" here in this verse line is with reference to the standpoint of each of the hundred thousand *koṭīs* of Śākyamuni Buddhas each of whom looks to and acknowledges Rocana Buddha as their original teacher.

23. Here the speaker switches from Rocana Buddha, the reward-body buddha to our Śākyamuni Buddha, the transformation-body buddha.

24. Zhuhong points out that: "As for 'the precepts already being complete,' with a single thought of the mind of faith, the myriad delusions are completely banished. The guarding against wrong and the stopping of evil completely reside in this." (戒已具足者。一念信心萬惑俱遣。防非止惡。盡在於斯。 / X38n0679_p0161b16)

25. Although "teachers among the Saṃgha" (師僧) could conceivably also be translated as "teachers and the Saṃgha," the commentators are fairly unanimous in agreeing that here it is referring to "teachers among the Saṃgha" and more specifically to those from whom one receives the precepts. For example, Zhuhong defines "teachers among the Saṃgha" as referring to one's *upādhyāya*, the monastic officiant from whom one receives the precepts. He then adds: "This does not refer to members of the Saṃgha in general." (師僧者。是已和尚。非泛僧也。 / X38n0679_p0162c03–04.)

26. This is a reference to the devas of the eighteen form realm heavens.

27. The text of the scripture itself does not include any titles for any of the precepts. In the English translation, I will be using Zhiyi's (ZY) title choices for each of these numbered precepts while also including Fazang's (FZ) title choices in these endnotes. As it happens, for most of these ten major precepts, their title choices are the same. Here FZ's title is identical: "The Precept against Killing." (ZY: "第一殺戒." / FZ: "殺戒第一.")

28. Lest one wonder about the relevance of "filial respect," more traditionally rendered as "filial piety," one may reflect that, across the course of countless previous lifetimes, it is probable that all beings that one encounters have served as one's own relatives. Therefore they should be regarded as deserving of an attitude of filial respect.

29. Both ZY (X38n0676_p0011b10), one of the very earliest commentaries, and ZH (X38n0679_p0168b24), as well as the Song and Yuan editions contain this "on the contrary" phrase also seen as standard in many of the later precepts, hence my emendation here.

30. Here again, FZ's title is identical to that of ZY: "The Precept against Stealing. (ZY: "第二盜戒." / FZ: "盜戒第二.")

31. Here again, FZ's title is identical to that of ZY: "The Precept against Sexual Relations." (ZY: "第三婬戒." / FZ: "婬戒第三.")

32. Depending on the commentator "sexual conduct contrary to the path" (非道行婬) may mean either sexual conduct involving the wrong orifice (oral or anal sexual relations), sexual relations with one's mother,

daughter, or sister, or sexual relations at the wrong times such as when one's wife is pregnant or nursing, etc.

33. Per Hirakawa (0573), "Liberate all beings" (救度一切眾生) corresponds to the Sanskrit *sarva-sattva-dhātu-paritrāṇatā*.

34. Here again, FZ's title is identical to that of ZY: "The Precept against False Speech." (ZY: "第四妄語戒." / FZ: "妄語戒第四.")

35. Here again, FZ's title is identical to that of ZY: "The Precept against Dealing in Intoxicants." (ZY: "第五酤酒戒." / FZ: "酤酒戒第五.")

Throughout the title and text of this fifth major precept, what I translate by the general term "intoxicants" (酒) would ordinarily more literally be translated as "alcoholic beverages" which would include wine, liquor, beer, spirits, etc. I instead translate it as "intoxicants" because the precept is clearly intended to include any recreationally or habitually consumed substances which becloud, dull, derange, or addict the mind or body. As such, this would of course also include substances such as *cannabis* and its active ingredient, THC, as well as methedrine, opiates, MDMA, DMT, and also psychedelics consumed in a non-therapeutic setting.

36. While ZY's title specifies that this refers to "transgressions committed by members of the four assemblies," FZ's "The Precept against Speaking of [Others'] Transgressions" is more general. (ZY: "第六說四眾過戒." / "說過戒第六.")

37. The "Two Vehicles" refers to the individual-liberation vehicles aimed at achieving either the spiritual liberation of an arhat or that of a *pratyekabuddha*.

38. Here again, FZ's title is identical to that of ZY: "The Precept against Praising Oneself and Disparaging Others." (ZY: "第七自讚毀他戒." / FZ: "自讚毀他戒第七.")

39. Whereas ZY's title is "The Precept against Acting Miserly and Insulting others," FZ specifies only, "The Precept against Deliberately Acting Miserly." (ZY: "第八慳惜加毀戒." / FZ: "故慳戒第八.")

40. Here, while ZY specifies, "The Precept against Acting with a Hateful Mind and Refusing to Accept Apologies," FZ's title has only "The Precept Against Hatefulness." (ZY: "第九瞋心不受悔戒." / FZ: "瞋戒第九.")

41. I include in brackets "kindness and" (慈) and "and a mind of filial respect" (孝順心) to show the probable original reading of the text as quoted in the early commentaries of ZY, ZH, and ZX. "Kindness and" also reflects the text as preserved in the Song, Yuan, and Ming editions.

42. Although the ZY title and the FZ title are basically the same ("The Precept against Slander of the Three Jewels"), in his commentary, ZY acknowledges the existence of two other alternative titles ("The Precept against Slandering the Dharma of the Bodhisattva" and "The Precept against Wrong Views and Wrong Speech"). (ZY: "第十謗三寶戒." [亦云 "謗菩薩法戒," 或云 "邪見邪說戒."] / FZ: "謗三寶戒第十.")
43. Here again the ZY and FZ titles are nearly identical in meaning but with slight differences in phrasing. Whereas ZY specifies both seniors and peers: "The Precept against Disrespecting Teachers and [Dharma] Friends," FZ only specifies those who are senior as the objects of proscribed disrespect: "The Precept against Slighting Arrogance toward Teachers and Seniors." (ZY: "第一不敬師友戒." / FZ: "輕慢師長戒第一.")
44. "Senior member of the Saṃgha" translates *shangzuo* (上座), literally "senior seated one" which usually refers to a bhikshu of at least thirty years tenure since receiving higher ordination.
45. An *upādhyāya* is a monastic preceptor or instructor.
46. An *ācārya* is a monastic who is a teacher of monastics.
47. Because the variant reading "a greatly virtuous fellow student…" (大德同學) found in the Song, Yuan, and Ming editions is recorded in Zhiyi's commentary as recorded by his amanuensis, Guanding (at X38n0676_p0015c22), I believe it is reasonable to accept this variant reading as possessing canonical primacy.
48. ZH explains that "one holding the same views" (同見) refers to "one whose mind possesses the same single understanding" (心同一解也。 / X38n0679_p0179c22).
49. Again, the presence of the Song, Yuan, and Ming variant reading "hateful mind" (瞋心) in the ZY commentary (X38n0676_p0015c23) is evidence of its relative antiquity and hence I include it here due to its apparent canonical authenticity.
50. ZY and FZ both refer to this precept as "The Precept against Consuming (lit. "drinking") Intoxicants. (ZY: "第二飲酒戒." / FZ: "飲酒戒第二.")

    Again, as in the earlier major precept prohibiting dealing in "intoxicants," throughout the title and text of this second minor precept, what I translate by the general term "intoxicants" (酒) would ordinarily more literally be translated as "alcoholic beverages" which typically would include wine, liquor, beer, spirits, etc. As with that previous precept, I instead translate it as "intoxicants" because the precept is clearly intended to include any recreationally or habitually consumed substances which becloud, dull, derange, or addict the mind or body. As such, this would of course also include substances such as *cannabis* and its active ingredient, THC, as well as methedrine, opiates, MDMA, DMT, and also psychedelics consumed in a non-therapeutic setting..

51. ZY and FZ are identical here where they both refer to this precept as "The Precept against Eating Meat." (ZY: "第三食肉戒." / FZ: "食肉戒第三.")
52. I follow the Ming edition's reading also found in the text as recorded in ZY, ZH, and ZX by emending this line to read as follows: "Eating meat cuts off the great kindness and compassion and the seed of the buddha nature (夫食肉者。斷大慈悲。佛性種子。). Without this emendation this sentence would have no subject and would make no sense.
53. Here the ZY and FZ titles are identical: "The Precept against Eating the Five Kinds of Pungent Plants." (ZY: "第四食五辛戒." / FZ: "食五辛戒第四.")
54. "The five kinds of pungent plants" (五辛) refers for the most part to plants from the *Allium* species. The plant names specified in the definitions of the five names given here are somewhat contradictory depending on one's dictionaries of choice. In any case, it is clear that they are for the most part intended to refer to the various types of garlic, onions, chives, shallots, leeks, etc., with *asafoetida* being the one exception which derives its pungence from a different part of a different species of plant, namely from the dried oleoresin found in the root and rhizomes of the *ferula asafoetida* plant found mostly in Southern Iran.
55. *Allium victorialis*, a.k.a. "alpine broad-leaf allium," or "victory onion."
56. The reasons why these five kinds of pungent plants are proscribed come down to their being associated with an increase in sexual desire and anger along with a tendency of Dharma protecting spirits to avoid practitioners who eat them. The *Śūraṅgama Sutra* also mentions that hungry ghosts and demons are attracted to those who eat these five kinds of pungent plants and as a result one becomes much more liable to being harassed by ghosts and demons. (See T19n0945_p0141c04–13.)
57. The ZY and FZ titles are essentially the same, but with slightly different wording. Here FZ's title is: "The Precept against Failure to Bring Up Offenses and Teach Repentance." (ZY: "第五不教悔罪戒." / FZ: "不舉教懺戒品第五.")

58. These seven heinous offenses (七逆罪) are explained below (1008c01–c03) as: drawing the blood of a buddha; killing one's father; killing one's mother; killing one's *upādhyāya*, killing one's *ācārya*; breaking up a Dharma-wheel-turning Saṃgha proceeding; and killing an *ārya*, i.e. killing anyone who has realized one of the fruits of the path.

59. The "eight difficulties" (八難) refer to eight conditions of rebirth in which being able to take up the Buddha's path to awakening is likely to be nearly impossible, these being birth: 1) in the hells; 2) as a hungry ghost (*preta*); 3) as an animal; 4) in the long-life heavens; 5) in the continent of Uttarakuru; 6) as blind, deaf, or dumb; 7) as one possessed of merely worldly wisdom and eloquence; or 8) birth before or after the appearance of a buddha.

60. The *upoṣadha* ceremony is the meeting held every two weeks in which monastics recite their moral codes.

61. The ZY and FZ titles are close in meaning, but somewhat different in wording. Here FZ has: "The Precept against Failing to Be Respectful and Request [the Teaching of] Dharma." (ZY: "第六不供給請法戒." / FZ: "不敬請法戒第六.")

62. Literally: "a hundred *li* or a thousand *li*" (百里千里).

63. Here I translate the Chinese *liang* (兩) as "ounce" assuming that this is referring to the so-called "old *liang*" which, according to Pleco Dictionary, is equivalent to 1.102 ounces.

64. ZY clarifies that "three times" refers to before noon, in the afternoon, and in the early evening. (三時者中前中後初夜… / X38n0676_p0017a09.)

65. The ZY and FZ titles are slightly different here. FZ has: "The Precept against Failure to Listen to the Sutras and Moral Codes." (ZY: "第七懈怠不聽法戒." / FZ: "不聽經律戒第七.")

66. I emend the text here by adding "Dharma" (法) based on strong evidence that it was in the original text provided by it's presence in the Song, Yuan, Ming, and Gong editions as well as in the commentaries of ZY, ZH, and ZX.

67. The "*vinaya*" is the portion of the Buddhist canon that preserves the Buddhist moral code.

68. Here the ZY and FZ titles express the same idea with different terminology. FZ's title reads: "The Precept against Turning Away from What Is Right and Turning toward What is Wrong." (ZY: "第八背大向小戒." / FZ: "背正向邪戒第八.")

69. Here the titles are mostly the same in meaning, but slightly different in wording. Here FZ has: "The Precept against Failure to Attend to

the Suffering of the Sick." (ZY: "第九不看病戒." / FZ: "不瞻病苦戒第九.")

70. The eight fields of merit are: the Buddha; the *āryas* (those who have awakened to one of the four stages of the path to arhatship or any of the irreversible stages on the bodhisattva path to buddhahood), the Saṃgha, *upādhyāyas, ācāryas,* one's father, one's mother, and the sick.

71. Again, the ZY and FZ titles have the same meaning but slightly different wording. Here FZ has: "The Precept against Collecting Weapons Used for Killing." (ZY: "第十畜殺眾生具戒." / FZ: "畜諸殺具戒第十.")

72. In accordance with the Song, Yuan, Ming, and Gong editions as well as the text as quoted in the commentaries of ZY, ZH, and ZX, I emend the reading of the Chinese text by substituting *sha* (殺) for *yu* (餘) at T24n1484_p1005c16.

73. The FZ title here is ambiguous. Perhaps it could be translated as "The Precept against Going among the Military with Communications from One's Country." (ZY: "第十一國使戒." / FZ: "通國入軍戒第十一.")

74. Here, because FZ states explicitly what ZY includes only implicitly, I "improve" the ZY title by adding "uncompassionate kinds of" in brackets. ZY's more complete title name is: "The Precept against Carrying On Uncompassionate Kinds of Trade." (ZY: "第十二販賣戒." / FZ: "傷慈販賣戒第十二.")

75. Lists of "the six kinds of domestic animals" (六畜) vary. Perhaps the most common listing mentions horses, cattle, sheep, pigs, dogs, and chickens.

76. Here the meanings of the ZY and FZ title are the same with FZ's differing only slightly in wording. FZ's title is: "The Precept against Baseless Slander." (ZY: "第十三謗毀戒." / FZ: "無根謗人戒第十三.")

77. The Zhiyi, Zhuhong, and Zhixu commentaries all interpret the intended meaning of this passage according to my bracketed emendation by which the practitioner is instructed to bring forth filial and compassionate thoughts not just to his six close relatives, but rather to all beings.

78. The "six close relatives" (六親) are usually listed as father, mother, elder brothers, younger brothers, wife, and children. Perhaps a more inclusive interpretation would substitute "elder siblings and younger siblings" for "elder brothers and younger brothers."

79. The ZY and FZ titles mean the same. However FZ includes what ZY only implies ("destructive"), hence I had to "improve" the ZY title with brackets. FZ's title is "The Precept against Destructive Fires." (ZY: "第十四放火燒戒." / FZ: "放火損燒戒.")

80. ZY points out that between the fourth and ninth month there are many kinds of bugs and other such things that would be killed by lighting such fires. (X38n0676_p0018b06.)

81. Arguing that "anything that belongs to anyone" (一切有主物) must be a scribal error, ZY emends the text to read: "One must not deliberately burn any living thing" (一切有生物). However, because the immediately preceding sentence has already switched away from concerns about setting fires that may kill beings to exclusively admonishing against burning things belonging to others ("other people's houses or dwellings, cities, villages, Saṃgha residences, fields, groves, or the possessions of ghosts, spirits, or officials"), I find ZY's line of reasoning here to be unconvincing. Therefore I do not follow his implicit suggestion to emend the text here.

82. Here both the meaning and wording of the ZY and FZ titles are different. FZ's title is: "The Precept against Teaching the Dharma in Opposition to the Doctrine." (ZY: "第十五僻教戒." / FZ: "法化違宗戒第十五.")

83. The ZY and FZ titles for this precept are slightly different in both meaning and wording. FZ's title is: "The Precept against Being Selfish with the Dharma Due to Scheming for Personal Benefit." (ZY: "第十六為利倒說戒." / FZ: "惜法規利戒第十六.")

84. Hungry ghosts (*pretas*) constitute one of the three wretched destinies (the other two being the animals and the hell realms). Their lives are characterized by constant insatiable hunger and are said to be the karmic retribution for extreme greed in previous existences.

85. Again, the ZY and FZ titles are similar in meaning, but slightly different in wording. FZ's title here is: "The Precept against Forceful Begging in Reliance on Officials." (ZY: "第十七恃勢乞求戒." / FZ: "依官強乞戒第十七.")

86. The ZY and FZ titles here are almost identical in meaning with only slightly different wording. FZ's title is: "The Precept against Serving as a Teacher with Insufficient Knowledge." (ZY: "第十八無解作師戒." / FZ: "無知為師戒第十八.")

87. As it happens, what the Chinese here call "divisive speech" or more literally "double-tongued speech" (兩舌) usually translates the Sanskrit *paiśunya* which is more often understood to mean "slander." Here FZ's has a rather differently worded title: "The Precept against Contentiousness-invoking Slander and Deception of Worthies." (ZY: "第十九兩舌戒." / FZ: "鬪謗欺賢戒第十九.")

88. The ZY and FZ titles here are the same in meaning but slightly different in wording. FZ's version of the title is: "The Precept Against

Being Unable to Rescue Beings." (ZY: "第二十不行放救戒." / FZ: "不能救生戒第二十.")

89. I emend the text here by adding "He should reflect in this manner" (應作是念) to accord with the Song, Yuan, Ming, and Gong editions as well with the text as quoted in ZY's commentary (at X38n0676_p0019b06–7).

90. I emend the reading of this line to restore its original wording as reflected in the Song, Yuan, Ming, and Gong editions as well as in nearly all the major commentaries beginning with ZY (at X38n0676_p0019b12–13).

91. The ZY and FZ titles here differ in both meaning and wording. FZ's title is: "The prohibition against having no compassion or patience and taking revenge." (ZY: "第二十一瞋打報仇戒." / FZ: "無慈忍酬怨戒第二十一.")

92. "Or other close relatives" here translates what one might instead translate more literally (and clumsily) as "or others among one's six types of close relatives" (六親)."

93. FZ points out that, although this would be an offense is committed by either a layperson or a monastic, monastics in particular are brought up here to emphasize that this would be an especially deep fault if committed by a monastic. (T40n1813_p0644a16–18.)

94. The ZY and FZ titles are somewhat different in both meaning and wording. FZ's title is: "The Precept against Looking on Others with Arrogance and Looking Lightly on the Dharma." (ZY: "第二十二憍慢不請法戒." / FZ: "慢人輕法戒第二十二.")

95. My modification of the faulty Taisho reading here to include "great wealth" (大富) so that the line then reads: "…great merit, great wealth, or bounteous riches including the seven precious things…" (大福。大富。饒財七寶。) is based on its presence in the very early commentary of Zhiyi as well as in the later commentaries of Zhuhong, and Zhixu.

96. Assuming that the first character in the FZ title is a graphic similarity scribal error in which *jing* (經), "scripture, etc." was accidentally substituted for *qing* (輕), "to slight," FZ's title here is: "The Precept against Slighting Beginning Students Seeking Instruction." (ZY: "第二十三憍慢僻說戒." / FZ: "經新求學戒第二十三.")

97. I emend the text here to accord with the ZY commentary and the Song, Yuan, Ming, and Gong editions as reflected in the Taisho endnote: "[1006:037] 心＝以【宋】【元】【明】【宮】."

98. "Auspicious signs" here is literally "good signs" (好相) which clearly means "signs betokening good omen," hence "auspicious signs."

99. "To see auspicious signs" beginning here and then hereafter (in this precept) is more literally "to obtain auspicious signs" (得好相) which really just means "to obtain a vision of auspicious signs," hence, to avoid clumsiness, I simplify this to "to see auspicious signs."

100. I emend the text here by adding *zhi* (至), "ultimately," to accord with text as quoted in the ZY commentary and as it appears in the Song, Yuan, Ming, and Gong editions.

101. "Within three" is an approximate translation of the Chinese "within one thousand *li*" (千里內). In fact, "one thousand *li*" in the period in question was equal to about two hundred and fifty-eight modern international miles. (At that time, a Chinese mile was equal to four hundred and sixteen meters.)

102. I emend the text here to accord with the ZY commentary and the Song, Yuan, Ming, and Gong editions as reflected in the Taisho endnote: "[1006: 043] 前＋（自誓）【宋】【元】【明】【宮】."

103. Here the FZ title is: "The Precept against Turning Away from What Is Right toward What Is Wrong." (ZY: "第二十四不習學佛戒." / FZ: "背正向邪戒第二十四")

104. I emend the reading of the Taisho text to read "the Dharma of the Great Vehicle" (instead of "the right Dharma of the Great Vehicle" in accordance with the ZY commentary and the Song, Yuan, Ming, and Gong editions, this in accordance with the Taisho endnote: "[1006: 044]（正）－【宋】【元】【明】【宮】."

105. Here the FZ title is: "The Precept against Failure to Maintain Correct Deportment When Serving as Host." (ZY: "第二十五不善和眾戒." / FZ: "為主失儀戒第二十五.")

106. Here the FZ title is: "The Precept against Acting Contrary to Correct Form When Entertaining Guests." (ZY: "獨受利養戒." / FZ: "待賓乖式戒第二十六.")

107. To accord with the most probable original reading as reflected in the ZY and ZH commentaries as well as in the Song, Yuan, Ming, and Gong editions, I emend the text here (at T24n1484_p1007a06) by adding *mu chuang* (木床), "wooden bed."

108. The Song, Yuan, Ming, and Gong editions include this line that is also quoted as part of the text in the ZY Sui Dynasty commentary (at X38n0676_p0020c15–16), the ZH commentary, and the ZX commentary : "… or should even be willing to cut off and sell his own flesh." (… 女+[身應割自身肉賣] / X38n0676_p0020c15–16.) Given that this is quoted in these early standard commentaries, I feel it is reasonable to include it here as an emendation reflecting the most probable original reading of the text.

109. A *dānapati* is a benefactor who provides gifts, food, or other types of donations to members of the monastic Saṃgha.

110. A *śramaṇa* is one who has left the home life to pursue the path of spiritual liberation. In these texts, *śramaṇa* is synonymous with being a Buddhist monk.

111. Here the FZ title is identical to that of ZY: "The Precept against Accepting Discriminatory Invitations." (ZY: "第二十七受別請戒." / FZ: "受別請戒第二十七.")

112. I emend the text here to accord with the text as quoted in the ZY commentary and the Song, Yuan, Ming, and Gong editions as reflected in the Taisho endnote: "[1007: 012] 田＋（中）【宋】【元】【明】【宮】."

113. Lists of the "eight fields of merit" (八福田) vary. The most common list refers to the Buddha, the *āryas* (those who have attained stages of the path equivalent to that of the streamwinner and above), the *upādhyāyas* (precept transmitting monks), the *ācāryas* (teaching monks during a transmission of the precepts), members of the Saṃgha, one's father, one's mother, and the sick.

114. An *ārya* is one of those who have awakened to one of the four stages of the path to arhatship or any of the irreversible stages on the bodhisattva path to buddhahood.

115. Here the FZ title is: "The Precept against Deliberately Extending Discriminatory Invitations to Members of the Saṃgha." (ZY: "第二十八別請僧戒." / FZ: "故別請僧戒第二十八.")

116. I emend the text here to accord with the text as quoted in the ZY commentary and the Song, Yuan, Ming, and Gong editions as reflected in the Taisho endnote: "[1007: 013] 欲＋（請僧求願知事報言）【宋】【元】【明】【宮】."

117. A "worthy" (*bhadra*) is a cultivator who has progressed beyond the level of a common worldling, but who has not as yet become an *ārya*, one who has become irreversible on the path to complete spiritual awakening.

118. "Common person" here translates *fanfu* (凡夫) for which the Sanskrit antecedent is *pṛthagjana* which itself refers to everyone who has not become enlightened to any stage of the path equivalent to that of a streamwinner or higher.

119. Here the FZ title is: "The Precept against Bad Skills That Harm Beings." (ZY: "第二十九邪命自活戒." / FZ: "惡伎損生戒第二十九.")

120. "Gold and silver poison" is variously interpreted with some claiming this is just the name of a particular poison, some saying it is a kind of potion to drive away snakes every year in the fifth month of the year,

and others claiming that gold and silver themselves are so toxic as to be used to poison people.

121. As for "*gu* poison" (蠱毒), this refers to a kind of poison used in black magic to mobilize ghosts and spirits against others.

122. It seems that, at least beginning with the early integrated text-with-commentary edition of the Zhiyi commentary recorded by his amanuensis, Guanding, this precept is usually given the title of "The Precept against not Respecting the Right Time" (不敬好時戒). Later on, in the commentary of Zhixu, this precept is found with the title of "The Precept against Managing (or "Exerting Influence on") the Laity" (經理白衣戒), this clearly in reference to a line found in the text of the precept as it comes down in most editions beginning with that of Zhiyi, but still missing in the text of Taisho T1484. (See below where I have included this line in end-noted brackets in my translation of this precept.)

    Here the FZ title is: "The Precept against Acting in Opposition to the Prohibitions by Doing What Is Wrong." (ZY: "第三十不敬好時戒." / FZ: "違禁行非戒.")

123. Although this bracketed line which seems to mean, "[if he serves as one who] exerts influence on the laity..." (經理白衣) is not included in the T1484 Taisho text, it is found as a quotation of the precept text embedded in the text of most commentaries (with the notable exception of Fazang's commentary).

124. As for the "six days of abstinence" (六齋日), they are the eighth, the fourteenth, the fifteenth, the twenty-third, the twenty-ninth, and the thirtieth days of the lunar month. These are considered auspicious days for the laity to observe the eight precepts proscribing: killing; stealing; sexual activity; false speech; consumption of intoxicants; adornment with flowers or wearing perfumes etc.; singing, dancing, and going to watch such things; sleeping or sitting on large grand beds; and eating at the wrong time (i.e., not after midday).

125. The "three long months of abstinence" (三長齋月) refers to the first, fifth, and ninth lunar months.

126. Here the FZ title is: "The Precept against Failure to Rescue [Sacred Objects or Individuals] When Witnessing Their Endangerment." (ZY: "第三十一不行救贖戒." / FZ: "見厄不救戒第三十一.")

127. The FZ title here is: "The Precept against Collecting Things Used in Actions Contrary to the Dharma." (ZY: "第三十二損害眾生戒." / FZ: "畜作非法戒第三十二.")

128. Raccoon dogs are probably prohibited here because in addition to being carnivorous predators that kill other animals they are also raised to be killed for their fur pelts.

129. Here the precept is probably not prohibiting raising dogs as companion animals. More likely, it intends to prohibit raising dogs for their flesh (a practice still common in parts of China) or as attack animals.

130. The Sanskrit antecedent for what I translate here as "thought" in ZY's suggested title is *vitarka-vicāra* in which *vitarka* (覺) refers to initial ideation and *vicāra* (觀) refers to secondary discursion, usually in the form of subsequent thinking on the topic of that initial ideation.

It seems that, at least for this precept, FZ's suggested title may be preferable: "33. The Precept against Watching, Listening, or Doing What is Unwholesome" (ZY: "第三十三邪業覺觀戒." / FZ: "觀聽作惡戒第三十三.")

131. *Prasena* is an ancient Indian military board game.

132. According to *Foguang* Dictionary, this "fingernail mirror" is a kind of fortune telling technique in which one smears an elixir on one's fingers and then recites a mantra by which one's palm then radiates light like a mirror which is able to manifest all sorts of images due to which one can foretell a person's auspicious, inauspicious, unfortunate, or fortunate future.

133. The FZ title here is "The Precept Requiring Solidly Upholding and Guarding One's [Bodhi] Resolve." (ZY: "第三十四暫離菩提心戒." / FZ: "堅持守心戒第三十四.")

134. This refers to the story of bhikshus who had been set upon by thieves who stole everything they had, including even their robes, but who feared that, in running away, they might be pursued and caught by the monks. Then one of the thieves who happened to have previously been a monk remembered that monks are forbidden to harm even live plants, whereupon those thieves tied all the monks down with live rushes so that, fearing they might kill the plants in freeing themselves from their vegetal bondage, the monks would all remain tied down rather than risk breaking the precept against injuring live plants. As it happened, the monks never broke the precepts for others eventually came by and released them so that they did not have to die in their dedication to refrain from violating even this minor precept. The story is related in a number of places in the Tripitaka, probably the earliest and most detailed recital being at T04n0201_p0268c06–269c24.

135. The FZ title here is: "The Precept against Failure to Make the Great Vows." (ZY: "第三十五不發願戒." / FZ: "不發大願戒第三十五.")

136. Here, to restore the most probable original reading of the Chinese text as it appears in the Song, Yuan, Ming, and Gong editions as well as in the very early commentary of ZY echoed by the commentaries of ZH and ZX, I emend it by dropping the character *you* (友) which then leaves the Chinese for what I translate as "good spiritual guide" (善知識) which is the standard rendering for the Sanskrit *kalyāṇamitra.*

137. The FZ title here is "The Precept against Failure to Bring Forth the Ten Vows." (ZY: "第三十六不發誓戒." / FZ: "不起十願戒第三十六.")

138. FZ, ZY, ZH, and ZX all agree that "these ten great vows" refers to the vows implicitly listed in the previous precept. While FZ's analysis is a bit too complex for this endnote, ZY, ZH, and ZX are unanimous in agreeing on the following list for which I provide ZX's precise wording: 1) The vow to maintain filial respect toward one's parents and one's teachers among the Saṃgha; 2) The vow to acquire good teachers; 3) The vow to acquire fellow students and excellent [good spiritual] friends; 4) The vow to see that they will teach me the Great Vehicle sutras and moral codes; 5) The vow to understand the stages of advancement; 6) The vow to understand the developmental stages; 7) The vow to understand the vajra stages; 8) The vow to understand the grounds; 9) The vow to cultivate in accordance with the Dharma; and 10) The vow to solidly uphold the Buddha's moral precepts. (X38n0694_p0679c23–680a02.)

139. The FZ title here is "The Precept against Deliberately Entering Dangerous Places." (ZY: "第三十七冒難遊行戒." / FZ: "故入難處戒第三十七.")

140. The "*dhūta* austerities" are spiritually purifying practices exemplified by the twelve *dhūta* austerities which, per *The Sutra on the Twelve Dhūta Austerities,* (T17n0783_p0720b13 – 722a07) consist of: "(1) dwelling in a secluded forest dwelling (i.e. in an *araṇya*); (2) always obtaining one's food on the alms round; (3) always going in sequential order (never skipping houses) when on the alms round; (4) eating only one meal per day; (5) never eating more than a fixed quantity of food; (6) never drinking soups or other sorts of beverages after midday; (7) wearing robes made of cast-off rags; (8) only wearing the three robes; (9) dwelling in a graveyard [or charnel ground]; (10) dwelling beneath a tree; (11) dwelling out on the open ground; and (12) only sitting and never lying down to sleep." (T17n0783_p0720c06 – 720c10)

141. All of the major commentaries agree that "two times" is intended to refer to the seasons of spring and fall.

142. The tin-headed staff (*khakharaka*) has metal rings that emit a jingling sound as a warning to insects, etc.

143. A "rope bed" (繩床) is most likely referring to hammock made of rope which can be strung between two trees and allow one to sleep without being so easily bothered and bitten by ants, scorpions, and other such bothersome creepy-crawlies.

144. A "*kāśāya* robe" is a dyed robe, one which ideally is dyed an ochre color.

145. The FZ title here is: "The Precept against Deviating from Propriety in the Saṃgha's Seating Arrangements." (ZY: "第三十八乖尊卑次序戒." / FZ: "眾坐乖儀戒第三十八.")

146. I include the bracketed phrase "does not accord with the Dharma in each and every case" (一一不如法) to reflect the version of the text recorded in nearly all of even the earliest commentaries, but which seems to have been lost in all but the Ming edition of the sutra text proper.

147. The FZ title here is: "The Precept against Failure to Explain [the Dharma] When It Should Be Explained." (ZY: "第三十九不修福慧戒." / FZ: "應講不講戒第三十九."

148. According to PDB, a *rākṣasa* is "a species of demigod in Buddhist mythology (the female form is an "ogress," or rākṣasī) usually described as a flesh-eating demon that is able to fly, run like the wind, and possess superhuman strength during the night."

149. The "three phases of karmic retribution" (三報) refer to: 1) Retribution to be experienced in the present life; 2) Retribution to be experience upon rebirth, i.e., when one dies; and 3) Retribution to be experienced in subsequent lives. The Yuan and Ming editions as well as the commentaries of Zhiyi, Zhuhong, and Zhixu quote the sutra text as instead having "three wretched destinies" (三惡 [道]) here, namely retribution entailing rebirth among the animals, among the hungry ghosts (*pretas*), or in the hells.

150. These seven heinous offenses (七逆罪) are explained below (1008c01–c03) as: drawing the blood of a buddha; killing one's father; killing one's mother; killing an *upādhyāya*, killing an *ācārya*; breaking up a Dharma-wheel-turning Saṃgha proceeding; and killing an *ārya*, i.e. killing anyone who has realized one of the fruits of the path.

151. The "eight difficulties" (八難) refer to eight conditions of rebirth in which being able to take up the Buddha's path to awakening is likely to be nearly impossible, these being birth: 1) in the hells; 2) as a hungry ghost (*preta*); 3) as an animal; 4) in the long-life heavens; 5) in the continent of Uttarakuru; 6) as blind, deaf, or dumb; 7) as one possessed of merely worldly wisdom and eloquence; or 8) birth before or after the appearance of a buddha.

152. *Brahmadaṇḍa* (梵壇 or 梵怛 or 梵杖, etc.) is explained in numerous places in the canon as referring to an extreme method of censure for monks or nuns who have repeatedly broken the precepts which involves refusing to have any interaction at all with them, including refusing to even speak with them.

153. The FZ title here is: "The Precept against Impropriety in Transmitting the Precepts." (ZY: "第四十揀擇受戒戒." / FZ: "受戒非儀戒第四十.")

154. Although the Taisho edition itself does not have the "attitude affected by hatred" phrase (瞋心), because it is contained in the Song, Yuan, Ming, and Gong editions as well as in the bodhisattva precepts text as quoted in all the Tiantai commentaries, it is reasonable to assume that it is part of the original text. Hence I choose to at least insert the phrase in brackets here.

155. The FZ title here is: "The Precept against Acting as a Teacher with Insufficent Virtue." (ZY: "第四十一為利作師戒." / FZ: "無德詐師戒第四十一.")

156. One of the Ming Dynasty commentators, Zhixu, points out that, in the transmission of these bodhisattva precepts, it is actually Śākyamuni Buddha who is the *upādhyaya* and Maitreya Bodhisattva who is the *ācarya*. This is a fairly common understanding of what is going on in the realm of the unseen when transmitting these precepts. However, Zhixu goes so far as to say that one should alter the punctuation and hence the reading of the Chinese text to accommodate this interpretation. Because neither Zhiyi nor Fazang say much about this idea and because they are arguably the two most revered of all the early commentators, I refrain from making any such changes to the straightforward translation of the text I have chose to make.

157. The "seven obstructive offenses" (七遮罪) is an alternative name for the "seven heinous offenses" (七逆罪). Perhaps this refers to the fact that those who have committed these offenses are thereby usually prevented from taking the bodhisattva precepts.

158. The habitually acquired lineage corresponds to the Sanskrit *samudānīta-gotra*.

159. In accordance with the text as it appears in the ZY, ZH, and ZX commentaries as well as in the Song, Yuan, Ming, and Gong editions, I emend the Chinese text to include the Chinese for this "intrinsic lineage" (性種性). The intrinsic lineage corresponds to the Sanskrit *prakriṭistha-gotra*.

160. The lineage of the path corresponds to the Sanskrit *bodhi-gotra* or *mārga-gotra*.

161. In accordance with the text as it appears in the ZY, ZH, and ZX commentaries as well as in the Song and Gong editions, I emend the Chinese text to include the character for "Dharma" (法) in "right Dharma nature."

162. The ten limbs of *dhyāna* (十禪支) consist of: initial attention (*vitarka*); sustained attention (*vicāra*); joy (*pramuditā*); bliss (*sukha*); single-mindedness (*citta-eka-agratā*); inward purity (*adhyātma-saṃprasāda*); equanimity (*upekṣa*); mindfulness; clear comprehension; the sensation of neither pleasure nor pain (*aduḥkha-asukha vedanā*).

163. The FZ title here is: "The Precept against Speaking the Precepts in the Wrong Place." (ZY: "第四十二為惡人說戒." / FZ: "非處說戒戒第四十二.")

164. ZY explains that "evil non-Buddhists" (外道惡人) refers to members of the ninety-five types of non-Buddhists (外道惡人即九十五種. / X38n0676_p0025a07–08.)

165. The FZ title here is: "The Precept against Deliberately Violating the Precepts." (ZY: "第四十三無慚受施戒." / FZ: "故毀禁戒戒第四十三.")

166. I emend the Taisho edition of the text to insert *gu* (故), "deliberately," which was originally present in the text as quoted in the commentaries of FZ, ZH, and ZX.

167. The FZ title here is: "The Precept against Failure to Respect the Sutras and Moral Codes." (ZY: "第四十四不供養經典戒." / FZ: "不敬經律戒第四十四.")

168. Mulberry paper has traditionally been made by hand from the inner fiber of the mulberry to produce an exceptionally fine and translucent paper.

169. The FZ title here is identical to ZY's: "The Precept against Failure to Teach Beings." (ZY: "第四十五不化眾生戒." / FZ: "不化眾生戒第四十五.")

170. The FZ title here is: "The Precept against Speaking the Dharma in Ways That Do Not Accord with Propriety." (ZY: "第四十六說法不如法戒." / FZ: "說法乖儀戒第四十六.")

171. The "fourfold assembly" (四衆 / *catasraḥ parṣadaḥ*) refers to the bhikshus, bhikshunis, *upasakas*, and *upāsikās* otherwise known as the monks, nuns, laymen, and laywomen.

172. The FZ title here is: "The Precept against Establishing Regulations That Contradict the Dharma." (ZY: "第四十七非法制限戒." / FZ: "非法立制戒第四十七.")

173. I emend the text by including in curly braces ({}) my translation of this very long sixty-one character passage of text included in the Taisho

endnote: "[1009:016] 律+（立統制眾安藉記僧比丘菩薩地立白衣高座廣行非法如兵奴事主而菩薩應受一切人供養而反為官走使非法非律若國王百官好心受佛戒者莫作是）六十一字【宋】】【元】【明】." It is clear from its inclusion in the Song, Yuan, and Ming editions, as well as from its inclusion in the text as quoted in the commentaries of Zhiyi, Zhuhong, and Zhixu that this passage was considered integral to this bodhisattva precepts text at least as early as 200 years after the time of its translation and was thus more than likely part of the original text translated by Kumārajīva around the beginning of the fifth century.

174. The FZ title here is "The Precept against Damaging the Dharma from Within." (ZY: "第四十八破法戒." / FZ: "自壞內法戒第四十八.")

175. I emend the text here to drop the "seven" (七) of "precepts of the seven buddhas" found in the Taisho text, doing so because it appears to be a relatively modern interpolation, for it is not found in the text as quoted in the early commentaries of ZY, ZH, or ZX, nor is it found in the Song, Yuan, Ming, or Gong editions.

176. I emend the text here by the addition of "precept" (戒) to allow it to read "bodhisattva-precept disciples" (菩薩戒弟子) in accordance with its wording as reflected in the way it is quoted in the early commentaries of ZY, ZH, and ZX.

177. I emend the text here through the addition of "rules like those appropriate for prisoners or rules like those appropriate for soldiers or servants" (如獄囚法兵奴之法) to restore the most probable original reading as reflected in the Song, Yuan, and Ming editions and in the commentaries of ZY, ZH, and ZX.

178. I emend the Chinese text here by inserting "...[and harms it] in a way that no other parasite coming from without could ever do. A son of the Buddha such as this does more damage to the Buddha's Dharma himself..." (非餘外蟲如是佛子自破佛法) to restore its most probable reading as quoted in the early commentaries of ZY, ZH, and ZX.

179. I emend the Chinese text here by inserting "One cannot damage them" (不可毀破) to restore its most probable reading as quoted in the early commentaries of ZY, ZH, and ZX as well as in the Song, Yuan, and Ming editions.

180. I emend the Chinese text here by removing "when" (時) and inserting "the sound" (之聲) to restore its most probable reading as quoted in the early commentaries of ZY, ZH, and ZX.

181. I emend the chinese text here by inserting "slander" (謗) to restore its most probable reading as quoted in the early commentaries of ZY, ZH, and ZX.

182. I emend the text with the addition of "Great Assembly" (大眾) in accordance with its wording as preserved in the Ming Edition and as quoted in the Tiantai commentaries of Zhiyi, Zhuhong, and Zhixu.
183. Per Zhixu's commentary (p692a11) the Chinese "three thousand" (三千) refers not to the number of listeners in the audience, but rather to a world system of a billion worlds (三千大千世界 / *trisāhasra-mahāsāhasra-loka-dhātu*) throughout which the Buddha's recitation was heard by an audience of countless students of the Dharma.
184. I follow Zhixu's suggestion that there is a missing four-character phrase here: "They also spoke in the same way." ("微塵世界下。闕亦如是說四字。" [Zhixu: 0692a24]). Both Zhiyi and Zhuhong instead suggest that the missing four-character phrase is "They also studied in the same way" (文末闕亦如是學。), but that does not seem to fit as well as Zhixu's suggestion.
185. To restore the most probable original reading, I emend the Chinese text here by replacing *ru ru* (如如) with *ru shi* (如是), "in this same way," as reflected in the early commentaries of ZY, ZH, and ZX as well as in the Song, Yuan, Ming, and Gong editions.
186. To restore the most probable original reading, I emend the Chinese text here by inserting *qi heng* (七行), "seven practices," as reflected in the early commentaries of ZY, ZH, and ZX.
187. The "precepts of the nature" generally refers to the personal moral standards which come naturally to the deeply spiritual person and which therefore should not require one to first become acquainted with the moral-virtue precepts formally laid down by the Buddha. These ordinarily would include: refraining from killing; not stealing; refraining from sexual misconduct; and not engaging in false speech.
188. The complete cessation absorption (滅盡定 / *nirodha-samāpatti*), otherwise known as "the absorption of the cessation of feeling and perception" may be seized upon as if it were nirvāṇa when in fact it is really just an exotic trap which keeps its practitioners stranded in a very subtle level of cyclic existence for inconceivably long periods of time.
189. To restore the most probable original reading as preserved in the text as quoted in the commentaries of ZY, ZH, and ZX as well as in the text of the Song, Yuan, Ming, and Gong editions, I emend the Chinese text here by substituting *e* (惡), "evils," for *chu* (處), "place," and substitute *cong* (從), "from," for *you* (由), "from."
190. *Sarvajña* means "all-knowledge."
191. "Lord of the Āryas" (聖主) is an honorific title for a buddha.

The Bodhisattva's Practice of Moral Virtue

Part One Supplement:

The Semimonthly Bodhisattva Precepts Recitation Ceremony

Annotated English Translation by Bhikshu Dharmamitra

正體字

X38 n0696_p0767a01 ‖
X38 n0696_p0767a02 ‖ No. 696
767a03 ‖ [1]附半月誦菩薩戒儀式註
767a05 ‖ 毗補提囉怛娜伽耶婆那摩賀
767a06 ‖ 冐地質多沙門　弘贊　注
767a15 ‖ 眾中當差堪能誦者誦之。眾既雲集。先舉香讚畢。
767a16 ‖ 三稱云。
767a17 ‖ **南無梵網教主盧舍那佛。**
767a18 ‖ 次舉開經偈。

[菩薩淨戒難得聞，經於無量俱胝劫，讀誦受持亦如是，如說修行者更難。]

Alternate **開經偈**:

[無上甚深微妙法，百千萬劫難遭遇，我今見聞得受持，願解如來真實義。]

其誦者昇座。白眾云。

767a19 ‖ **某甲稽首和南。敬白大眾。僧差誦戒。恐有錯悞。願同**
767a20 ‖ **誦者。慈悲指示。**
767a21 ‖ ○初歸敬三寶　二策修　三作前方便
767a22 ‖ 四誦戒序　五結問　六正誦戒經。

简体字

Downloaded 02/22/2024 from: https://www.zjailv.com/fxbd/462/2000.html

附半月诵菩萨戒仪式注

弘赞作品集

附半月诵菩萨戒仪式注

古文典藏app下载, 加公众号便于联系

毗补提啰怛娜伽耶婆那摩贺

冒地质多沙门　弘赞　注

众中当差堪能诵者诵之。众既云集。先举香赞毕。三称云。

南无梵网教主卢舍那佛。

次举开经偈。其诵者升座。白众云。

某甲稽首和南。敬白大众。僧差诵戒。恐有错误。愿同诵者。慈悲指示。

○初归敬三宝　二策修　三作前方便　四诵戒序　五结问　六正诵戒经。

The Semimonthly Bodhisattva Precepts Recitation Ceremony

(As quoted in the commentary on this ceremony by Śramaṇa[1] Hong Zan [1611–1685] of Guangzhou's Jeweled Elephant Monastery.)[2]

From among the members of the Assembly, one should appoint someone who is able to recite it to perform the recitation. Once the Assembly has gathered, after having first recited the incense praise, they should recite the following [invocation] three times:

Namo Rocana Buddha, Lord of the Brahmā's Net Teachings. (x3)

Next, recite the scripture-opening verse.[3]

[The bodhisattva's precepts of purity are but rarely heard
even when passing through measureless *koṭīs* of kalpas.
So too it is with reading, reciting, receiving, and upholding them.
Rarer still is one who cultivates them in accordance with how they were taught.]

[An alternate sutra-opening verse:[4]

The unsurpassed, extremely profound, and sublime Dharma
is rarely ever met even in a hundred thousand myriads of kalpas.
Having now seen, heard, and been enabled to receive and uphold it,
may we comprehend the Tathāgata's true and actual meaning.]

The reciter should then ascend to the high seat and address the Assembly, saying:

I, so-and-so,[5] bow in reverence and respectfully address the Great Assembly, for I have been entrusted with the recitation of the precepts. Fearing that I may err in reciting them, I hope that those reciting along with me will, with kindness and compassion, point out any errors.

List of Contents:

Part One: Taking Refuge in and Revering the Three Jewels;
Part Two: Instigation to Cultivation;
Part Three: Perform the Preliminary Procedures;
Part Four: Recite the Preface to the Precepts;
Part Five: Questioning [the Assembly];
Part Six: The Actual Recitation of the Precept Scripture.

正體字

767a23‖ ○初歸敬三寶
767a24‖ 菩薩戒眾等。諦聽。
767b01‖ 歸命盧舍那。十方金剛佛。亦禮前論主。當覺慈氏尊。
767b02‖ 今說三聚戒。菩薩咸共聽。
767c01‖ 戒如大明燈。能消長夜闇。戒如真寶鏡。照法盡無遺。
767c02‖ 戒如摩尼珠。雨物濟貧窮。離世速成佛。唯此法為最。
767c03‖ 是故諸菩薩。應當勤護持。
767c21‖ ○二策修
767c22‖ 諸大德。春分四月日為一時。
768a09‖ 半月日[巳>已]過。
768a14‖ 少一夜。餘有一夜三月半在。
768b06‖ 老死至近。佛法欲滅。諸大德。優婆塞。優婆夷。為得道
768b07‖ 故。一心勤求精進。所以者何。諸佛一心勤求精進。故
768b08‖ 得阿耨多羅三藐三菩提。何況餘善道法。各聞強健
768b09‖ 時。努力勤修善。如何不求道。安可須待老。欲何樂乎。
768c05‖ 是日[巳>已]過。命亦隨減。如少水魚。斯有何樂。

简体字

○初归敬三宝

菩萨戒众等。谛听。

归命卢舍那。十方金刚佛。亦礼前论主。当觉慈氏尊。今说三聚戒。菩萨咸共听。戒如大明灯。能消长夜闇。戒如真宝镜。照法尽无遗。戒如摩尼珠。雨物济贫穷。离世速成佛。唯此法为最。是故诸菩萨。应当勤护持。

○二策修

诸大德。春分四月日为一时。

半月日已过。

少一夜。余有一夜三月半在。

老死至近。佛法欲灭。诸大德。优婆塞。优婆夷。为得道故。一心勤求精进。所以者何。诸佛一心勤求精进。故得阿耨多罗三藐三菩提。何况余善道法。各闻强健时。努力勤修善。如何不求道。安可须待老。欲何乐乎。

是日已过。命亦随减。如少水鱼。斯有何乐。

Part One: Taking Refuge in and Revering the Three Jewels

The members of this bodhisattva precept assembly should listen carefully:

We take refuge in Rocana Buddha,
in the Vajra Buddhas throughout the ten directions,
and also pay reverence to the former treatise master
and future Honored One, Maitreya.

As we now speak the three collections of moral precepts,[6]
You bodhisattvas should all listen together.
The precepts are like a great bright lamp
that is able to dispel the darkness of the long night.

The precepts are like a true precious mirror
that completely reflects all dharmas without exception.
The precepts are like a *maṇi* jewel
that rains down gifts to rescue all the poor.

To leave the world and quickly become a buddha—
It is only this Dharma that is supreme.
Therefore all those who are bodhisattvas
Should diligently guard and uphold them.

Part Two: Instigation to Cultivation

Greatly Virtuous Ones, spring's full moon day of the fourth month will mark [the completion of] one season.[7]

[Now],this month's half-moon day has already passed except for [this] one period of the night. There still remains this one period of the night followed by the three and a half months remaining [in this spring season].

Old age and death are growing near. The Buddha's Dharma is on the verge of dying out. For the sake of reaching enlightenment,[8] all of you Greatly Virtuous ones and all of you *upāsakas* and *upāsikās* should single-mindedly and diligently pursue it with vigor. Why? It is due to single-mindedly and diligently pursuing it with vigor that all buddhas have realized *anuttara-samyak-saṃbodhi*,[9] how much the more so all of the other good dharmas of the path. Having heard it when still strong and healthy, one should energetically and diligently cultivate what is good. How could one not seek the path? How could one suppose it is necessary to wait to do so until one is old? What sort of happiness do you wish to attain?

This day has already passed and one's life has also diminished correspondingly. This is like being a fish stranded in ever shallower water. What bliss is there in this?

正體字

768c22‖ ○三作前方便
768c23‖ 僧集不。
769a03‖ 和合不。
769a07‖ 僧集和合。何所作為。
769a10‖ 說戒布薩。
769a18‖ 此中未受菩薩戒。及不清淨者出不。
769a24‖ 不來囑授菩薩。有幾人說欲。及清淨。
769b16‖ ○四誦戒序
769b17‖ 諸佛子等。合掌至心聽。我今欲說諸佛大戒序。眾集
769b18‖ 默然聽。自知有罪。當悔懺。悔懺即安樂。不懺悔。罪益
769b19‖ 深。無罪者默然。默然故。當知眾清淨。諸大德。優婆塞。
769b20‖ 優婆夷等。諦聽。
769c09‖ 佛滅度後。於末法中應當尊敬波羅提木叉。波羅提
769c10‖ 木叉者。即是此戒。持此戒時。如闇遇明。如貧人得寶。
769c11‖ 如病者得瘥。如囚繫出獄。如遠行者得歸。當知此。即
769c12‖ 是眾等大師。若佛住世。無異此也。
770a12‖ 怖心難生。善心難發。

简体字

○三作前方便

僧集不。

和合不。

僧集和合。何所作为。

说戒布萨。

此中未受菩萨戒。及不清净者出不。

不来嘱授菩萨。有几人说欲。及清净。

○四诵戒序

诸佛子等。合掌至心听。我今欲说诸佛大戒序。众集默然听。自知有罪。当悔忏。悔忏即安乐。不忏悔。罪益深。无罪者默然。默然故。当知众清净。诸大德。优婆塞。优婆夷等。谛听。

佛灭度后。于末法中应当尊敬波罗提木叉。波罗提木叉者。即是此戒。持此戒时。如闇遇明。如贫人得宝。如病者得瘥。如囚系出狱。如远行者得归。当知此。即是众等大师。若佛住世。无异此也。

怖心难生。善心难发。

Part Three: Perform the Preliminary Procedures

Q: "Has the Saṃgha assembled or not?"

Q: "Has the Saṃgha come together in harmony or not?"

A: "The Saṃgha has assembled and it is in harmony."

Q: "What is the purpose for which they have done so?"

A: "This is in order to participate in the *upoṣadha* recitation of the precepts."

Q: "Are there any among you who have not yet taken the bodhisattva precepts or who are not pure who have not yet departed?"

[A: "All who have not taken the bodhisattva precepts or who are impure have already left."]

Q: "Of those bodhisattvas who could not come but who have communicated through an intermediary, how many of them declared that they wished to attend and did affirm their purity?"[10]

[A: Answer as appropriate.]

Part Four: Recite the Preface to the Precepts

Preface to the Brahmā's Net Sutra Bodhisattva Precepts

All you sons of the Buddha, place your palms together and listen with a mind of utmost sincerity. I now wish to speak the preface to the great precepts of all buddhas. Having gathered together here, the Assembly should listen in silence. If one becomes aware that one has committed an offense one should repent, for, having repented, one then becomes peaceful and happy. If one does not repent, his offenses become increasingly grave. Those who are free of offenses may remain silent. By such silence it will be known that the members of this assembly are pure. Greatly Virtuous Ones,[11] *upāsakas*, and *upāsikās*,[12] listen attentively:

After the Buddha's nirvāṇa, during the Semblance Dharma Age,[13] one should revere the *prātimokṣa*.[14] The *prātimokṣa* is just these very precepts. When one upholds these precepts, it is just as when one who is in darkness encounters the light, just as when one who is poor obtains a jewel, just as when one who is sick finds a cure, just as when one who has been imprisoned emerges from prison, and just as when one who has traveled afar is then able to return home. One should realize that these [precepts] serve as the great master for all those in the Assembly, no differently than if the Buddha himself were still dwelling in the world.[15]

It is difficult to develop a mind that is fearful [of committing offenses] and it is difficult to develop a mind that is devoted to

正體字

故經云。勿輕小罪。以為無殃。水
770a13‖ 滴雖微。漸盈大器。剎那造罪。殃墮無間。一失人身。萬
770a14‖ 劫不復。
770a24‖ 壯色不停。猶如奔馬。人命無常。過於山水。今日雖存。
770b01‖ 明亦難保。
770b06‖ 眾等。各各一心。勤求精進。慎勿懈怠懶惰。睡眠縱意。
770b07‖ 夜即攝心。存念三寶。莫以空過。徒設疲勞。後代深悔。
770b08‖ 眾等。各各一心。謹依此戒。如法修行。應當學。
770b18‖ ○五詰問
770b19‖ 諸大德。今(白黑)月十(五四)日。作布薩。說菩薩戒。眾當一心
770b20‖ 善聽。有罪者發露。無罪者默然。默然故。當知諸大德
770b21‖ 清淨。堪說菩薩戒。[巳>已]說菩薩戒序竟。今問諸大德。是
770b22‖ 中清淨不(三問)。

简体字

故经云。勿轻小罪。以为无殃。水滴虽微。渐盈大器。刹那造罪。殃堕无间。一失人身。万劫不复。

壮色不停。犹如奔马。人命无常。过于山水。今日虽存。明亦难保。

众等。各各一心。勤求精进。慎勿懈怠懒惰。睡眠纵意。夜即摄心。存念三宝。莫以空过。徒设疲劳。后代深悔。众等。各各一心。谨依此戒。如法修行。应当学。

○五诘问

诸大德。今(白黑)月十(五四)日。作布萨。说菩萨戒。众当一心善听。有罪者发露。无罪者默然。默然故。当知诸大德清净。堪说菩萨戒。已说菩萨戒序竟。今问诸大德。是中清净不(三问)。

goodness. Therefore a sutra says: "Do not consider minor offenses to be insignificant, taking them to be free of misfortune, for, although drops of water are tiny, they will gradually fill up even a large vessel."[16] An offense committed in a *kṣaṇa* may bring about the misfortune of falling into the Uninterrupted [Hells].[17] Having once lost the human body, one may not regain it even after a myriad kalpas. Like the passing of a galloping horse, a strong body does not remain for long. A person's life passes more quickly[18] than the [rapidly flowing] waters of a mountain stream. Although it may remain today, it would be difficult to guarantee it will still be here tomorrow.

Members of the Assembly, each of you should single-mindedly and diligently seek to cultivate with vigor. Take care and do not become indolent or lazy or allow your mind to become uncontrolled when sleeping. At night, one should focus the mind and remain mindful of the Three Jewels.[19] One must not allow it to occur that, by letting the time go by fruitlessly, one's efforts are expended in vain so that, later on, one will be bound to experience deep regret. Members of the Assembly, you should each single-mindedly and diligently abide by these precepts. You should train in them by cultivating them in accordance with the Dharma.

Part Five: Questioning the Assembly

Greatly Virtuous Ones: Today is the ________ day of the ______ month. We are performing the *upoṣadha* ceremony in which we speak the bodhisattva precepts. The Assembly should listen single-mindedly and well. Those who have committed offenses should reveal them whereas those who are free of offenses should remain silent. By their silence we will know that the Great Assembly is pure and that therefore we can proceed with speaking the bodhisattva precepts. We have finished speaking the preface to the bodhisattva precepts. We now ask the Greatly Virtuous Ones: "Are those within this assembly pure, or not?) (Ask three times.)

正體字

770c20	○六正誦戒經
770c21	謂誦心地品下。從爾時起。至共成佛道。
771a06	既誦戒畢。下座謝眾云。
771a07	某甲敬謝大眾。僧差誦戒。三業不勤。戒文生澁。坐久
771a08	延遲。令眾生惱。望眾慈悲。布施歡喜。
771a09	
771a10	附半月誦菩薩戒儀式註(終)

****
【經文資訊】卍新纂續藏經第 38 冊 No. 0696 半月誦菩薩戒儀式註
【版本記錄】CBETA 電子佛典 Rev. 1.4 (Big5)，完成日期：2007/07/10
【編輯說明】本資料庫由中華電子佛典協會（CBETA）依卍新纂續藏經所編輯
【原始資料】CBETA 人工輸入，CBETA 掃瞄辨識
【其他事項】本資料庫可自由免費流通，詳細內容請參閱【中華電子佛典協會資料庫版權宣告】
****
[0767001]（梵網經菩薩戒略疏卷八之附。[○@編]）

简体字

○六正诵戒经
谓诵心地品下。从尔时起。至共成佛道。
既诵戒毕。下座谢众云。
某甲敬谢大众。僧差诵戒。三业不勤。戒文生涩。坐久延迟。令众生恼。望众慈悲。布施欢喜。
附半月诵菩萨戒仪式注(终)

Part Six: The Actual Recitation of the Precept Scripture

This refers to reciting the second fascicle of the Mind Ground Chapter beginning with "At that time…" on through to "May all of those who hear this Dharma swiftly succeed in realizing buddhahood."

After having finished the recitation of the precepts, the reciter should descend from the high seat and thank the Assembly, saying:

I, so-and-so, respectfully thank the Great Assembly. Although I was appointed by the Saṃgha to recite the precepts, because of my lack of diligence in cultivating the three modes of action, my recitation of the precept text may not have been smooth. Perhaps then I have made the Assembly sit for an overly long time through an extended recitation and thus caused them unnecessary discomfort. I hope the Assembly will have compassion on me and feel satisfied with my recitation.

(End of the Semi-monthly Recitation of the Bodhisattva Precepts)

Recitation Ceremony Endnotes

1 "Commentary by the Great Bodhicitta Śramaṇa Hongzan." (冐地質多沙門　弘贊　注.)

2 At the end of his introductory paragraph to his commentary on this ceremony (X38_n0696), Śramaṇa Hongzan attributes the origin of the ceremony to members of the Tiantai School at the end of the Tang Dynasty or the beginning of the Song Dynasty (X38n0696_p0767a14).

3 This ceremony text does not specify which of several alternate sutra-opening verses should be used. The sutra-opening verse that I insert here is one that is most directly relevant to the bodhisattva precepts and which therefore is commonly recited at the beginning of bodhisattva precept recitations: 菩薩淨戒難得聞，經於無量俱胝劫，讀誦受持亦如是，如說修行者更難。

4 An alternative sutra-opening verse sometimes used here is: 無上甚深微妙法，百千萬劫難遭遇，我今見聞得受持，願解如來真實義。

5 Here "so-and-so" (某甲) indicates that, when the Assembly is reciting the precepts, whoever has been appointed to do so should replace "so-and-so" with his or her name and title, as for instance: "I, Bhikshu Dharmadīpa (or Bhikshuni Upāsika John Smith, or Upāsikā Jane Brown, etc.), bow in reverence ... etc."

6 "The three collections of moral precepts" (三聚戒), most often referred to as "the three collections of the precepts of purity" (三聚淨戒), refers to the three different sorts of moral precepts and the three important functions they serve: 1) "The precepts of restraint" (*saṃvaraśīla* / 攝律儀戒) consisting of those that serve to bring about the stopping of whatever is wrong or evil; 2) "The precepts that gather good dharmas" (*kuśala-dharma-saṃgrāhaka-śila* / 攝善法戒) consisting of those that serve to bring about the cultivation of good moral qualities; and 3) "The precepts that gather in beings" (*sattva-artha-kriyā-śīla* / 攝眾生戒) consisting of those that serve to gather in other beings by benefiting them.

7 Zhuhong's parenthetical note (at 0153c02–04) explains: "This is relying on [the calendar of] India (*xiyu* - 西域) where one year is divided into three seasons and a single season has four months. From the sixteenth day of the twelfth lunar month (*la yue* - 臘月) to the fifteenth day of the fourth month constitutes the spring season. From the sixteenth day of the fourth month to the fifteenth day of the eighth month constitutes the summer season. From the sixteenth day of the eighth month to the fifteenth day of the twelfth lunar month constitutes the winter season. Now here [in this text as we have received it] it is referring to the spring season. One should accord with [India's]

three-season calendar in making changes [to this statement in the ceremony so that it corresponds to the actual time of year in which one is conducting the recitation of the precepts]."

8 Here, "reaching enlightenment" (bodhi) is "gaining the path" (得道) which usually translates *abhisaṃbuddha.*

9 *Anuttara-samyak-saṃbodhi* is the "utmost, right, and perfect enlightenment" of a buddha.

10 In another parenthetical note (0153c14–17), Zhuhong explains that "those bodhisattvas who could not come but who have communicated through an intermediary" refers to those who let it be known to the most senior monastic (上座) via intermediaries that, although they wished to attend the *upoṣadha* ceremony, they could not come for reasons such as because they are taking care of matters for the Three Jewels, because they are caring for parents who are ill, or because of other such causes and conditions preventing their attendance. Although such individuals could not personally attend, they nonetheless send an intermediary to represent them in declaring their purity.

11 "Greatly Virtuous Ones" is a literal translation of the Chinese (大德) which in turn translates the Sanskrit *bhadanta* which, at least in this context, is a form of address for eminent monastics.

12 "Upāsakas" and "upāsikās" are the Sanskrit designations for male (*upāsaka*) and female (*upāsikā*) lay disciples who have at least taken the Three Refuges.

13 "Semblance Dharma Age" [像法] refers to the second of the three Dharma ages: the Right Dharma Age, the Semblance Dharma Age, and the Dharma-ending Age. It is a period in which appearances (ornate temples, etc.) tend to be more and more prominent, whereas deep practice and attainment of realizations tend to be less common.

Note: Although, by its own admission, the Ming Dynasty commentary by Śramaṇa Hong Zan has substituted "Dharma-ending Age" here, I have preferred to stay with text of the preface as preserved in the Taisho edition of the original text translated by Kumārajīva.

14 "*Prātimokṣa*" (波羅提木叉) is the Sanskrit word for the code of monastic precepts. As translated into Chinese (別解脫), it was considered to mean "individual liberation." The actual meaning of the Sanskrit word is "leading to liberation." Thus, just as the monastic precepts taken at the time of ordination are described as "*prātimokṣa* precepts" which lead the practitioner toward liberation, so too it is with these ten major bodhisattva precepts.

15 More literally, this says: "One should realize that these serve as the great master for all those in the congregation. If the Buddha were dwelling in the world, it would be no different from this." But this doesn't really seem to fully express the intended meaning, hence my slightly free translation intended to encourage the reader to revere these precepts just as one would revere the Buddha himself if he were still here among us.

16 This is a quote from the seventeenth chapter of the Dhammapada (**法句經, 惡行品**) found at T04n0210_p0565a02-03 as "莫輕小惡，以為無殃，水[1]渧雖微，漸盈大器".

17 "Uninterrupted [Hells]" (無間[地獄]) refers to the Avīci Hells.

18 "Passes more quickly" here is more literally "is more impermanent than" (人命**無常過於**山水。).

19 The "Three Jewels" refers to the Buddha, the Dharma, and the Saṃgha.

Part One Bibliography

The Dharmapada – 法句經 (T04n0210)

Fazang's commentary – 梵網經菩薩戒本疏 (T40n1813)

Hongzan's Semimonthly Bodhisattva Precept Ceremony commentary – 半月誦菩薩戒儀式註 (X38n0696)

Kumārajīva's Bodhisattva Precepts Translation – 梵網經盧舍那佛說菩薩心地戒品第十 (T24n1484)

The Sutra on the Twelve Dhūta Austerities – 十二頭陀經 (T17n0783)

Zhixu's Bodhisattva Precepts Commentary – 佛說梵網經菩薩心地品合註 (X38n0694)

Zhiyi's Bodhisattva Precepts Commentary – 菩薩戒義疏 (T40n1811)

Zhuhong's Bodhisattva Precepts Commentary – 梵網經心地品菩薩戒義疏發隱 (X38n0679)

Part One Glossary

ācārya – An *ācārya* is a monastic who is a teacher of monastics.

amṛta – *Amṛta* means "the deathless" and is otherwise a reference to the devas' "elixir of immortality." Here it is euphemism for nirvāṇa, the idea being that careful observance of the precepts constitutes the gateway to ultimate success on the path to buddhahood and the nirvāṇa of a buddha.

anuttara-samyak-saṃbodhi – *Anuttara-samyak-saṃbodhi* is the "utmost, right, and perfect enlightenment" of a buddha.

ārya – An *ārya* is one those who have awakened to one of the four stages of the path to arhatship or any of the irreversible stages on the bodhisattva path to buddhahood.

avīci hells – The *avīci* hells, otherwise known as "the uninterrupted hells, are hells in which the sufferings undergone by its denizens are uninterrupted and terribly intense.

bhadanta (大德) – "Greatly Virtuous Ones," a respectful form of address for eminent monastics.

bhikshu – a "bhikshu" is a fully ordained Buddhist monk.

bhikshuni – a "bhikshuni" is a fully ordained Buddhist nun..

bodhi tree – "bodhi tree" is the name given to the tree under which the Buddha became enlightened.

Dharma – By convention, "Dharma" when written with a capital "D" refers to the teachings of the Buddha.

Dharma master – A "Dharma master" is another name for a fully ordained Buddhist monk (or nun) who is learned in Buddhist doctrine and texts and is devoted to teaching the Dharma to others.

dānapati – A *dānapati* is a benefactor who provides gifts, food, or other types of donations to members of the monastic Saṃgha.

devaputra – A *devaputra* is literally "a son of the devas." hence a young deva.

dhūta austerities – The "*dhūta* austerities" are spiritually purifying practices exemplified by the twelve *dhūta* austerities which, per "The Sutra on the Twelve Dhūta Austerities," (T17n0783_p0720b13 – 722a07) consist of: "(1) dwelling in a secluded forest dwelling (i.e. in an *araṇya*); (2) always obtaining one's food on the alms round; (3) always going in sequential order (never skipping houses) when on the alms round; (4) eating only one meal per day; (5) never eating more than a fixed quantity of food; (6) never drinking soups or other sorts of beverages after midday; (7) wearing robes made of cast-off rags; (8) only wearing the three robes; (9) dwelling in a graveyard [or charnel ground]; (10) dwelling beneath a tree; (11) dwelling out on the open ground; (12) only sitting and never lying down to sleep." (T17n0783_p0720c06 – 720c10)

dhyāna – "*Dhyāna*" refers to the practice of meditation.

dhyāna heavens – The "*dhyāna* heavens" are the various levels of heavens to which the various levels of *dhyāna* absorptions tend to lead when one is reborn.

eight difficulties – The "eight difficulties" (八難) refer to eight conditions of rebirth in which being able to take up the Buddha's path to awakening is likely to be nearly impossible, these being birth: 1) in the hells; 2) as a hungry ghost (*preta*); 3) as an animal; 4) in the long-life heavens; 5) in the continent of Uttarakuru; 6) as blind, deaf, or dumb; 7) as one possessed of merely worldly wisdom and eloquence; or 8) birth before or after the appearance of a buddha.

eight types of ghosts and spiritual beings – The "eight types of ghosts and spiritual beings" (八部鬼神) consist of gods, dragons, *yakṣas, gandharvas, asuras, garuḍas, kiṃnaras,* and *mahoragas*.

field of merit – A field of merit is any person or institution which, if supported constitutes a source of merit for the benefactor who supports them. Examples include the Buddha, the Dharma, and the Saṃgha as well as pure monks and nuns. There is a common list of "the eight fields of merit" which consist of: the Buddha; the *āryas* (those who have awakened to one of the four stages of the path to arhatship or any of the irreversible stages on the bodhisattva path to buddhahood), the Saṃgha, *upādhyāyas, ācāryas,* one's father, one's mother, and the sick.

five precepts – The five precepts are the formally received proscriptions against killing, stealing, sexual misconduct, false speech, and intoxicants.

fourfold assembly – The "fourfold assembly" (四眾 / *catasraḥ parṣadaḥ*) refers to the bhikshus, bhikshunis, *upasakas,* and *upāsikās* otherwise known as the monks, nuns, laymen, and laywomen.

hungry ghosts – Hungry ghosts (*pretas*) constitute one of the three wretched destinies (the other two being the animals and the hell realms). Their lives are characterized by constant insatiable hunger and are said to be the karmic retribution for extreme greed in previous existences.

ineffable – An "ineffable" (不可說) translates the Sanskrit *anabhilāpya,* an ineffably large number among the very largest of the one hundred and twenty-plus numbers described in the Asaṃkhyeya Chapter of the Avataṃsaka Sutra.

kāṣāya – A "*kāśāya* robe" is a dyed robe, one which ideally is dyed an ochre color.

koṭi – A very large number which, according to PDB is variously defined "as one hundred thousand, ten million, one hundred million, or an infinity."

kṣaṇa – A *kṣaṇa*, per Soothill, is "the shortest span of time, a moment, the ninetieth part of a thought and a 4,500th part of a minute."

merit – "Merit" (*puṇya*) is the accumulation of wholesome karma from virtuous acts of body, mouth, and mind which conduces to progress on the path and fortunate outcomes in lifespan, health, mental and physical capacities, and repeated rebirths in proximity to good spiritual mentors, right Dharma, and conditions conducing to further advancement on the path to spiritual awakening.

pārājika offense – A *pārājika* offense is one entailing expulsion from the community.

prātimokṣa – "*Prātimokṣa*" (波羅提木叉) is the Sanskrit word for the code of monastic precepts. As translated into Chinese (別解脫), it was considered to mean "individual liberation." The actual meaning of the Sanskrit word is "leading to liberation." Thus, just as the monastic precepts taken at the time of ordination are described as "*prātimokṣa* precepts" which lead the practitioner toward liberation, so too it is with these ten major and forty-eight minor bodhisattva precepts.

pratyekabuddha – A *pratyekabuddha* is a person who, without the presence of a buddha in the world and without receiving the teaching of any fully enlightened buddha, nonetheless, all on his own, attains enlightenment to at least the arhat's level of awakening.

Rocana Buddha – Rocana Buddha is the reward body buddha (*sambhogakāya*) of Vairocana Buddha (the Dharma body buddha).

Śākyamuni Buddha – Śākyamuni Buddha, the historical Buddha, is one of countless transformation body buddhas.

samādhi – samādhi is a state of one-pointed concentration on a single object.

Saṃgha – The Sanskrit spelling of "Sangha." In the context of the Three Refuges, this refers to "the *ārya* Saṃgha" consisting of those who have awakened to one of the stages of the path. Otherwise it may refer simply to "the common Saṃgha" consisting of monks and nuns.

sarvajña – *Sarvajña* means "all-knowledge."

semblance Dharma age – "Semblance Dharma age" refers to the second of the three Dharma ages: the right Dharma age, the semblance Dharma age, and the Dharma ending age. It is a period in which appearances (ornate temples, etc.) tend to be more and more prominent, whereas deep practice and attainment of realizations tend to be less common.

seven heinous offenses – These seven heinous offenses (七逆罪) are explained in bodhisattva precept number forty (1008c01–c03) as: drawing the blood of a buddha; killing one's father; killing one's mother; killing one's *upādhyāya*, killing one's *ācārya*; breaking up a Dharma-wheel-turning Saṃgha proceeding; and killing an *ārya*, i.e. killing anyone who has realized one of the fruits of the path.

seven obstructive offenses The "seven obstructive offenses" (七遮罪) is an alternative name for the "seven heinous offenses" (七逆罪). This may refer to the fact that those who have committed these offenses are usually thereby prevented from taking the bodhisattva precepts.

six close relatives – The "six close relatives" (六親) are usually listed as father, mother, elder brothers, younger brothers, wife, and children. Perhaps a more inclusive interpretation would substitute "elder siblings and younger siblings" for "elder brothers and younger brothers."

six kinds of domestic animals – Lists of "the six kinds of domestic animals" (六畜) vary. Perhaps the most common listing mentions horses, cattle, sheep, pigs, dogs, and chickens.

sons of the Buddha – This is a very literal translation of the Chinese *fozi* (佛子) which translates the Sanskrit *buddha-putra*.

śramaṇa – A *śramaṇa* is one who has left the home life to pursue the path of spiritual liberation. In these texts, *śramaṇa* is synonymous with being a Buddhist monk.

Three collections of moral precepts – See "Three collections of the precepts of purity."

Three collections of the precepts of purity – "The three collections of the precepts of purity" (三聚淨戒) also known as "the three collections of moral precepts" (三聚戒), refers to the three different sorts of moral precepts and the three important functions they serve: 1) "The precepts of restraint" (*saṃvaraśīla* / 攝律儀戒) consisting of those that serve to bring about the stopping of whatever is wrong or evil; 2) "The precepts that gather good dharmas" (*kuśala-dharma-saṃgrāhaka-śila* / 攝善法戒) consisting of those that serve to bring about the cultivation of good moral qualities; and 3) "The precepts that gather in beings" (*sattva-artha-kriyā-śīla* / 攝眾生戒) consisting of those that serve to gather in other beings by benefiting them.

Three Jewels – The "Three Jewels" refers to the Buddha, the Dharma, and the *ārya* Saṃgha.

Two Vehicles – The "Two Vehicles" refers to the individual-liberation vehicles aimed at achieving the spiritual liberation of an arhat or a *pratyekabuddha*.

Uninterrupted Hells – "Uninterrupted Hells" (無間地獄) refers to the

Avīci Hells and the uninterrupted experience of agonizing pain experienced by those who are reborn there.

upādhyāya – An *upādhyāya* is a monastic preceptor or instructor.

upāsakas, and *upāsikās* – "*Upāsakas*" and "*upāsikās*" are the Sanskrit designations for male (*upāsaka*) and female (*upāsikā*) lay disciples who have at least taken the three refuges. More often than not, they may well have taken the five precepts as well.

upoṣadha – The *upoṣadha* ceremony is the meeting held every two weeks in which monastics recite their moral codes.

vajra spirits – "*Vajra* spirits" (金剛神) or "*vajra*-wielding spirits" (執金剛) are a type of guardian spirit who usually holds a weapon in his hand that is called a *vajra*.

Vinaya – The "*vinaya*" is the portion of the Buddhist canon that preserves the Buddhist moral code.

Worthy – A "worthy" (*bhadra*) is a cultivator who has progressed beyond the level of a common worldling, but who has not as yet become an *ārya,* one who has become irreversible on the path to complete spiritual awakening.

Part One: The Brahmā's Net Sutra Bodhisattva Precepts Variant Readings in Other Chinese Editions

[1003003] 此序宋元明宮四本俱無
[1003004] （菩薩心地品之下）＋爾【宋】【元】【明】【宮】
[1003005] 佛＋（子）【宋】【元】【明】【宮】
[1003006] 〔及〕－【宋】【元】【明】【宮】
[1003007] 光＋（光）【宋】【元】【明】
[1003008] （所）＋說【宋】【元】【明】【宮】
[1003009] （法門）＋海【宋】【元】【明】【宮】
[1003010] 〔從座起〕－【宮】
[1003011] 定＝足【宋】
[1003012] 〔牟尼佛〕－【宋】【元】【宮】
[1003013] 〔王〕－【宋】【元】【明】【宮】
[1003014] 〔王〕－【宋】【宮】
[1003015] 其＝共【元】
[1003016] 〔花光王〕－【宋】【元】【宮】
[1003017] 〔法門品〕－【宋】【元】【宮】
[1003018] 〔品〕－【明】
[1003019] 〔有〕－【明】
[1004001] 則＝即【明】
[1004002] 佛即＝即佛【宋】【元】，〔佛〕－【宮】
[1004003] （諸）＋佛【明】
[1004004] 〔乘〕－【宮】
[1004005] 〔佛〕－【宋】【元】【宮】
[1004006] 誦＝言【元】
[1004007] 〔無〕－【宋】【元】
[1004008] 非＋（無）【宮】
[1004009] （行）＋菩【宋】【元】【明】【宮】
[1004010] 薩＋（道）【明】
[1004011] 〔故〕－【宋】【元】【宮】
[1004012] （應）＋善【明】
[1004013] 〔子〕－【宋】【元】【宮】
[1004014] （我）＋已【宋】【元】【明】【宮】
[1004015] 〔是事〕－【明】
[1004016] 言＝告【宋】【元】【宮】
[1004017] 便＋（殺）【明】

[1004018] 因殺緣殺法殺業＝業殺報殺因殺緣【宋】【元】，
＝業殺法殺因殺緣【宮】
[1004019] 〔一切眾生〕－【宋】【元】【宮】
[1004020] 自＝反【宋】【元】
[1004021] 〔者〕－【宋】【元】【宮】＊[＊ 1 2 3 4 5 6 7 8
9 10 11 12 13 14 15 16]
[1004022] 盜＋（呪盜）【明】
[1004023] 盜因盜緣盜法盜業＝盜業盜報盜因盜緣【宋】【元】，
＝盜業盜法盜因盜緣【宮】
[1004024] 〔呪盜〕－【明】
[1004025] 主＋（物）【宋】【元】【明】【宮】
[1004026] 應＝常【宋】【元】【宮】
[1004027] 順＋（心）【宋】【元】【明】【宮】
[1004028] 〔財〕－【宋】【元】【宮】
[1004029] 婬緣婬法婬業＝婬業婬法婬緣【宋】【元】【宮】
[1004030] 妄語緣妄語法妄語業＝妄語業妄語法妄語緣【宋】
【元】【宮】
[1004031] 〔正見〕－【宋】【元】【明】【宮】
[1004032] 〔邪〕－【宋】【元】【宮】
[1004033] 酤酒緣酤酒法酤酒業＝酤酒業酤酒法酤酒緣【宋】
【元】【宮】
[1004034] 〔一切〕－【宋】【元】【宮】
[1004035] 〔之〕－【宋】【宮】
[1004036] 子＋（口）【宋】【元】【明】【宮】＊[＊ 1]
[1004037] 罪過緣罪過法罪過業＝罪過業罪過法罪過緣【宋】
【元】【宮】
[1004038] 悲＝慈【明】
[1004039] 毀他緣毀他法毀他業＝毀他業毀他法毀他緣【宋】
【元】【宮】
[1004040] 〔應〕－【宮】
[1004041] 慳緣慳法慳業＝慳業慳法慳緣【宋】【元】【宮】
[1005001] 〔以〕－【宋】【元】【宮】
[1005002] 瞋緣瞋法瞋業＝瞋業瞋法瞋緣【宋】【元】【宮】
[1005003] （慈）＋悲【宋】【元】【明】
[1005004] 杖＝仗【宋】【元】【明】【宮】＊[＊ 1 2]
[1005005] 謗緣謗法謗業＝謗業謗法謗緣【宋】【元】【宮】
[1005006] 仁＝人【宋】【宮】
[1005007] 〔失〕－【宋】
[1005008] 〔如〕－【宋】【元】【明】【宮】

[1005009] 〔佛言〕－【宋】【元】【明】【宮】
[1005010] 和上＝和尚【明】下同
[1005011] 阿闍梨＝阿闍黎【明】下同
[1005012] 大＋（德）【宋】【元】【明】
[1005013] 〔應起…心〕十九字－【宮】
[1005014] 慢心癡＝癡心慢【宋】【元】
[1005015] 心＋（瞋心）【宋】【元】【明】
[1005016] 酒＋（一切酒不得飲）【宋】【元】【明】
[1005017] 食＋（夫食肉者）【明】
[1005018] （佛）＋性【宋】【元】【明】【宮】
[1005019] 慈葱蘭葱＝韮薤【宮】
[1005020] 〔若〕－【宋】【元】【宮】
[1005021] 共＝同【宋】【元】【明】【宮】
[1005022] （不）＋教悔【宋】【元】【明】【宮】
[1005023] 〔起〕－【宮】
[1005024] 〔醫藥〕－【宋】【元】【明】【宮】
[1005025] 講＋（法）【宋】【元】【明】【宮】
[1005026] 〔常應〕－【宮】，〔常〕－【宋】【元】
[1005027] 〔疾〕－【宋】【元】【明】【宮】
[1005028] （供）＋養【宋】【元】【明】【宮】
[1005029] 惡心瞋恨不＝瞋恨心不看乃【宋】【元】【明】【宮】
[1005030] 救＋（濟）【宋】【元】【明】【宮】
[1005031] 網羅＝羅網【宋】【元】【明】【宮】
[1005032] 餘＝殺【宋】【元】【明】【宮】
[1005033] 生＋（不得畜殺眾生具）【明】
[1005034] 〔一切刀杖〕－【明】，〔一切〕－【宋】【元】【宮】
[1005035] 六＋（度）【明】【宮】
[1005036] 當廣明＝廣開明【宋】，〔當〕－【元】【明】，＝廣開【宮】
[1005037] （尚）＋不【宋】【元】【明】【宮】
[1005038] 不＋（應）【明】
[1005039] 自＝故【宋】【元】【宮】
[1005040] 〔若故作者〕－【宋】【元】【宮】，若故＋（自作教人）【明】
[1006001] 〔於〕－【宋】【元】【明】【宮】
[1006002] 曠野＝野田【宮】
[1006003] 〔人〕－【宋】【元】【宮】，（惡）＋人【明】
[1006004] 受＝授【宋】【元】【明】【宮】

[1006005] 〔應〕－【宋】【元】【明】【宮】
[1006006] 發＋（趣）【宋】【元】【明】【宮】
[1006007] （於）＋三【宋】【元】【明】【宮】
[1006008] 〔他〕－【宋】【元】【明】【宮】
[1006009] 〔從〕－【宋】【元】【宮】
[1006010] 虎狼＋（口）【宋】【元】【宮】
[1006011] 子＋（口中）【宋】【元】【宮】
[1006012] （然）＋後【宋】【元】【明】【宮】
[1006013] 故＋（為名聞故）【宋】【元】【明】
[1006014] 物＝財【宋】【元】【明】【宮】＊ [＊ 1]
[1006015] 學＝應學十二部經【宋】【元】【明】
[1006016] 者日夜＝日日【宋】【元】【明】【宮】
[1006017] 偈＋（及）【明】
[1006018] 法＋（知）【宋】【元】，（不知）【明】
[1006019] 授＝受【宋】【元】【明】【宮】
[1006020] 〔若故作者〕－【宋】【元】【宮】，
〔若故作〕－【明】
[1006021] 業＋（應作是念）【宋】【元】【明】【宮】
[1006022] 生＋（業）【宋】【元】【明】【宮】
[1006023] 〔常住之法教人放生〕－【宋】【元】【明】【宮】
[1006024] 〔應〕－【宋】【元】【宮】
[1006025] 經＋（律）【宋】【元】【明】【宮】
[1006026] （其）＋亡【宋】【元】【宮】
[1006027] 〔廣〕－【宮】
[1006028] 〔相〕－【宋】【元】【宮】
[1006029] 慈＋（心）【宋】【元】【明】【宮】
[1006030] 讎＝詶【宋】【元】【明】【宮】
[1006031] 〔中〕－【宮】
[1006032] （作）＋報【宋】【元】【明】【宮】
[1006033] 〔初〕－【宮】
[1006034] 〔恃〕－【宋】【元】【宮】
[1006035] 福＝富【宋】【元】【明】【宮】
[1006036] 窮＋（下賤）【明】
[1006037] 心＝以【宋】【元】【明】【宮】
[1006038] 相＋（時）【宋】【元】【明】【宮】
[1006039] 應＝以【宋】【元】【宮】
[1006040] 〔何以故〕－【宋】【元】【宮】
[1006041] 〔以〕－【宋】【元】【明】【宮】＊ [＊ 1]
[1006042] 生＋（至）【宋】【元】【明】【宮】

[1006043] 前＋（自誓）【宋】【元】【明】【宮】
[1006044] 〔正〕－【宋】【元】【明】【宮】
[1006045] 習＝集【宋】【元】
[1006046] （一切）＋書【明】
[1006047] 若故作者＝者故作【宋】【宮】
[1006048] 滅＋（度）【宋】【元】【明】【宮】
[1006049] 房＝坊【明】＊ [＊ 1 2 3 4 5]
[1006050] （為）＋教【宋】【元】【明】【宮】
[1006051] 訟＝諍【宋】【元】【明】【宮】
[1007001] 在＝住【宋】【元】【宮】
[1007002] 後＝又【宋】【宮】，＝若【元】【明】
[1007003] 邑＋（若）【明】
[1007004] 床＋（木床）【宋】【元】【明】【宮】
[1007005] 女＋（身應割自身肉賣）【宋】【元】【明】【宮】
[1007006] 〔以〕－【宋】【元】【宮】
[1007007] 檀越＋（主）【宋】【宮】
[1007008] 請＋（而）【宋】【元】【明】【宮】
[1007009] 僧＋（者）【明】
[1007010] 姓＝性【宋】【宮】
[1007011] 〔若故作者〕－【宋】【元】【明】【宮】
[1007012] 田＋（中）【宋】【元】【明】【宮】
[1007013] 欲＋（請僧求願知事報言）【宋】【元】【明】【宮】
[1007014] 〔故〕－【宋】【元】【明】【宮】＊ [＊ 1 2]
[1007015] 〔合〕－【宮】
[1007016] 銀＋（毒）【明】
[1007017] 慈＋（惘心無孝順）【明】
[1007018] 〔若故作者〕－【宋】【元】【宮】
[1007019] 謗＝傍【明】
[1007020] 色＋（作諸）【明】
[1007021] 〔如〕－【宋】【元】【宮】
[1007022] 〔於〕－【宋】【元】【宮】
[1007023] 販＝及【明】
[1007024] 〔生〕－【宋】【元】【宮】
[1007025] 慈＋（悲）【明】
[1007026] 〔發心菩薩〕－【宋】【元】【明】【宮】
[1007027] 秤＝稱【宋】【元】【宮】
[1007028] 作＝養【宋】【元】【明】【宮】
[1007029] 將＝鬪【宋】【元】【宮】

[1007030] 得＝聽【宋】【元】【宮】
[1007031] 賽＝塞【宋】【元】【明】
[1007032] 戲＝戰【元】
[1007033] 毬＝毱【宋】【元】【明】【宮】
[1007034] 壺＋（牽道）【宋】【元】【明】【宮】
[1007035] 城＝成【宋】【元】【宮】
[1007036] 爪＝瓜【元】
[1007037] 蓍＝芝【宋】【宮】
[1007038] 〔得〕－【宋】【元】【宮】
[1007039] 度＝渡【宋】【元】【明】【宮】
[1007040] 〔善〕－【宋】【元】【宮】
[1007041] 〔三寶〕－【宋】【元】【明】【宮】
[1007042] 〔友〕－【宋】【元】【明】【宮】
[1007043] （此）＋破【明】＊ [＊ 1 2 3 4 5 6 7 8 9]
[1007044] 〔飲〕－【宮】
[1007045] 刺＋（身）【宋】【元】【明】【宮】
[1007046] 〔經百〕－【宋】【元】【宮】
[1007047] 鎚＝椎【宋】【宮】
[1007048] （此）＋破【宋】【元】【明】【宮】
[1008001] 〔遍〕－【明】
[1008002] 劓＝身攙【宋】【元】
[1008003] 〔之〕－【宋】【元】【宮】＊ [＊ 1 2]
[1008004] 〔悉得〕－【宋】【元】【明】【宮】
[1008005] 〔而〕－【宋】【元】【明】【宮】
[1008006] 〔此〕－【宋】【元】【明】【宮】
[1008007] 輕＋（若誦）【明】
[1008008] 前＋（誦）【宋】【元】【明】【宮】
[1008009] 人＝及【宋】【元】【明】【宮】
[1008010] 〔乃〕－【宋】【元】【明】【宮】
[1008011] 〔難及以〕－【宋】【元】【明】【宮】
[1008012] 入＋（一切難處）【宋】【宮】
[1008013] 若＝故【宋】【宮】
[1008014] 悉＝亦【宋】【元】【明】【宮】
[1008015] 入＋（此難處況行頭陀者是難處）【宋】【元】【宮】
[1008016] 若＝而【宋】【元】【宮】
[1008017] 不＝一一不如法【明】
[1008018] 疾病＝病疾【宋】【宮】
[1008019] 日乃至七＝四七五【宋】【元】【宮】，
＝日四五七日乃至七【明】

[1008020] 應讀誦講說＝講【宋】【元】【宮】，＝應講【明】
[1008021] 律＋（而）【宋】【元】【宮】，（一切）【明】
[1008022] 〔所燒〕－【宋】【元】【明】【宮】
[1008023] 所[漂*寸]＝焚漂【宋】【元】【明】，＝燒漂【宮】
[1008024] 〔應〕－【宋】【元】【明】【宮】
[1008025] 報＝惡【元】【明】
[1008026] 七逆八難＝八難七逆【宋】【元】【明】【宮】
[1008027] 讀誦講說＝講【宋】【元】【明】【宮】
[1008028] 〔如〕－【宋】【元】【宮】＊ [＊ 1]
[1008029] 壇＝坦【宮】
[1008030] 蕑＝簡【宋】【宮】，＝揀【元】【明】
[1008031] 〔天〕－【宋】【宮】
[1008032] 〔子〕－【宋】【宮】
[1008033] 其俗服＝其國土衣服色異與俗服【宋】【元】【宮】
[1008034] 〔師〕－【宋】【元】【明】【宮】
[1008035] 〔汝〕－【宋】【元】【明】【宮】
[1008036] 和上＝和尚【元】【明】＊ [＊ 1]
[1008037] 遮＝逆【明】
[1008038] 〔現〕－【宮】
[1008039] 〔盡〕－【宋】【元】【宮】
[1008040] 禮＋（拜）【宋】【元】【宮】
[1008041] （法）＋師【宋】【元】【明】【宮】
[1008042] 心＋（瞋心）【宋】【元】【明】【宮】
[1008043] 〔者〕－【宋】【宮】
[1008044] 誡＝戒【宋】【宮】＊ [＊ 1]
[1008045] 遮＋（罪者）【明】
[1008046] 〔應〕－【宮】
[1008047] 受＝授【明】＊ [＊ 1]
[1008048] 〔戒〕－【宋】【元】【宮】
[1008049] （若）＋無【明】
[1008050] 受＝與授戒【明】
[1008051] 十＋（重）【元】【明】
[1008052] 〔應〕－【宋】【元】【明】【宮】
[1008053] 重＝戒【宋】【宮】＊
[1008054] 若＝苦【宋】【元】【明】【宮】
[1008055] 相＋（者）【宋】【元】【明】【宮】
[1008056] 〔見〕－【宋】【元】【明】【宮】
[1008057] 增＋（長）【宋】【元】【明】【宮】
[1008058] 戒＋（善）【宋】【元】【宮】，（益）【明】

[1008059] 首＝手【宮】
[1008060] 懺罪＝懺悔罪便得【明】
[1008061] 性＋（性種性）【宋】【元】【明】【宮】
[1008062] 正＋（法）【宋】【宮】，（覺）【元】【明】
[1009001] 〔多求〕－【宋】【元】【宮】
[1009002] 〔故〕－【宋】【宮】
[1009003] 〔若〕－【宋】【元】【宮】
[1009004] 〔若〕－【宋】【元】【明】【宮】
[1009005] 人＋（皆）【明】
[1009006] （故）＋毀【明】
[1009007] 析＝折【宮】
[1009008] 〔竹帛〕－【宮】
[1009009] 〔應〕－【宮】
[1009010] 〔當〕－【宋】【元】【明】【宮】
[1009011] 應＋（在）【明】
[1009012] 眾＋（白衣）【宋】【元】【明】【宮】
[1009013] 如＋（敬）【宮】
[1009014] 法＋（說）【元】【明】
[1009015] 〔佛〕－【宋】【元】【明】【宮】
[1009016] 律＋（立統制眾安藉記僧比丘菩薩地立白衣高座廣行非法如兵奴事主而菩薩應受一切人供養而反為官走使非法非律若國王百官好心受佛戒者莫作是）六十一字【宋】【元】【明】
[1009017] （不）＋以【宋】【元】【明】
[1009018] 〔七〕－【宋】【元】【明】【宮】
[1009019] 戒＋（者）【明】
[1009020] 菩薩＋（戒）【明】
[1009021] 作繫縛事＝繫縛【宋】【元】【宮】
[1009022] （如獄囚法兵奴之法）＋如【宋】【元】【明】
[1009023] 肉＋（非餘外蟲如是佛子自破佛法）【明】，〔肉〕－【宮】
[1009024] 母＋（不可毀破）【宋】【元】【明】
[1009025] 時＝之聲【明】
[1009026] 〔經〕－【宋】【元】【宮】
[1009027] （於）＋百【明】
[1009028] 不用一聞＝不一聞【宋】【元】【宮】，＝不聞一【明】
[1009029] 〔而〕－【宋】【元】【明】【宮】

[1009030] 破＋（破）【宋】【元】【宮】
[1009031] 〔諸〕－【宋】【元】【宮】
[1009032] 諦聽此＝聽【宋】【元】【明】【宮】
[1009033] 十重＝十戒【宋】【宮】
[1009034] 〔輕〕－【宋】【宮】
[1009035] 等＋（大眾）【明】
[1009036] 廣＝已【宋】【元】【宮】
[1009037] 士＝者【宋】【元】【宮】
[1009038] 十＝下【宋】【元】【明】【宮】
[1009039] 如如＝如是【宋】【元】【明】【宮】
[1009040] 王＋（七行）【明】
[1009041] 諸＝諍【宋】，＝淨【元】【宮】
[1010001] 佛行處＝諸佛子【宋】【元】【明】【宮】
[1010002] 計＝討【元】
[1010003] 信＝生【宋】【宮】，＝主【元】
[1010004] 盡＝壽【宋】【元】【明】【宮】
[1010005] 亦＝又【宋】【元】【宮】
[1010006] 處＝惡【宋】【元】【明】【宮】
[1010007] 由＝從【宋】【元】【明】【宮】
[1010008] 以＝已【宋】【元】【宮】
[1010009] （（梵網…下））十八字＝（（梵網經卷下））五字【宋】【宮】，（（佛說梵網經卷下））七字【元】【明】

The Bodhisattva's Practice of Moral Virtue

Part Two:

Nāgārjuna on the Perfection of Moral Virtue

As Translated into Chinese by Tripiṭaka Master Kumārajīva
From Ārya Nāgārjuna's Mahāprajñāpāramitā Upadeśa

Annotated English Translation by Bhikshu Dharmamitra

Part Two:
Nāgārjuna on the Perfection of Moral Virtue

General Table of Contents

Directory to Chapter One Subchapters

I. Ch.1, Subchapter 21: Explanation of the Meaning of Śīla Pāramitā 163
A. The Sutra Text 163
B. Nāgārjuna's Commentary 163
1. General Definition of Moral Virtue (*Śīla*) 163
2. Proscribed Behavior Categories 163
3. Levels of Precept Observance and the Consequences 163
4. The Necessity of Scrupulous Observance 165
5. Uselessness of Unprecepted Asceticism 165
6. The Irrelevance of Social Station 167
7. The Breaker of Precepts 167
8. The Observer of the Precepts 169
9. The Man with the Marvelous Vase (Story) 171
10. The Good Fortune of the Observer of Precepts 173
11. The Wretched State of the Precept Breaker: 32 Analogies 175
II. Ch.1, Subchapter 22: On the Details and Import of the Moral Precepts 181
A. Precepts Defined: Cessaton of and Restraint from Evil 181
1. The Layperson's Precepts 181
a. The Five Precepts 181
1) The Precept Against Killing 181
a) Killing Defined 181
b) Abhidharmic Analysis of Killing Precept 183
c) Additional Abhidharma Analytic Data 185
d) Resumption of Expository Killing Precept Discussion 189
i) Objection: Killing is Justified. Why Abstain? 189
ii) Refutation of Arguments for Killing 189
e) The Merchant Who Lost His Jewels (Story) 191
f) Killing as the Worst and Not Killing as the Finest of Actions 191
g) Ten Karmic Effects from Killing 193
h) The Butcher's Son Refuses to Kill (Story) 197
2) The Precept Against Stealing 199
a) Stealing Defined 199
b) The Benefits of Not Stealing 199
c) Two Main Categories of Stealing 201
d) The Reprehensibility of Robbery in Particular 201
e) Objection: But Isn't the Very Boldness Admirable? 203
f) Condemnation of Theft of Any Sort 203
g) Sexual Misconduct Defined 205
h) Objection: How Could This Apply to One's Wife? 205
i) In Instances of the One-day Precept 207
ii) In Instances of Pregnancy or Nursing 207

iii) In Instances Involving Inappropriate Orifice or Force 207
i) Objection: If Her Husband Doesn't Know, What's the Problem? 207
i) Offense Is Based on the Act Itself 207
ii) Alienation of Affections Entails Theft 207
iii) Disrepute, Hatred, Unhappiness, Fear, Danger, Lies, Censure 209
iv) Identity of Lovers Makes It Pointless 209
v) Present and Future Happiness Is Lost 209
vi) One Should Have Sympathy for the Prospective Cuckold 209
vii) The Karmic Retribution Is Horrible 209
j) Ten Karmic Effects of Sexual Misconduct 211
3) The Precept Against False Speech 211
a) False Speech Defined 211
b) The Inherent Faults in False Speech 213
c) Kokālika's Slanderous Offense (Story) 215
d) Rāhula's Lesson About False Speech (Story) 221
e) Ten Karmic Effects of False Speech 223
4) The Precept Against Intoxicants 223
a) Alcoholic Beverages Defined 223
b) Objection: With So Many Benefits, Why Abstain? 225
c) Thirty-Five Karmic Effects of Consuming Intoxicants 225
5) Additional Five-Precept Topics 229
a) Summation of the Primary Basis of Lay Morality 229
b) Eight Precepts, Other Mouth Karmas, Pure Livelihood 229
i) Limited Capacities of Lay Buddhists 229
ii) How the False Speech Precept Subsumes the Others 229
iii) Lay Life's Inherent Connection to Harsh Speech 231
iv) Five Degrees of Five-Precept Acceptance 231
v) Buddha's Verse on Five-Precept Karmic Rewards 231
(1) Buddhahood is the Goal; Why Praise Heavens? 235
(2) Three Endeavors Entailing Certain Rewards 235
(3) Attraction to Karmic Rewards Conducing to the Path 235
b. The Specific-Term Practice of Eight Precepts 237
1) The Ceremony for Life-Long Five-Precept Practice 241
c. Comparison of Five and Eight Precepts 247
1) The Middling Grade of Lay Precept Observance 249
2) The Superior Grade of Lay Precept Observance 251
a) How These Precepts Are the Causes for Nirvāṇa 251
b) **[Chapter 1, Subchapter 23: On the Meaning of Chapter One's Praise of Śīla Pāramitā. Part One: Additional Precept Specifics]** _ _ _ _
How Can Precepts Be Foremost in the Eightfold Path? 253
3) The Superior-Superior Grade of Lay Precept observance 253
2. The Monastic Precepts 253
a. The Value of the Monastic Precepts 255
1) Inherent Path-Defeating Difficulties in Lay Life 255
2) Comparison of Lay and Monastic Situations 255

3) Difficulties Specific to the Monastic Life 257
4) Utpalavarṇā Promotes Monasticism (Story) 257
5) An Inebriated Brahman Becomes a Monk (Story) 261
6) Concluding Statement on Lay Life versus Monasticism 261
b. The Four Categories of Monastic Precepts 261
1) The Origin of the Śikṣamāṇā Postulant Nun Category 263
a) Why Wouldn't a Pregnant Śikṣamāṇā Be as much a Liability? 263
b) Two Subcategories of Śikṣamāṇā 265
B. Conclusion of Precept Details Discussion 265
III. Ch.1, Subchapter 23, Pt. 2: A Continued Explanation of the Perfection of Moral Virtue 267
A. Definition of the Perfection of Moral Virtue 267
1. Indifference to Sacrificing One's Life in Upholding Precepts 267
2. Buddha's Past Life as a Dragon (Illustrative Story) 267
B. More Defining Characteristics of Śīla Pāramitā 269
1. How Śīla Generates All Six Perfections 271
2. Śīla's Generation of Śīla Pāramitā 271
3. Śīla's Generation of Dāna Pāramitā 271
a. The Three Types of Giving 271
1) The Giving of Wealth 273
2) The Giving of Dharma 273
3) The Giving of Fearlessness 273
b. The Altruistic Vow of the Bodhisattva 273
4. Śīla's Generation of Kṣānti Pāramitā 273
a. The Precepts' Dependence on Establishing Patience 273
b. The Execution wagon Analogy 275
c. The Walking Stick Analogy 277
5. Śīla's Generation of Vīrya Pāramitā 277
a. Śīla's Expulsion of Negligence 277
b. Śīla's Engendering of Renunciation 277
c. A Coyote Makes His Escape (Illustrative Story) 277
d. The Mind's Self-Exhortation to Action 279
e. The Archery Analogy 279
f. Śīla's Natural Promotion of Diligent Self-control 281
6. Śīla's Generation of Dhyāna Pāramitā 281
a. Rectification of Mind Through Physical and Verbal Goodness 281
b. The Grass-in-Sesame Analogy 281
c. The Fetter-Diminishing Effect of the Precepts 281
d. The Invalid's-Fragility Analogy 283
e. The Clarity-Promoting Effects of Moral Restraint 283
f. Śīla's Production of Higher Rebirth and Path Acquisition 283
g. The Cooperative Link Between Precepts and Dhyāna 283
1) The Precepts-as-Stairs Analogy 283
2) The Fetter-Induced Mental Wind Analogy 283
7. Śīla's Generation of *Prajñāpāramitā* 285

a. A Wisdom Generating Contemplation of Precepts 285
b. The Lotus-from-Mud Analogy 285
c. Making Precept Practice Reflect Prajñā 285
d. The Keen Mind, Lacking Precepts, Becomes Dull 285
e. The Dull Mind, Imbued with Precepts, Becomes Keen 285
8. Concluding Statement on the Nature of Śīla Pāramitā 287
C. Unfindability of Offense and Non-Offense 287
1. Objection: Offense and Non-offense Do Exist 287
2. The Meaning of Unfindability of Offense and Non-Offense 287
a. The Link to Unfindability of Beings and Unfindability of Precepts 287
b. Objection: How Can One Claim Beings Don't Exist? 289
c. Clarification of Unfindability of Beings 289
1) Refutation: Incompatibility of Singularity and Multiplicity 289
2) Refutation of Beings: Impossibility of Karmic Retribution 289
3) Refutation of Non-Aggregate Beings: Eternalist Fallacy 289
4) Objection: Aggregate-Based Beings Are Like a Finger-Based Fist 291
5) Refutation: Absence of Any Apprehensible "Being" Dharma 291
a) Synopsis of Related Non-Buddhist Positions 291
b) A Deceased Guru Disguised (Illustrative Story) 293
6) Refutation Based on Consequence of Beings' Impermanence 293
7) Refutation Based on Later Arising of Aggregates 293
3. Concluding Discussion of Unfindability and Its Import 295

正體字

T25n1509_p0153b02║ 大智度論釋初品[6]中尸羅波羅蜜
153b03║ [7]義第二十一(卷第十三)
153b04║
153b05║ [*]龍樹菩薩造
153b06║ [*]後秦龜茲國三藏鳩摩羅什
153b07║ [*]奉 詔譯
153b08║ [8]【經】罪不罪不可得故。應具足尸羅波羅蜜
153b09║ [9]【論】尸羅([10]秦言性善)好行善道不自放逸。是名
153b10║ 尸羅。或受戒行善或不受戒行善。皆名尸羅。
153b11║ 尸羅者。略說身口律儀有八種。不惱害不劫
153b12║ 盜不邪婬不妄語不兩舌不惡口不綺語不飲
153b13║ 酒及淨命。是名戒[11]相。若不護放捨。是名破
153b14║ 戒。破此戒者墮三惡道中。若下持戒生人
153b15║ 中。中持戒生六欲[12]天中。

简体字

This Dazhidulun Fascicle 13 and 14 Text from the Qianlong Zang Downloaded on 03/08/2024 from this site: https://www.fojingzaixian.com/qianlongdazangjing.html at this site url: https://www.fojingzaixian.com/q1300.html

大乘论·第1163部 大智度论一百卷（第一卷～第二十卷） 龙树菩萨造姚秦三藏法师鸠摩罗什译

大智度论卷第十三

释初品中尸罗波罗蜜

【经】“罪不罪不可得故，应具足尸罗波罗蜜。”

【论】尸罗（此言性善），好行善道，不自放逸，是名尸罗。或受戒行善，或不受戒行善，皆名尸罗。尸罗者，略说身、口律仪有八种：不恼害，不劫盗，不邪淫，不妄语，不两舌，不恶口，不绮语，不饮酒及净命，是名戒。若不护放舍，是名破戒。破此戒者，堕三恶道中。若下持戒生人中，中持戒生六欲天中，

The Perfection of Moral Virtue
By Ārya Nāgārjuna

Ch. 1, Subchapter 21: Explanation of the Meaning of Śīla Pāramitā

I. Ch.1, Subchapter 21: Explanation of the Meaning of Śīla Pāramitā

A. The Sutra Text

Sutra: It is based on the unfindability of offense and non-offense that one should pursue the perfection of moral virtue (*śīla pāramitā*).

B. Nāgārjuna's Commentary

Exegesis:

1. General Definition of Moral Virtue (*Śīla*)

Śīla refers to being fond of coursing along in the way of goodness while not allowing oneself to be negligent (*pramāda*). This is what is meant by *śīla*. Perhaps one takes on the moral precepts and practices goodness or perhaps one refrains from taking on the moral precepts and yet still practices goodness. Both of these cases qualify as "*śīla*." (Chinese textual note: In our language, ["*śīla*"] means "to be good by nature.")[1]

2. Proscribed Behavior Categories

As for *śīla*, generally described, the regulation behaviors specific to the body and mouth are of eight kinds. They include refraining from taking life (*prāṇātipāta*), refraining from taking what is not given (*adattādāna*), refraining from engaging in sexual misconduct (*kāmamithyācāra*), refraining from engaging in false speech (*mṛṣāvāda*), refraining from engaging in divisive speech (*paiśunyavāda*),[2] refraining from engaging in harsh speech (*pāruṣyavāda*), refraining from engaging in frivolous speech (*saṃbhinnapralāpa*),[3] and refraining from partaking of intoxicants (*madyapāna*). This includes pure livelihood (*pariśuddhājīva*) as well. These are the specific characteristics of the moral precepts.

If one fails to guard them and so lets go of and relinquishes them, this amounts to "breaking" the moral precepts. One who breaks these moral precepts is bound to fall into the three wretched destinies.

3. Levels of Precept Observance and the Consequences

If one upholds the moral precepts at an inferior level, then one is born among humans. If one upholds the precepts at a middling level, one is born among the six desire realm heavens. If one upholds the

正體字

上持戒又行四禪
153b16 四空定。生色無色界清淨天中。上持戒有三
153b17 種。下清淨持戒得阿羅漢。中清淨持戒得辟
153b18 支佛。上清淨持戒得佛道。不著不[13]猗不破
153b19 不缺聖所讚愛。如是名為上清淨[14]持戒。若
153b20 慈愍眾生故。為度眾生故。亦知戒實相
153b21 故心不猗著。如此持戒[15]將來[16]令人至佛
153b22 道。如是名為得無上佛道戒。若人求大善
153b23 利。當堅持戒如惜重寶。如護身命。何以
153b24 故譬如大地一切萬物有形之類。皆依地而
153b25 住。戒亦如是戒為一切善法住處。復次譬如
153b26 無足欲行無翅欲飛無船[17]欲渡。是不可
153b27 得。若無戒欲[18]得好果亦復如是。若人棄
153b28 捨此戒。雖山居[19]苦行食果服藥。與禽獸
153b29 無異。或有人但服水為戒。

简体字

上持戒又行四禅、四空定，生色、无色界清净天中。上持戒有三种：下清净持戒得阿罗汉，中清净持戒得辟支佛，上清净持戒得佛道。不著不猗，不破不缺，圣所赞爱，如是名为上清净持戒。若慈愍众生故，为度众生故，亦知戒实相故，心不猗著；如此持戒，将来至佛道。如是名为得无上佛道戒。若人求大善利，当坚持戒，如惜重宝，如护身命。何以故？譬如大地，一切万物有形之类，皆依地而住；戒亦如是，戒为一切善法住处。

复次，譬如无足欲行，无翅欲飞，无船欲度，是不可得；若无戒欲求好果，亦复如是。若人弃舍此戒，虽山居苦行，食果服药，与禽兽无异。或有人但服水为戒，

precepts at a superior level and also cultivates the four *dhyānas* and the four emptiness absorptions, one is born in the pure heavens of the form or formless realms.

The superior observance of the moral precepts is of three types: If one adheres to the lesser level of pure observance of the precepts, one achieves arhatship. If one adheres to the middle level of pure observance of the precepts, one attains *pratyekabuddhahood*. If one adheres to the superior level of pure observance of the precepts, one attains the path to buddhahood.

If one neither attaches to them nor leans upon them and if one neither breaks them nor has deficiencies with respect to them, he is one who is praised and cherished by the Āryas. Instances such as these illustrate what is meant by superior purity in the observance of the moral precepts.

If one acts out of kindness and sympathy for beings, if one is motivated by the intention to bring beings across to liberation, and if one knows in accordance with reality the true character of the moral precepts, then one's mind does not lean upon or attach to them. If one upholds the precepts in this way, in the future one will cause people to reach the path to buddhahood. This is what is meant by gaining the moral precepts of the unsurpassed buddha path.

4. The Necessity of Scrupulous Observance

If one wishes to obtain great wholesome benefit, then one should uphold the moral precepts solidly, just as if one were cherishing a valuable treasure and as if one were guarding one's own physical life. Why? Just as the myriad beings possessed of physical form all rely upon the earth and abide there, so too it is with the moral precepts. The moral precepts are the dwelling place of all wholesome dharmas.

Moreover, [dispensing with moral precepts] is like wishing to walk without legs, like wishing to fly without wings and like wishing to cross over a body of water without a boat. This cannot be done. If one is lacking in the moral precepts and yet one wishes to obtain a fine result, it is just the same. If a person casts off and relinquishes these moral precepts, although he may abide in the mountains, practicing ascetic practices and eating fruits and taking herbs, he is still no different from the birds or the animals.

5. Uselessness of Unprecepted Asceticism

There may be people who take on the observance of ascetic practices and thus who adopt the discipline of drinking only water, of

正體字

或服乳或服氣
153c01 或剃髮或長髮。或頂上留少許髮。或著袈
153c02 裟或著白衣或著草衣或木皮衣。或冬入
153c03 水或夏火炙。若自墜高巖若於恒河中洗。
153c04 若日三浴再供養火。種種祠[20]祀種種呪願受
153c05 行苦行。以無此戒空無所得。若有人雖
153c06 處高堂大殿好衣美食。而能行此戒者得
153c07 生好處。及得道果。若貴若賤若小若大。[21]能
153c08 行此淨戒皆得大利。若破此戒無貴無賤
153c09 無大無小。皆不得隨意生善處。復次破戒
153c10 之人。譬如清涼池而有毒蛇不中澡浴。亦
153c11 如好華果樹而多逆刺。若人雖在貴家生
153c12 身體端[22]政廣學多聞。而不樂持戒無慈愍
153c13 心。亦復如是如偈說
153c14 貴而無智則為衰　　智而憍慢亦為衰

简体字

或服乳，或服气；或剃发，或长发，或顶上留少许发；或著袈裟，或著白衣，或著草衣，或木皮衣；或冬入水，或夏火炙；若自坠高岩，若于恒河中洗；若日三浴，再供养火，种种祠祀，种种咒愿，受行苦行；以无此戒，空无所得。若有人虽处高堂大殿，好衣美食，而能行此戒者，得生好处及得道果。若贵若贱，若小若大，能行此净戒，皆得大利。若破此戒，无贵无贱，无大无小，皆不得随意生善处。

复次，破戒之人，譬如清凉池而有毒蛇，不中澡浴；亦如好华果树，而多逆刺。若人虽在贵家生，身体端正，广学多闻，而不乐持戒，无慈愍心，亦复如是。如偈说：

“贵而无智则为衰，智而憍慢亦为衰，持戒之人而毁戒，今世后世一切衰！”

drinking only milk, of consuming only vital energy, of shaving off the hair, of letting the hair grow long, of reserving a only a small patch of hair atop the head, of wearing a *kāṣāya* robe, of wearing a white robe, of wearing clothes made of grass, of wearing clothes made of tree bark, of plunging into water in winter, of burning themselves with fire in the summer, of throwing themselves off of a high cliff, of washing themselves in the Ganges River, of taking three baths each day, of repeatedly making offerings to fire, of carrying out all kinds of sacrificial offerings, or of resorting to all sorts of spells and prayers. However, insofar as they may not have taken on these moral precepts, those practices are useless and thus there is nothing to be gained through pursuing them.

6. The Irrelevance of Social Station

Although a person may abide in an exalted position, living in a grand palace, wearing fine clothes, and consuming exquisite cuisine, if he is nonetheless able to cultivate these moral precepts, he will be able to be reborn into a fine place and eventually will achieve the fruits of cultivating the path. No matter whether one is of noble or humble social station and no matter whether one has little status or great status, if one is able to cultivate these precepts of purity, he will gain from it a great resulting benefit.

However, if one breaks these moral precepts, there are no considerations reserved for noble or humble class or greater or lesser status. In every case, one will remain unable to succeed in being born in a good place that accords with one's aspirations.

7. The Breaker of Precepts

Moreover, the circumstance of a person who breaks the precepts is comparable to a clear and cool pool containing a poisonous snake. One refrains from bathing in such a place. It is also like a tree bearing fine flowers and fruit but an abundance of thorns. Although a person may abide in a family of the nobility, may possess a body that is handsome and fine, and may have accumulated an abundance of learning, if he finds no pleasure in upholding the moral precepts and his mind is devoid of kindness and pity, he is just like this. His situation is as described in this verse:

> If one is of noble birth, but has no wisdom, this is ruination.
> If one is intelligent, but is arrogant, this too is ruination.
> If one is an upholder of precepts, but then violates the precepts,
> In this life and in later lives, all is ruination.

正體字

153c15 持戒之人而毀戒　今世後世一切衰
153c16 人雖貧賤。而能持戒勝於富貴。而破戒者
153c17 華香木香不能遠聞。持戒之香周遍十方。
153c18 持戒之人具足安樂。名聲遠聞天人敬愛。現
153c19 世常得種種快樂。若欲天上人中富貴長壽。
153c20 取之不難。持戒清淨所願皆得。復次持戒
153c21 之人。見破戒人刑獄[23]考掠種種苦惱。自知
153c22 永離此事以為欣慶。若持戒之人。見善人
153c23 得譽名聞快樂。心自念言。如彼得譽。我亦
153c24 有分。持戒之人壽終之時刀風解身筋脈斷
153c25 絕。自知持戒清淨心不怖畏。如偈說
153c26 大惡病中　戒為良藥　大恐怖中
153c27 戒為守護　死闇冥中　戒為明燈
153c28 於惡道中　戒為橋樑　死海水中
153c29 戒為大船
154a01 復次持戒之人。常得今世人所敬養

简体字

人虽贫贱而能持戒，胜于富贵而破戒者。华香、木香不能远闻；持戒之香，周遍十方。持戒之人，具足安乐，名声远闻，天人敬爱，现世常得种种快乐。若欲天上、人中、富贵、长寿，取之不难；持戒清净，所愿皆得。

复次，持戒之人，见破戒人刑狱拷掠种种苦恼，自知永离此事，以为欣庆。若持戒之人，见善人得誉，名闻快乐，心自念言："如彼得誉，我亦有分。"持戒之人，寿终之时，刀风解身，筋脉断绝，自知持戒清净，心不怖畏。如偈说：

"大恶病中，戒为良药；大恐怖中，戒为守护；
死暗冥中，戒为明灯；于恶道中，戒为桥梁；
死海水中，戒为大船。"

复次，持戒之人，常得今世人所敬养，

8. The Observer of the Precepts

Although one may be poor and of low social station, if one is able to uphold the moral precepts, this is superior to being wealthy or of noble birth while yet still being a breaker of the precepts.

The fragrance of flowers and the fragrance of the trees is such that one is unable to smell them from afar. However, the fragrance from upholding the precepts universally pervades throughout the ten directions. The person who upholds the moral precepts perfects the realization of peacefulness and happiness. His name is heard in faraway quarters and he is revered and cherished by both men and gods. In this present life, he always achieves all manner of happiness. If he desires wealth, nobility, and long life in the heavens or among people, it is not difficult for him to obtain it. If one is pure in upholding the moral precepts, he gains whatever he wishes.

Moreover, a person who upholds the moral precepts observes the precept breaker's suffering and affliction encountered through punishments, confinements, beatings, and floggings, knows with respect to himself that he has forever transcended such vulnerabilities, and is overjoyed on that account.

If a person who upholds the precepts sees a good person gaining a good name, fame, and happiness, and thinks to himself, "In just the same fashion as he has come by a good reputation, I too have a measure of that." When the life of a person who upholds the moral precepts comes to an end, when the knife-like wind cuts loose the body, and when the sinews and blood vessels are severed, he knows that he has upheld the precepts purely. His mind remains free of fearfulness. This situation is as described in a verse:

In an epidemic of great evil,
the moral precepts serve as fine medicine.
In a circumstance of great fearfulness,
the precepts are a guardian protector.

In the midst of the darkness of death,
the precepts serve as a bright lamp.
Where one might fall into the wretched destinies,
the precepts act as a bridge.

Within the waters of the sea of mortality,
the precepts are a great ship.

Furthermore, the person who upholds the precepts always finds that he is revered and supported by people of his time. His mind

正體字

心樂不
154a02 悔。衣食無乏。死得生天後得佛道。持
154a03 戒之人無事不得。破戒之人一切皆失。譬
154a04 如有人常供養天。其人貧窮一心供養滿
154a05 十二歲求索富貴。天愍此人自現其身而
154a06 問之曰。汝求何等。答言。我求富貴。欲令
154a07 心之所願一切皆得。天與一器名曰德瓶。
154a08 而語之言。所須之物從此瓶出。其人得已
154a09 應意所欲無所不得。得如意已具作好
154a10 舍象馬車乘。七寶具足。供給賓客事事
154a11 無乏。客問之言。汝先貧窮。今日[1]所由得
154a12 如此富。答言。我得天瓶。瓶能出此種種
154a13 眾物故富如是。客言。出瓶見示并所出物。
154a14 即為出瓶。瓶中引出種種眾物。其人憍泆
154a15 立瓶上舞。瓶即破壞。一切眾物亦一時滅。
154a16 持戒之人亦復如是。種種妙樂無願不得。
154a17 若人破戒憍泆[2]自恣

简体字

心乐不悔，衣食无乏，死得生天，后得佛道。持戒之人，无事不得；破戒之人，一切皆失。譬如有人常供养天，其人贫穷，一心供养满十二岁，求索富贵。天愍此人，自现其身而问之曰："汝求何等？"答言："我求富贵，欲令心之所愿，一切皆得！"天与一器，名曰德瓶，而语之言："所须之物，从此瓶出。"其人得已，应意所欲，无所不得。得如意已，具作好舍，象马、车乘、七宝具足，供给宾客，事事无乏。客问之言："汝先贫穷，今日何由得如此富？"答言："我得天瓶，瓶能出此种种众物，故富如是。"客言："出瓶见示，并所出物！"即为出瓶，瓶中引出种种众物。其人憍泆，立瓶上舞，瓶即破坏，一切众物亦一时灭。持戒之人，亦复如是，种种妙乐，无愿不得；若人破戒，憍泆自恣，

remains blissful and free of regrets. He has no shortage of either clothing or food. When he dies, he is born in the heavens and then subsequently gains realization of the path to buddhahood. For the person who upholds the precepts, there is no matter in which he is not successful. For a person who breaks the precepts, everything is lost.

9. The Man with the Marvelous Vase (Story)

This situation is analogous to that of the man who constantly devoted himself to making offerings to a particular deity. As this man was poverty-stricken, for twelve full years he single-mindedly made offerings out of a desire to gain wealth and nobility. The god was moved to feel pity for this man, manifested himself before him, and then asked, "What is it that you seek?"

The man replied, "I'm seeking to gain wealth and nobility. I desire to have it occur that I may obtain everything I wish for."

The god then gave him a vessel known as "the vase of virtue" and told the man, "Everything you need will come forth from this vase."

After the man got it, there was nothing which he wished for that he did not succeed in obtaining. After he had acquired the ability to get anything he wished for, he built himself a fine house complete with elephants, horses, and carriages, and also came to possess an abundance of the seven kinds of jewels. He gave generously to all of his guests so that they were never wanting in any respect.

One of his guests inquired of him, "You used to be poverty-stricken. How is it that now you have come by such wealth?"

The man replied, "I received this celestial vase. The vase is able to bring forth all of these different kinds of things. It is on account of this that I have gained such wealth."

The guest asked, "Would you show me the vase and something which it has brought forth?"

He immediately brought out the vase. From within the vase, he drew forth all manner of objects. Then, in prideful carelessness, he began to dance about on the top rim of the vase, whereupon the vase was immediately shattered. At the very same time, all of the different sorts of things which it had produced all simultaneously disappeared.

One who upholds the moral precepts is just like this. He receives all manner of marvelous bliss and there is no wish which he does not realize. However, if a person breaks the precepts—if he becomes pridefully careless and gives free rein to willfulness—he will

正體字

亦如彼人破瓶失[3]物。
154a18 | 復次持戒之人名稱之香。今世後世[4]周滿天
154a19 | 上及在人中。復次持戒之人。人所樂施不
154a20 | 惜財物。不修世利而無所乏得生天上。
154a21 | 十方佛前入三乘道而得解脫。唯種種邪
154a22 | 見。持戒後無所得。復次若人雖不出家。但
154a23 | 能修行戒法。亦得生天。若人持戒清淨[5]行
154a24 | 禪智慧。欲求度脫老病死苦此願必得。持
154a25 | 戒之人雖無兵仗眾惡不加。持戒之財
154a26 | 無能奪者。持戒親親雖死不離。持戒莊嚴
154a27 | 勝於七寶。以是之故。當護於戒如護身
154a28 | 命如愛寶物。破戒之人受苦萬端。如向貧
154a29 | 人破瓶失物。[6]以是之故應持淨戒。復次
154b01 | 持戒之人。觀破戒人罪應自勉勵一心持戒。

简体字

亦如彼人破瓶失利。

复次，持戒之人，名称之香，今世、后世，周满天上及在人中。

复次，持戒之人，人所乐施，不惜财物，不修世利而无所乏；得生天上，十方佛前，入三乘道而得解脱。唯种种邪见持戒，后无所得。

复次，若人虽不出家，但能修行戒法，亦得生天。若人持戒清净，禅定、智慧，欲求度脱老病死苦，此愿必得。持戒之人，虽无兵仗，众恶不加。持戒之财，无能夺者。持戒亲亲，虽死不离。持戒庄严，胜于七宝。以是之故，当护于戒，如护身命，如爱宝物。破戒之人，受苦万端，如向贫人破瓶失物。

复次，持戒之人，观破戒人罪，应自勉励，一心持戒。

become just like this man who broke his vase and consequently lost everything.

10. The Good Fortune of the Observer of Precepts

Furthermore, the reputation of the person who upholds the precepts spreads like a fragrance and pervades both the heavens and the human realm in both current and later lives. Additionally, the person who upholds the precepts is one to whom people enjoy making gifts, not stinting in giving even their valuable possessions. He does not cultivate worldly profit and yet there is nothing for which he is wanting. He succeeds in being born in the heavens. He enters the way of the Three Vehicles in the presence of the Buddhas of the ten directions and then succeeds in achieving liberation. It is only in a case where all manner of erroneous views figure in one's upholding of precepts that there might be nothing gained later.

Then again, even though a person may not have left behind the home life, if he is only able to cultivate the dharma of the precepts, he too will succeed in being reborn in the heavens. If a person is pure in his upholding of the precepts while also cultivating *dhyāna* and wisdom, and if he seeks thereby to cross himself over to liberation from the suffering of aging, sickness, and death, this wish will certainly be realized. Even though a person who upholds the precepts may not be under the protection of the military's weaponry, awful events will not befall him.

The wealth of upholding precepts is such that none can steal it away. The upholding of precepts is the most intimate of intimates. Even when one dies, one still does not become estranged from it. The adornment furnished by the upholding of precepts is superior to that of the seven precious things. It is for these sorts of reasons that one should remain just as protective of the moral precepts as one is protective of one's own physical life and just as cherishing of them as one is in cherishing precious possessions.

The person who breaks the precepts undergoes a myriad forms of suffering. He is like that man who used to be poor, subsequently became rich, but then broke the vase, and lost everything as a consequence. It is for these reasons that one should uphold the precepts of purity.

Moreover, when the person who upholds the precepts observes the karmic punishments of those who have broken the precepts, he should encourage himself on that account to devote himself to single-minded observance of the moral precepts.

正體字

154b02 云何名為破戒人罪。破戒之人人所不敬。
154b03 其家如塚人所不到。破戒之人失諸功德。
154b04 譬如枯樹人不愛樂。破戒之人如霜蓮花
154b05 人不喜見。破戒之人惡心可畏譬如羅剎。
154b06 破戒之人人不歸向。譬如渴人不向枯井。
154b07 破戒之人心常疑悔。譬如犯事之人常畏罪
154b08 至。破戒之人如田被雹不可依仰。破戒之
154b09 人譬如苦[7]苽。雖形似甘種而不可食。破
154b10 戒之人如賊聚落不可依止。破戒之人譬
154b11 如大病人不欲近。破戒之人不得免苦。譬
154b12 如惡道難可得過。破戒之人不可共止。譬
154b13 如惡賊難可親近。破戒之人譬如[8]大坑行
154b14 者避之。破戒之人難可共住譬如毒蛇。破
154b15 戒之人不可近觸譬如大火。破戒之人譬
154b16 如破船不可乘渡。破戒之人譬如吐食不
154b17 可更噉。

简体字

云何名为破戒人罪？破戒之人，人所不敬，其家如冢，人所不到。破戒之人，失诸功德，譬如枯树，人不爱乐。破戒之人，如霜莲华，人不喜见。破戒之人，恶心可畏，譬如罗刹。破戒之人，人不归向，譬如渴人，不向枯井。破戒之人，心常疑悔，譬如犯事之人，常畏罪至。破戒之人，如田被雹，不可依仰。破戒之人，譬如苦瓜，虽形似甘种而不可食。破戒之人，如贼聚落，不可依止。破戒之人，譬如大病，人不欲近。破戒之人，不得免苦，譬如恶道难可得过。破戒之人，不可共止，譬如恶贼难可亲近。破戒之人，譬如火坑，行者避之。破戒之人，难可共住，譬如毒蛇。破戒之人，不可近触，譬如大火。破戒之人，譬如破船，不可乘度。破戒之人，譬如吐食，不可更啖。

11. The Wretched State of the Precept Breaker: 32 Analogies

What is meant by "the karmic punishments of those who have broken the moral precepts"?

A person who breaks the precepts is not respected by others. His house becomes like a tomb in that people do not choose to go there.

The person who breaks the moral precepts loses all of his meritorious qualities. He becomes like a dead and leafless tree in which people take no pleasure.

A person who breaks the precepts becomes like a frost-damaged lotus which people take no delight in viewing.

The person who breaks the precepts possesses an evil and fearsome mind like that of a *rākṣasa* ghost.

Just as thirsty people avoid a dried-up well, so too do people avoid returning into the presence of a precept-breaker.

The mind of the person who breaks the precepts is constantly beset with doubts and regrets. He is comparable to a criminal in that he is always fearful that punishment may come his way.

The person who breaks the precepts becomes like farmland struck by a hail storm which people cannot rely on for sustenance.

A person who breaks the precepts is like a bitter melon which, though resembling the sweet varieties, is inedible.

A person who breaks the precepts is like a village populated by thieves in which one cannot remain.

A person who breaks the precepts is like a person afflicted with a serious disease in that one does not wish to draw close to him.

The breaker of the precepts is unable to avoid suffering. It is just as with a wretchedly bad path on which it is difficult to travel.

One cannot remain together with a person who breaks the precepts. Just as with an evil thief, it is difficult to grow close to him.

A person who breaks the precepts is like a great abyss. Those who travel by avoid it.

A person who breaks the precepts is difficult to dwell together with. In this he is comparable to a poisonous snake.

A person who breaks the precepts cannot be approached or touched. Thus he is comparable to a huge conflagration.

A person who breaks the precepts is like a wrecked boat in which one cannot ride to ferry on across the waters.

A person who breaks the precepts is like food which has been vomited up and which cannot be feasted on again.

正體字

破戒之人在好眾中。譬如惡馬在
154b18 | 善馬[9]群。破戒之人與善人異。如驢在牛
154b19 | 群。破戒之人在精進眾。譬如[10]儜兒在健人
154b20 | 中。破戒之人雖似比丘。譬如死屍在眠人
154b21 | 中。破戒之人譬如偽珠在真珠中。破戒之人
154b22 | 譬如伊蘭在栴檀[11]林。破戒之人雖形似善
154b23 | 人內無善法。雖復剃頭染衣次第捉籌名
154b24 | 為比丘。實非比丘。破戒之人若著法衣。則
154b25 | 是熱銅鐵[12]鍱以纏其身。若持鉢盂則是盛
154b26 | 洋銅器。若所噉食則是吞燒鐵丸。飲熱洋
154b27 | 銅。若受人供養供給。則是地獄獄[13]鬼守之。
154b28 | 若入精舍則是入大地獄。若坐眾僧床榻。
154b29 | 是為坐熱鐵床上。復次破戒之人。常懷怖
154c01 | 懅如重病人常畏死至。亦如五逆罪人。心
154c02 | 常自念我為佛賊。藏覆避隈如賊畏人。歲
154c03 | 月日過常不安隱。

简体字

破戒之人，在好众中，譬如恶马在善马群中。破戒之人，与善人异，如驴在牛群。破戒之人，在精进众，譬如儜儿在健人中。破戒之人，虽似比丘，譬如死尸在眠人中。破戒之人，譬如伪珠在真珠中。破戒之人，譬如伊兰在栴檀林中。破戒之人，虽形似善人，内无善法；虽复剃头、染衣，次第捉筹，名为比丘，实非比丘。破戒之人，若著法衣，则是热铜铁鍱以缠其身；若持钵盂，则是盛洋铜器；若所啖食，则是吞烧铁丸，饮热洋铜；若受人供养供给，则是地狱狱卒守人；若入精舍，则是入大地狱；若坐众僧床榻，是为坐热铁床上。

复次，破戒之人，常怀怖懅，如重病人，常畏死至。亦如五逆罪人，心常自念："我为佛贼，藏覆避隈。"如贼畏人，岁月日过，常不安隐。

When a person who breaks the precepts is present within a group of good people, it is like when a bad horse is present in a herd of good horses.

A person who breaks the precepts is different from good people. It is just as when a donkey is present within a herd of cattle.

When a person who breaks the precepts is present within the vigorous assembly, it is like when a weakling child is present among strong men.

Although a person who breaks the precepts may look like a bhikshu, he is like a corpse in the midst of a group of sleeping men.

A person who breaks the precepts is like a counterfeit pearl in the midst of true pearls.

A person who breaks the precepts is like an *eraṇḍa* tree[4] in the midst of a forest of sandalwood.

Although the person who breaks the precepts resembles a good person in appearance, he contains no good dharmas within. Although he may shave his head, dye the robes, take up vouchers according to seniority, and be referred to as a bhikshu, he is not really a bhikshu.

If a person who breaks the precepts dons the Dharma robes, [it is as if] he were to encase his body in sheets of hot brass.

If he takes up the bowl, then it is [as if it were] a vessel filled with molten brass.

If he consumes food, it is as if he were swallowing burning iron pellets and drinking molten brass.

If he accepts offerings or support from people, [it is as if] they are just the minion ghosts of hell who imprison him.

If he enters a monastic dwelling, [then it is as if] he is entering a great hell.

If he sits on a seat belonging to the members of the Saṃgha, [it is as if] he is sitting down on a bed of hot iron.[5]

Additionally, a person who breaks the precepts constantly experiences a feeling of fearfulness. Like a person with a serious illness, he is always afraid that death is about to come.

He is also just like a person who has committed the five heinous transgressions.[6] He constantly thinks to himself, "I am a thief who steals from the Buddha. He stays in hiding and avoids contact by staying in less-frequented places. He is just like a thief who is fearful of others. As the months and days of each year go by, he always feels ill at ease and insecure.

正體字

破戒之人雖得供養利
154c04 ‖ 樂是樂不淨。譬如愚人供養莊嚴死屍。智
154c05 ‖ 者聞之[14]惡不欲見。如是種種無量。破戒之
154c06 ‖ 罪不可稱說。行者應當一心持戒

简体字

破戒之人，虽得供养利乐，是乐不净；譬如愚人，供养庄严死尸，智者闻之，恶不欲见。如是种种无量破戒之罪，不可称说，行者应当一心持戒。

Although a person who breaks the precepts may gain the benefit and pleasure of offerings, this pleasure is not pure. This circumstance is comparable to when a fool makes offerings to a corpse and then proceeds to adorn it. When the wise hear of such a thing, they find it disgusting and do not even wish to lay eyes on it.

The measurelessly many different kinds of punishments resulting from breaking the precepts are indescribably numerous. Thus the practitioner should be single-minded in upholding the moral precepts.

正體字

154c07 [15]大智度論釋初品中戒相義[16]第二十二之一
154c08 問曰。已知如是種種功德果報。云何[17]名為
154c09 戒[18]相。答曰。惡止不更[19]作。若心生若口言若
154c10 從他受。息身口惡是為戒[*]相。云何名為
154c11 惡。若實是眾生。知是眾生發心欲殺而奪
154c12 其命。生身業有作色。是名殺生罪。其餘繫
154c13 閉鞭打等。是助殺法。復次殺他得殺罪。非
154c14 自殺身心知眾生而殺。是[20]名殺罪。不如
154c15 夜中見人謂為杌樹而殺者。故殺生得殺
154c16 罪。非不[21]故也。快心殺生得殺罪非狂癡。
154c17 命根斷是殺罪。

简体字

释戒相义

问曰：已知如是种种功德果报，云何名为戒相？

答曰：恶止不更作，是名为戒。若心生，若口言，若从他受，息身、口恶，是为戒相。云何名为恶？若实是众生，知是众生，发心欲杀而夺其命，生身业，有作色，是名杀生罪。其余系闭、鞭打等，是助杀法。

复次，杀他得杀罪，非自杀身。心知众生而杀是杀罪，不如夜中见人，谓为杌树而杀者，故杀生得杀罪，非不故也。快心杀生得杀罪，非狂痴。命根断，是杀罪，

Ch. 1, Subchapter 22: On the Details and Import of the Precepts

II. Ch. 1, Subchapter 22: On the Details and Import of the Moral Precepts

A. Precepts Defined: Cessaton of and Restraint from Evil

Question: We are already aware of the many sorts of meritorious qualities and resultant rewards [associated with the moral precepts]. What are the characteristic features of the moral precepts?

Response: They consist of the stopping of evil and the refraining from any further commission of it. This is the case whether it comes forth from the mind, whether it involves utterances by the mouth, or whether it involves external influences. It includes the putting to rest of evil on the part of the body and the mouth. These are what constitute the characteristic features of the precepts.

1. The Layperson's Precepts

a. The Five Precepts

1) The Precept Against Killing

a) Killing Defined

What constitutes evil? In this case, it is where there actually is a being, one knows it is a being, one brings forth the thought desirous of killing it and taking its life. One then brings forth the physical action and there does exist a visible physical form (*vijñapti-rūpa*). This constitutes the offense of killing a being. The other factors: the tying up, the confining, the whipping, the beating, and so forth—these are dharmas which are auxiliary to killing.

Additionally, it is when one kills another being that one incurs the offense of killing. In a circumstance where one kills one's own body—even if one knows it to be a being and then performs the act of killing, it is still not the case that this constitutes the offense of killing.

It does not qualify as an offense when one sees a person at night, thinks him to be a leafless tree trunk, and then kills him. It is when one deliberately kills a being that one incurs the killing offense. It is not the case [that an offense is incurred] when the act is not intentional. When one kills a being and does so with a pleased mind, one incurs the offense of killing. In a circumstance where one is not in a state of crazed delusion and then the root of life is cut off, this constitutes the offense of killing.

正體字

非作瘡身業是殺罪。非但口
154c18 教勅口教是殺罪。非但心[22]生如是等名殺
154c19 [23]罪。不作是罪名為戒。若人受戒心生口
154c20 言。我從今日不復殺生。若身不動口不言。
154c21 而獨心生自誓。我從今日不復殺生。是名
154c22 不殺生戒。有人言。是不殺生戒或善或無記。
154c23 問曰。如阿毘曇中說。一切戒律儀皆善。今何
154c24 以言無記。答曰。如迦栴延子阿毘曇中言一
154c25 切善。如餘阿毘曇中言。不殺戒或善或無記。
154c26 何以故。若不殺戒常善者。持此戒人應如
154c27 得道人常不墮惡道。以是故或時應無記。
154c28 無記無[24]果報故。不生天上人中。問曰。不
154c29 以戒無記故墮地獄。更有惡心生故墮地
155a01 獄。答曰。不殺生得無量善法。作無作福

简体字

非作疮。身业是杀罪，非但口教敕。口教是杀罪，非但心生恶。如是等名杀罪相；不作是罪，名为戒。若人受戒，心生、口言："我从今日不复杀生！"若身不动，口不言，而独心生自誓："我从今日不复杀生！"是名不杀生戒。有人言："是不杀生戒，或善、或无记。"

问曰：如阿毗昙中说：一切戒律仪皆善。今何以言无记？

答曰：如迦旃延子阿毗昙中，言一切善；如余阿毗昙中，言不杀戒，或善、或无记。何以故？若不杀戒常善者，持此戒人，应如得道人，常不堕恶道。以是故，或时应无记；无记无报故，不生天上人中。

问曰：不以戒无记故堕地狱，更有恶心生故堕地狱？

答曰：不杀生，得无量善法，作、无作福

It is not the case that the physical action of creating a wound in itself constitutes the offense of killing. It is not the case that when one has only given the verbal instructions as an order [to kill] that those verbal instructions in and of themselves constitute the offense of killing. Nor is it the case that merely the mind's generation of these sorts of things constitutes a killing offense. It is refraining from committing this offense that constitutes [upholding] the precept.

In an instance in which a person takes the precept, the thought arises and the mouth speaks, saying, "From this day on, I will not again kill beings." If it happens that the body does not actually move and the mouth does not actually speak, but the mind alone makes the vow to oneself, resolving that "From this very day onward, I will refrain from ever again killing beings," this *does* constitute the precept against killing.

There are those who say that this precept against killing may be categorized as "good" or it may be categorized as "neutral."

Question: According to the testimony of the Abhidharma, all moral regulations associated with the precepts are good. Why then do you now say that they may be "neutral"?

b) Abhidharmic Analysis of Killing Precept

Response: According to the Abhidharma of Kātyāyanīputra they are all categorized as "good."[7] According to the statements contained in other *abhidharmas*, the precept of not killing may be good or it may be neutral. Why? If it were the case that the not killing precept were always good, then it ought to be the case that those who uphold this precept should never fall into the wretched destinies just as in the case of those who have already gained realization of the path. Using this rationale as a basis, there may be times when it should be neutral. Because that which is neutral has no resulting retribution, it may be the case that one has no resulting rebirth in the heavens or in the human realm [solely traceable to having adhered to this particular moral precept].

Question: It is not the case that one would fall into the hells based solely on the neutrality of a precept. It is because of the additional factors associated with the generation of evil thoughts that one falls into the hells.

Response: By not killing beings, one develops an immeasurable number of good dharmas. This is because the creating of merit through non-commission of the offense is accumulating constantly

正體字

常日
155a02 夜生故。若作少罪有限有量。何以故。隨有
155a03 量而不[1]隨無量。以是故知。不殺戒中或有
155a04 無記。復次有人不從師受戒。而但心生自
155a05 誓。我從今日不復殺生。如是不殺或時[2]無
155a06 記。問曰。是不殺戒何界繫。答曰。如迦栴延
155a07 子阿毘曇中言一切受戒律儀。皆欲界繫。餘
155a08 阿毘曇中言。或欲界繫或不繫。以實言之應
155a09 有三種。或欲界繫或色界繫或[3]無漏。殺生法
155a10 雖欲界。不殺戒應隨殺在欲界。但色界不
155a11 殺。無漏不殺遠遮故。是真不殺戒。復次有人
155a12 不受戒。而從生已來不好殺生。或善或無
155a13 記是名無記。是不殺生[4]法非心非心數法
155a14 亦非心相應。或共心生或不共心生。迦栴
155a15 延子阿毘曇中言。不殺生是身口業。

简体字

常日夜生故；若作少罪，有限、有量。何以故随有量而不随无量？以是故，知不杀戒中，或有无记。

复次，有人不从师受戒，而但心生自誓："我从今日不复杀生。"如是不杀，或时无记。

问曰：是不杀戒何界系？

答曰：如迦旃延子阿毗昙中言：一切受戒律仪，皆欲界系。余阿毗昙中言：或欲界系，或不系。以实言之，应有三种：或欲界系，或色界系，或不系。杀生法虽欲界，不杀戒，应随杀在欲界；但色界不杀，无漏不杀，远遮故，是真不杀戒。

复次，有人不受戒，而从生已来，不好杀生，或善、或无记，是名无记。是不杀生法，非心、非心数法，亦非心相应；或共心生，或不共心生。迦旃延子阿毗昙中言：不杀生是身、口业，

day and night. However, if one is simultaneously committing a few karmic offenses, one's merit then becomes limited and measurable. How is this so? The relative balance gravitates toward that which is measurable and does not go the way of the immeasurable. It is on this basis that one can realize that within the sphere of the not killing precept, there may be instances in which it becomes "neutral."

Moreover, there are those people who do not receive the precepts from a Master but who only bring forth in their minds a vow to themselves, "From this day on, I shall no longer kill any beings." The refraining from killing under this sort of circumstance may have times when it is only neutral.

Question: To which of the realms is this precept requiring abstention from killing connected?

Response: According to the statements in the Abhidharma of Kātyāyanīputra, all moral regulations associated with received precepts are connected to the desire realm. According to statements in other *abhidharmas,* it may be connected to the desire realm or may not be connected to any realm at all. To speak of it in a manner corresponding to reality, there are three ways of classifying it: It may be connected to the desire realm; it may be connected to the form realm; or it may be connected to states beyond the contaminants (*āsrava*).

Although it would seem that the not-killing precept should be most properly associated with the desire realm where killing is actually carried out, because in the form realm and realms free of the contaminants one is far removed from actually engaging in killing, it is those spheres which best exemplify the true implementation of the not-killing precept.

Additionally, there are those people who do not actually take the killing precept but who, from birth onwards, nonetheless find no pleasure in killing beings. [Abstention from killing] may be either "good" or "neutral." This is one of those circumstances qualifying as "neutral."

c) Additional Abhidharma Analytic Data

This dharma of abstention from killing is not mind, is not a mind dharma, and is not a dharma associated with the mind. It may arise in association with the mind or it may be that it does not arise in association with the mind.

It is stated in the Abhidharma of Kātyāyanīputra that abstention from killing beings is either body karma or mouth karma, that

正體字

或作色
155a16 ‖ 或無作色。或[5]時隨心行或不隨心行。[6](丹注云隨心行
155a17 ‖ 定共戒不隨心意五戒)非先世業報。二種修應修。二種證
155a18 ‖ 應證。[7](丹注云身證慧證)思惟斷一切欲界最後得見
155a19 ‖ 斷時斷。凡夫聖人所得是色法。或可見或不
155a20 ‖ 可見法。或有對法或無對法。有報法有果法。
155a21 ‖ 有漏法有為法有上法。[8](丹注云非極故有上)非相應因。
155a22 ‖ 如是等分別是名不殺戒。問曰。八直道中戒
155a23 ‖ 亦不殺生。何以獨言不殺生戒有報有漏。答
155a24 ‖ 曰。此中但說受戒律儀[9]法。不說無漏[10]戒
155a25 ‖ 律儀。復次餘阿毘曇中言。不殺法常不逐心
155a26 ‖ 行。非身口業。不隨心業行。或有報或無報
155a27 ‖ [11]非心相應法或有漏或無漏。是為異法。餘
155a28 ‖ 者[12]皆同。

简体字

或作色，或无作色，或随心行，或不随心行，非先世业报。二种修应修，二种证应证。思惟断，一切欲界最后得；见断、时断，凡夫圣人所得。是色法，或可见，或不可见法；或有对法，或无对法；有报法，有果法，有漏法，有为法，有上法，非相应因。如是等分别，是名不杀戒。

问曰：八直道中戒，亦不杀生，何以独言不杀生戒有报、有漏？

答曰：此中但说受戒律仪法，不说无漏戒律仪。

复次，余阿毗昙中言：不杀法常不逐心行，非身口业；不随心业行，或有报，或无报；或有漏，或无漏；是为异法，余者皆同。

it may involve visible or invisible form, that it may conform with actions of the mind or may not conform with the actions of the mind. It is not the case that it constitutes karmic retribution from earlier lives. (Chinese textual note: The notes in red state that "conforming with the mind" refers to "precepts linked to meditative absorption" whereas "not conforming with the mind" refers to the five precepts.)

There are two types of cultivation that should be cultivated and two types of realization that should be realized. (Chinese textual note: The notes in red state that this refers to "physical realization" and "wisdom realization.") There is severance through thought. In all desire realms, it is the last to be achieved. This may involve severance through cognition or severance linked to a particular temporal circumstance.

That which is gained by both the common person and an *ārya* is a form dharma. It may be visible or it may be invisible. It may involve a dharma that is opposable or it may involve a dharma that is not opposable. It is a dharma that has a reward. It is a dharma that has a fruition. It is a dharma that may involve the contaminants. It is a conditioned dharma. It is a surpassable dharma. (Chinese textual note: The notes in red state that it is surpassable because it is not ultimate.) It is a non-corresponding cause. Analyses such as these are employed [in *abhidharma* writings] to describe the precept forbidding killing.

Question: The killing of beings is also forbidden by the moral-precept standard included in the eightfold right path. Why do you merely note here that the precept of abstention from killing beings has a retribution and may involve the contaminants?

Response: We discuss herein only the regulatory dharmas associated with taking the precepts. We do not discuss here the regulations associated with beings who have become free of the contaminants. Moreover, in other *abhidharmas,* it is stated that the dharma of abstention from killing is practiced through the mind's constantly avoiding pursuit [of ideation tending toward killing], that it is not the case that it constitutes karma of the body or mouth, that it is practiced through refraining from following along with the karma associated with one's mind, that it may or may not involve karmic retribution, that it is not a dharma associated with the mind, and that it may or may not involve the contaminants. These are dharmas that vary [in their analysis from author to author]. They are in agreement on the other issues.[8]

正體字

復有言。諸佛賢聖不戲論諸法。
155a29 | [13](丹注云種種異說名為戲也)現前眾生各各惜命。
是故佛言。
155b01 | 莫奪他命。奪他命世世受諸苦痛。眾生有
155b02 | 無後當說。問曰。人能以力勝人并國殺怨。
155b03 | 或田獵皮肉所濟處大。[14]令不殺生得何等
155b04 | 利。答曰。得無所畏安樂無怖。我以無害
155b05 | 於彼故。彼亦無害於我。以是故無怖無
155b06 | 畏。好殺之人雖復位極人王。亦不自安。如
155b07 | 持戒之人。單[15]行獨遊無所畏難。復次好殺
155b08 | 之人。有命之屬皆不喜見。若不好殺。一切
155b09 | 眾生皆樂依附。復次持戒之人。命欲終時其
155b10 | 心安樂無疑無悔。若生天上若在人中常
155b11 | 得長壽。是為得道因緣。乃至得佛住壽無
155b12 | 量。復次殺生之人。今世後世受種種身心苦
155b13 | 痛。不殺之人無此眾難。是為大利。

简体字

复有言："诸佛贤圣不戏论诸法，现前众生各各惜命，是故佛言莫夺他命；夺他命，世世受诸苦痛。"众生有、无后当说。

问曰：人能以力胜人，并国杀怨，或田猎皮肉，所济处大；今不杀生，得何等利？

答曰：得无所畏，安乐无怖。我以无害于彼故，彼亦无害于我，以是故，无怖无畏。好杀之人，虽复位极人王，亦不自安；如持戒之人，单独游行，无所畏难。

复次，好杀之人，有命之属皆不喜见。若不好杀，一切众生皆乐依附。

复次，持戒之人，命欲终时，其心安乐，无疑无悔；若生天上，若在人中，常得长寿；是为得道因缘，乃至得佛，住寿无量。

复次，杀生之人，今世、后世受种种身心苦痛。不杀之人，无此众难，是为大利。

d) Resumption of Expository Killing Precept Discussion

There are yet others who make the point that the Buddhas, the Worthies, and the Āryas are not inclined toward frivolous debate about dharmas and that, no matter which being one may encounter, in all cases it is inclined to cherish its own life. Therefore the Buddha said, "Do not take another's life. If one takes another's life, one will be bound to undergo all manner of bitter pain in life after life." The issue of whether or not beings actually exist shall be discussed later on. (Chinese textual note: The notes in red state that the "frivolous" [in "frivolous debate"] refers to all sorts of divergent discussions.)

i) Objection: Killing is Justified. Why Abstain?

Question: People are able to use their strength to be victorious over others, annex adjacent countries, and kill their enemies. The skins and meat hunted in the field may provide great benefits in rescuing [people from hunger]. What then is the value of preventing one from killing beings?

ii) Refutation of Arguments for Killing

Response: One gains from this a state of fearlessness. One becomes peaceful, happy and free of dread. Because there has been no harm on my part toward others, they harbor no harmful intentions toward me, either. On account of this, one is never terrified and abides in fearlessness. Although a man who likes to kill may rise to the highest position in which he becomes a king among men, he is still not at peace with himself. However, if one is a man who upholds the precepts, he may travel by himself and roam about alone, fearing nothing, and encountering no calamities.

Moreover, any being who possesses a life span does not enjoy encountering a person who takes pleasure in killing. If one dislikes killing, all beings happily rely on him. Again, when the life of a person who upholds the precepts is about to come to its end, his mind is at peace, happy, free of doubts, and free of regrets. Then, whether he is reborn in the heavens or among men, he always gains a long life span. This behavior constitutes a cause and condition for realizing the path. When such a person finally achieves buddhahood, his lifespan in the world is incalculably long.

Additionally, in both present and future lives, a person who kills beings experiences all kinds of physical and mental bitterness and pain. A person who refrains from killing remains free of such manifold difficulties. This amounts to a great benefit.

正體字

復次行
155b14 者思惟。我自惜命愛身。彼亦如是與我何
155b15 異。以是之故不應殺生。復次若[16]人殺生者。
155b16 為善人所訶怨家所嫉。負他命故常有
155b17 怖畏為彼所憎。死時心悔當墮地獄若畜
155b18 生中。若出為人常當短命。復次假令後世
155b19 無罪。不為善人所訶怨家所嫉。尚不應
155b20 故奪他命。何以故。善相之人所不應行。何
155b21 況[17]兩世有罪弊惡果報。復次殺為罪中之
155b22 重。何以故人有死急不惜重寶。但以活命
155b23 為先。譬如賈客[18]入海採寶。垂出大海其
155b24 船卒壞珍寶失盡。而自喜慶舉手而言。幾失
155b25 大寶。眾人怪言。汝失財物裸形得脫。云何
155b26 喜言幾失大寶。答言。一切寶中人命第一。人
155b27 為命故求財。不為財故求命。以是故。佛
155b28 說十不善道中殺[19]罪最在初。五戒中亦最在
155b29 初。若人種種修諸福德。而無不殺生戒

简体字

复次，行者思惟："我自惜命、爱身，彼亦如是，与我何异？以是之故，不应杀生。"

复次，若杀生者，为善人所诃，怨家所嫉；负他命故，常有怖畏，为彼所憎；死时心悔，当堕地狱，若畜生中；若出为人，常当短命。

复次，假令后世无罪，不为善人所诃、怨家所嫉，尚不应故夺他命。何以故？善相之人所不应行；何况两世有罪，弊恶果报！

复次，杀为罪中之重。何以故？人有死急，不惜重宝，但以活命为先。譬如贾客入海采宝，垂出大海，其船卒坏，珍宝失尽，而自喜庆，举手而言："几失大宝！"众人怪言："汝失财物，裸形得脱，云何喜言几失大宝？"答言："一切宝中，人命第一；人为命故求财，不为财故求命。"以是故，佛说十不善道中，杀最在初；五戒中亦最在初。若人种种修诸福德，而无不杀生戒，

Furthermore, the practitioner reflects to himself, "I cherish my own life and am fond of this body. Others are the same in this respect. How are they any different from me? I should therefore refrain from killing any being."

Moreover, if one is a killer of beings, he is denounced by good people and is hated by his enemies. Because he is responsible for taking the lives of others, he is constantly afflicted with fearfulness and is detested by those beings.[9] When he dies, his mind is full of regrets and he is bound to fall into the hells or into the realm of animals. When he emerges from those realms, his lifespan is bound to always be brief.

Then again, even if one were able to cause there to be no karmic retributions in later lives, no denunciation by good people, and no detestation by enemies, one should still refrain from deliberately taking another's life. Why? This is a thing which should not be done by those who are good. How much the more so is this the case where one encounters in both eras[10] the resulting retribution arising from the baseness and evil of one's own offenses.

Furthermore, killing amounts to the most serious of all offenses. How is this so? When a person encounters a life-threatening situation, he will not spare even the most valuable treasures [in the quest to save his own life]. He takes simply being able to survive as what is of primary importance.

e) The Merchant Who Lost His Jewels (Story)

This principle is illustrated by the case of the merchant who went to sea to gather jewels. When he had just about gotten back from the great sea, his boat suddenly broke apart and the precious jewels were all lost. He was nonetheless overjoyed and exultant, throwing up his hands and exclaiming, "I almost lost a great jewel!"

Everyone thought this strange and said, "You lost all your valuable possessions and escaped without even any clothes on your back. How can you joyfully exclaim, "I almost lost a great jewel!"

He replied, "Among all the jewels, a person's life is foremost. It is for the sake of their lives that people seek wealth. It is not that they seek to live for the sake of wealth."

f) Killing as the Worst and Not Killing as the Finest of Actions

It is for this reason that the Buddha said that, among the ten bad karmic actions, the offense of killing is foremost. It is also foremost among the five precepts. Even if a person cultivates all sorts of merit, so long as he does not have the precept against taking life,

正體字

則
155c01 無所益。何以故。雖在富貴處生勢力豪強。
155c02 而無壽命誰受此樂。以是故知。諸餘罪中
155c03 殺罪最重。諸功德中不殺第一。世間中惜命
155c04 為第一。何以知之。一切世人甘受刑罰[20]刑
155c05 殘[*]考掠以護壽命。復次若有人受戒心[21]生。
155c06 從今日不殺一切眾生。是於無量眾生中。
155c07 [22]已以所愛重物施與。所得功德亦復無量。
155c08 如佛說有五大施。何等五。一者不殺生是為
155c09 最大施。不盜不邪婬不妄語不飲酒亦復如
155c10 是。復次行慈三昧其福無量。水火不害刀
155c11 兵不傷。一切惡毒所不能[23]中。以五大施
155c12 故所得如是。復次三世十方中尊佛為第
155c13 一。如佛語難提迦優婆塞。殺生有十罪。何
155c14 等為十。一者心常懷毒世世不絕。二者眾
155c15 生憎惡眼不喜見。三者常懷惡念思惟惡
155c16 事。四者眾生畏之如見蛇虎。

简体字

则无所益。何以故？虽在富贵处生，势力豪强而无寿命，谁受此乐？以是故，知诸余罪中，杀罪最重；诸功德中，不杀第一。世间中惜命为第一，何以知之？一切世人，甘受刑罚、刑残拷掠以护寿命。

复次，若有人受戒，心生口言："从今日不杀一切众生。"是于无量众生中，以所爱重物施与，所得功德亦复无量。如佛说："有五大施。何等五？一者、不杀生，是为最大施；不盗、不邪淫、不妄语、不饮酒，亦复如是。"

复次，行慈三昧，其福无量，水火不害，刀兵不伤，一切恶毒所不能中；以五大施故，所得如是。

复次，三世十方中尊，佛为第一。如佛语难提迦优婆塞："杀生有十罪。何等为十？一者、心常怀毒，世世不绝；二者、众生憎恶，眼不喜见；三者、常怀恶念，思惟恶事；四者、众生畏之，如见蛇虎；

there is nothing to be gained from it. Why? Even though one might be born into a circumstance in which one enjoys karmic blessings and noble birth attended by the power of aristocratic connections, if he still does not have a long lifespan, who would be able [to survive long enough] to experience such bliss?[11]

For these reasons, one knows that, among all of the offenses, the offense of killing is the most serious and, among all of the meritorious practices, refraining from killing is foremost. In the world, it is the preserving of one's own life which is the primary concern. How do we know this? Everyone in the world would agree to undergo the physical cruelty of corporeal punishment, including even beating and flogging, in order to spare their own lives.

Then again, if the thought to take on the moral precepts arises in a person in such a way that he thinks, "From this very day onward, I shall not kill any beings," by doing this he has already given a gift to an incalculable number of beings of something that they prize as valuable. The merit which he gains thereby is also incalculable.

According to what the Buddha said, there are five great gifts. What are the five? The first is not killing beings. This is the greatest gift. Not stealing, not engaging in sexual misconduct, not lying, and not drinking intoxicants are the others which are the similar in this respect.

Additionally, the merit of practicing the samādhi of kindness (*maitrī-samādhi*) is incalculable. Water and fire will not harm one. Knives and military weapons will not injure one. No matter what the evil poison, one is unable to be poisoned by it. These are the sorts of things that one gains from giving the five great gifts.

g) Ten Karmic Effects from Killing

Moreover, the Buddha, foremost among all revered throughout the three periods of time and ten directions, told the *upāsaka* Nandika, "There are ten punishments that accrue from killing beings. What are the ten?

1. In life after life without cease, one's mind constantly nurtures a poisonous disposition.
2. Beings detest, regard as evil, and find no joy in seeing such a person.
3. One constantly cherishes malicious thoughts and contemplates evil endeavors.
4. Beings fear one just as if they had encountered a snake or tiger.

正體字

五者睡時心
155c17 怖覺亦不安。六者常有惡夢。七者命終之時
155c18 狂怖惡死。八者種短命業因緣。九者身壞命
155c19 終墮[24]泥梨中。十者若出為人常當短命。復
155c20 次行者心念。一切有命乃至[25]昆虫皆自惜身。
155c21 云何以衣服飲食。自為身故而殺眾生。復
155c22 次行者當學大人法。一切大人中佛為最
155c23 大。何以故。一切智慧成就十力具足。能度眾
155c24 生常行慈愍。持不殺戒自致得佛。亦教弟
155c25 子行此慈愍。行者欲學大人行故亦當不
155c26 殺。問曰。不侵我者殺心可息。若為侵害強
155c27 奪逼迫。是當云何。答曰。應當量其輕重。若
155c28 人殺己先自思惟。[26]全戒利重[＊]全身為重。
155c29 破戒為失喪身為失。如是思惟已。知持戒
156a01 為重[＊]全身

简体字

五者、睡时心怖，觉亦不安；六者、常有恶梦；七者、命终之时，狂怖恶死；八者、种短命业因缘；九者、身坏命终，堕泥犁中；十者、若出为人，常当短命。”

复次，行者心念：“一切有命，乃至蜫虫，皆自惜身；云何以衣服、饮食自为身故而杀众生？”

复次，行者当学大人法。一切大人中，佛为最大。何以故？一切智慧成就，十力具足，能度众生，常行慈愍，持不杀戒，自致得佛，亦教弟子行此慈愍。行者欲学大人行故，亦当不杀。

问曰：不侵我者，杀心可息；若为侵害、强夺、逼迫，是当云何？

答曰：应当量其轻重。若人杀己，先自思惟：“全戒利重？全身为重？破戒为失？丧身为失？”如是思惟已，知持戒为重，全身

5. One becomes terrified when asleep and unable to be at peace when awake.
6. One always has bad dreams.
7. As one's life draws to an end, one descends into madness and terror of dying.
8. One plants the karmic causes and conditions for having only a brief life.
9. When the body deteriorates and one's life ends, one falls into *niraya* (the hells).
10. When one emerges and finally regains human rebirth, one is bound to always have only a short life.

h) Contemplations to Reinforce Not Killing

Additionally, the practitioner thinks to himself, "All things possessed of life, including even the insects, cherish their own physical bodies. How could one kill beings for clothing, food and drink, or for the sake of one's own body?"

Moreover, the practitioner should study the dharmas of the great men. Among all the great men, the Buddha is the greatest. How is this so? He has perfected every sort of wisdom and has brought the ten powers to complete fulfillment. He is able to liberate beings and he constantly implements kindness and pity. It was through upholding the precept against killing that he arrived at the achievement of buddhahood. He then also instructed his disciples to course in this kindness and pity. Because the practitioner wishes to emulate the practices of the great men, he too ought to refrain from killing.

i) Objection: What If My Life Is Threatened?

Question: If it is not a case of my being attacked, then the thought of killing may be put to rest. However, if one has been attacked, overcome by force, and is then being coerced by imminent peril, what should one do then?

Reply: One should weigh the relative gravity of the alternatives. If someone is about to take one's life, one should first consider whether the benefit from preserving the precept is more important or whether the benefit from preserving one's physical life is more important, considering also whether it is precept breakage that determines loss or whether it is physical demise that determines what amounts to a loss.

After having reflected in this manner, one realizes that maintaining the precept is momentous and that preserving one's physical

正體字

為輕。若苟免[*]全身身何所得。
156a02 是身名為老病死藪。必當壞敗。若為持戒
156a03 失身其利甚重。又復思惟。我前後失身世世
156a04 無數。或作惡賊禽獸之身。但為財利諸不善
156a05 事。今乃得為持淨戒故。不惜此身捨命
156a06 持戒。勝於毀禁[*]全身。百千萬[1]倍不[2]可
156a07 為喻。如是定心應當捨身。以護淨戒。如
156a08 一須陀洹人。生屠殺家年向成人。應當修
156a09 其家業而不肯殺生。父母與刀并一口羊
156a10 閉著屋中。而語之言。若不殺羊。不令汝出
156a11 得見日月生活飲食。兒自思惟言。我若殺
156a12 此一羊。便當終為此業。豈以身故為此大罪。
156a13 便以刀自殺。父母開戶見。羊在一面立兒
156a14 已命絕。當自殺時即生天上。若如此者是
156a15 為不惜壽命[*]全護淨戒。如是等義是名
156a16 不殺生戒。

简体字

为轻。若苟免全身，身何所得？是身名为老病死薮，必当坏败！若为持戒失身，其利甚重。又复思惟：“我前后失身，世世无数，或作恶贼、禽兽之身，但为财利诸不善事；今乃得为持净戒故，不惜此身，舍命持戒，胜于毁禁全身百千万倍，不可为喻。”如是定心，应当舍身以护净戒。如一须陀洹人，生屠杀家；年向成人，应当修其家业而不肯杀生。父母与刀，并一口羊，闭著屋中而语之言：“若不杀羊，不令汝出、得见日月、生活饮食！”儿自思惟言：“我若杀此一羊，便当终为此业，岂以身故为此大罪？”便以刀自杀。父母开户，见羊在一面立，儿已命绝。当自杀时，即生天上。若如此者，是为不惜寿命，全护净戒。如是等义，是名不杀生戒。

life is a minor matter. If in avoiding peril one is able only to succeed in preserving one's body, then what advantage is gained with having preserved the body? This body is the swamp of senescence, disease, and death. It will inevitably deteriorate and decay. However, if it is for the sake of upholding the precept that one loses one's body, the benefit of that is extremely consequential.

Furthermore, one should consider thus: "From the past on up to the present, I have lost my life an innumerable number of times. At turns, I have taken birth as a malevolent brigand or as a bird or beast where I have lived solely for profit or all manner of other unworthy pursuits.

"I have now encountered a situation in which [loss of life] might be for the sake of preserving the purity of the moral precepts. To not be stinting of this body and to sacrifice my life to uphold the precepts would be a billion times better than, and in fact incomparable, to merely safeguarding my body at the expense of violating the prohibitions." Thus one may decide in this manner that one should forsake the body in order to protect the integrity of the pure precepts.

j) The Butcher's Son Refuses to Kill (Story)

For example, there once was a man who, having reached the rank of *srota-āpanna*,[12] had taken rebirth into the family of a butcher and then grown up to the threshold of adulthood. Although he was expected to pursue his household occupation, he was unable to kill animals. His father and mother gave him a knife and a sheep and shut him up in a room, telling him, "If you do not kill the sheep, we will not allow you to come out and see the sun or the moon, or to have the food and drink necessary for your own survival."

The son thought to himself, "If I kill this sheep, then I will be compelled to pursue this occupation my entire life. How could I commit such a great crime solely for the sake of this body?" He then took up the knife and killed himself. The father and mother eventually opened the door to take a look only to discover that the sheep was standing off to one side whilst the son was laying there, already deceased.[13]

Having killed himself, he then took rebirth in the heavens. If one were to act in this manner, this would amount to not sparing even one's own life in safeguarding the integrity of the pure precepts.

Concepts such as we have treated here form the bases for the precept against killing.

正體字

不與取者。知他物生盜心。取物
156a17 | 去離本處物屬我。是名盜。若不作是名不
156a18 | 盜。其餘方便[3]計挍。乃至手捉未離地[4]者
156a19 | 名助盜法。財物有二種。有屬他有不屬
156a20 | 他。取屬他物是[5]為盜罪。屬他物亦有二
156a21 | 種。一者聚落中二者空地。此二處物。盜心取
156a22 | 得盜罪若物在空地當撿挍。知是物近誰
156a23 | 國。是物應當[6]有屬不應取。如毘尼中說
156a24 | 種種不盜。是名不盜相。問曰。不盜有何等
156a25 | 利。答曰。人命有二種。一者內。二者外。若奪
156a26 | 財物是為奪外命。何以故。命依飲食衣[7]被
156a27 | [8]等故活。若劫若奪是名奪外命。如[9]偈說
156a28 | 一切諸眾生　衣食以自活
156a29 | 若奪若劫取　是名劫奪命
156b01 | 以是事故有智之人不應劫奪。

简体字

不与取者，知他物，生盗心，取物去离本处，物属我，是名盗。若不作，是名不盗。其余方便校计，乃至手捉未离地者，是名助盗法。财物有二种：有属他，有不属他。取属他物，是盗罪。属他物亦有二种：一者、聚落中，二者、空地。此二处物，盗心取，得盗罪。若物在空地，当检校知是物近谁国？是物应当有属，不应取。如毗尼中说种种不盗，是名不盗相。

问曰：不盗有何等利？

答曰：人命有二种：一者、内，二者、外。若夺财物，是为夺外命。何以故？命依饮食、衣被等故活，若劫若夺，是名夺外命。如偈说：

“一切诸众生，衣食以自活；若夺若劫取，是名劫夺命。”

以是事故，有智之人不应劫夺。

2) The Precept Against Stealing

a) Stealing Defined

As for taking what is not given, if one knows it is something belonging to another, if one brings forth a thought intent on stealing it, if one takes that thing away from its original location, and if the thing is then considered to be "mine," this is what is meant by stealing. If one does not do this, then this amounts to refraining from stealing. The other associated factors, from the planning of the act on up to and including grasping it with the hand when it has not yet left the ground—these constitute dharmas auxiliary to stealing.

Valuable objects are of two types: those which belong to someone else and those which do not belong to someone else. If one takes a thing which belongs to someone else, this constitutes an offense of stealing.

Things which belong to someone else are also of two kinds: those which are within the boundaries of a village and those which are in the wilderness. If one's taking of things from either of these places is accompanied by a mind intent on stealing, then one incurs the offense of stealing. If the object is in the wilderness, then one should consider critically and come to an understanding as to whose kingdom this object might be in close proximity to, and as to whether or not it has an owner and thus should not be taken. Accordance with the Vinaya[14] discussions of the various circumstances not constituting stealing defines the character of what does not qualify as stealing.

b) The Benefits of Not Stealing

Question: What are the benefits of refraining from stealing?

Response: There are two parts to a person's life, that which is inward and that which is outward. If one steals someone's valuables, this amounts to stealing his outward life. How is this so? Life depends upon drink, food, clothing, bedding, and other such things by which he is therefore able to survive. If one robs someone of these things or steals them, this amounts to stealing the outward bases of his life. This is as described in a verse:

Each and every one of all the beings
depends on clothes and food for his own survival.
Whether one takes by stealing or by robbing,
this amounts to robbing or stealing someone's life.

On account of this fact, a wise person should refrain from robbing or stealing.

正體字

復次當自
156b02 思惟。劫奪得物以自供養。雖身充足會亦
156b03 當死。死入地獄。家室親屬雖共受樂。獨自
156b04 受罪。亦不能救。已得此觀應當不盜。復
156b05 次是不與取有二種。一者偷。二者劫。此二共
156b06 名不與取。於不與取中盜為最重。何以故。
156b07 一切人以財自活。而或[10]穿踰盜取是最不
156b08 淨。何以[11]故。無力勝人畏死。盜取故。劫奪之
156b09 中盜為[12]罪重。如偈說
156b10 飢餓身羸瘦　　受罪大苦[13]劇
156b11 他物不可觸　　譬如大火聚
156b12 若盜取他物　　其主泣[14]懊惱
156b13 假使天王等　　猶亦以為苦
156b14 殺生人罪雖重。然於所殺者是賊。偷盜人
156b15 於一切有物人中賊。若犯餘戒。於異國中
156b16 有不以為罪者。[15]若偷盜人。一切諸國無不
156b17 治罪。

简体字

复次，当自思惟：“劫夺得物，以自供养，虽身充足，会亦当死；死入地狱，家室亲属虽共受乐，独自受罪，亦不能救。”已得此观，应当不盗。

复次，是不与取有二种：一者、偷，二者、劫，此二共名不与取。于不与取中，盗为最重。何以故？一切人以财自活，而或穿窬盗取，是最不净。何以故？无力胜人，畏死盗取故。劫夺之中，盗为重罪，如偈说：

“饥饿身羸瘦，受罪大苦处；他物不可触，譬如大火聚。

若盗取他物，其主泣懊恼，假使天王等，犹亦以为苦。”

杀生人罪虽重，然于所杀者是贼，偷盗人于一切有物人中贼。若犯余戒，于异国中有不以为罪者；偷盗人，一切诸国无不治罪。

Moreover, one ought to reflect, "If it is by robbing or by stealing that one obtains the things that he gives to himself, even though he may be personally well provided for, he will nonetheless come to that time when he too must die. On dying, he will enter the hells. Then, even though his family might still be experiencing bliss, he will be compelled to undergo punishment all by himself and will then be ensconced in a situation from which he cannot be rescued." Having contemplated in this fashion, one should then refrain from stealing.

c) Two Main Categories of Stealing

Additionally, this [offense of] "taking what is not given" falls into two categories: The first is stealing. The second is robbery. They are both generally referred to as "taking what is not given."

d) The Reprehensibility of Robbery in Particular

Within the sphere of taking what is not given, robbery is the most serious form of the offense. How is this so? All people rely upon their wealth to keep themselves alive. If one nonetheless breaks in and commits robbery, this constitutes the most defiled sort of conduct. Why? It is because one has no power in such circumstances to allay the victim's fear of being murdered. It is because, in the course of committing robbery, one [forcefully] seizes possessions that robbery is the most serious class of stealing offense. This is as described in a verse:

> Hungry and starving, one's body emaciated and thin,
> one undergoes punishment amidst intensely great suffering.[15]
> The belongings of others cannot even be touched,
> for they are like a great flaming bonfire.
>
> If one seizes through robbery the possessions of others,
> their owners start weeping in anguished affliction.
> Even if one were a king of the gods or one of that sort,
> one would still look on this as freighted with suffering.

e) The Gravity and Universal Condemnation of Theft

Although one does commit a serious offense by killing, still, from the standpoint of the victim of the killing, he is seen as having acted as a thief [of a life]. A person who steals is a thief to all people who own material possessions. If one transgresses against other precepts, it may be that in other countries there are those who do not take that to constitute an offense. However, if one is a person who steals, there is no country that does not punish it as an offense.

正體字

問曰。刧奪之人。今世有人讚美其健。
156b18 於此刧奪何以[16]不作。答曰。不與[17]而盜是
156b19 不善相。刧盜之中雖有差降俱為不善。譬
156b20 如美食雜毒惡食雜毒。美惡雖殊雜毒不
156b21 異。亦如明闇蹈火晝夜雖異燒足一也。今
156b22 世愚人不識罪福二世果報。無仁慈心。見
156b23 人能以力相侵強奪他財。讚以為[18]強。諸佛
156b24 賢聖慈愍一切。了達三世殃[19]禍不朽。所不
156b25 稱譽。以是故知刧盜之罪俱為不善。善人行
156b26 者之所不為。如佛說。不與取有十罪。何等
156b27 為十。一者物主常瞋。二者重疑[20](丹注云重罪人疑)三
156b28 者非[21]行時不籌量。

简体字

问曰：劫夺之人，今世有人赞美其健，于此劫夺，何以放舍？

答曰：不与而偷盗，是不善相；劫盗之中，虽有差降，俱为不善。譬如美食杂毒，恶食杂毒，美恶虽殊，杂毒不异。亦如明闇蹈火，昼夜虽异，烧足一也。今世愚人，不识罪、福二世果报，无仁慈心；见人能以力相侵，强夺他财，赞以为强。诸佛贤圣，慈愍一切，了达三世殃祸不朽，所不称誉。以是故，知劫盗之罪，俱为不善，善人行者之所不为。如佛说："不与取有十罪。何等为十？一者、物主常瞋；二者、重疑（重罪人疑）；三者、非时行，不筹量；

f) Objection: But Isn't the Very Boldness Admirable?

Question: As for people who engage in robbery by force, there are people in the present era who praise them and see their boldness as admirable. Why then should one refrain from engaging in this sort of thievery?

g) Condemnation of Theft of Any Sort

Response: If one takes something which has not been given, this is an act characterized by unwholesomeness. Although there are lesser infractions within the realm of stealing, all of them are inherently bad. This is comparable to mixing poison into fine food or mixing poison into bad food. Although there may be distinctions between fine and poor cuisine, still, in the sense that they have both been mixed with poison, they do not differ at all.

This is also comparable to stepping into fire when it is light out and when it is dark. Although there is the difference of day as opposed to night, they are the same as regards the burning of one's feet. The foolish people of the present age are not aware of the resultant retribution from offenses and merit as it occurs in the two periods of time. Devoid of thoughts of humanity and kindness, they observe that a man is able to use his strength to invade and take another's wealth by force and then praise it as being a measure of his power.

The Buddhas, the Worthies, and the Āryas maintain kindness and pity for all. They have completely understood that there is no fading away of the [inevitability of] encountering disasters and misfortunes [as karmic retributions for such acts] as one moves through the three periods of time. Hence they do not praise such acts. One should therefore realize that all stealing offenses are inherently bad. Any practitioner who is a good person will refrain from engaging in these actions.

h) Ten Karmic Effects of Stealing

As described by the Buddha, taking what is not given has ten associated punishments.

1. The owner always nourishes hatred.
2. One is repeatedly called into doubt. (Chinese textual note: The notes in red state, "With repeated offenses, people harbor doubts".)
3. Even when not engaged in the act, one is liable to encounter unforeseen events.[16]

正體字

四者[22]朋黨惡人遠離
156b29 賢善。五者破善相。六者得罪於官。七者財
156c01 物沒入。八者種貧窮業因緣。九者死入地
156c02 獄。十者若出為人勤苦求財。五家所共若王
156c03 若賊若火若水若不愛子用。乃至藏埋亦失。
156c04 邪婬者。[23]若女人為父母兄弟姊妹夫主兒子
156c05 世間法王法守護。若犯者是名邪婬。若有雖
156c06 不守護以法為守。云何法守。一切出家女
156c07 人在家。受一日戒。是名法守。若以力若以
156c08 財若[24]誑誘若自有妻受戒有[25]娠乳兒非
156c09 道。[26]如是犯者名為邪婬。如是種種乃至以
156c10 華鬘與婬女為要。如是犯者名為邪婬。如
156c11 是種種不作。名為不邪婬。問曰。人守人瞋

简体字

四者、朋党恶人，远离贤善；五者、破善相；六者、得罪于官；七者、财物没入；八者、种贫穷业因缘；九者、死入地狱；十者、若出为人，勤苦求财，五家所共，若王、若贼、若火、若水、若不爱子用，乃至藏埋亦失。”

邪淫者，若女人为父母、兄弟、姊妹、夫主、儿子，世间法、王法守护，若犯者是名邪淫。若有虽不守护，以法为守。云何法守？一切出家女人，在家受一日戒，是名法守。若以力，若以财，若诱诳；若自有妻受戒，有娠，乳儿，非道；乃至以华鬘与淫女为要；如是犯者，名为邪淫。如是种种不作，名为不邪淫。

问曰：人守人瞋，

4. One associates with evil men and departs far from those who are worthy and good.
5. One destroys one's own wholesome qualities.
6. One becomes known as a criminal by the authorities.
7. One's valuables are bound to be lost.
8. One plants the karmic causes and conditions for being poor and destitute [in the future].
9. When one dies, he enters the hells.
10. When one emerges and takes a human rebirth again, he undergoes intense bitterness in the quest for wealth. Then, even so, that wealth ends up being shared with five different groups consisting of the King, thieves, fire, water, and unloving sons. Even if one hides it away or buries it, it is still bound to be lost.

3) The Precept Against Sexual Misconduct

a) Sexual Misconduct Defined

As for the precept against sexual misconduct, if one violates [the "protected" status) of a female under the protection of the father, the mother, the elder or younger brother, the elder or younger sister, the husband as head of the family, a son, the law of the world, or the law of a king, this constitutes sexual misconduct.

Sometimes there are those who, although they are not "under protection" in this sense, are nonetheless under the protection of the Dharma. How is it that one is under the protection of the Dharma? This refers to all women who have left the home life and to those who are householders but who have taken the "one day" precept. This is referred to as being under the protection of the Dharma.

If one uses force, or if one uses money, or if one engages in deceptive seduction, or if one has a wife who has taken the precept, who is pregnant or who is nursing an infant, or if one engages in sexual activity involving an inappropriate orifice—if one transgresses in such ways, this constitutes sexual misconduct.

All sorts of situations like these even extending to the giving of a flower garland to a courtesan as an indication of intent—if one transgresses in such ways, this constitutes sexual misconduct. If in all sorts of situations such as these one refrains from taking such actions, this qualifies as not engaging in sexual misconduct.

b) Objection: How Could This Apply to One's Wife?

Question: When the woman is under the protection of a man, one engenders the man's hatred. When she is under the protection of the

正體字

156c12 | 法守破法應名邪婬。人自有妻何以為邪。
156c13 | 答曰。既聽受一日戒。墮於法中。本雖是婦
156c14 | 今不自在。過受戒時則非法守。有[*]娠婦
156c15 | 人以其身重。厭本所習。又為傷[*]娠。乳兒
156c16 | 時婬其母乳則竭。又以心著婬欲不復護
156c17 | 兒。非道之處則非女根女心不樂。強以非
156c18 | 理故名邪婬。是事不作名為不邪婬。問曰。
156c19 | 若夫主不知不見不惱。他有何罪。答曰。以
156c20 | 其邪故既名為邪。是為不正。是故有罪。復
156c21 | 次此有種種罪過。夫妻之情異身同體。奪他
156c22 | 所愛破其本心。

简体字

法守破法，应名邪淫。人自有妻，何以为邪？

答曰：既听受一日戒，堕于法中；本虽是妇，今不自在；过受戒时，则非法守。有娠妇人，以其身重，厌本所习，又为伤娠。乳儿时淫其母，乳则竭；又以心著淫欲，不复护儿。非道之处，则非女根，女心不乐，强以非理，故名邪淫。是事不作，名为不邪淫。

问曰：若夫主不知，不见不恼，他有何罪？

答曰：以其邪故；既名为邪，是为不正，是故有罪。

复次，此有种种罪过，夫妻之情，异身同体，夺他所爱，破其本心，

Dharma, one violates the Dharma. In these cases, it should qualify as sexual misconduct. However, when it involves a man's own wife, how can it constitute misconduct?

i) In Instances of the One-day Precept

Response: When one has agreed to the taking of the one day precept, one falls under the jurisdiction of the Dharma. Although originally, she may indeed be one's spouse, now one no longer exercises sovereign independence in the matter. Once the time has passed when that precept is in force, then that situation no longer qualifies as one of being "under the protection of the Dharma."

ii) In Instances of Pregnancy or Nursing

There are cases where the wife is pregnant and, because the body is heavy, there is aversion for what was originally practiced. Moreover, it can be injurious to the pregnancy. If one engages in sexual relations with the mother during the time she is nursing an infant, the milk may dry up. Moreover, if the mind becomes attached to sexual desire, then there may not be continued protective regard for the infant.

iii) In Instances Involving Inappropriate Orifice or Force

If one resorts to a place which is not the [genital] orifice, then that is not the female organ and the mind of the woman is not pleased. [Also,], if one resorts to force, because that is unprincipled, that would qualify as sexual misconduct. If one does not engage in such things, this constitutes refraining from sexual misconduct.

c) Objection: If Her Husband Doesn't Know, What's the Problem?

Question: If the husband does not know, does not observe it, and is not afflicted by it, what offense do others incur?

i) Offense Is Based on the Act Itself

Response: It is because it is wrong [that it is regarded as an offense]. Because it is wrong, this is a case of having done what is not right. It is because of this that one [who does this] is deemed to have committed an offense.

ii) Alienation of Affections Entails Theft

Moreover, there are all sorts of transgressions inherent in this. The feelings existing between husband and wife are such that, although they are of different bodies, they are substantially the same [unified entity]. If one steals the object of another person's love and destroys her original thoughts [of affection for him], one qualifies thereby

正體字

是名為賊。復有重罪。惡名
156c23 醜聲為人所憎少樂多畏。或畏刑戮又畏
156c24 夫主傍人所知多懷妄語。聖人所呵罪中之
156c25 罪[27](丹注云婬罪邪婬破戒故名罪中之罪)
復次婬[28]泆之人當自思
156c26 惟。我婦他妻同為女人。骨肉情[29]態彼此無
156c27 異。而我何為橫生惑心隨逐邪意邪婬之
156c28 人。破失今世後世之樂。(好名善譽身心安樂今世得也。
生天得道涅槃之利
156c29 後世得也)復次迴己易處以自制心。若彼侵我妻
157a01 我則忿[1]恚。我若侵彼彼亦何異。恕己自制
157a02 故應不作。復次如佛[2]所說。邪婬之人後墮
157a03 劍樹地獄眾苦備受。得出為人。家道不穆。
157a04 常值婬婦邪僻殘[3]賊

简体字

是名为贼。复有重罪，恶名丑声，为人所憎；少乐多畏，或畏刑戮，又畏夫主傍人所知；多怀妄语，圣人所诃，罪中之罪。

复次，淫泆之人，当自思惟：“我妇他妻，同为女人，骨肉情态，彼此无异，而我何为横生惑心，随逐邪意？”邪淫之人，破失今世、后世之乐（好名善誉，身心安乐，今世得也。生天得道，涅槃之利，后世得也）。

复次，回己易处，以自制心：“若彼侵我妻，我则忿毒；若我侵彼，彼亦何异？”恕己自制，故应不作。

复次，如佛说：“邪淫之人，后堕剑树地狱，众苦备受；得出为人，家道不穆，常值淫妇，邪僻残贼，

as a thief. Thus one simultaneously commits yet another serious offense.

iii) Disrepute, Hatred, Unhappiness, Fear, Danger, Lies, Censure

One gains a bad name and an ugly reputation. One is detested by others and thus experiences diminished happiness and increased fearfulness. One may live in fear of brutal punishment. Additionally, one is fearful that the husband and other people will find out about it. Hence one is much involved in maintaining lies. It is an activity which is denounced by the Āryas. It involves offenses within offenses. (Chinese textual note: The notes in red say, "As for this lust-related offense, it is because one breaks [yet other] precepts while committing sexual misconduct that it refers to 'offenses within offenses.'")

iv) Identity of Lovers Makes It Pointless

Furthermore, the sexually dissolute person ought to reflect, "My wife and his wife are both women. In terms of bone and flesh, feelings and demeanor, that one and this one are no different. So why do I perversely bring forth these deluded thoughts and pursue such incorrect intentions?"

v) Present and Future Happiness Is Lost

A person who engages in sexual misconduct destroys and loses any happiness in both this life and later lives. (Chinese textual note: [As for what is lost, it is] a fine name, a reputation for goodness, and peace and happiness of body and mind that might otherwise be gained in the present life [as well as] the benefits of heavenly rebirth, realization of the path, and reaching nirvāṇa [that might otherwise be] realized in later lives.)

vi) One Should Have Sympathy for the Prospective Cuckold

Then again, as a means of controlling one's mind, one should turn one's situation around and change places, considering: "If he were to violate my wife, I would be enraged. Therefore, if I were to violate his wife, how is it that he would feel any differently?" Through the natural self-control arising from realizing one's own situation, one should be motivated to refrain from such acts.

vii) The Karmic Retribution Is Horrible

What's more, as the Buddha himself declared, a person who engages in sexual misconduct later falls into the hell of sword trees in which he undergoes an abundance of many sorts of sufferings. When he finally succeeds in emerging and becoming a human again, his family life will not be harmonious and he will always meet up with a licentious wife who is devious, remote, and ruthlessly cruel.

正體字

邪婬為患。譬如蝮蛇
157a05 亦如大火。不急避之禍害將及。如佛所說。
157a06 邪婬有十罪。一者常為所婬夫主欲危害
157a07 之。二者夫婦不穆常共鬪諍。三者諸不善法
157a08 日日增長。於諸善法日日損減。四者不守
157a09 護身妻子孤寡。五者財產日耗。六者有諸惡
157a10 事常為人所疑。七者親屬知識所不愛憙。
157a11 八者種怨家業因緣。九者身壞命終死入地
157a12 獄。十者若出為女人多人共夫。若為男子
157a13 婦不貞潔。如是等種種因緣不作。是名不
157a14 邪婬。妄語者。不淨心欲誑他。覆隱實出異
157a15 語生口業。是名妄語。妄語之罪從言聲相
157a16 [4]解生。若不相解雖不實語。無妄語罪。是
157a17 妄語。知言不知不知言知。見言不見

简体字

邪淫为患。譬如蝮蛇，亦如大火，不急避之，祸害将及！”如佛所说：“邪淫有十罪：一者、常为所淫夫主欲危害之；二者、夫妇不穆，常共斗诤；三者、诸不善法日日增长，于诸善法日日损减；四者、不守护身，妻子孤寡；五者、财产日耗；六者、有诸恶事，常为人所疑；七者、亲属、知识所不喜爱；八者、种怨家业因缘；九者、身坏命终，死入地狱；十者、若出为女人，多人共夫；若为男子，妇不贞洁。”如是等种种因缘不作，是名不邪淫。

妄语者，不净心，欲诳他，覆隐实，出异语，生口业，是名妄语。妄语之罪，从言声相解生；若不相解，虽不实语，无妄语罪。是妄语，知言不知，不知言知；见言不见，

d) Ten Karmic Effects of Sexual Misconduct

Sexual misconduct is a calamity analogous to a venomous snake or a great fire which, should one fail to immediately avoid it, it then entails the encroachment of disastrous harm. As stated by the Buddha, sexual misconduct has ten resulting karmic punishments:

1. The husband of [the offender's] sexual conquest is constantly bent on destroying him.
2. The husband and wife are not harmonious and are constantly engaged in mutual strife.
3. Bad dharmas proliferate with each passing day, whereas good dharmas diminish with each passing day.
4. One fails to protect one's own physical health as one also widows one's wife and orphans one's children.
5. One's wealth and business deteriorate daily.
6. All sorts of unfortunate situations develop as one is also constantly doubted by others.
7. One's relatives and friends no longer feel affection or fondness for him.
8. One plants the karmic causes and conditions for having enemies.
9. At the break-up of the body when the life comes to an end, one dies and enters the hells.
10. If, when one emerges, one takes rebirth as a woman, one becomes the victim of gang rape. If one takes birth as a man, one's wife is not chaste.

If one refrains from all such causes and conditions as these, then this qualifies as refraining from sexual misconduct.

4) The Precept Against False Speech

a) False Speech Defined

As for false speech, if one has a thought that is not pure in which one wishes to deceive someone else, if one hides the truth, and if one utters words that differ from the truth, thereby generating the karma of the mouth, this is what constitutes "false speech." The offense of false speech arises from the sound of the words and mutual understanding. If there is no mutual understanding, then although they are untrue words, there is no offense of false speech.

As for this false speech: if one actually does know, yet nonetheless claims that he does not know; if one does not know, yet claims that he does know; if one has seen, yet claims that he has not seen;

正體字

不

157a18 見言見。聞言不聞不聞言聞。是名妄語。
157a19 若不作是名不妄語。問曰。妄語有何等罪。
157a20 答曰。妄語之人。先自誑身然後誑人。以實
157a21 為虛以虛為實。虛實顛倒不受善法。譬如
157a22 覆瓶水不得入。妄語之人心無慚愧。閉塞
157a23 天道涅槃之門。觀知此罪。是故不作。復次
157a24 觀知實語其利甚廣。實語之利自從己出甚
157a25 為易得。是為一切出家[5]人[6]力。如是功德
157a26 居家出家人共有此利。善人之相。復次實語
157a27 之人其心端直。其心端直易得免苦。譬如
157a28 稠林曳木直者易出。問曰。若妄語有如是
157a29 罪。人何以故妄語。答曰。有人愚癡少智。遭
157b01 事苦厄妄語求脫不知事發。今世得罪
157b02 不知後世有大罪報。復有人雖知妄語罪。
157b03 慳貪瞋恚愚癡多故而作妄語。

简体字

不见言见；闻言不闻，不闻言闻；是名妄语。若不作，是名不妄语。

问曰：妄语有何等罪？

答曰：妄语之人，先自诳身，然后诳人；以实为虚，以虚为实，虚实颠倒，不受善法。譬如覆瓶，水不得入。妄语之人，心无惭愧，闭塞天道、涅槃之门。观知此罪，是故不作。

复次，观知实语，其利甚广，实语之利，自从己出，甚为易得，是为一切出家人力。如是功德，居家、出家人，共有此利，善人之相。

复次，实语之人，其心端直，其心端直，易得免苦；譬如稠林曳木，直者易出。

问曰：若妄语有如是罪，人何以故妄语？

答曰：有人愚痴少智，遭事苦厄，妄语求脱；不知事发今世得罪，不知后世有大罪报。复有人虽知妄语罪，悭贪、瞋恚、愚痴多故，而作妄语。

if one has not seen, yet claims that he has seen; if one has heard, yet claims that he has not heard; or if one has not heard, yet claims that he has heard—these all constitute instances of false speech. If one has not acted in such a manner, then this qualifies as refraining from committing false speech.

b) The Inherent Faults in False Speech

Question: What faults are there in false speech?

Response: The person who commits false speech first of all cheats himself, and then proceeds to deceive others. He takes what is real as false and what is false as real. He turns false and real upside down and refuses to accept good dharmas. He is comparable to an inverted vase into which water cannot be poured.

The mind of a person who commits false speech is devoid of a sense of shame or a dread of blame. He blocks off both the way to the heavens and the gate to nirvāṇa. One contemplates this matter, realizes the existence of these disadvantages, and therefore does not engage in it.

Additionally, one contemplates this matter and realizes that the benefits of true speech are extremely vast. The benefits of true speech naturally come forth from one's self and are extremely easily gained. This is the power of all who have left the home life. Both householders and those who have left the home life possess the benefits of this sort of merit. It is the mark of a good person.

Moreover, the mind of a person whose words are true is correct and straight. Because his mind is correct and straight, it is easy for him to succeed in avoiding suffering. It is just as when pulling forth logs from a dense forest. The straight ones come forth easily.

c) Why Then Do People Engage in False Speech?

Question: If false speech entails disadvantages such as these, why then do people engage in false speech?

Response: There are those who are foolish and deficient in wisdom who, when they encounter anguishing difficulties, tell lies as a stratagem to escape them. They fail to recognize the manner in which matters are bound to unfold. When they commit a transgression in this present life, they do not realize that there will be an immense retribution in a later life which is brought on as a result of that transgression.

Then again, there are people who, although they are aware of the fact that false speech entails a transgression, nonetheless course in lies due to an abundance of greed, hatred, or delusion.

正體字

復有人雖
157b04 不貪恚。而妄證人罪心謂實爾。死墮地
157b05 獄如提婆達多弟子俱伽離。常求舍利弗目
157b06 揵連過失。是時二人夏安居竟。遊行諸國
157b07 值天大雨。到陶作家宿盛陶器舍。此舍中
157b08 先有一女人在闇中宿。二人不知。此女人
157b09 其夜夢失不淨。晨朝趣水澡[7]洗。是時俱伽
157b10 離偶行見之。俱伽離能相知人交會情狀。而
157b11 不知夢與不夢。是時俱伽離顧語弟子。此
157b12 女人昨夜與人情通。即問女人汝在何處
157b13 臥。答言。我在陶師屋中寄宿。又問共誰。答
157b14 言。二比丘。是時二人從屋中出。俱伽離見
157b15 已。又以相驗之。意謂二人必為不淨。先懷
157b16 嫉妬既見此事。遍諸城邑聚落告之。次到
157b17 [8]祇洹唱此惡聲。於是中間梵天王來欲見
157b18 佛。佛入靜室寂然三昧。諸比丘眾亦各閉
157b19 房三昧。皆不可覺。即自思惟。我[9]故來見
157b20 佛。佛入三昧

简体字

复有人虽不贪恚，而妄证人罪，心谓实尔，死堕地狱。如提婆达多弟子俱伽离，常求舍利弗、目揵连过失。是时，二人夏安居竟，游行诸国，值天大雨，到陶作家，宿盛陶器舍。此舍中先有一女人在暗中宿，二人不知。此女人其夜梦失不净，晨朝趣水澡洗。是时，俱伽离偶行见之。俱伽离能相，知人交会情状，而不知梦与不梦。是时，俱伽离顾语弟子："此女人昨夜与人情通。"即问女人："汝在何处卧？"答言："我在陶师屋中寄宿。"又问："共谁？"答言："二比丘。"是时，二人从屋中出，俱伽离见已，又以相验之，意谓二人必为不净。先怀嫉妒，既见此事，遍诸城邑聚落告之；次到祇洹，唱此恶声。于是中间，梵天王来欲见佛。佛入静室，寂然三昧；诸比丘众，亦各闭房三昧，皆不可觉。即自思惟："我故来见佛，佛入三昧，

d) Kokālika's Slanderous Offense (Story)

Additionally, there are people who, although not afflicted with greed or hatred, nonetheless falsely testify to another man's transgression because, in their own minds, they are of the opinion that their testimony is true. When they die, they plummet into the hells just as did Kokālika, a disciple of Devadatta. He constantly sought to find fault with Śāriputra and Maudgalyāyana.

At that time, those two men had just reached the end of the summer retreat and so they proceeded to travel about, journeying through the various states. Having encountered a great rain storm, upon arriving at the home of a potter, they spent the night in a pottery storage building.

Before they had arrived, unbeknownst to these two, a woman had already gone in and fallen asleep in a darkened part of the building. That night, this woman had an orgasm in her dreams. In the early morning, she went to get water with which to bathe. Kokālika happened to be walking by at the time and took notice of her. Kokālika possessed the ability to know about a person's sex life simply by observing one's countenance. Even so, he couldn't deduce whether the activity had happened in a dream state or while awake.

Kokālika then mentioned to a disciple, "This woman had sex with someone last night," whereupon he asked the woman, "So, where did you spend the night last night?"

She replied, "I spent the night over in the pottery building."

Next, he asked, "Who else was there?"

She replied, "There were a couple of bhikshus there." At just that time, those very two men happened to emerge from inside that building. Having noticed them, Kokālika examined their countenances and convinced himself that the two men were definitely not pure. It so happened that he had formerly nurtured jealousy toward them. Having observed this situation, he proceeded to spread it all about in the various cities, villages and hamlets. Next, he went to the Jeta Grove where he openly proclaimed this evil rumor.

At this time, it so happened that Brahmā, the King of the Gods, had come wishing to have an audience with the Buddha. However, the Buddha had entered into a silent room where he remained very still, immersed in samādhi. All of the bhikshus too had shut their doors and entered samādhi. None of them could be roused. Then he thought to himself, "I originally came to see the Buddha, but, as it happens, the Buddha has gone into samādhi."

正體字

且欲還去。即復念言。佛從定
157b21 ‖ 起亦將不久。於是小住。到俱伽離房前。扣
157b22 ‖ 其戶而言。俱伽離俱伽離。舍利弗目揵連心
157b23 ‖ 淨柔軟。汝莫謗之而長夜受苦。俱伽離問
157b24 ‖ 言。汝是何人。答言。我是梵天王。問言。佛說
157b25 ‖ 汝得阿那含道。汝何以故來。梵王心念而說
157b26 ‖ 偈言
157b27 ‖ 　無量法欲量　　不應以相取
157b28 ‖ 　無量法欲量　　是[10]野人覆沒
157b29 ‖ 說[11]此偈已。到佛所具說其[12]事。佛言。善哉
157c01 ‖ 善哉。快說此偈。爾時世尊復說此偈
157c02 ‖ 　無量法欲量　　不應以相取
157c03 ‖ 　無量法欲量　　是[*]野人覆沒
157c04 ‖ 梵天王聽佛說已。忽然不現即還天上。爾
157c05 ‖ 時俱迦離到佛所。頭面禮佛足却住一面。
157c06 ‖ 佛告俱伽離。舍利弗目揵連心淨柔軟。汝莫
157c07 ‖ 謗之而長夜受苦。俱伽離白佛言。我於佛
157c08 ‖ 語不敢不信。但自目見了了。定知二人實
157c09 ‖ 行不淨。

简体字

且欲还去。”即复念言：“佛从定起，亦将不久。”于是小住，到俱伽离房前，扣其户而言：“俱伽离！俱伽离！舍利弗、目揵连心净柔软，汝莫谤之而长夜受苦！”俱伽离问言：“汝是何人？”答言：“我是梵天王。”问言：“佛说汝得阿那含道，汝何以故来？”梵王心念而说偈言：

“无量法欲量，不应以相取；无量法欲量，是野人覆没！”

说是偈已，到佛所，具说其意。佛言：“善哉！善哉！快说此偈！”尔时，世尊复说此偈：

“无量法欲量，不应以相取；无量法欲量，是野人覆没！”

梵天王听佛说已，忽然不现，即还天上。尔时，俱伽离到佛所，头面礼佛足，却住一面。佛告俱伽离：“舍利弗、目揵连，心净柔软，汝莫谤之而长夜受苦！”俱伽离白佛言：“我于佛语不敢不信，但自目见了了，定知二人实行不净。”

He was about to return [to his celestial abode] when he had another thought, "It won't be long before the Buddha arises from meditative absorption. I'll just wait here a for a little while longer." He then went over to the entrance to Kokālika's room, knocked on the door, and called out, "Kokālika! Kokālika! The minds of Śāriputra and Maudgalyāyana are pure and pliant. Do not slander them or you will be bound to spend the long night [of your future lifetimes] enduring sufferings."

Kokālika asked, "Who are you?"

He replied, "I am Brahmā, King of the Gods."

He asked, "The Buddha has said that you have realized the path of the *anāgāmin* (lit. "never-returner").[17] Why then have you returned here?"

Brahmā, King of the Gods, thought for a moment and then uttered this verse:

In wishing to fathom immeasurable dharmas,
one should not seize on what is mere appearance.
In wishing to fathom immeasurable dharmas,
a boor of this sort is bound to capsize and drown.

After he had spoken this verse, he went to where the Buddha was and set forth the entire matter. The Buddha said, "Good indeed. Good indeed. This verse should be proclaimed straightaway." The Bhagavat himself then repeated the verse:

In wishing to fathom immeasurable dharmas,
one should not seize on what is mere appearance.
In wishing to fathom immeasurable dharmas,
a boor of this sort is bound to capsize and drown.

After Brahmā, King of the Gods, had heard the Buddha proclaim this, he suddenly disappeared and immediately returned to the heavens.

Kokālika then went to where the Buddha was, prostrated in reverence before the Buddha, and then stood off to one side. The Buddha told Kokālika, "The minds of Śāriputra and Maudgalyāyana are pure and pliant. Do not slander them or you will spend the long night [of future lifetimes] undergoing sufferings."

Kokālika addressed the Buddha, saying, "I don't dare disbelieve the words of the Buddha. However, I saw this clearly with my own eyes. I know definitely that these two men have actually committed impure acts."

正體字

佛如是三呵。俱伽離亦三不受。即
157c10 從坐起而去。還其房中舉身生瘡。始如芥
157c11 子漸大如豆如棗如[13]奈。轉大如苽。翕然
157c12 爛壞如大火燒。叫喚[14]嘷哭其夜即死。入大
157c13 蓮華地[15]獄。有一梵[16]天夜來白佛。俱伽離
157c14 已死復有一梵天言。墮大蓮華地獄。其夜
157c15 過已佛命僧集而告之言。汝等欲知俱伽
157c16 離所墮地獄壽命長短不。諸比丘言。願樂欲
157c17 聞。佛言。有六十斛胡麻。有人過百歲取
157c18 一胡麻。如是至盡。阿浮陀地獄中壽故未
157c19 盡。二十阿浮陀地獄中壽。為一尼羅浮陀地
157c20 獄中壽。如二十尼羅浮陀地獄中壽為一
157c21 [17]阿羅邏地獄中壽。二十[*]阿羅邏地獄中壽。
157c22 為一[*]阿婆婆地獄中壽。二十[*]阿婆婆地獄
157c23 中壽。為一休休地獄中壽。二十休休地獄中
157c24 壽。為一漚波羅地獄中壽。二十漚波羅地獄
157c25 中壽。為一分陀梨迦地獄中壽。二十分陀梨
157c26 迦地獄中壽。為一摩呵波頭摩地獄中壽。俱
157c27 伽離墮是摩呵波頭摩地獄中。出其大舌
157c28 以[18]百釘釘之。五百具犁耕之。爾時世尊
157c29 說此偈言
158a01 [1]夫士之生　斧在口中　所以斬身
158a02 由其惡言　應呵而讚　應讚而呵
158a03 口集諸惡　終不見樂

简体字

佛如是三诃，俱伽离亦三不受，即从座起而去。还其房中，举身生疮，始如芥子，渐大如豆、如枣、如柰，转大如瓜，翕然烂坏；如大火烧，叫唤号啕，其夜即死，入大莲华地狱。有一梵天夜来白佛：“俱伽离已死。”复有一梵天言：“堕大莲华地狱。”其夜过已，佛命僧集而告之言：“汝等欲知俱伽离所堕地狱寿命长短不？”诸比丘言：“愿乐欲闻！”佛言：“有六十斛胡麻，有人过百岁取一胡麻，如是至尽，阿浮陀地狱中寿故未尽。二十阿浮陀地狱中寿，为一尼罗浮陀地狱中寿。如二十尼罗浮陀地狱中寿，为一呵罗逻地狱中寿。二十呵罗逻地狱中寿，为一呵婆婆地狱中寿。二十呵婆婆地狱中寿，为一休休地狱中寿。二十休休地狱中寿，为一沤波罗地狱中寿。二十沤波罗地狱中寿，为一分陀黎迦地狱中寿。二十分陀黎迦地狱中寿，为一摩呵波头摩地狱中寿。俱伽离堕是摩呵波头摩地狱中，出其大舌，以五百钉钉之，五百具犁耕之。”尔时，世尊说此偈言：

“夫士之生，斧在口中；所以斩身，由其恶言。
应呵而赞，应赞而呵；口集诸恶，终不见乐！

The Buddha rebuked him in this manner three times and Kokālika three times still refused to accept it. He then got up from his place, left, and returned to his room. His entire body then broke out in sores. At first, they were the size of sesame seeds. They gradually became as big as beans, as big as dates, as big as mangoes, and finally, as big as melons. Then, they all simultaneously broke open, leaving him looking as if he had been burned by a great fire. He wailed and wept. Then, that very night, he died and entered the Great Lotus Blossom Hell. A Brahma Heaven god came and informed the Buddha, "Kokālika has already died."

Then yet another Brahma Heaven god declared, "He has fallen into the Great Lotus Blossom Hell." After that night had passed, the Buddha ordered the Saṃgha to assemble, and then asked, "Do you all wish to know the length of the life in that hell into which Kokālika has fallen?"

The Bhikṣus replied, "Pray, please tell us. We wish to hear it."

The Buddha said, "It is as if there were sixty bushels of sesame seeds and then a man came along only once every hundred years and took away but a single sesame seed. If this went on until all of the sesame seeds were gone, the lifespan endured in the Arbuda Hells would still not have come to an end. Twenty Arbuda Hell lifespans equal the lifespan in the Nirarbuda Hells. Twenty Nirarbuda Hell lifespans equal the lifespan in the Aṭaṭa Hells. Twenty Aṭaṭa Hell lifespans equal the lifespan in the Hahava Hells. Twenty Hahava Hell lifespans equal the lifespan in the Huhuva Hells. Twenty Huhuva Hell lifespans equal the lifespan in the Utpala Hells. Twenty Utpala Hell lifespans equal the lifespan in the Puṇḍarīka Hells. Twenty Puṇḍarīka Hell lifespans equal the lifespan in the Mahāpadma Hells. Kokālika has fallen into these Mahāpadma Hells.[18] His tongue is drawn forth and nailed down with a hundred nails where it is plowed by five hundred plows." The Bhagavat then spoke forth this verse:

> When a person takes rebirth there,
> hatchets are plunged into his mouth.
> The reason for the body's being hacked
> is found in his utterance of evil words.
>
> What should be criticized, he nonetheless has praised.
> What should be praised, he nonetheless has criticized.
> The mouth thus piles up all manner of evil deeds,
> with the result that one is never able to experience any bliss.

正體字

158a04 ‖ 心口業生惡　墮尼羅浮獄
158a05 ‖ 具滿百千世　受諸[2]毒苦痛
158a06 ‖ 若生阿浮陀　具滿三[3]十六
158a07 ‖ 別更有[4]五世　皆受諸苦毒
158a08 ‖ 心依邪見　破賢聖語　如竹生實
158a09 ‖ 自毀其[5]形
158a10 ‖ 如是等心生疑謗。遂至決定亦是妄語。妄語
158a11 ‖ 人乃至佛語而不信受。受罪如是。以是故
158a12 ‖ 不應妄語。復次如佛子羅睺羅。其年幼稚
158a13 ‖ 未知慎口。人來問之。世尊在不。詭言不在。
158a14 ‖ 若不在時。人問羅睺羅。世尊在不。詭言佛
158a15 ‖ 在。有人語佛。佛語羅睺羅。澡[6]槃取水與吾
158a16 ‖ 洗足。洗足已。語羅睺羅。覆此澡[*]槃。如勅
158a17 ‖ 即覆。佛言。以水注之。注已問言。水入中不。
158a18 ‖ 答言。不入。佛告羅睺羅。無慚愧人妄語覆
158a19 ‖ 心道法不入。亦復如是。

简体字

心口业生恶，堕尼罗浮狱；具满百千世，受诸苦毒痛。

若生阿浮陀，具满三十六；别更有五世，皆受诸苦毒。

心依邪见，破贤圣语；如竹生实，自毁其形。”

如是等心生疑谤，遂至决定，亦是妄语。妄语人，乃至佛语而不信受，受罪如是！以是故，不应妄语。

复次，如佛子罗睺罗，其年幼稚，未知慎口。人来问之：“世尊在不？”诡言不在。若不在时，人问罗睺罗：“世尊在不？”诡言佛在。有人语佛，佛语罗睺罗：“澡盘取水，与吾洗足！”洗足已，语罗睺罗：“覆此澡盘！”如敕即覆。佛言：“以水注之！”注已，问言：“水入中不？”答言：“不入！”佛告罗睺罗：“无惭愧人，妄语覆心，道法不入，亦复如是！”

The actions of mind and mouth generate evil.
One plummets then into the Nirarbuda Hells.
For a term of fully a hundred thousand lifetimes,
he endures there all manner of excruciating pain.

When one takes rebirth into the Arbuda Hells,
he is bound to endure it for a full thirty-six lives,
and then suffer for yet another additional five lives
where, in all of them he suffers all manner of suffering anguish.

The mind comes to rely upon erroneous views,
and speaks then in a way destroying the Worthies and Āryas.
In this, it's like that bamboo which, in putting forth its fruit,
thereby brings on the destruction of its very own physical form.

In just such a manner, the mind generates doubts and slanders. Once they have become rigidly established, they also become manifest in false speech. Thus a person who engages in false speech refuses to believe in or accept even the words of the Buddha. He becomes bound then to undergo punishments just such as these. It is for these reasons that one must refrain from engaging in false speech.

e) Rāhula's Lesson About False Speech (Story)

Then again, a case in point is that of the Buddha's son Rāhula who, being in years but a child, had still not yet understood the importance of taking care with his words. When people would come and ask him, "Is the Bhagavat here, or not?" he would deceive them by saying, "He's not here."

If in fact he was not present, when others would ask Rāhula, "Is the Bhagavat here or not?" he would deceive them by saying, "The Buddha is here."

Someone informed the Buddha about this. The Buddha then told Rāhula, "Get a wash basin, fill it with water, and then wash my feet for me." After his feet had been washed, he instructed Rāhula, "Now put the lid on this wash basin."

Then, obeying the command, he immediately covered it. The Buddha then said, "Get some more water and pour it in." After it had been poured, he asked, "Did the water go in or not?"

Rāhula replied, "No, it didn't go in."

The Buddha told Rāhula, "The lies of a person without any sense of shame or dread of blame cover over his mind so that, in just this same manner, the Dharma of the path is unable to enter into it."

正體字

如佛說。妄語有十
158a20 罪。何等為十。一者口氣臭。二者善神遠之
158a21 非人得便。三者雖有實語人不信受。四者
158a22 智人[7]語議常不參豫。五者常被誹謗。醜惡
158a23 之聲周聞天下。六者人所不敬。雖有教勅
158a24 人不承用。七者常多憂愁。八者種誹謗業
158a25 因緣。九者身壞命終當墮地獄。十者若出
158a26 為人常被誹謗。如是種種不作。是為不妄
158a27 語。名口善律儀。不飲酒者。酒有三種。一者
158a28 穀酒。二者果酒。三者藥草酒。果酒者。[8]蒱桃
158a29 阿梨咤樹果。如是等種種名為果酒。藥草酒
158b01 者。種種藥草。合和米[9]麴甘蔗汁中。能變成
158b02 酒。同[10]蹄畜乳酒。一切乳熱者可中作酒。略
158b03 說。若乾若濕若清若濁。如是等能令人心動
158b04 放逸。是名為酒。

简体字

如佛说："妄语有十罪。何等为十？一者、口气臭；二者、善神远之，非人得便；三者、虽有实语，人不信受；四者、智人谋议，常不参预；五者、常被诽谤，丑恶之声，周闻天下；六者、人所不敬，虽有教敕，人不承用；七者、常多忧愁；八者、种诽谤业因缘；九者、身坏命终，当堕地狱；十者、若出为人，常被诽谤。"如是种种不作，是为不妄语，名口善律仪。

不饮酒者，酒有三种：一者、穀酒，二者、果酒，三者、药草酒。果酒者，葡萄、阿梨吒树果，如是等种种，名为果酒。药草酒者，种种药草，合和米曲、甘蔗汁中，能变成酒，同蹄畜乳酒，一切乳热者可中作酒。略说若干、若湿，若清、若浊，如是等能令人心动放逸，是名为酒。

f) Ten Karmic Effects of False Speech

As stated by the Buddha, false speech has ten karmic retributions. What are the ten? They are as follows:

1. The breath always smells bad.
2. The good spirits depart far from him and the non-humans are then free to have their way with him.
3. Even though there may be instances when he does speak the truth, people nonetheless do not believe or accept it.
4. He can never participate in discussions with the wise.
5. He is always slandered and his ugly and foul reputation is heard throughout the land.
6. He is one not respected by others. Although he may issue instructions and orders, people do not accept or follow them.
7. He is constantly afflicted with many worries.
8. He plants the karmic causes and conditions resulting in his being slandered.
9. When his body deteriorates and his life comes to an end, he is bound to fall into the hells.
10. When he emerges and becomes a person, he is always the object of slander.

If one does not engage in the various different sorts of actions as these, this is what constitutes refraining from false speech. This is a moral regulation defining goodness in the sphere of mouth karma.

5) The Precept Against Intoxicants

a) Alcoholic Beverages Defined

As for abstention from alcoholic beverages, alcoholic beverages are of three kinds, the first being alcoholic beverages made from grain, the second being alcoholic beverages made from fruit, and the third being alcohol beverages made from botanical herbs.

As for alcoholic beverages made from fruit, this includes grapes and the fruit of the *ariṣṭaka* tree. All other such varieties also qualify as alcoholic beverages made from fruit. As for alcoholic beverages made from botanical herbs, when mixed into rice or wheat and sugar cane juice, all sorts of botanical herbs are capable then of being transformed into alcoholic beverages. This is also true of milk from hooved animals, for any sort of fermented milk may be used in the same fashion to make alcoholic beverages.

To summarize, whether they be dry, wet, clear, or turbid, any such things possessing the capacity to influence a person's mind to move or backslide are collectively referred to as alcoholic beverages.

正體字

一切不應飲。是名不飲酒。
158b05 問曰。酒能破冷益身令心歡喜。何[11]以不
158b06 飲。答曰。益身甚少所損甚多。是故不應
158b07 飲。譬如美飲其中雜毒。是何等毒。如佛語
158b08 難提迦優婆塞。酒有三十五失。何等三十五。
158b09 一者[12]現世財物虛竭。何以故。人飲酒醉心
158b10 無節限。用費無度故。二者眾[13]病之門。三者
158b11 鬪諍之本。四者裸露無恥。五者醜名惡聲人
158b12 所不敬。六者覆沒智慧。七者應所得物而
158b13 不得。已所得物而散失。八者伏匿之事盡向
158b14 人說。九者種種事業廢不成辦。十者醉為
158b15 愁本。何以故。醉中多失。醒已慚愧憂愁。十
158b16 一者身力轉少。十二者身色壞。十三者不知
158b17 敬父。十四者不知敬母。

简体字

一切不应饮，是名不饮酒。

问曰：酒能破冷益身，令心欢喜，何以故不饮？

答曰：益身甚少，所损甚多，是故不应饮。譬如美饮，其中杂毒，是何等毒？如佛语难提迦优婆塞："酒有三十五失。何等三十五？一者、现在世财物虚竭，何以故？人饮酒醉，心无节限，用费无度故；二者、众疾之门；三者、斗诤之本；四者、裸露无耻；五者、丑名恶声，人所不敬；六者、覆没智慧；七者、应所得物而不得，已所得物而散失；八者、伏匿之事，尽向人说；九者、种种事业，废不成办；十者、醉为愁本，何以故？醉中多失，醒已惭愧、忧愁；十一者、身力转少；十二者、身色坏；十三者、不知敬父；十四者、不知敬母；

One must not drink any of them. This is what is meant by abstention from alcoholic beverages.

b) Objection: With So Many Benefits, Why Abstain?

Question: Alcohol is able to dispel coldness, benefit the body, and cause the mind to be delighted. Why then should one refrain from drinking it?

Response: The benefits to the body are extremely minor. The harmful aspects are extremely numerous. Therefore, one should not drink it. It is analogous to a marvelous beverage into which one has mixed poison. What sorts of "poison" are being referred to here? As told by the Buddha to the *upāsaka,* Nandika, alcohol has thirty-five faults. What are the thirty-five? They are:

c) Thirty-Five Karmic Effects of Consuming Intoxicants

1. Valuables owned in the present life are squandered. Why? When people consume intoxicants, their minds know no limits. Consequently they indulge in unconstrained wastefulness.
2. It is the entry point for affliction with the many sorts of diseases.
3. It is the basis for generating strife.
4. One's nakedness is allowed to become shamelessly exposed.
5. One develops an ugly name and terrible reputation leading to not being respected by others.
6. It obscures and submerges one's wisdom.
7. Those things which ought to be obtained are nonetheless not obtained, whilst whatever has already been obtained becomes scattered and lost.
8. Matters which should remain confidential are told in their entirety to others.
9. All sorts of endeavors deteriorate and are not brought to completion.
10. Intoxication is the root of worry. How so? When one is inebriated, much is lost. After one returns to a condition of mental clarity, one feels a sense of shame and dread of blame and abides in a state of worry.
11. The strength of the body decreases.
12. The appearance of the body deteriorates.
13. One does not know to respect one's father.
14. One does not know to respect one's mother.

正體字

十五者不敬沙
158b18 門。十六者不敬婆羅門。十七者不敬伯叔
158b19 及尊長。何以故。醉悶[14]恍惚無所別故。十八
158b20 者不尊敬佛。十九者不敬法。二十者不敬
158b21 僧。二十一者朋黨惡人。二十二者踈遠賢
158b22 善。二十三者作破戒人。二十四者無慚無愧。
158b23 二十五者不守六情。二十六者縱[15]色放逸。
158b24 二十七者人所憎惡不喜見之。二十八者
158b25 貴重親屬及諸知識所共擯棄。二十九者行
158b26 不善法。三十者棄捨善法。三十一者明人智
158b27 士所不信用。何以故。酒放逸故。三十二者
158b28 遠離涅槃。三十三者種狂癡因緣。三十四者
158b29 身壞命終墮惡道泥梨中。三十五者若得為
158c01 人所生之處常當狂騃。如是等種種過失。
158c02 是故不飲。如偈說

158c03 酒失覺知相　身色濁而惡
158c04 智心動而亂　慚愧已被劫

简体字

十五者、不敬沙门；十六者、不敬婆罗门；十七者、不敬伯、叔及尊长，何以故？醉闷恍惚，无所别故；十八者、不尊敬佛；十九者、不敬法；二十者、不敬僧；二十一者、朋党恶人；二十二者、疏远贤善；二十三者、作破戒人；二十四者、无惭、无愧；二十五者、不守六情；二十六者、纵己放逸；二十七者、人所憎恶，不喜见之；二十八者、贵重亲属，及诸知识所共摈弃；二十九者、行不善法；三十者、弃舍善法；三十一者、明人、智士所不信用，何以故？酒放逸故；三十二者、远离涅槃；三十三者、种狂痴因缘；三十四者、身坏命终，堕恶道泥犁中；三十五者、若得为人，所生之处，常当狂騃。”如是等种种过失，是故不饮。如偈说：

“酒失觉知相，身色浊而恶，智心动而乱，惭愧已被劫。

15. One does not respect *śramaṇas*.
16. One does not respect brahmans.
17. One does not respect one's uncles or venerable elders. Why is this? One is so stupefied by drunkenness as to fail to make any such distinctions.
18. One does not honor or respect the Buddha.
19. One does not respect the Dharma.
20. One does not respect the Saṃgha.
21. One associates with bad people.
22. One remains distant from worthy and good people.
23. One becomes a breaker of the precepts.
24. One becomes devoid of a sense of shame or dread of blame.
25. One fails to guard the six sense faculties [through appropriate restraint].
26. One falls away into sexual profligacy.
27. One becomes so detested and abhorred by others that they find no delight in laying eyes on him.
28. One becomes abandoned and rejected by those who are esteemed, by one's relatives, and by one's friends.
29. One courses in those dharmas which are not good.
30. One relinquishes good dharmas.
31. One is neither trusted nor employed by intelligent people or wise personages. Why? Because, through intoxication, one has fallen into neglectful ways.
32. One departs far from nirvāṇa.
33. One plants the causes and conditions for becoming crazy and stupid.
34. When the body deteriorates and the life comes to an end, one is bound to fall into the wretched destinies and, in particular, into *niraya* (the hells).
35. When one finally succeeds in taking human rebirth again, wherever one is reborn, one is crazy and stupid.

It is due to all sorts of faults such as these that one should abstain from drinking. This is as described in the following verse:

Intoxicants cause the loss of the signs of awakening.
One's physical appearance becomes murky and detestable.
While one's intelligence becomes agitated and confused,
one is robbed of both sense of shame and a dread of blame.

正體字

158c05 失念增瞋心　失歡毀宗族
158c06 如是雖名飲　實為飲死毒
158c07 不應瞋而瞋　不應笑而笑
158c08 不應哭而哭　不應打而打
158c09 不應語而語　與狂人無異
158c10 奪諸善功德　知愧者不飲
158c11 如是四罪不作。是身善律儀。妄[16]語不作是
158c12 口善律儀。名為優婆塞五戒律儀。問曰。若八
158c13 種律儀。及淨命是名為戒。何以故優婆塞。
158c14 於口律儀中。無三律儀及淨命。答曰。白衣
158c15 居家。受世間樂兼修福德。不能盡行戒
158c16 法。是故佛令持五戒。復次四種口業中妄語
158c17 最重。復次妄語心生故作。餘者或故作或不
158c18 故作。復次但說妄語已攝三事。復次諸善
158c19 法中實為

简体字

失念增瞋心，失欢毁宗族；如是虽名饮，实为饮死毒。

不应瞋而瞋，不应笑而笑，不应哭而哭，不应打而打，

不应语而语，与狂人无异；夺诸善功德，知愧者不饮。”

如是四罪不作，是身善律仪；妄言不作，是口善律仪；名为优婆塞五戒律仪。

问曰：若八种律仪及净命，是名为戒，何以故优婆塞于口律仪中无三律仪，及净命？

答曰：白衣居家，受世间乐，兼修福德，不能尽行戒法，是故佛令持五戒。

复次，四种口业中，妄语最重。

复次，妄语心生故作；余者或故作，或不故作。

复次，但说妄语，已摄三事。

复次，诸善法中，实为

One loses one's mindfulness, multiplies hate-ridden thoughts,
forfeits one's happiness, and does damage to the clan.
Thus, although it may be referred to as "drinking,"
in truth, it is synonymous with consuming deadly poison.

Where one should not be hateful, one is nonetheless hateful.
Where one should not laugh, one nonetheless laughs.
Where one should not cry, one nonetheless cries.
Where one should not inflict blows, one nonetheless inflicts blows.

What one should not say, one nonetheless says.
One becomes indistinguishable from a crazy person.
All of one's good qualities are stolen away.
Thus, whoever knows a sense of shame abstains from drink.

6) Additional Five-Precept Topics

a) Summation of the Primary Basis of Lay Morality

In this manner, abstention from four offenses constitutes accordance with the moral regulations governing goodness in physical actions whereas abstention from false speech constitutes accordance with the moral regulations governing goodness in verbal actions. These collectively constitute the moral regulations comprising the *upāsaka's* five precepts (*upāsakapañcaśīla*).

b) Eight Precepts, Other Mouth Karmas, Pure Livelihood

Question: If it is the case that eight moral regulations and pure livelihood collectively constitute the precepts, why is there no mention here for the *upāsaka* of either the other three moral regulations associated with the mouth[19] or of pure livelihood?

i) Limited Capacities of Lay Buddhists

Response: The laity (lit. "the white-robed ones") dwell in the midst of the home life where they accept the pleasures of the world while also concurrently cultivating merit. Hence they are unable to fully practice the Dharma as prescribed by the moral precepts. Therefore the Buddha decreed that they should uphold the five precepts.

ii) How the False Speech Precept Subsumes the Others

Moreover, within the four moral regulations associated with mouth karma, false speech is the most serious. Additionally, with false speech, the thought arises and then one deliberately engages in it. As for the others, one may deliberately engage in them or may do so without any particular deliberate intention.

Then again, when one mentions only false speech, one thereby already implicitly subsumes within it the other three related endeavors. Moreover, among all good dharmas, truthfulness is the

正體字

最大。若說實語四種正語皆已攝
158c20 得。復次白衣處世。當官理務家業作使。是
158c21 故難持不惡口法。妄語故作[17]事重故不應
158c22 作。是五戒有五種受。名五種優婆塞。一者
158c23 一分行優婆塞。二者少分行優婆塞。三者多
158c24 分行優婆塞。四者滿行優婆塞。五者斷婬優
158c25 婆塞。一分行者。於五戒中受一戒。不能
158c26 受持四戒。少分行者。若受二戒若受三戒。
158c27 多分行者。受四戒。滿行者。盡持五戒。斷婬
158c28 者。受五戒已師前更作[18]自誓言。我於自
158c29 婦不復行婬。是名五戒。如佛偈說
159a01 不殺亦不盜　亦不有邪婬
159a02 實語不飲酒　正命以淨心
159a03 若能行此者　二世憂畏除
159a04 戒福恒隨身　常與天人俱
159a05 世間六時華　榮曜色相發
159a06 以此一歲華　天上一日具

简体字

最大；若说实语，四种正语皆已摄得。　　　复次，白衣处世，当官理务，家业作使，是故难持不恶口法。妄语故作，重事故不应作。是五戒有五种受，名五种优婆塞：一者、一分行优婆塞，二者、少分行优婆塞，三者、多分行优婆塞，四者、满行优婆塞，五者、断淫优婆塞。一分行者，于五戒中受一戒，不能受持四戒；少分行者，若受二戒，若受三戒；多分行者，受四戒；满行者，尽持五戒；断淫者，受五戒已，师前更作誓言：“我于自妇不复行淫。”是名五戒。

如佛偈说：

“不杀亦不盗，亦不有邪淫，实语不饮酒，正命以净心。

若能行此者，二世忧畏除，戒福恒随身，常与天人俱。

世间六时华，荣耀色相发，以此一岁华，天上一日具。

one of greatest importance. If one utters true speech, all four types of right speech are completely subsumed and acquired.

iii) Lay Life's Inherent Connection to Harsh Speech

Additionally, the layperson abides in the world where he becomes responsible for oversight and management. He takes responsibility for the family business and issues orders. Hence it is difficult to uphold the dharma that requires abstention from harsh speech. False speech, however, is a thing that is intentionally done. Because it is a serious matter, one must not engage in it.

iv) Five Degrees of Five-Precept Acceptance

There are five degrees of acceptance of the five precepts which determine the five kinds of *upāsaka*. The first is the single-practice *upāsaka*. The second is the lesser-practice *upāsaka*. The third is the greater-practice *upāsaka*. The fourth is the full-practice *upāsaka*. And the fifth is the celibate *upāsaka*.

As for the first, the single-practice *upāsaka*, it refers to taking on one precept from among the five moral precepts while being unable to take on and uphold the other four precepts. As for the lesser-practice *upāsaka*, it refers to taking on two or three precepts. The greater-practice *upāsaka* is one who takes on four precepts. The full-practice *upāsaka* completely upholds all five precepts. As for the celibate *upāsaka*, after taking on the five precepts, in the presence of his spiritual teacher, he additionally makes a vow for himself, saying, "I will no longer engage in sexual activity even with my own wife. This is what is meant by the five precepts. They are as described by the Buddha in verse:

v) Buddha's Verse on Five-Precept Karmic Rewards

One does not kill, does not steal,
nor does one engage in sexual misconduct.
One maintains true speech, abstains from alcohol,
and upholds right livelihood. One thereby purifies his mind.

For whoever is able to put this into practice,
during the two eras,[20] worry and fear will be dispensed with,
precept merit will constantly follow along with him,
and he will always enjoy the company of gods and men.

In the six-seasoned flower of the worldly existence,
glory and physical appearance bloom together.
This single flower of all of our years
is contained in a single day of celestial existence.[21]

正體字

159a07 天樹自然生　花鬘及瓔珞
159a08 丹葩如燈照　眾色相間錯
159a09 天衣無央數　其色若干種
159a10 鮮白映天日　輕密無間[1]壟
159a11 金色[2]映繡文　斐亹如雲氣
159a12 如是上妙服　悉從天樹出
159a13 明珠天耳璫　寶磔曜手足
159a14 隨心所好[3]愛　亦從天樹出
159a15 金華琉璃莖　金剛為華[4]鬚
159a16 柔軟香芬熏　悉從寶池出
159a17 琴瑟箏箜篌　七寶為挍飾
159a18 器妙故音清　皆亦從樹出
159a19 波[(匕/示)*(入/米)]質姤樹　天上樹中王
159a20 在彼歡喜園　一切無有比
159a21 持戒為耕田　天樹從中出
159a22 天廚甘露味　飲食除飢渴
159a23 天女無監礙　亦無[5]妊身難
159a24 [6]嬉怡縱逸樂　食無便利患
159a25 持戒常攝心　得生自恣地

简体字

天树自然生，华鬘及缨络，丹葩如灯照，众色相间错。
天衣无央数，其色若干种，鲜白映天日，轻密无间垄。
金色照文绣，斐亹如云气，如是上妙服，悉从天树出。
明珠天耳珰，宝磔耀手足，随心所好服，亦从天树出。
金华琉璃茎，金刚为华须，柔软香芬熏，悉从宝池出。
琴瑟筝箜篌，七宝为校饰，器妙故音清，皆亦从树出。
波[颖-页+汆]质妒树，天上树中王，在彼欢喜园，一切无有比。
持戒为耕田，天树从中出，天厨甘露味，饮食除饥渴。
天女无监碍，亦无妊身难，熙怡纵逸乐，食无便利患。
持戒常摄心，得生自恣地，

The celestial trees spontaneously produce
flower garlands and necklaces.
The crimson flowers bloom as radiantly as lamps
and their many colors are each embedded among all the others.

The countless varieties of celestial apparel,
in hues of so many sorts,
are fresh and pure, reflecting the heavenly sun,
and are light, tightly-woven, and free of any wrinkles.

The golden light is reflected in embroidered motifs.
The graceful color patterns appear like formations of airy clouds.
Such supremely marvelous apparel
all comes forth from the trees in the heavens.

Bright jewels, celestial earrings,
And precious bracelets brighten the hands and feet.
Whatever the mind finds delightful
Comes forth as well from the heavenly trees.

There are flowers of gold with stems of *vaiḍūrya*,
with floral stamens and pistils made from *vajra*.
Soft and pliant, exuding a pervasive fragrance,
they all grow forth from pools of jewels.

The guitar, bass, harp, and lute[22]
are inlaid with ornaments of seven precious things.
The instruments are marvelous, the ancient sounds clear.
All of these also come forth from the trees.

The Pārijātaka tree[23]
is the king of the trees in the heavens.
It grows there within the "Garden of Delight" (Nandanavana)
where it remains unmatched by any other.

Upholding the precepts amounts to the tilling of the fields
from which these heavenly trees all grow forth.
The celestial kitchens issue flavors of sweet-dew ambrosia.
Their drink and food dispel both hunger and thirst.

The heavenly maidens have no interference from guardians,
nor do they have the hindrance of a pregnancy-prone body.
One may enjoy oneself, relax, and be unrestrained in pleasures
while eating there remains free of the troubles of elimination.

If one upholds the precepts and constantly controls the mind,
one may be born in a land where one may be freely indulgent.

正體字

159a26 無事亦無難　常得肆樂志
159a27 諸天得自在　憂苦不復生
159a28 所欲應念至　身光照幽冥
159a29 如是種種樂　皆由施與戒
159b01 若欲得此報　當勤自勉勵
159b02 問曰。今說尸羅波羅蜜當以成佛。何以[7]故
159b03 乃讚天福。答曰。佛言。三事必得報果不虛。
159b04 布施得大[8]富。持戒生好處。修定得解脫。若
159b05 單行尸羅得生好處。若修定智慧慈悲和
159b06 合得三乘道。今但讚持戒。現世功德名聞安
159b07 樂。後世得報。如偈所讚。譬如小兒蜜塗苦
159b08 藥然後能服。今先讚戒福然後人能持戒。
159b09 [9]能持戒已立大誓願得至佛道。是為尸
159b10 羅生尸羅波羅蜜。又以一切人皆著樂世間
159b11 之樂天上為最。若聞天上種種快樂。便能受
159b12 行尸羅。

简体字

无事亦无难，常得肆乐志。
诸天得自在，忧苦不复生，所欲应念至，身光照幽冥。
如是种种乐，皆由施与戒，若欲得此报，当勤自勉励！”

问曰：今说尸罗波罗蜜，当以成佛，何以乃赞天福？

答曰：佛言三事必得报果不虚；布施得大福，持戒生好处，修定得解脱。若单行尸罗，得生好处；若修定、智慧、慈悲、和合，得三乘道。今但赞持戒现世功德，名闻、安乐后世得报，如偈所赞。譬如小儿，蜜涂苦药，然后能服；今先赞戒福，然后人能持戒。持戒已，立大誓愿，得至佛道，是为尸罗生尸罗波罗蜜。又以一切人皆著乐，世间之乐天上为最。若闻天上种种快乐，便能受行尸罗；

There are no tasks to be done, there are no difficulties,
and one is ever able to fulfil one's aspirations for bliss.

All of the gods achieve sovereign freedom.
Distress and suffering no longer arise there.
Whatever one desires comes forth in response to one's thoughts,
while the light from one's body illuminates all darkness.

All sorts of such pleasures as these
all come from giving and observance of the precepts.
If one wishes to gain this reward,
one ought to be diligent and exhort oneself in this.

(1) Since Buddhahood is the Goal, Why Praise the Heavens?

Question: Now we are discussing the *śīla pāramitā*. It should be for the purpose of realizing buddhahood. Why is there now this praising of the merits of the heavens?

(2) Three Endeavors Entailing Certain Rewards

Response: The Buddha said that there are three endeavors that certainly entail rewards and for which the gaining of results is not a false matter: If one gives, one gains great fortune. If one upholds the precepts, one will be reborn in a fine place. If one cultivates the meditative absorptions, one will gain liberation.

If one practices *śīla* alone, one will succeed in being born in a fine place. If one additionally implements the combined practice of the absorptions, wisdom, kindness and compassion, one will succeed in gaining the path of the Three Vehicles.

(3) Attraction to Karmic Rewards Conducing to the Path

We are just now praising the upholding of precepts in particular. This brings meritorious qualities, fame, peace, and bliss in the present life while gaining in later lives rewards such as were praised in the verse. This is analogous to smearing honey on bitter medicine for a small child so that he then becomes able to swallow it. We now initially praise the merit from the precepts so that a person then becomes able to uphold the precepts. After one has been able to uphold the precepts, he makes the great vow to succeed in reaching the path to buddhahood. This amounts to the practice of *śīla* finally producing *śīla pāramitā*.

Also, because all people are attached to bliss and because, among all of the world's blisses, those in the heavens are the most supreme, if people hear of all of the various sorts of pleasure and happiness in the heavens, they will then be able to take on the practice of *śīla*.

正體字

後聞天上無常。厭患心生能求解
159b13 脫。更聞佛無量功德。若慈悲心生。依尸羅
159b14 波羅蜜。得至佛道。以是故雖說尸羅報無
159b15 咎。問曰。白衣居家唯此五戒。更有餘法耶。
159b16 答曰。有一日戒六齋日持功德無量。若十二
159b17 月一日至十五日。受持此戒其福[10]甚多。問
159b18 曰。云何受一日戒。答曰。受一日戒法長跪
159b19 合掌應如是言。我某甲今一日一夜。歸依
159b20 佛歸依法歸依僧。如是二如是三歸依。我
159b21 某甲歸依佛竟。歸依法竟。歸依僧竟。如
159b22 是二如是三歸依竟。我某甲若身業不善。若
159b23 口業不善。若意業不善。貪欲瞋恚愚癡故。若
159b24 今世若[11]過世有如是罪。今日誠心懺悔。身
159b25 清淨口清淨心清淨。受行八戒是則布薩。
159b26 [12]秦言[13]共住。

简体字

后闻天上无常，厌患心生，能求解脱；更闻佛无量功德，若慈悲心生，依尸罗波罗蜜得至佛道。以是故，虽说尸罗报无咎。

问曰：白衣居家，唯此五戒，更有余法耶？

答曰：有一日戒，六斋日持，功德无量；若十二月一日至十五日，受持此戒，其福最多。

问曰：云何受一日戒？

答曰：受一日戒法，长跪合掌，应如是言："我某甲今一日一夜，归依佛、归依法、归依僧！"如是二、如是三归依。"我某甲归依佛竟、归依法竟、归依僧竟。"如是二、如是三归依竟。"我某甲若身业不善，若口业不善，若意业不善，贪欲、瞋恚、愚痴故。若今世，若先世，有如是罪，今日诚心忏悔。身清净，口清净，心清净，受行八戒。是则布萨，此言善宿。

Later, when they have heard of the impermanence of the heavens, thoughts of aversion and abhorrence will develop, and they will finally be able to take up the quest for liberation.

When people additionally hear of the incalculable meritorious qualities of the Buddha, it may be then that thoughts of kindness and compassion will arise in them. As a result, they may then become able to rely upon *śīla pāramitā* as the means to succeed in reaching the path to buddhahood. It is on account of these factors that, although we do discuss the rewards associated with *śīla,* there is no fault inherent in it.[24]

b. The Specific-Term Practice of Eight Precepts

Question: Is it that the householder has only these these five precepts, or are there other relevant dharmas in addition to these?

Response: There are also the one-day precepts and the six days of abstinence. The merit gained from upholding those is incalculable. If one is able to observe these precepts from the first through the fifteenth of the twelfth month, his merit will become extremely abundant.

1) The Ceremony for Specific-Term Eight-Precept Practice

Question: How does one go about taking the one-day precepts?

Response: The dharma for accepting the one-day precepts entails kneeling on both knees with the palms joined while making a statement such as this: "I, so-and-so, now, for one day and one night, take refuge in the Buddha, take refuge in the Dharma, and take refuge in the Saṃgha." One proceeds in this manner, proclaiming the taking of the refuges for a second and a third time.

Next, one proclaims, "I, so-and-so, have now taken refuge in the Buddha. I have now taken refuge in the Dharma. I have now taken refuge in the Saṃgha." One proceeds in this manner, declaring the completion of the refuges for a second and a third time.

Next, one proclaims, "I, so-and-so, whether it be bad karma of the body, bad karma of the mouth, or bad karma of the mind, whether it be on account of greed, on account of hatred, or on account of stupidity, and whether it be that I have offenses such as these in the present life or in former lives, today, with a sincere mind, I repent of them all in order to achieve purity of the body, purity of the mouth and purity of the mind."

If one then takes on the practice of the eight precepts this constitutes the *upavāsa.* (Chinese textual note: In our language, this means "dwelling together.")

正體字

如諸佛盡壽不殺生。我某甲
159b27 一日一夜。不殺生亦如是。如諸佛盡壽不
159b28 盜。我某甲一日一夜。不盜亦如是。[14]如諸
159b29 佛盡壽不婬。我某甲一日一夜不婬亦如
159c01 是。如諸佛盡壽不妄語。我某甲一日一夜
159c02 不妄語亦如是。如諸佛盡壽不飲酒。我
159c03 某甲一日一夜不飲酒亦如是。如諸佛盡
159c04 壽不坐高大床上。我某甲一日一夜。不坐
159c05 高大床上亦如是。如諸佛盡壽不著花瓔
159c06 珞。不香塗身不著香熏衣。我某甲一日一
159c07 夜。不著花瓔珞不香塗身不著香熏衣亦
159c08 如是。如諸佛盡壽不自歌舞作樂[15]亦不
159c09 往觀聽。我某甲一日一夜。不自歌舞作樂
159c10 不往觀聽亦如是。已受八戒。如諸佛盡
159c11 壽不過中食。我某甲一日一夜。不過中食
159c12 亦如是。我某甲受行八戒隨學諸佛法。名
159c13 為布薩。願持是布薩福報。[16]願生生不墮
159c14 三惡八難。我亦不求轉輪聖王梵釋天王世
159c15 界之樂。

简体字

如诸佛尽寿不杀生，我某甲一日一夜不杀生亦如是；如诸佛尽寿不盗，我某甲一日一夜不盗亦如是；如诸佛尽寿不淫，我某甲一日一夜不淫亦如是；如诸佛尽寿不妄语，我某甲一日一夜不妄语亦如是；如诸佛尽寿不饮酒，我某甲一日一夜不饮酒亦如是；如诸佛尽寿不坐高大床上，我某甲一日一夜不坐高大床上亦如是；如诸佛尽寿不著华缨络、不香涂身、不著香熏衣，我某甲一日一夜不著华缨络、不香涂身、不著香熏衣亦如是；如诸佛尽寿不自歌舞作乐、不往观听，我某甲一日一夜不自歌舞作乐、不往观听亦如是。已受八戒，如诸佛尽寿不过中食，我某甲一日一夜不过中食亦如是。我某甲受行八戒，随学诸佛法，名为布萨。愿持是布萨福报，生生不堕三恶八难。我亦不求转轮圣王、梵释天王世界之乐；

Next, one proclaims, "Just as the Buddhas, for the remainder of their entire lives, did not kill beings, in the same manner, I, so-and-so, for one day and one night, will not kill beings.

"Just as the Buddhas, for the remainder of their entire lives, did not steal, in the same manner, I, so-and-so, for one day and one night, will not steal.

"Just as the Buddhas, for the remainder of their entire lives, did not engage in sexual activity, in the same manner, I, so-and-so, for one day and one night, will not engage in sexual activity.

"Just as the Buddhas, for the remainder of their entire lives, did not commit false speech, in the same manner, I, so-and-so, for one day and one night, will not commit false speech.

"Just as the Buddhas, for the remainder of their entire lives, did not drink intoxicants, in the same manner, I, so-and-so, for one day and one night, will not drink intoxicants.

"Just as the Buddhas, for the remainder of their entire lives, did not sit on a high or grand couch, in the same manner, I, so-and-so, for one day and one night, will not sit on a high or grand couch.

"Just as the Buddhas, for the remainder of their entire lives, did not wear flowers or necklaces, did not perfume their bodies, and did not perfume their robes, in the same manner, I, so-and-so, for one day and one night, will not wear flowers or necklaces and will not perfume my body or my robes.

"Just as the Buddhas, for the remainder of their entire lives, did not themselves sing or dance or make music and did not go to watch or listen to it, in the same manner, I, so-and-so, for one day and one night, will not myself sing or dance or make music or go and observe or listen to it."

At this point, one completes the taking of the eight precepts.

One then continues by proclaiming, "Just as the Buddhas, for the remainder of their entire lives, did not eat past midday, in the same manner, I, so-and-so, for one day and one night, will not eat past midday.

"I, so-and-so, accept and practice the eight precepts and pursue the study of the Dharma of the Buddhas. This constitutes the *upavāsa*. I pray I will be able to sustain the meritorious retribution of this *upavāsa* and so pray that in life after life I will not fall into the three wretched destinies or experience the eight difficulties.

"I do not seek the pleasures of a wheel-turning sage king, of Brahmā or Śakradevendra, the kings of the gods, or of worldly

正體字

願諸煩惱盡逮[17]得薩婆若成就佛
159c16 道。問曰。云何受五戒。答曰。受五戒法。長跪
159c17 合[18]掌言。我某甲歸依佛歸依法歸依僧。
159c18 如是[19]二如是三。我某甲歸依佛竟。歸依
159c19 法竟。歸依僧竟。如是二如是三。我是釋迦
159c20 牟尼佛優婆塞證知我。[20]我某甲從今日盡
159c21 壽歸依。戒師應言。汝優婆塞聽。是多陀阿
159c22 伽度阿羅呵三藐三佛陀知人見人。為優婆
159c23 塞說五戒如是。[21]是汝盡壽持。何等五。盡
159c24 壽不殺生是優婆塞戒。是中盡壽不應故
159c25 殺生。是事若能當言諾。盡壽不盜。是優婆
159c26 塞戒。是中盡壽不應盜。是事若能當言諾。
159c27 盡壽不邪婬。是優婆塞戒。是中盡壽不應
159c28 邪婬。是事若能當言諾。盡壽不妄語。是優
159c29 婆塞戒。是中盡壽不應妄語。是事若能當
160a01 言諾。盡壽不飲酒。是優婆塞戒。是中盡壽
160a02 不應飲酒。是事若能當言諾。

简体字

愿诸烦恼尽，逮萨婆若，成就佛道。”

问曰：云何受五戒？

答曰：受五戒法，长跪合掌言：“我某甲，归依佛、归依法、归依僧！”如是二、如是三。“我某甲归依佛竟、归依法竟、归依僧竟。”如是二、如是三。“我是释迦牟尼佛优婆塞，证知我某甲，从今日尽寿归依。”戒师应言：“汝优婆塞听！是多陀阿伽度、阿罗诃、三藐三佛陀，知人见人，为优婆塞说五戒如是，汝尽寿持！何等五？尽寿不杀生，是优婆塞戒，是中尽寿不应故杀生；是事若能，当言诺。尽寿不盗，是优婆塞戒，是中尽寿不应盗；是事若能，当言诺。尽寿不邪淫，是优婆塞戒，是中尽寿不应邪淫；是事若能，当言诺。尽寿不妄语，是优婆塞戒，是中尽寿不应妄语；是事若能，当言诺。尽寿不饮酒，是优婆塞戒，是中尽寿不应饮酒；是事若能，当言诺。

existence. I pray that I will be able to bring an end to all afflictions, will be able to succeed in gaining *sarvajñāna* (omniscience), and will be able to succeed in perfect realization of the path to buddhahood."

2) The Ceremony for Life-Long Five-Precept Practice

Question: How does one go about taking the five precepts?

Response: The dharma for accepting the five precepts is as follows: Kneeling on both knees with the palms joined, one then proclaims, "I, so-and-so, take refuge in the Buddha, take refuge in the Dharma, and take refuge in the Saṃgha." One proceeds in this fashion for a second and a third time.

Next, one proclaims, "I, so-and-so, have now taken refuge in the Buddha, have now taken refuge in the Dharma, and have now taken refuge in the Saṃgha." One proceeds thus a second and a third time.

Next, one states, "I am an *upāsaka* disciple of Śākyamuni Buddha. Pray, certify and be aware that I, so-and-so, take these refuges from this day onward, for the rest of my life."

The Precept Master then says, "You, Upāsaka, hear me: The Tathāgatha, the Arhat and Samyāksambuddha, is a man of knowledge and a man of vision. He proclaimed the five precepts for the *upāsaka* in just this way. They are to be upheld for the rest of your life.

"What are the five? They are: To not kill beings for the rest of one's life is an *upāsaka* precept. Herein, for the rest of one's life, one must not deliberately kill beings. If you are able to carry out this matter, then you should say, 'I do so swear.'

"To not steal for the rest of one's life is an *upāsaka* precept. Herein, for the rest of one's life, one must not steal. If you are able to carry out this matter, then you should say, 'I do so swear.'

"To not engage in sexual misconduct for the rest of your life is an *upāsaka* precept. Herein, for the rest of your life, you must not engage in sexual misconduct. If you are able to carry out this matter, then you should say, 'I do so swear.'

"To not engage in false speech for the rest of one's life is an *upāsaka* precept. Herein, for the rest of one's life, one must not engage in false speech. If you are able to carry out this matter, then you should say, 'I do so swear.'

"To not drink intoxicants for the rest of one's life is an *upāsaka* precept. Herein, for the rest of one's life, one must not drink intoxicants. If you are able to carry out this matter, then you should say, 'I do so swear.'

正體字

是優婆塞五
160a03 戒盡壽受持。當供養三寶佛寶法寶比丘
160a04 僧寶勤修福[1]業以來佛道。問曰。何以故。六
160a05 齋日受八戒修福德。答曰。是日惡鬼逐人
160a06 欲奪人命。疾病凶衰令人不吉。是故劫初
160a07 聖人。教人持齋修善作福以避凶衰。是時
160a08 齋法不受八戒。直以一日不食為齋。後佛
160a09 出世教語之言。汝當一日[2]一夜如諸佛持
160a10 八戒過中不食。是功德將人至涅槃。如四
160a11 天王經中佛說。月六齋日使者太子及四天
160a12 王。自下觀察眾生布施持戒孝順父母。少者
160a13 便上忉利以啟帝釋。帝釋諸天心皆不[3]悅
160a14 言。阿修羅種多諸天種少。若布施持戒孝順
160a15 父母多者。諸天帝釋心皆歡喜說言。增益
160a16 [4]天眾減損阿修羅。是時釋提婆那民[5]見諸
160a17 天歡喜。說此偈言
160a18 六日神足月　受持清淨戒
160a19 是人壽終後　功德必如我

简体字

是优婆塞五戒尽寿受持。当供养三宝：佛宝、法宝、比丘僧宝；勤修福德，以求佛道！”

问曰：何以故六斋日受八戒、修福德？

答曰：是日恶鬼逐人，欲夺人命，疾病凶衰，令人不吉。是故劫初圣人教人持斋，修善作福，以避凶衰。是时斋法不受八戒，直以一日不食为斋，后佛出世，教语之言：“汝当一日一夜，如诸佛持八戒，过中不食，是功德将人至涅槃。”如四天王经中佛说：月六斋日，使者太子及四天王，自下观察众生。布施、持戒、孝顺父母少者，便上忉利，以启帝释。帝释诸天心皆不悦，说言：“阿修罗种多，诸天种少。”若布施、持戒、孝顺父母多者，诸天帝释心皆欢喜，说言：“增益诸天众，减损阿修罗。”是时，释提婆那民见诸天欢喜，说此偈言：

“六日神足月，受持清净戒；是人寿终后，功德必如我！”

"These five precepts of the *upāsaka* are to be accepted and upheld for the remainder of one's life. One should make offerings to the Triple Jewel, the Buddha Jewel, the Dharma Jewel, and the Bhikshu Saṃgha Jewel. One should diligently cultivate meritorious karma and thereby come forth into the path to buddhahood."

3) Why Eight Precepts Are Observed on Six Days

Question: Why is it that, on the six days of abstinence, one takes the eight precepts and cultivates merit?

Response: It is on these days that evil ghosts pursue people desiring to rob them of their lives. They bring acute illnesses and calamitous ruination and thus cause people misfortune. Therefore the sages at the beginning of the kalpa instructed people to observe days of abstinence, cultivate good, and do meritorious deeds to thereby avoid calamity and ruination.

At that time, the abstinence dharma did not involve taking these eight precepts. It only took going one day without food as constituting abstinence. Later, when the Buddha came forth into the world, he instructed people, saying, "In the manner of the Buddha, you should uphold the eight precepts for one day and one night while also refraining from eating after midday. This merit will take a person to nirvāṇa."

According to what the Buddha said in *The Sutra of the Four Heavenly Kings*, on these six monthly abstinence days the retainers, princes, and the four heavenly kings themselves descend, observe, and investigate the status of beings' giving, maintenance of the precepts, and filial piety toward their fathers and mothers. In an instance where it is deficient, they then ascend to the Trāyastriṃśa Heaven and inform Śakra of this. In such a case, Śakra and the other gods are all disappointed and proclaim, "The clan of the *asuras*[25] is on the increase and the clan of the gods is diminishing."

If, however, it is the case that the giving, maintenance of precepts, and filial piety toward fathers and mothers is greater, then the gods and Śakra are all delighted and thus proclaim, "There is increase in the company of the gods and a decrease among the *asuras*. At one such time, Śakradevendra observed the delight among the gods and uttered a verse, saying:

If, on six days and [on fifteen] in "spiritual" months,[26]
someone is able to uphold the pure precepts—
After this person's life has come to an end,
his merit will certainly be comparable to mine.

正體字

160a20 佛告諸比丘。釋提桓因不應說如是偈。所
160a21 以者何。釋提桓因[6]三衰三毒未除。云何妄
160a22 言持一日戒功德福報必得如我。若受持
160a23 此戒心應如佛。是則實說。諸大尊天歡喜
160a24 因緣故。得福增多。復次此六齋日。惡鬼害
160a25 人惱亂一切。若所在丘聚郡縣國邑。有持
160a26 齋受戒[7]行善人者。以此因緣惡鬼遠去。住
160a27 處安隱。以是故六日持齋受戒得福增多。
160a28 問曰。何以故諸惡鬼[8]神輩。以此六日惱害
160a29 於人。答曰。天地本起經說。劫初成時有異梵
160b01 天王子。諸鬼神父。修梵志苦行。滿天上十
160b02 二歲。於此六日。割肉出血以著火中。以是
160b03 故諸惡鬼神。於此六日輒有勢力。問曰。諸
160b04 鬼神父。何以於此六日割身肉血以著火
160b05 中。答曰。諸神中摩醯首羅神最大第一。諸神
160b06 皆有日分。摩醯首羅。一月有四日分。八日
160b07 二十三日十四日二十九日。餘神一月有二
160b08 日分。月一日十六日

简体字

佛告诸比丘："释提桓因，不应说如是偈。所以者何？释提桓因，五衰、三毒未除，云何妄言持一日戒，功德福报必得如我？若受持此戒，必应如佛，是则实说。"诸大尊天欢喜因缘故，得福增多。

复次，此六斋日，恶鬼害人，恼乱一切。若所在丘聚、郡县、国邑，有持斋受戒善人者，以此因缘，恶鬼远去，住处安隐。以是故，六日持斋受戒，得福增多。

问曰：何以故诸恶鬼辈，以此六日恼害于人？

答曰：天地本起经说：劫初成时，有异梵天王子诸鬼神父，修梵志苦行，满天上十二岁，于此六日，割肉、出血以著火中。以是故，诸恶鬼神于此六日辄有势力。

问曰：诸鬼神父，何以于此六日割身肉、血以著火中？

答曰：诸神中摩醯首罗神最大第一，诸神皆有日分。摩醯首罗一月有四日分：八日、二十三日、十四日、二十九日。余神一月有二日分：月一日、十六日，

The Buddha told the Bhikshus, "Śakradevendra should not have uttered a verse such as this. Why? Śakradevendra has not yet gotten rid of the five signs of deterioration[27] or the three poisons. How could he falsely state, 'If there is one who upholds the one-day precepts, he will certainly gain a meritorious reward comparable to mine.'? If one upholds these precepts, he ought as a result to become similar in mind to the Buddha. If he had said this, then it would have qualified as true speech."

Because the great and revered gods are delighted, one gains an increased amount of merit. Additionally, on these six abstinence days, evil ghosts bring harm to people and strive to visit affliction and confusion upon everyone. If, in the open country, village, prefecture, province, country, or city-state where one abides, there is a person who observes the days of abstinence, takes the precepts, and practices goodness, because of this, the evil ghosts depart far away and the place in which one dwells becomes peaceful and secure. For this reason, if one observes the abstinences and takes the precepts on these six days, one thereby gains increased merit.

4) Why Ghosts Act Up Six Days Each Month (Story)

Question: Why do the evil ghosts and spirits take advantage of these six days to visit affliction and harm on people?

Response: In *The Sutra on the Origins of Heaven and Earth*, it states that when this kalpa first began, there was a different "Brahmā" diety's son who was the father of the ghosts and spirits. He cultivated a form of *brahmacārin* ascetic practice whereby, for a full twelve heavenly years, on the occasion of these six days, he cut away portions of his own flesh, drew off a measure of his own blood, and then placed them in a fire. It was because of this that the evil ghosts and spirits would suddenly come into possession of particularly strong powers on these six days.

Question: Why on these six days did the father of the ghosts and spirits cut away the flesh and blood of his own body, placing them into a fire?

Response: Among all the ghosts and spirits, the Maheśvara spirit is the greatest and the most primary in status. All of the spirits have an allotted number of days. Maheśvara has an allotment of four days out of each month: the eighth, the twenty-third, the fourteenth, and the twenty-ninth.

The other spirits have an allotment of two days out of each month: their first day out of the month is the sixteenth and their

正體字

月二日十七日。其十五
160b09 日三十日屬一切神。摩醯首羅為諸神主。又
160b10 得日多故數其四日為齋。二日是一切諸
160b11 神日。亦數以為齋。是故諸鬼神。於此六日
160b12 輒有力勢
160b13 復次諸鬼[9]神父於此六日割肉出血以著
160b14 火中。過十二歲已。天王來下語其子言。汝
160b15 求何願。答言。我求有子。天王言。仙人供養
160b16 法。以燒香甘果諸清淨事。汝云何以肉血
160b17 著火中。如罪惡法。汝破善法樂為惡事。
160b18 令汝生惡子噉肉飲血。當說。是時火中
160b19 有八大鬼出。身黑如墨髮黃眼赤有大光
160b20 明。一切鬼神皆從此八鬼生。以是故。於此
160b21 六日割身肉血以著火中而得勢力。如佛
160b22 法中日無好惡。隨世惡日因緣故。教持齋
160b23 受[10]八戒。問曰。五戒一日戒何者為勝。答曰。
160b24 有因緣故二戒俱等。但五戒

简体字

月二日、十七日。其十五日、三十日，属一切神。摩醯首罗为诸神主，又得日多故，数其四日为斋；二日是一切诸神日，亦数以为斋。是故诸鬼神于此六日，辄有力势。

复次，诸鬼神父，于此六日割肉、出血，以著火中；过十二岁已，天王来下，语其子言："汝求何愿？"答言："我求有子！"天王言："仙人供养法，以烧香、甘果诸清净事；汝云何以血、肉著火中，如罪恶法？汝破善法，乐为恶事，令汝生恶子，啖肉、饮血。"当说是时，火中有八大鬼出，身黑如墨，发黄、眼赤，有大光明。一切鬼神，皆从此八鬼生。以是故，于此六日，割身肉、血以著火中而得势力。如佛法中，日无好恶，随世恶日因缘故，教持斋受戒。

问曰：五戒、一日戒，何者为胜？

答曰：有因缘故，二戒俱等。但五戒

second day out of the month is the seventeenth. The fifteenth and the thirtieth belong collectively to all spirits.

Because Maheśvara is the lord of all of the spirits and because he has been allotted the most days, his four days came to be counted as abstinence days. The other two days also counted as abstinence days are the days belonging collectively to all of the spirits. Hence, all of the ghosts and spirits suddenly possess strong powers on these six days.

Furthermore, after the father of ghosts and spirits had continued for twelve years his practice of cutting away his own flesh, drawing off his blood, and placing them in fire, the king of the gods descended and asked his son, "What prayer do you seek to fulfill by doing this?"

He replied, "I seek to have sons."

The king of the gods said, "It is the offering method of the *rishis* to employ the burning of incense, the offering up of sweet fruits, and the carrying out of all manner of pure endeavors. Why do you employ this method of placing flesh and blood into fire, a method associated with offensive and evil dharmas? Your destruction of the dharma of goodness and your taking pleasure in carrying out evil endeavors will cause you to give birth to evil sons who feast on flesh and drink blood."

Then, in accordance with his proclamation, eight huge ghosts came forth at that very moment from within the fire. Their bodies were as black as ink. Their hair was yellow, their eyes were red, and they shone with abundant light. Then, all manner of ghosts and spirits were subsequently born from these eight ghosts. Thus it was that this practice of carving off his own flesh, drawing his own blood, and then placing them into fire resulted in the generation of such power.

As for the Dharma of the Buddha, though, these days are devoid of any particular auspiciousness or adversity. But nonetheless, as an adaptation to the world's treatment of these as inauspicious days, one is instructed to observe the abstinences and take the eight precepts on these days.

c. Comparison of Five and Eight Precepts

Question: Which is superior, the five precepts or the one-day precepts?

Response: There may be causal bases whereby the two precept categories can be considered equal. However, the five precepts are

正體字

終身持。八戒一
160b25 日持。又五戒常持時多而戒少。一日戒時少
160b26 而戒多。復次若無大心雖復終身持戒。不
160b27 如有大心人一日持戒也。譬如軟夫為將。
160b28 雖復[11]將兵終身。智勇不足卒無功名。若
160b29 如英雄奮發禍亂立定。一日之勳功蓋天下。
160c01 是二種戒。名居家優婆塞法。居家持戒凡有
160c02 四種。有下中上。有上上。下人持戒為今世
160c03 樂故。或為怖畏稱譽名聞故。或為家法曲
160c04 隨他意故。或避苦[12]役求離[13]危難故。如
160c05 是種種是下人持戒。中人持戒。為人中富貴
160c06 歡娛適意。或期後世福樂。[14]剋己自勉為
160c07 苦。日少所得甚多。

简体字

终身持，八戒一日持。又五戒常持，时多而戒少，一日戒时少而戒多。

复次，若无大心，虽复终身持戒，不如有大心人一日持戒也。譬如软夫为将，虽复持兵终身，智勇不足，卒无功名；若如英雄奋发，祸乱立定，一日之勋，功盖天下。是二种戒，名居家优婆塞法。居家持戒，凡有四种：有下、中、上，有上上。下人持戒，为今世乐故；或为怖畏，称誉名闻故；或为家法，曲随他意故；或避苦役，求离厄难故。如是种种，是下人持戒。中人持戒，为人中富贵，欢娱适意；或期后世福乐，克己自勉，为苦日少，所得甚多，

taken for the rest of one's life, whereas the eight precepts are upheld for only a single day at a time. But then again, although the five precepts are constantly upheld over a longer period of time, the precepts observed are fewer in number. With the one-day precepts, the time is less, but the number of precepts observed is greater.

As another consideration, if one is not possessed of a great mind, although one may uphold the precepts for one's entire life, the goodness involved does not measure up to that of a person of the great mind upholding the precepts for but a single day.[28]

This is analogous to a weak man serving as a general. Although he may serve as a general of the troops for the rest of his life, because of his inadequacies in wisdom and bravery, the shock troops will have no reputation for meritorious service. But if a greatly heroic man brings forth high resolve to immediately stabilize a disastrous and chaotic situation, through just a single day of devoted service, his meritorious reputation may spread throughout the world.

1) Four Grades of Lay Precept Observance

These two categories of precepts are dharmas intended for the householder, the *upāsaka*. The upholding of precepts on the part of the householder is commonly of four degrees. There are the lesser, the middling, the superior, and the superior among the superior.

2) The Lesser Grade of Lay Precept Observance

When a lesser person upholds the precepts, it may be for the sake of gaining pleasures in the present life, or perhaps it may be out of fearfulness, out of a desire to be praised, or out of a motivation to gain a prestigious reputation. Or it may be that for the sake of adhering to family standards, he will constrain himself to go along with someone else's ideas. It may also be done out of a desire to avoid a misery-ridden period of conscription or may be done because one seeks to avoid dangerous circumstances. All sorts of factors such as these may characterize the lesser person's observance of moral precepts.

3) The Middling Grade of Lay Precept Observance

When the middling person upholds the precepts, it is for the sake of wealth and noble status in the human realm and for the sake of gaining delights and pleasures that accord with his aspirations. Or perhaps, hoping for good fortune and bliss in later lives, one will endure self-denial and encourage himself, thinking, "The days one must suffer this are but few, whereas the gains to be achieved are extremely great."

正體字

如是思惟堅固持戒。譬
160c08 如商人遠出深入得利必多。持戒之福令人
160c09 受後世福樂亦復如是。上人持戒為涅槃
160c10 故。知諸法一切無常故。欲求離苦常樂無
160c11 為故。復次持戒之人其心不悔。心不悔故
160c12 得喜樂。[15]得喜樂故得一心。得一心故得
160c13 實智。得實智故得厭心。得厭心故得離
160c14 欲。得離欲故得解脫。得解脫故得涅槃。
160c15 如是持戒為諸善法根本。復次持戒為八正
160c16 道初門入道初門必至涅槃

简体字

如是思惟坚固持戒。譬如商人，远出深入，得利必多；持戒之福，令人受后世福乐，亦复如是。上人持戒，为涅槃故；知诸法一切无常故，欲求离苦，常乐无为故。

复次，持戒之人，其心不悔，心不悔故得喜乐，得喜乐故得一心，得一心故得实智，得实智故得厌心，得厌心故得离欲，得离欲故得解脱，得解脱故得涅槃。如是持戒，为诸善法根本。

复次，持戒为八正道初门，入道初门，必至涅槃。

Through making such considerations, one may come to uphold the precepts solidly. This is comparable to a merchant's traveling far and investing heavily. The profit to be gained is bound to be great. The merit from upholding the precepts causes people to receive good fortune and bliss in later lives in just this fashion.

4) The Superior Grade of Lay Precept Observance

When the superior person observes the moral precepts, it is for the sake of nirvāṇa and because he knows that all dharmas are impermanent. It is because he wishes to transcend suffering and gain eternal enjoyment of the unconditioned.

a) How These Precepts Are the Causes for Nirvāṇa

Furthermore, the mind of the person who observes the moral precepts remains free of regrets. Because his mind remains free of regrets, he gains delight and enjoyment. Because he gains delight and enjoyment from it, he achieves single-mindedness. Because he achieves single-mindedness, he gains real wisdom. Because he gains real wisdom, he develops the mind of renunciation. Because he develops the mind of renunciation, he succeeds in transcending desire. Because he succeeds in transcending desire, he gains liberation. Because he gains liberation, he gains nirvāṇa. In this manner, upholding the precepts constitutes the foundation for all the good dharmas.

Moreover, the upholding of precepts constitutes the initial entryway onto the eightfold right path. This initial entryway onto the path certainly extends all the way to nirvāṇa.

正體字

160c17 [16]大智度論釋初品中讚尸[17]羅波羅蜜義
160c18 [18]第二十[19]三
160c19 問曰。如八正道。正語正業在中。正見正行在
160c20 初。今何以言戒為八正道初門。答曰。以數
160c21 言之大者為始。正見最大。是故在初。復次
160c22 行道故以見為先。諸法次第故戒在前。譬
160c23 如作屋棟梁雖大以地為先。上上人持戒
160c24 憐愍眾生。為佛道故。以知諸法求實相
160c25 故。不畏惡道不求樂故。如是種種。是上
160c26 上人持戒。是四總名優婆塞戒。出家戒亦有
160c27 四種。一者沙彌沙彌尼戒。二者式叉摩那戒。
160c28 三者比丘尼戒。四者比丘僧戒。問曰。若居家
160c29 戒得生天上。得

简体字

释赞尸罗波罗蜜义

问曰：如八正道，正语、正业在中，正见、正行在初，今何以言戒为八正道初门？

答曰：以数言之，大者为始，正见最大，是故在初。

复次，行道故，以见为先；诸法次第，故戒在前。譬如作屋，栋梁虽大，以地为先。上上人持戒，怜愍众生，为佛道故；以知诸法，求实相故，不畏恶道，不求乐故。如是种种，是上上人持戒。是四，总名优婆塞戒。

出家戒亦有四种：一者、沙弥、沙弥尼戒，二者、式叉摩那戒，三者、比丘尼戒，四者、比丘僧戒。

问曰：若居家戒得生天上，得

Ch. 1, Subchapter 23:
On the Meaning of Chapter One's Praise of Śīla Pāramitā

Part One: Additional Precept Specifics[29]

b) How Can Precepts Be Foremost in the Eightfold Path?

Question: According to the sequence in the eightfold right path, right speech and right livelihood are in the middle whereas right views [leading to] right practice are at the beginning. Why then do you now state that the precepts serve as the initial entryway into the eightfold right path?

Response: When we speak of numerical priorities, those of greatest significance are listed first. Right views is the one which is of greatest significance. Therefore it is placed at the beginning. Moreover, because one is traveling along a path, one takes seeing clearly as the foremost priority. Because all dharmas involve a particular sequence, it is the moral precepts that come first. This is analogous to the construction of a building in which, although the beams and rafters may be huge, one nonetheless must take the ground itself as the first priority.

5) The Superior-Superior Grade of Lay Precept observance

In the case of a person who is the most superior among the superior in the upholding of precepts, it is done out of pity for beings and for the sake of the path to buddhahood. It is in order to understand all dharmas and fathom their true character in accordance with reality. It is not done on account of fear of the wretched destinies and it is not done because one seeks to gain pleasures.

All sorts of motives such as these characterize the practice of one who is the most superior among the superior in the upholding of the precepts. These four categories generally constitute an *upāsaka's* practice of the precepts.

2. The Monastic Precepts

The precepts of those who have left the home life involve four categories: The first consists of the precepts of a *śrāmaṇera* and *śrāmaṇerikā*. The second consists of the precepts of a *śikṣamāṇā*. The third consists of the precepts of a bhikshuni. The fourth consists of the precepts of the Bhikshu Saṃgha.

Question: If by relying on the householder's precepts, one succeeds in being reborn in the heavens, succeeds in gaining the

正體字

菩薩道亦得至涅槃。復何
161a01 用出家戒。答曰。雖俱得度然有難易。居家
161a02 生[1]業種種事務。若欲專心道法家業則廢。
161a03 若欲專修家業道事則廢。不取不捨乃應
161a04 行法。是名為難。若出家離俗絕諸[2]紛亂。一
161a05 向專心行道為易
161a06 復次居家憒鬧多事多務。結使之根眾惡之
161a07 府。是為甚難。若出家者。譬如有人出在空
161a08 野無人之處而一其心。無思無慮內想既
161a09 除。外事亦去。如偈說
161a10 閑坐林樹間　寂然滅眾惡
161a11 恬澹得一心　斯樂非天樂
161a12 人求富貴利　名衣好床褥
161a13 斯樂非安隱　求利無厭足
161a14 納衣行乞食　動止心常一

简体字

菩萨道，亦得至涅槃，复何用出家戒？

答曰：虽俱得度，然有难易。居家生业种种事务，若欲专心道法，家业则废；若欲专修家业，道事则废；不取不舍，乃应行法，是名为难。若出家离俗，绝诸忿乱，一向专心，行道为易。

复次，居家愦闹，多事多务，结使之根，众恶之府，是为甚难。若出家者，譬如有人，出在空野无人之处而一其心，无思无虑，内想既除，外事亦去。如偈说：

“闲坐林树间，寂然灭众恶；恬澹得一心，斯乐非天乐。

人求富贵利，名衣好床褥；斯乐非安隐，求利无厌足。

纳衣行乞食，动止心常一；

bodhisattva path, and also succeeds in reaching nirvāṇa, of what further use are the monastic precepts?

a. The Value of the Monastic Precepts

1) Inherent Path-Defeating Difficulties in Lay Life

Response: Although one may gain liberation through both approaches, still, there are ways that are difficult and ways that are easier.

The actions involved in the life of a householder involve all kinds of endeavors and responsibilities. If one wishes to focus one's mind especially on the dharmas of the path, then the business of the family deteriorates. If one desires to focus one's mind especially on cultivating the business of the family, then the matters associated with the path deteriorate.

2) Comparison of Lay and Monastic Situations

Neither seizing on nor forsaking anything—it is in this manner that one should cultivate the Dharma. This is renowned for its difficulty. However, if one leaves the home life, separates from the circumstances of the laity, cuts off all complexity and chaos, and maintains a focused mind, then cultivating the path becomes easy.

Moreover, the befuddlement and boisterousness of the householder's life involves many endeavors and much responsibility. It is the root of the fetters and the repository of the manifold ills. This is an extremely difficult situation.

When one leaves the home life, it is analogous to a person being able to go forth into the unpopulated and empty wilderness to unify his mind. He is then able under those circumstances to become free of immersion in ideation and mental discursion. Once the inward thoughts have been gotten rid of, the outward matters depart as well. This is as described in a verse:

When sitting undisturbed within the forest,
in a state of stillness, one extinguishes the manifold ills.
Calmly and contentedly, one gains unity of mind.
This sort of bliss is unequaled even by the bliss of the heavens.

People seek after the benefit of wealth and noble status,
for famous fashions and for fine furnishings.
This sort of pleasure affords no peace or security.
One thus pursues one's own benefit, but finds no satisfaction.

The one with the patchwork robes practices reliance on alms,
and, whether moving or still, his mind is thus always unified.

正體字

161a15║ 自以智慧眼　觀知諸法實
161a16║ 種種法門中　皆以等觀入
161a17║ 解慧心寂然　三界無能及
161a18║ 以是故知出家修戒行道為易。復次出家修
161a19║ 戒。得無量善律儀。一切具足滿。以是故白
161a20║ 衣等應[3]當出家受[4]具足戒。復次佛法中出
161a21║ 家法第一難修。如閻浮呿提梵志問舍利
161a22║ 弗。於佛法中何者最難。舍利弗答曰。出家
161a23║ 為難。又問。出家[5]有何等難。答曰。出家樂法
161a24║ 為難。既得樂法復何者為難。修諸善法難。
161a25║ 以是故應出家。復次若人出家時。魔王驚
161a26║ [6]愁言。此人諸結使欲薄。必得涅槃墮僧寶
161a27║ 數中。復次佛法中出家人。雖破[7]戒墮罪。罪
161a28║ 畢得解脫。如[8]優鉢羅華比丘尼本生經中
161a29║ 說。

简体字

自以智慧眼，观知诸法实。

种种法门中，皆以等观入；解慧心寂然，三界无能及！”

以是故，知出家修戒，行道为易。

复次，出家修戒，得无量善律仪，一切具足满。以是故，白衣等应出家受戒。

复次，佛法中，出家法第一难修。如阎浮呿提梵志问舍利弗：“于佛法中，何者最难？”舍利弗答曰：“出家为难！”又问：“出家何等难？”答曰：“出家乐法为难。”“既得乐法，复何者为难？”“修诸善法难。”以是故，应出家。

复次，若人出家时，魔王惊疑言：“此人诸结使欲薄，必得涅槃，堕僧宝数中。”

复次，佛法中出家人，虽破形堕罪，罪毕得解脱。如郁钵罗华比丘尼本生经中说：

He spontaneously employs the eye of wisdom,
and so contemplates and knows the true character of all dharmas.

Among all the different entryways into the Dharma,
all are entered through contemplation of their equality.
When the understanding and wise mind abides in stillness,
nothing anywhere in the three realms is able to equal this.

For these reasons, one should realize that it is easiest to practice the path through leaving behind the home life and cultivating the precepts under those circumstances.

Additionally, if one leaves the home life and cultivates the monastic precepts, one becomes able to achieve the complete perfection of an incalculable number of aspects of good moral conduct. It is for these reasons that members of the lay community should leave the home life and take on the complete precepts.

3) Difficulties Specific to the Monastic Life

Then again, it is also the case that, within the Dharma of the Buddha, the particular dharma of leaving the home life is the one that is the most difficult to cultivate. This is as alluded to in the questions of the *brahmacārin* Jambukhādaka to Śāriputra, in which he asked, "In the Dharma of the Buddha, what is most difficult?"

Śāriputra replied, "Leaving behind the home life is difficult."

He then also asked, "What are the difficulties involved in leaving the home life?"

He replied, "Having left the home life, it is delighting in the Dharma that is difficult."

"If one succeeds in delighting in the Dharma, then what beyond this is difficult?"

"To cultivate all good dharmas is difficult."

For the above reasons, one should leave behind the home life. Moreover, when one leaves behind the home life, the king of the *māras* becomes frightened and worried, saying, "The fetters of this man are about to become scant. He will certainly gain nirvāṇa and thus fall in among the members of the Saṃgha Jewel."

4) Utpalavarṇā Promotes Monasticism (Story)

Also, although among those who have left the home life in the Dharma of the Buddha there are those who break the precepts and fall into offenses, once the corresponding karmic retribution has come to an end, they then succeed in gaining liberation. This is as described in *The Bhikshuni Utpalavarṇā Jātaka Sutra.*

正體字

佛在世時。此比丘尼得六神通阿羅漢。入
161b01 | 貴人舍常讚出家法。語諸貴人婦女言。姊
161b02 | 妹可出家。諸貴婦女言。我等少壯容色盛美
161b03 | 持戒為難。或當破戒。比丘尼言。但出家破
161b04 | 戒便破。問言。破戒當墮地獄。云何可破。答
161b05 | 言。墮地獄便墮。諸貴婦[9]女笑之言。地獄受
161b06 | 罪云何可墮。比丘尼言。我自憶念本宿命。
161b07 | 時作戲女著種種衣服而說舊語。或時著
161b08 | 比丘尼衣以為戲笑。以是因緣故。迦葉佛
161b09 | 時作比丘尼。自恃貴姓端[＊]政。心生憍慢而
161b10 | 破禁戒。破戒罪故墮地獄受種種罪。受罪
161b11 | 畢竟值釋迦牟尼佛。出家得六神通阿羅漢
161b12 | 道。以是故知。出家受戒。雖復破戒以戒因
161b13 | 緣故。得阿羅漢道。

简体字

佛在世时，此比丘尼得六神通阿罗汉，入贵人舍，常赞出家法，语诸贵人妇女言：“姊妹可出家！”诸贵妇女言：“我等少壮，容色盛美，持戒为难，或当破戒！”比丘尼言：“但出家，破戒便破。”问言：“破戒当堕地狱，云何可破？”答言：“堕地狱便堕！”诸贵妇女皆笑之言：“地狱受罪，云何可堕？”比丘尼言：“我自忆念本宿命时作戏女，著种种衣服而说旧语，或时著比丘尼衣以为戏笑。以是因缘故，迦葉佛时作比丘尼，自恃贵姓端正，心生憍慢而破禁戒；破戒罪故，堕地狱受种种罪。受罪毕竟，值释迦牟尼佛出家，得六神通阿罗汉道。以是故，知出家受戒，虽复破戒，以戒因缘故得阿罗汉道；

When the Buddha was still abiding in the world, this bhikshuni gained the six superknowledges and arhatship. She made a practice of going into the households of the nobility where she constantly praised the tradition of leaving the home life. In doing so, she spoke to the wives and daughters of the nobility, saying, "Sisters, you could leave behind the home life."

The wives and daughters among the nobility replied, "But we are young and strong. Our countenances and physical forms are full and beautiful. It would be difficult to uphold the precepts. It might happen that we would break the precepts."

The Bhikshuni then replied, "Just go ahead and leave the home life, anyway. If it does happen that you end up breaking the precepts, then so it is: You break them."

They responded, "If we break the precepts, we'll fall into the hells. How could it be conceivable that they might be broken?"

She replied, "If it happens that you end up falling into the hells, then you fall."

The wives and daughters of the nobility all laughed at this, saying, "When one falls into the hells, one is compelled to undergo punishments. How then could one even contemplate a situation where one might fall?"

The Bhikshuni replied, "I recall that in a previous life I was an actress who put on all sorts of costumes in which I would play traditional parts. There were times when I would put on the robes of a bhikshuni and then regarded that as laughable. It was due to these causal circumstances that, at the time of Kāśyapa Buddha, I was actually able to become a bhikshuni. However, on account of my noble birth and beauty, I was overcome with arrogance and then broke the restrictive prohibitions. On account of the karmic offenses associated with having broken the precepts, I fell into the hells where I underwent all sorts of punishments as retribution.

"When I had finished undergoing retribution for those offenses, I was able to encounter Śākyamuni Buddha and leave the home life again, whereupon I then succeeded in gaining the six superknowledges and the path of arhatship. Based on this, one should realize that, if one leaves the home life and takes those precepts, even though one may happen to break the precepts, one is nonetheless bound to succeed in gaining the path of arhatship as a result of the causal circumstances associated with having taken those precepts in the first place.

正體字

若但作惡無戒因緣不
161b14 得道也。我乃昔時世世墮地獄。地獄出為
161b15 惡人。惡人死還入地獄都無所得。今以此
161b16 證知出家受戒。雖復破戒以是因緣可得
161b17 道果。復次如佛在[10]祇洹。有一醉婆羅門。來
161b18 到佛所求作比丘。佛勅阿難與剃頭著法
161b19 衣。醉酒既醒驚怪己身忽為比丘即便走
161b20 去。諸比丘問佛。何以聽此醉婆羅門作比
161b21 丘。佛言。此婆羅門無量劫中初無出家心。今
161b22 因醉故暫發微心。以是因緣故[11]後當出家
161b23 得道。如是種種因緣。出家之利功德無量。以
161b24 是故白衣雖有五戒不如出家。是出家律
161b25 儀有四種。沙彌沙彌尼式叉摩[12]那比丘尼比
161b26 丘。

简体字

若但作恶，无戒因缘，不得道也。我乃昔时世世堕地狱，地狱出为恶人，恶人死还入地狱，都无所得。”今以此证知出家受戒，虽复破戒，以是因缘可得道果。

复次，如佛在祇洹，有一醉婆罗门来到佛所，求作比丘。佛敕阿难与剃头，著法衣。醉酒既醒，惊怪己身忽为比丘，即便走去。诸比丘问佛：“何以听此醉婆罗门作比丘？”佛言：“此婆罗门，无量劫中初无出家心，今因醉故暂发微心，以是因缘故当出家得道。”如是种种因缘，出家之利，功德无量。以是故，白衣虽有五戒，不如出家。是出家律仪有四种：沙弥、沙弥尼，式叉摩那，比丘尼，比丘。

"However, if one merely commits evil deeds, but yet does so in the absence of that causal circumstance of having taken the precepts, then one will not succeed in realization of the path. And so it was that I fell into the hells in many previous lifetimes, only to emerge from the hells and become an evil person again, whereupon I would fall right back down into the hells. As a consequence, I failed in those instances to gain anything worthwhile as a result."

Now, based on this, we can verify that, if one simply leaves behind the home life and takes the precepts, even though one might eventually break the precepts, one will nonetheless finally succeed in gaining the fruition of the path through the force of those causal circumstances."

5) An Inebriated Brahman Becomes a Monk (Story)

Then again, this point is also illustrated by that time when the Buddha dwelt in the Jeta Grove and a drunken brahman came before the Buddha requesting to become a bhikshu. The Buddha ordered Ānanda to administer tonsure and outfit the man in the Dharma robes. When that brahman awoke from his inebriation, he was startled and amazed that he had suddenly become a bhikshu, whereupon he immediately ran off.

The other bhikshus then inquired of the Buddha, "Why did the Buddha permit this drunken brahman to become a bhikshu?"

The Buddha replied, "Even in innumerable eons, this brahman has never thought to leave the home life. Now, due to his inebriation, he briefly generated a feeble intention to do so. On account of this causal circumstance, he will later become able to leave the home life and achieve realization of the path."

6) Concluding Statement on Lay Life versus Monasticism

Based on all sorts of causal circumstances such as these, one can see that the benefits and merit of leaving the home life are incalculable. Hence, although the members of the lay community do possess the five precepts, they cannot be compared to those associated with leaving the home life.

b. The Four Categories of Monastic Precepts

The moral regulations of those who have left the home life consist of four categories: those of the *śrāmaṇera* and *śrāmaṇerikā* (male and female novices); those of the *śikṣamāṇā* (a postulant novice nun); those of the bhikshuni (fully-ordained nun); and those of the bhikshu (a fully ordained monk).

正體字

云何沙彌沙彌尼。出家受戒法。白衣來欲
161b27 求出家。應求二師。一[13]和上。一[14]阿闍梨。和
161b28 上如父阿闍梨如母。以棄本生父母。當求
161b29 出家父母。著袈[15]裟[16]剃除鬚髮。應兩[17]手捉
161c01 和上兩足。何以捉足。天竺法以捉足。為第
161c02 一恭敬供養。阿闍梨應教十戒。如受戒法。
161c03 沙彌尼亦如是。唯以比丘尼為和上。式叉
161c04 摩那受六法二歲。問曰。沙彌十戒便受具
161c05 足戒。比丘尼法中。[18]何以有式叉摩那。然後
161c06 得受具足戒。答曰。佛在世時。有一長者婦。
161c07 不覺懷妊出家受具足戒。其後身大轉現。
161c08 諸長者譏嫌比丘。因此制。有二[19]歲學戒
161c09 受六法。然後受具足戒。問曰。若為譏嫌。式
161c10 叉摩那豈不致譏。答曰。式叉摩那未受具
161c11 足[20]戒。譬如小兒亦如給使。雖有罪穢人
161c12 不譏嫌。[21]是[22]名式叉摩那[23]受六法。

简体字

云何沙弥、沙弥尼出家受戒法？白衣来欲求出家，应求二师：一和尚，一阿阇黎。和尚如父，阿阇黎如母；以弃本生父母，当求出家父母。著袈裟衣，剃除须发，应两手捉和尚两足。何以捉足？天竺法以捉足为第一恭敬供养。阿阇黎应教十戒，如受戒法。沙弥尼亦如是，唯以比丘尼为和尚。式叉摩那受六法二岁。

问曰：沙弥十戒，便受具足戒；比丘尼法中，何以有式叉摩那，然后得受具足戒？

答曰：佛在世时，有一长者妇，不觉怀妊，出家受具足戒。其后身大转现，诸长者讥嫌比丘；因此制有二年学戒，受六法，然后受具足戒。

问曰：若为讥嫌，式叉摩那岂不致讥？

答曰：式叉摩那未受具足，譬如小儿，亦如给使；虽有罪秽，人不讥嫌。

What are the means by which a *śrāmaṇera* and *śrāmaṇerikā* leave the home life and take on those precepts? The lay follower who comes seeking to leave the home life should request two masters: one *upādhyāya* and one *ācārya*. The *upādhyāya* is comparable to one's father whereas the *ācārya* is comparable to one's mother. Having set aside one's original parents, one should thus seek out among the monastics those capable of serving in those roles.

One next dons the *kāṣāya* robe while also cutting off the hair and beard. [In bowing down in respect], one should then grasp the feet of the *upādhyāya* with his two hands. Why does one grasp his feet? It is the custom of India that to grasp the feet demonstrates the most superior form of reverential offering. The *acārya* should then provide instruction in the ten precepts. This is done in accordance with the protocols for receiving those precepts. For the *śrāmaṇerikā* it is just the same, the difference being that she takes a bhikshuni to serve as her *upādhyāya*. As for the *śikṣamāṇā*, she takes on six dharmas for a [pre-novitiate probationary] period of two years.

1) The Origin of the Śikṣamāṇā Postulant Nun Category

Question: The *śrāmaṇera* first takes the ten precepts and then takes the complete precepts. Why, within the dharma of the bhikshuni, does there exist the *śikṣamāṇā* stage, and only afterwards, the receiving of the complete precepts?

Response: When the Buddha was in the world, there once was the wife of an elder who, unaware that she had already become pregnant, nonetheless left the home life and received the complete precepts. Afterwards, her body swelled and her pregnancy began to show. On account of this, the elders ridiculed and criticized the bhikshus. It was on account of this that it was laid down that, [for nuns], there would be a two-year period of studying the precepts and accepting six dharmas after which one would progress toward taking the complete precepts.

a) Why Wouldn't a Pregnant Śikṣamāṇā Be as much a Liability?

Question: If the community had been ridiculed and criticized in the former circumstance, how is it that a *śikṣamāṇā* would not bring about ridicule in a similar situation?

Response: The *śikṣamāṇā* has not yet taken the complete precepts. Her circumstance is analogous to that of a small child or a servant whom people still do not ridicule or criticize even though they may incur the defilement of an offense. This is the situation when a *śikṣamāṇā* takes on the discipline of six dharmas.

正體字

是式叉
161c13 摩那有二種。一者十八歲童女受六法。二
161c14 者夫家十歲得受六法。若[24]欲受具足戒
161c15 應二部僧中。[25]用五衣鉢[26]盂。比丘尼。為和
161c16 上及教師。比丘為戒師。餘如受戒法。略說
161c17 則五[27]百戒。廣說則八萬戒。第三[28]羯磨訖。即
161c18 得無量律儀。成就比丘尼。比丘則有三衣
161c19 鉢[*]盂。三師十僧如受戒法。略說二百五十。
161c20 廣說則八萬。第三羯磨[29]訖。即得無量律儀
161c21 法。是總名為戒。是為尸羅
161c22 大智度論卷第十三

简体字

是式叉摩那有二种：一者、十八岁童女受六法，二者、夫家十岁得受六法。若受具足戒，应二部僧中用五衣钵盂；比丘尼为和尚及教师，比丘为戒师，余如受戒法。略说则五百戒，广说则八万戒。第三羯磨讫，即得无量律仪，成就比丘尼。比丘则有三衣钵盂，三师十僧，如受戒法。略说二百五十，广说则八万。第三羯磨讫，即得无量律仪法。是总名为戒，是为尸罗。

b) Two Subcategories of Śikṣamāṇā

This *śikṣamāṇā* category is of two types: The first is the eighteen-year-old virgin girl who has taken on six dharmas. The second is a woman who has been with the husband's family for a period of ten years but who is then able to take on the discipline of six dharmas.

2) The Bhikshuni Ordination

When she wishes to take the complete precepts, she should do so in the midst of the two divisions of the Saṃgha, wearing the five-stripe robe and carrying the bowl. Bhikshunis serve as the *upādhyāya* and as the teacher providing instruction. A bhikshu serves as the precept master.

The rest corresponds to the standard protocol for receiving the precepts. Generally speaking, this involves five hundred precepts. Extensively speaking, there are eighty thousand precepts. At the conclusion of the third *karmavācanā*, one then accesses an incalculable number of moral regulations in becoming a bhikshuni.

3) The Bhikshu Ordination

In the case of the bhikshu, there are three robes and a bowl. There are three masters along with an additional ten members of the Saṃgha, this in accordance with the standard protocol for receiving the precepts. [For the bhikshu], generally speaking, there are two hundred and fifty precepts. To speak of it in extensive terms, there are eighty thousand. At the conclusion of the third *karmavācanā*, one then accesses an incalculable number of moral regulation dharmas.

B. Conclusion of Precept Details Discussion

This has been a general presentation of what constitutes the moral precepts. These comprise [the bases] of what is intended by "*śīla*" (moral virtue).

正體字

T25n1509_p0162a02║ 大智度論釋初品中尸羅波羅蜜
162a03║ [1]義之餘(卷第十四)
162a04║
162a05║ [＊]龍樹菩薩造
162a06║ [＊]後秦龜茲國三藏鳩摩羅什
162a07║ [＊]奉　詔譯
162a08║ 問曰。已知尸羅相。云何為尸羅波羅蜜。答
162a09║ 曰。有人言。菩薩持戒寧自失身不毀小戒。
162a10║ 是為尸羅波羅蜜。如[2]上蘇陀蘇摩王經中
162a11║ 說。不惜身命以[3]全禁戒。如菩薩本身曾
162a12║ 作大力毒龍。若眾生在前。身力弱者眼視便
162a13║ 死。身力強者氣[4]往而死。是龍受一日戒。出
162a14║ 家求靜入林樹間。思惟坐久疲懈而睡。龍法
162a15║ 睡時形狀如蛇。身有文章七寶雜色。獵者
162a16║ 見之驚喜言曰。以此希有難得之皮。獻上
162a17║ 國王以為[5]服飾不亦宜乎。便以杖[6]按其
162a18║ 頭以刀剝其皮。龍自念言。我力如意。傾覆
162a19║ 此國其如反掌。此人小物豈能困我。我今
162a20║ 以持戒故不計

简体字

大智度论卷第十四

释初品中尸罗波罗蜜义之余

问曰：已知尸罗相，云何为尸罗波罗蜜？

答曰：有人言："菩萨持戒，宁自失身，不毁小戒，是为尸罗波罗蜜。"如上苏陀苏摩王经中说，不惜身命以全禁戒。如菩萨本身，曾作大力毒龙。若众生在前，身力弱者，眼视便死；身力强者，气往而死。是龙受一日戒，出家求静，入林树间思惟；坐久，疲懈而睡。龙法，睡时形状如蛇，身有文章，七宝杂色。猎者见之惊喜，言曰："以此希有难得之皮，献上国王以为服饰，不亦宜乎？"便以杖按其头，以刀剥其皮。龙自念言："我力如意，倾覆此国，其如反掌。此人小物，岂能困我？我今以持戒故，不计

Ch.1, Subchapter 23, Pt.2:
A Continued Explanation of the Perfection of Moral Virtue[30]

III. Ch.1, Subchapter 23, Pt. 2: A Continued Explanaton of the Perfection of Moral Virtue

A. Definition of the Perfection of Moral Virtue

Question: Now that we have already become aware of the specific aspects involved in "*śīla*" itself, what is it then that constitutes "*śīla pāramitā*" (the perfection of moral virtue)?

1. Indifference to Sacrificing One's Life in Upholding Precepts

Response: There are those who say that when the bodhisattva upholds the precepts and would rather lose his physical life than damage minor precepts, it is this which constitutes *śīla pāramitā*. As described in the previously-cited *The Sutra of King Sutasoma,* one does not spare even one's own physical life in order to preserve the integrity of the restrictive precepts.

2. Buddha's Past Life as a Dragon (Illustrative Story)

For example, in a former life, the Bodhisattva was a greatly powerful poisonous dragon. Whenever any being came to stand before him, in the case of those who were physically weak, if he so much as gazed upon them, they would die on the spot. As for those who were physically strong, if he breathed on them, they would die.

This dragon had taken the one-day precepts. He left his dwelling seeking quietude and had gone into the forest. He had been sitting in contemplation for a long time, became tired and lax, and then had fallen asleep. It is the way of dragons that when they fall asleep their bodies appear like those of snakes. His body had patterns on it which were composed of the various colors of the seven precious things.

It so happened that some hunters noticed him and, both startled and delighted, said, "Wouldn't it be appropriate to take this skin, so rare and difficult to come by, and offer it up to the King as an adornment for his robes?" They then held its head down with a staff and used a knife to strip away its skin.

The dragon thought to himself, "My strength is such that, were I only to wish it, turning this entire country upside down would be as easy as turning over one's hand. These people are but little creatures. How could they be able to put me in difficult straits? Because I am now upholding the precepts, I shall relinquish all regard for

正體字

此身當從佛語。於是自
162a21 忍[7]眠目不視。閉氣不息憐愍此人。為持
162a22 戒故一心受剝不生悔意。既以失皮赤肉
162a23 在地。時日大熱宛轉土中欲趣大水。見諸
162a24 小蟲來食其身。為持戒故不復敢動。自思
162a25 惟言。今我此身以施諸蟲。為佛道故今以
162a26 肉施以充其身。後成佛時當以法施以益
162a27 其心。如是誓已身乾命[8]絕。即生第二忉利
162a28 天上。爾時毒龍釋迦文佛是。[9]是時獵者提婆
162a29 達等六師是也。諸小蟲輩。釋迦文佛初轉法
162b01 輪八萬諸天得道者是。菩薩護戒不惜身
162b02 命。決定不悔。其事如是。是名尸羅波羅蜜。
162b03 復次菩薩持戒。為佛道故作大要誓。必度
162b04 眾生不求今世後世之樂。不為名聞[10]虛譽
162b05 法故。亦不自為早求涅槃。但為眾生沒
162b06 在長流。恩愛所欺愚惑所誤。我當度之令
162b07 到彼岸。

简体字

此身，当从佛语！”于是自忍，眼目不视，闭气不息；怜愍此人，为持戒故，一心受剥，不生悔意。既以失皮，赤肉在地，时日大热，宛转土中；欲趣大水，见诸小虫来食其身，为持戒故，不复敢动。自思惟言：“今我此身以施诸虫，为佛道故，今以肉施以充其身。后成佛时，当以法施以益其心。”如是誓已，身干命终，即生第二忉利天上。尔时毒龙，释迦文佛是也；时猎者，提婆达等六师是也；诸小虫辈，释迦文佛初转法轮，八万诸天得道者是。菩萨护戒，不惜身命，决定不悔，其事如是，是名尸罗波罗蜜。

复次，菩萨持戒，为佛道故，作大要誓：“必度众生！不求今世、后世之乐，不为名闻称誉法故，亦不自为早求涅槃，但为众生没在长流，恩爱所欺，愚惑所误，我当渡之令到彼岸。”

this body. I should just follow along with the instructions of the Buddha."

And so he remained patient while this was going on, kept his eyes closed, and refrained from casting his gaze on them. He held his breath and, out of pity for these men, kept himself from breathing on them. For the sake of upholding the precepts, he single-mindedly endured the peeling away of his skin, and did not develop any thoughts of regret.

Then, having lost his skin, his bare flesh rested directly on the ground. It was during a season when the sun was very hot. He slithered along through the dirt desiring to make his way to a large body of water. He then noticed all the little insects that had come to eat his body. Then, for the sake of upholding the precepts, he did not dare to move any more.

He thought to himself, "Now I will just donate my body to the insects. For the sake of the path to buddhahood, I will now make a gift of this flesh so that their bodies may become full. Later, when I have achieved buddhahood, I will use the giving of Dharma to benefit their minds."

Having made this vow, his body dried up and his life was cut off. He was then born in the second level of the Trāyastriṃśa Heavens. That poisonous dragon was a former incarnation of Śākyamuni Buddha. In the present era, those hunters manifested as Devadatta and the six [non-Buddhist] masters. The little insects were the eighty-thousand gods who gained the path when Śākyamuni Buddha first turned the wheel of the Dharma.

B. More Defining Characteristics of Śīla Pāramitā

The bodhisattva guards the precepts, not sparing even his own physical life in doing so. He is decisive in this and has no regrets. When his endeavors are of this sort, this constitutes *śīla pāramitā*.

Then again, as he observes the precepts, the bodhisattva makes a great vow for the sake of the path to buddhahood: "I will certainly bring beings across to liberation, will not seek the pleasures of this or later lives, will not do it for the sake of fame or the dharmas of an empty reputation, and will not do it for the sake of seeking an early nirvāṇa for myself. I will do it solely for the sake of beings who are submerged in the long-continuing flow [of the river of cyclic existence], who are cheated by their affections, and who are deceived by their own delusion. I will bring them across to liberation and thereby enable them to reach the far shore."

正體字

一心持戒為生善處。生善處故
162b08 見善人。見善人故生[11]智慧。生[＊]智慧故得
162b09 行六波羅蜜。[12]得行六波羅蜜故得佛道。
162b10 如是持戒名為尸羅波羅蜜。復次菩薩持戒
162b11 心樂善清淨。不為畏惡道。亦不為生天。但
162b12 求善[13]淨以戒[14]熏心令心樂善。是為尸羅
162b13 波羅蜜。復次菩薩以大悲心持戒得[15]至佛
162b14 道。是名尸羅波羅蜜。復次菩薩持戒。能生
162b15 六波羅蜜。是則名為尸羅波羅蜜。云何持戒
162b16 能生戒。因五戒得沙彌戒。因沙彌戒得
162b17 [16]律儀戒。因[＊]律儀戒得禪定戒因禪定戒
162b18 得無漏戒。是為戒生戒。云何持戒能生於
162b19 檀。檀有三種。一者財施。二者法施。三者無畏
162b20 施。

简体字

一心持戒，为生善处，生善处故见善人，见善人故生善智，生善智故得行六波罗蜜，行六波罗蜜故得佛道。如是持戒，名为尸罗波罗蜜。

复次，菩萨持戒，心乐善清净，不为畏恶道，亦不为生天，但求善清净；以戒熏心，令心乐善，是为尸罗波罗蜜。

复次，菩萨以大悲心持戒，得至佛道，是名尸罗波罗蜜。

复次，菩萨持戒，能生六波罗蜜，是则名为尸罗波罗蜜。

云何持戒能生戒？因五戒得沙弥戒，因沙弥戒得律仪戒，因律仪戒得禅定戒，因禅定戒得无漏戒，是为戒生戒。

云何持戒能生于檀？檀有三种：一者、财施，二者、法施，三者、无畏施。

He is single-minded in his observance of the moral precepts and is consequently reborn in a good place. Through rebirth in a good place, he meets good people. Through meeting good people, he develops wisdom. By developing wisdom, he succeeds in practicing the six *pāramitās*. Because he succeeds in practicing the six *pāramitās*, he gains the realization of the path to buddhahood. When one upholds the moral precepts in this manner, it is this which constitutes *śīla pāramitā*.

Moreover, in the bodhisattva's observance of the moral precepts, it is done with a mind that finds happiness in goodness and purity. It is not motivated by fear of the wretched destinies nor is it motivated by a desire to be reborn in the heavens. He seeks only to embody goodness and purity. It is through the mind's being imbued with the moral precepts that it is caused to take pleasure in goodness. This is what constitutes *śīla pāramitā*.

Furthermore, it is by using the mind of great compassion in upholding the precepts that the bodhisattva succeeds in reaching the path to buddhahood. It is this which constitutes *śīla pāramitā*.

1. How Śīla Generates All Six Perfections

Moreover, the bodhisattva's upholding of the precepts is able to bring forth all six of the *pāramitās*. It is this then that qualifies as "*śīla pāramitā*."

2. Śīla's Generation of Śīla Pāramitā

How is it that observing the moral precepts is itself able to produce [perfection in] the practice of the moral precepts? It is because of the five precepts that one gets the *śrāmaṇera* (novice) precepts. It is because of the *śrāmaṇera* precepts that one accesses the [complete] moral regulation precepts. It is because of those moral regulation precepts that one gains the moral precept observance associated with *dhyāna* absorption. It is because of the moral precept observance associated with *dhyāna* absorption that one attains the moral precepts free of the contaminants. This is the process by which the moral precepts themselves produce [perfection in] the moral precepts.

3. Śīla's Generation of Dāna Pāramitā

a. The Three Types of Giving

How does upholding the precepts engender *dāna*? There are three kinds of *dāna*: The first kind involves the giving of material wealth. The second kind is the giving of Dharma. The third kind is the giving of fearlessness.

正體字

持戒自撿不侵一切眾生財物。是[17]名財
162b21‖ 施。眾生見者慕其所行。又為說法令其開
162b22‖ 悟。又自思惟。我當堅持淨戒。與一切眾生
162b23‖ 作供養福田。令諸眾生得無量福。如是種
162b24‖ 種名為法施。一切眾生皆畏於死。持戒不
162b25‖ 害。是則無畏施。復次菩薩自念。我當持戒
162b26‖ 以此戒報。為諸眾生作轉輪聖王。或作閻
162b27‖ 浮提王。若作天王令諸眾生。滿足於財無
162b28‖ 所乏短。然後坐佛樹下。降伏魔王破諸
162b29‖ 魔軍。成無上道。為諸眾生說清淨法。令無
162c01‖ 量眾生度老病死海。是為持戒因緣生檀波
162c02‖ 羅蜜。云何持戒生忍辱。持戒之人心自念言。
162c03‖ 我今持戒為[18]持心故。若持戒無忍當墮地
162c04‖ 獄。雖不破戒以無忍故不免惡道。

简体字

持戒自检，不侵一切众生财物，是则财施。众生见者，慕其所行，又为说法，令其开悟。又自思惟："我当坚持净戒，与一切众生作供养福田，令诸众生得无量福。"如是种种，名为法施。一切众生皆畏于死，持戒不害，是则无畏施。

复次，菩萨自念："我当持戒，以此戒报，为诸众生作转轮圣王，或作阎浮提王，若作天王，令诸众生满足于财，无所乏短；然后坐佛树下，降伏魔王，破诸魔军，成无上道，为诸众生说清净法，令无量众生渡老病死海。"是为持戒因缘生檀波罗蜜。

云何持戒生忍辱？持戒之人，心自念言："我今持戒为治心故。若持戒无忍，当堕地狱；虽不破戒，以无忍故，不免恶道。

1) The Giving of Wealth

When one observes the moral precepts, one is frugal oneself while also refraining from encroaching on the material wealth of any other being. This itself amounts to the giving of wealth.

2) The Giving of Dharma

When beings witness this [practice of observing the moral precepts], they respond with an admiring emulation of [the bodhisattva's] actions. He then also speaks Dharma for them, thus causing them to awaken. He then reflects: "I should be firm in adhering to the precepts of moral purity, thereby providing for all beings a field of karmic blessings for the offerings they make." As a result of this, he enables beings to acquire measureless merit. All sorts of circumstances such as these constitute the giving of Dharma.

3) The Giving of Fearlessness

All beings fear death. When one upholds the precepts, one refrains from bringing any harm to them. This in itself amounts to the giving of fearlessness.

b. The Altruistic Vow of the Bodhisattva

Moreover, the bodhisattva thinks to himself, "I shall uphold the precepts and, for the sake of all beings, shall employ the karmic reward from these precepts to become a wheel-turning sage king or perhaps a king of Jambudvīpa. In the event that I become a king among the the gods, then I will cause all beings to be amply supplied with wealth and to have nothing in which they are wanting.

"Later on, I will sit beneath the bodhi tree, vanquish the king of the *māras*, destroy *Māra's* armies, perfect the unsurpassed path, and speak the pure Dharma for the sake of all beings, thus causing an incalculable number of beings to cross beyond the sea of aging, sickness, and death."

These instances demonstrate how the causal factors associated with upholding the precepts bring forth *dāna pāramitā*.

4. Śīla's Generation of Kṣānti Pāramitā

a. The Precepts' Dependence on Establishing Patience

How is it that observing the moral precepts engenders patience (*kṣānti*)? A person who upholds the precepts reflects to himself: "I now uphold the precepts for the sake of maintaining my own mind. If I fail to maintain patience in my observance of the precepts, then I am bound to fall into the hells. Although I may not have actually broken any of the moral precepts, due to failing to maintain patience, I will still have failed to avoid the wretched destinies.

正體字

何可
162c05 縱忿不自制心。但以心故入三惡趣。是故
162c06 應當好自勉強懃修忍辱。復次行者欲令
162c07 戒德堅強。當修忍辱。所以者何。忍為大力。
162c08 能牢固戒令不動搖。復自思惟。我今出家
162c09 形與俗別。豈可縱心如世人法。宜自勉勵
162c10 以忍調心以身口忍心亦得忍。若心不忍
162c11 身口亦爾。是故行者當令身口心忍絕諸忿
162c12 恨。復次是戒略說則有八萬。廣說則無量。我
162c13 當云何能具持此無量戒法。唯當忍辱眾
162c14 戒自得。譬如有人得罪於王。王以罪人載
162c15 之刀車。六邊利刃[19]間不容間。奔逸馳[20]走行
162c16 不擇路。若能持身不為刀傷。是則殺而不
162c17 死。持戒之人亦復如是。戒為利刀忍為持
162c18 身。若忍心不固戒亦傷人。

简体字

何可纵忿不自制心？”但以心故入三恶趣，是故应当好自勉强，勤修忍辱。

复次，行者欲令戒德坚强，当修忍辱。所以者何？忍为大力，能牢固戒，令不动摇。复自思惟：“我今出家，形与俗别，岂可纵心如世人法？宜自勉励，以忍调心。”以身、口忍，心亦得忍；若心不忍，身、口亦尔。是故行者当令身、口、心忍，绝诸忿恨。

复次，是戒略说，则有八万，广说则无量。“我当云何能具持此无量戒法？唯当忍辱，众戒自得。”譬如有人得罪于王，王以罪人载之刀车，六边利刃，间不容间，奔逸驰走，行不择路。若能持身，不为刀伤，是则杀而不死。持戒之人，亦复如是，戒为利刀，忍为持身，若忍心不固，戒亦伤人。

"This being the case, how could I give free rein to anger and thus fail to control my own mind? It is solely on account of the mind that one enters into the three wretched destinies. I should therefore be skillful in strictly restraining myself while diligently cultivating patience."

Moreover, the practitioner who desires the virtue of his precept practice to be solid and strong should cultivate patience. Why? Patience constitutes a great power which is able to strengthen the precepts and cause one to remain unmoved and unshaken.

One additionally reflects to himself: "Now that I have left the home life, I have taken on a different mode from that of the common person. How then could I give free rein to the mind after the manner typical of worldly people?"

It is appropriate that one encourage oneself to employ patience to train the mind. It is through patience of body and mouth that the mind also succeeds in becoming patient. Again, if the mind itself fails to maintain patience, the body and mouth become just the same. Therefore, the practitioner should influence his body, mouth, and mind to maintain patience, thus severing all instances of anger and enmity.

Furthermore, briefly described, these moral precepts number eighty thousand. If one discusses them extensively, then they are found to be incalculably numerous. One might think: "How could I possibly succeed in perfectly observing these innumerable precept dharmas?" One need only exercise patience. As a consequence, all of the many precepts are naturally brought to realization.

b. The Execution wagon Analogy

This is analogous to a circumstance where a man has committed an offense in his relations with the King and the King has consequently ordered that miscreant placed in a wagon of knives in which he is surrounded on all six sides by sharp blades with no intervening space between himself and the blades. The wagon is then turned loose at a fast gallop, racing along aimlessly through the streets. If he is able to control his body and thus avoid being harmed by the knives, this would be a case of being slain yet still not dying. A person who upholds the precepts is just like this. The precepts are like the sharp knives. Patience is analogous to the controlling of the body. If one's mind of patience fails in its solidity, then the precepts themselves may injure a person.

正體字

又復譬如老人
162c19 ‖ 夜行無杖則[21]蹶。忍為戒杖扶人至道。福
162c20 ‖ 樂因緣不能動搖。如是種種。名為持戒生
162c21 ‖ 羼提波羅蜜。云何持戒而生精進。持戒之人
162c22 ‖ 除去放逸。自力懃修習無上法。捨世間樂
162c23 ‖ 入於善道。志求涅槃以度一切。大心不懈
162c24 ‖ 以求佛為本。是為持戒能生精進。復次持
162c25 ‖ 戒之人疲厭世苦老病死患。心生精進必
162c26 ‖ [22]求自脫。亦以度人。譬如野干在林樹間。
162c27 ‖ 依隨師子及諸虎豹。求其殘肉以自存活。
162c28 ‖ [23]有時空乏夜半踰城深入人舍。求肉不得
162c29 ‖ [24]屏處睡息不覺夜竟惶怖無計。走則慮不
163a01 ‖ 自免。住則懼畏死痛。便自

简体字

又复譬如老人夜行，无杖则蹶，忍为戒杖，扶人至道，福乐因缘不能动摇。如是种种，名为持戒生羼提波罗蜜。

云何持戒而生精进？持戒之人，除去放逸，自力勤修，习无上法，舍世间乐，入于善道，志求涅槃以度一切，大心不懈，以求佛为本，是为持戒能生精进。

复次，持戒之人，疲厌世苦、老病死患，心生精进，必自求脱，亦以度人。譬如野干在林树间，依随师子及诸虎豹，求其残肉以自存活。时间空乏，夜半逾城，深入人舍，求肉不得，屏处睡息，不觉夜竟；惶怖无计，走则虑不自免，住则惧畏死痛；便自

c. The Walking Stick Analogy

This is also analogous to an elderly person who might be prone to fall down if he walks along at night without the aid of a walking stick. Patience serves as a "walking stick" in one's practice of observing the moral precepts. It supports a person in successfully arriving at realization of the path. It insures that circumstances produced by merit-generated bliss remain unable to shake him [from his observance of the precepts].

All sorts of instances such as these demonstrate how upholding the moral precepts generates *kṣānti pāramitā.*

5. Śīla's Generation of Vīrya Pāramitā

a. Śīla's Expulsion of Negligence

How is it that one may engender vigor (*vīrya*) through observing the moral precepts? The person who upholds the precepts gets rid of negligence (*pramāda*). Through one's own power, one earnestly cultivates the unsurpassed Dharma. One relinquishes the pleasures of the world and enters into the path of goodness. One resolves to seek nirvāṇa for the sake of all. One possesses a great mind, refrains from laziness, and takes striving for buddhahood as one's fundamental priority. This is how observing the moral precepts is able to bring forth vigor.

b. Śīla's Engendering of Renunciation

Moreover, the person who observes the moral precepts becomes weary and abhorrent of the sufferings of the world and the calamities of aging, sickness, and death. His mind generates vigor and the resolve that he will certainly seek his own liberation while also bringing about the deliverance of others.

c. A Coyote Makes His Escape (Illustrative Story)

This is analogous to the case of the coyote who lived in the forest depending for his survival on following along after lions, tigers and leopards, scavenging the leftover carcasses of their prey. There happened to be a period of time when there was a shortage of available food for him. This led him to slip into the city in the middle of the night, making his way deep into a man's household. He was seeking for some meat but failed to find any.

He happened to fall asleep in a screened-off spot and, unaware that the night had already ended, awoke, startled, frightened, and at a loss for what to do. If he tried to run out, he figured he would be unable to save himself, but if he remained, he feared he would fall victim to the pain of being killed. Consequently, he then fixed

正體字

定心詐死在地
163a02 | 眾人來見有一人言。我須野干耳即便截
163a03 | 取。野干自念。截耳雖痛但令身在。次有一
163a04 | 人言。我須野干尾便復截去。野干復念。截
163a05 | 尾雖痛猶是小事。次有一人言。我須野
163a06 | [1]干牙。野干心念。取者轉多儻取我頭則無
163a07 | 活路。即從地起奮其智力。絕踊[2]間關徑
163a08 | 得自濟。行者之心求脫苦難亦復如是。若
163a09 | 老至時猶故自寬。不能慇懃決斷精進。病亦
163a10 | 如是。以有[3]差期未能決計。死欲至時自
163a11 | 知無冀。便能自勉果敢慇懃大修精進。從
163a12 | 死地中[4]畢至涅槃。復次持戒之法。譬如人
163a13 | 射。先得平地地平然後心安。心安然後挽滿。
163a14 | 挽滿然後陷深。戒為平地定意為弓。挽滿
163a15 | 為精進箭為智慧。賊是無明。

简体字

定心，诈死在地。众人来见，有一人言：“我须野干耳，即便截取。”野干自念：“截耳虽痛，但令身在。”次有一人言：“我须野干尾，便复截去。”野干复念：“截尾虽痛，犹是小事。”次有一人言：“我须野干牙。”野干心念：“取者转多，傥取我头，则无活路。”即从地起，奋其智力，绝踊间关，径得自济。行者之心，求脱苦难，亦复如是；若老至时，犹故自宽，不能殷勤决断精进；病亦如是，以有瘥期，未能决计；死欲至时，自知无冀，便能自勉，果敢殷勤，大修精进，从死地中得至涅槃。

复次，持戒之法，譬如人射，先得平地，地平然后心安，心安然后挽满，挽满然后陷深。戒为平地，定意为弓，挽满为精进，箭为智慧，贼是无明。

his mind on just laying there on the ground, pretending that he was dead.

Many people came to see this. There was one man who said, "I have need of the ears of a coyote." He then cut them off and took them away.

The coyote thought to himself, "Although it hurts to have one's ears cut off, still, the body is allowed to survive."

Next, there was a man who said, "I have need of the tail of a coyote." He then cut that off as well and departed.

The coyote next thought, "Although it hurts to have one's tail cut off, still, it's a relatively minor matter."

Next, there was a man who said, "I need a coyote's teeth."

The coyote thought, "The scavengers are becoming more numerous. Suppose they were to take my head. Were they to do that, I would have no way to survive." He then sprang up from the ground and, arousing the strength of his own intelligence, suddenly bolted for a narrow exit, thereby immediately saving himself.

d. The Mind's Self-Exhortation to Action

In seeking liberation from the trials of suffering, the mind of the practitioner is just like this. When old age arrives, he may still find reason to forgive himself and may still be unable to be diligent, earnest, and decisive in the application of vigor. It may be just the same when encountering sickness. Because there is still hope for a cure, he may still be unable to be resolute in carrying out his strategy.

But when death is about to arrive, he realizes that there is no further hope. He is then able to dare to be decisive and diligent in devoting himself mightily to the cultivation of vigor. Then, escaping from the spot where death is upon him, he finally succeeds in reaching nirvāṇa.

e. The Archery Analogy

Moreover, the dharma of observing the moral precepts is analogous to archery in which a person first finds a level spot of ground. Having found level ground, one then stabilizes the mind. After the mind has become stable, one draws back the bow completely. When one has drawn it back completely, the arrow then plunges deeply into the target. The precepts are analogous to level ground. The decisive mind is comparable to the bow. Drawing it back completely corresponds to vigor. The arrow is comparable to wisdom and the enemy [who is shot by the arrow] is analogous to ignorance.

正體字

若能如是展
163a16║力精進。必至大道以度眾生。復次持戒之
163a17║人能以精進自制五情不受五欲。若心已
163a18║去能攝令還。是為[5]持戒能護諸根。護諸
163a19║根則生禪定。生禪定則生智慧。生智慧
163a20║得至佛道。是為持戒生毘梨耶波羅蜜。云
163a21║何持戒生禪。人有三業作[6]諸善。若身口業
163a22║善。意業自然入善。譬如曲草生於麻中不
163a23║扶自直。持戒之力能羸諸結使。云何能羸。
163a24║若不持戒。瞋恚事來殺心即生。若欲事至婬
163a25║心即成。若持戒者雖有微瞋不生殺心。雖
163a26║有婬念婬事不成。是為持戒能令諸結使
163a27║羸。諸結使羸禪定易得。

简体字

若能如是展力精进，必至大道，以度众生。

复次，持戒之人，能以精进自制五情，不受五欲；若心已去，能摄令还，是为于戒能护诸根。护诸根则生禅定，生禅定则生智慧，生智慧得至佛道；是为持戒生毗梨耶波罗蜜。

云何持戒生禅？人有三业作诸善，若身、口业善，意业自然入善；譬如曲草生于麻中，不扶自直。持戒之力，能羸诸结使。云何能羸？若不持戒，瞋恚事来，杀心即生；若欲事至，淫心即成。若持戒者，虽有微瞋，不生杀心；虽有淫念，淫事不成，是为持戒能令诸结使羸。诸结使羸，禅定易得。

If one is able to bring forth one's strength and be vigorous in this manner, he will certainly arrive at realization of the great path and he will thereby become able to bring beings across to liberation.

f. Śīla's Natural Promotion of Diligent Self-control

Then again, the person who upholds the precepts is able to use vigor to self-regulate his own five sense faculties. He does not indulge in pursuit of the five types of desire. If his mind has already gone off course, he is able to draw it back and cause it to return. This is a case of observing the moral precepts being able to bring about a guarding of the sense faculties. If one guards the sense faculties, then one develops *dhyāna* absorption. If one develops *dhyāna* absorption, then one develops wisdom. If one develops wisdom, then one succeeds in arriving at realization of the path to buddhahood.

These are circumstances in which upholding the moral precepts brings forth *vīrya pāramitā.*

6. Śīla's Generation of Dhyāna Pāramitā

a. Rectification of Mind Through Physical and Verbal Goodness

How is it that upholding the precepts brings forth *dhyāna*? People possess the three karmic actions by which they may do what is good. If the actions of the body and mouth are good, then the actions of the mind naturally enter into goodness.

b. The Grass-in-Sesame Analogy

This is analogous to normally crooked grasses that may be caused to grow vertically when grown in the midst of sesame plants. Thus, even without being propped up, they then naturally grow straight in such circumstances.

c. The Fetter-Diminishing Effect of the Precepts

The power of observing the moral precepts is able to cause the fetters to waste away. How is this able to cause such wasting away? If one fails to observe the moral precepts, when a matter comes along that provokes rage, the intention to kill may immediately arise. If a situation arrives that conduces to lust, sensual thoughts are immediately conceived.

However, in the case of one who observes the moral precepts, although there may be slight anger, one refrains from bringing forth the intention to kill. Although there may be sensual thoughts, lustful activity is not indulged. This is how observing the moral precepts is able to cause the fetters to waste away. As the fetters waste away, *dhyāna* absorption is easily attained.

正體字

譬如老病失力死
163a28 事易得。[7]結使羸故禪定易得。復次人心未
163a29 息常求[8]逸樂。行者持戒棄捨世福心不
163b01 放逸。是故易得禪定。復次持戒之[9]人得生
163b02 人中。次生六欲天[10]上。次至色界。[11]若破色
163b03 相生無色界。持戒清淨。斷諸結使得阿羅
163b04 漢道。大心持戒愍念眾生是為菩薩。復次
163b05 戒為撿麁禪為攝細。復次戒攝身口。禪止
163b06 亂心。如人上屋非梯不昇。不得戒梯禪
163b07 亦不立。復次破戒之人。結使風強散亂其
163b08 心。其心散亂則禪不可得。持戒之人。煩惱風
163b09 軟心不大散。禪定易得。如是等種種因緣。
163b10 是為持戒生禪波羅蜜。

简体字

譬如老病失力，死事易得；结使羸故，禅定易得。

复次，人心未息，常求实乐；行者持戒，弃舍世福，心不放逸，是故易得禅定。

复次，持戒之人，得生人中，次生六欲天上，次至色界，破色相生无色界；持戒清净，断诸结使，得阿罗汉道；大心持戒，愍念众生，是为菩萨。

复次，戒为检粗，禅为摄细。

复次，戒摄身、口，禅止乱心；如人上屋，非梯不升，不得戒梯，禅亦不立。

复次，破戒之人，结使风强，散乱其心；其心散乱，则禅不可得。持戒之人，烦恼风软，心不大散，禅定易得。如是等种种因缘，是为持戒生禅波罗蜜。

d. The Invalid's Fragility Analogy

This is analogous to when someone has become aged and sick to the point where he has lost his typical vitality. In such a case, complete demise comes easily. Similarly, in a case where the fetters have wasted away, *dhyāna* absorption is easily established.

e. The Clarity-Promoting Effects of Moral Restraint

Moreover, when a person's thoughts have not yet been put to rest, he tends to constantly seek unrestrained indulgence in pleasures. However, when the practitioner observes the moral precepts, he renounces worldly karmic blessings. His mind refrains from falling into negligence. As a consequence, it becomes easy for him to succeed in developing *dhyāna* absorption.

f. Śīla's Production of Higher Rebirth and Path Acquisition

Also, the person who observes the moral precepts succeeds thereby in being reborn among humans. Next, he is reborn in the six desire heavens. Thereafter, he reaches the form realm. If he is then able to break through the characteristic aspects of form, he is able to be reborn in the formless realm. If he remains pure in his observance of the moral precepts, he cuts off the fetters and gains the path of arhatship. If he upholds the precepts with the great mind while maintaining sympathetic regard for beings, this is a bodhisattva.

g. The Cooperative Link Between Precepts and Dhyāna

Additionally, the precepts involve restraint with regard to what is coarse. *Dhyāna* involves focusing on the subtle. Also, the moral precepts restrain the body and the mouth. *Dhyāna* brings stillness to the scattered mind.

1) The Precepts-as-Stairs Analogy

This process is analogous to moving higher in a building. If there were no stairs, one would be unable to ascend. If one fails to gain the stairs of the precepts, *dhyāna* absorption cannot be established either.

2) The Fetter-Induced Mental Wind Analogy

Then again, in a person who breaks the precepts, the wind of the fetters is strong and so it scatters and confuses his mind. If his mind is scattered and confused, then *dhyāna* cannot be realized. In the case of a person who upholds the moral precepts, the wind of the fetters is weak and so his mind is not much scattered by it. Thus, for him, *dhyāna* absorption is easily gained.

All sorts of causal circumstances such as these illustrate how observing the moral precepts generates *dhyāna pāramitā.*

正體字

云何持戒能生智
163b11 慧。持戒之人觀此戒相從何而有。知從眾
163b12 罪而生。若無[12]眾罪。則亦無戒。戒相如是。
163b13 從因緣有。何故生著。譬如蓮華出自[13]污
163b14 泥。色雖鮮好出處不淨。以是悟心不令生
163b15 著。是為持戒生般若波羅蜜。復次持戒之
163b16 人心自思惟。若我以持戒貴而可取。破戒
163b17 賤而可捨[14]者。若有此心不應般若。以智
163b18 [15]慧籌量心不著戒無取無捨。是為持戒生
163b19 般若波羅蜜。復次不持戒人雖有利智以
163b20 營世務。種種欲求生業之事。慧根漸鈍。譬
163b21 如利刀以割泥土遂成鈍器。若出家持戒
163b22 不營世業。常觀諸法實相無

简体字

云何持戒能生智慧？持戒之人，观此戒相从何而有，知从众罪而生；若无众罪，则亦无戒。戒相如是从因缘有，何故生著？譬如莲华出自淤泥，色虽鲜好，出处不净；以是悟心，不令生著，是为持戒生般若波罗蜜。

复次，持戒之人，心自思惟："若我以持戒贵而可取，破戒贱而可舍，若有此心，不应般若。"以智筹量，心不著戒，无取、无舍，是为持戒生般若波罗蜜。

复次，不持戒人，虽有利智，以营世务，种种欲求生业之事，慧根渐钝；譬如利刀以割泥土，遂成钝器。若出家持戒，不营世业，常观诸法实相无

7. Śīla's Generation of *Prajñāpāramitā*

a. A Wisdom Generating Contemplation of Precepts

How is it that upholding the moral precepts is able to bring forth wisdom? The person who observes the precepts contemplates the origins of the specific aspects of the moral precepts. He realizes that they originate with the numerous sorts of karmic offenses. If none of those numerous karmic offenses had been committed in the first place, then there would not be any moral precepts, either. Since the specific aspects of the moral precepts exist in this manner—on the basis of causes and conditions—how could one become attached to them?

b. The Lotus-from-Mud Analogy

In this sense, the moral precepts are comparable to lotus blossoms growing forth from grime-ridden mud. Although their form is fresh and fine, the place from which they arise is impure. If one awakens one's mind in this fashion, then one does not allow it to develop attachments. This is an instance of the upholding of precepts bringing forth *prajñāpāramitā.*

c. Making Precept Practice Reflect Prajñā

Additionally, one who observes the moral precepts should reflect, "Were I to regard upholding precepts as noble and therefore a justification for grasping while regarding breaking precepts as base and therefore as a justification for rejection, such thought would not correspond to *prajñā*. This is because, when one relies on wisdom as the basis of one's analyses, one's mind refrains from seizing on the moral precepts and one remains free of either grasping or rejection." This [reflection] is an instance in which upholding the precepts serves as the basis for generating *prajñāpāramitā*.

d. The Keen Mind, Lacking Precepts, Becomes Dull

What's more, even though one who fails to uphold the precepts may possess sharp wisdom, because all manner of endeavors associated with managing worldly responsibilities involve creating karma through one's striving, the faculty of wisdom gradually grows dull. This is analogous to using a sharp blade to cut mud. As a consequence, it eventually becomes a dull instrument.

e. The Dull Mind, Imbued with Precepts, Becomes Keen

If one leaves behind the home life, upholds the precepts, desists from engaging in worldly endeavors, and constantly contemplates in accordance with reality the true character of dharmas as devoid

正體字

相。先雖鈍根
163b23 以漸轉利。如是等種種因緣。名為持戒生
163b24 般若波羅蜜。[16]如是名為尸羅波羅蜜生六
163b25 波羅蜜。復次菩薩持戒不以畏故。亦非愚
163b26 癡非疑非[17]惑。亦不自為涅槃故。持戒但
163b27 為一切眾生故。為得佛道故。為得一切
163b28 佛法故。如是相名為尸羅波羅蜜。復次若
163b29 菩薩[18]於罪不罪不可得[19]故。是時名為尸羅
163c01 波羅蜜。問曰。[20]若捨惡行善是為持戒。云何
163c02 言罪不罪不可得。答曰。非[21]謂邪見麁心
163c03 言不可得[22]也。若深入諸法相。行空三昧。
163c04 慧眼觀故罪不可得。罪無故不罪亦不可得。
163c05 復次眾生不可得故。殺罪亦不可得。罪不可
163c06 得故戒亦不可得。何以故。以有殺罪故則
163c07 有戒。若無殺罪則亦[23]無戒。

简体字

相；先虽钝根，以渐转利。如是等种种因缘，名为持戒生般若波罗蜜。如是等名为尸罗波罗蜜生六波罗蜜。

复次，菩萨持戒不以畏故，亦非愚痴，非疑、非戒盗，亦不自为涅槃故持戒，但为一切众生故，为得佛道故，为得一切佛法故。如是相，名为尸罗波罗蜜。

复次，若菩萨于罪不罪不可得，是时，名为尸罗波罗蜜。

问曰：若人舍恶行善，是为持戒，云何言罪不罪不可得？

答曰：非为邪见粗心言不可得。深入诸法相，行空三昧，慧眼观故，罪不可得；罪无故，不罪亦不可得。

复次，众生不可得故，杀罪亦不可得；罪不可得故，戒亦不可得。何以故？以有杀罪故，则有戒；若无杀罪，则亦无戒。

of any [inherently existent] characteristics, although one may have formerly had dull faculties, they gradually become ever sharper.

All sorts of causal circumstances similar to the above illustrate how upholding moral precepts engenders *prajñāpāramitā*. Causal circumstances of the sort cited previously illustrate how *śīla pāramitā* brings forth all six *pāramitās*.

8. Concluding Statement on the Nature of Śīla Pāramitā

Additionally, the bodhisattva's upholding of the moral precepts is not done on account of fear, nor is it the case that it is done out of stupidity, or doubt, or delusion, or out of a private quest for his own nirvāṇa. The upholding of the moral precepts is carried out solely for the sake of all beings, for the sake of success in the path to buddhahood, and for the sake of gaining all the dharmas of buddhahood. Characteristics such as these demonstrate what is meant by *śīla pāramitā*.

C. Unfindability of Offense and Non-Offense

Then again, if the bodhisattva's practice is based in the unfindability of either offense or non-offense, it is at this time that it qualifies as *śīla pāramitā*.

1. Objection: Offense and Non-offense Do Exist

Question: If one is able to relinquish evil and practice goodness, it is this which constitutes the upholding of the precepts. How then can it be said that offense and non-offense cannot be found?

2. The Meaning of Unfindability of Offense and Non-Offense

Response: This is not referring to the concept of "unfindability" described by those of erroneous views and coarse minds. If one enters deeply into the characteristics of all dharmas and courses in the samādhi of emptiness, because one employs the wisdom eye in one's contemplation, one discovers that offenses are not apprehensible. Because offenses themselves are [ultimately] nonexistent, non-offense cannot be found, either.[31]

a. The Link to Unfindability of Beings and Unfindability of Precepts

Moreover, because beings themselves cannot be gotten at, the offense of killing cannot be gotten at, either. Because the offense itself cannot be gotten at, the corresponding moral precept cannot be gotten at, either. How is this? It is on account of the existence of the offense of killing that the corresponding moral precept exists. If there were [ultimately] no offense of killing, then there would [finally] be no corresponding moral precept, either.

正體字

問曰。今眾生
163c08 現有。云何言眾生不可得。答曰。肉眼所見是
163c09 為非見。若以慧眼觀則不得眾生。如上檀
163c10 中說。無施者無受者。無財物此亦如是。
163c11 復次若有眾生是五眾耶離五眾耶。若是
163c12 五眾五眾有五眾生為一。如是者五[24]可為
163c13 一一可為五。譬如市易物。直五匹以一
163c14 匹取之則不可得。何以故。一[25]不得作五
163c15 故。以是故知五眾[*]不得作一眾生。復次五
163c16 眾生滅無常相眾生法從先世來至後世。
163c17 受罪福於三界。若五眾是眾生。譬如草木自
163c18 生自滅。如是則無罪縛亦無解脫。以是故
163c19 知非五眾是眾生。若離五眾有眾生。如先
163c20 說神常遍中已破。

简体字

问曰：今众生现有，云何言众生不可得？

答曰：肉眼所见，是为非见；若以慧眼观，则不得众生。如上檀中说无施者、无受者、无财物，此亦如是。

复次，若有众生，是五众耶？离五众耶？若是五众，五众有五，众生为一；如是者，五不可为一，一不可为五。譬如市易物值五匹，以一匹取之，则不可得。何以故？一不可得作五故，以是故，知五众不可得作一众生。

复次，五众生灭无常相。众生法，从先世来，至后世，受罪福于三界。若五众是众生，譬如草木自生自灭，如是则无罪缚，亦无解脱。以是故，知非五众是众生；若离五众有众生，如先说神常遍中已破。

b. Objection: How Can One Claim Beings Don't Exist?

Question: It is manifestly the case that "beings" *do* now exist. How can you claim that "beings" cannot be gotten at?

c. Clarification of Unfindability of Beings

Response: As for what is seen by the fleshly eye, this amounts to non-seeing. However, if one contemplates with the wisdom eye, then one does not find any "being." This is as explained above in the section on *dāna pāramitā* wherein it was stated that there is no donor, no recipient, and no material object offered as a gift.

1) Refutation: Incompatibility of Singularity and Multiplicity

Additionally, if, as you claim, a being *does* exist, is it identical with the five aggregates, or does it exist apart from the five aggregates? If it is supposedly identical with the five aggregates, [one must confront the fact that] the five aggregates are fivefold, whereas a "being" is a singular entity. If what you assert were actually the case, then [this would amount to the absurd and untenable assertion that] "five" would somehow equal "one" and "one" would somehow equal "five."

To use the trading of goods in the market as an analogy, a person is unable to get something worth five currency units in exchange for only a single currency unit. Why? It is because "one" cannot equal "five." As a consequence, one must realize that the five-fold aggregates cannot constitute a singular being.

2) Refutation of Beings: Impossibility of Karmic Retribution

Moreover, the five aggregates are characterized by the process of creation, destruction, and impermanence. It is the characteristic dharma of beings that they come forth from a former life and arrive at a later life and undergo karmic punishments and karmic blessings within the three realms. If the five aggregates make up a being, then they would be born naturally and die naturally after the manner of grass or trees. If this were actually the case, then there would be no being bound by offenses nor would there be any liberation to be gained. Based on this, one knows that it is not true that the five aggregates constitute a being.

3) Refutation of Non-Aggregate Beings: Eternalist Fallacy

And if one asserts the existence of a being distinct from the five aggregates, this is precisely what was already refuted in the prior discussion addressing the fallacy of a supposedly eternally existent and universally pervasive spiritual soul (*ātman*).

正體字

復次離五眾則我見心不
163c21 生。若離五眾有眾生。是為墮常。若墮常
163c22 者是則無生無死。何以故。生名先無今[26]有。
163c23 死名已生便滅。若眾生常者。應遍[27]滿五道
163c24 中。先[28]已常有云何今復來生。若不有生則
163c25 無有死。問曰。定有眾生。何以故言無。五眾
163c26 因緣有眾生法。譬如五指因緣[29]拳法生。答
163c27 曰。此言非也。若五眾因緣有眾生法者。除
163c28 五眾則別有眾生法然不可得。眼自見色
163c29 耳自聞聲鼻嗅香舌知味身知觸意知法
164a01 空無我法。離此六事更無眾生。諸外道輩
164a02 倒見故。言眼能見色是為眾生。乃至意能
164a03 知法是為眾生。又能憶念能受苦樂是為
164a04 眾生。但作是見不知眾生實。

简体字

复次，离五众则我见心不生。若离五众有众生，是为堕常；若堕常者，是则无生、无死。何以故？生名先无今有；死名已生便灭。若众生常者，应遍五道中先已常有，云何今复来生？若不有生，则无有死。

问曰：定有众生，何以故言无？五众因缘，有众生法；譬如五指因缘，拳法生。

答曰：此言非也！若五众因缘有众生法者，除五众，则别有众生法，然不可得；眼自见色，耳自闻声，鼻嗅香，舌知味，身知触，意知法，空无我法；离此六事，更无众生。诸外道辈倒见故，言眼能见色，是为众生；乃至意能知法，是为众生；又能忆念能受苦乐，是为众生；但作是见，不知众生实。

Furthermore, if one asserts that there exists such a being distinct from the five aggregates, then the thought imputing existence of a self therein would not even arise. If one asserts existence of a being apart from the five aggregates, one falls into an eternalist view.

If one falls into an eternalist view, then this entails the nonexistence of birth and the nonexistence of death. Why? Birth refers to something formerly nonexistent now coming into existence. Death refers to something already born then being extinguished. If it were the case that beings were eternally existent, then it ought to be the case that they exist everywhere filling up the five paths of rebirth.[32] If something already exists eternally, why would it then now come to birth yet again? And if it does not have a birth, then it has no death, either.

4) Objection: Aggregate-Based Beings Are Like a Finger-Based Fist

Question: It is definitely the case that beings exist. How can one claim that they are nonexistent? It is based on the causes and conditions of the five aggregates that the dharma of a being exists. This is analogous to the case of the causes and conditions of the five fingers generating the dharma of a fist.

5) Refutation: Absence of Any Apprehensible "Being" Dharma

Response: This statement is fallacious. If the dharma of a being exists among the causes and conditions associated with the five aggregates, then, aside from the five aggregates themselves, there exists some separate "being" dharma. However, no such thing can be found. The eye itself sees forms. The ear itself hears sounds. The nose smells fragrances. The tongue knows flavors. The body knows tangibles. The intellectual mind faculty knows dharmas as objects-of-mind. They are all empty and devoid of any dharma of a self. Apart from these six [sense-based] phenomena, there is no additional "being."

a) Synopsis of Related Non-Buddhist Positions

Based on inverted views, non-Buddhists claim, "When the eye is able to see forms, this involves a being," and so forth until we come to, "When the mind is able to know dharmas, this involves a being." They also claim that, when one remembers and when one is able to undergo suffering and pleasure, these circumstances involve a being. However, they merely create this view. They do not actually possess any direct knowledge of any genuinely-existent entity associated with this "being" the existence of which they posit.

正體字

譬如一長老
164a05 大德比丘。人謂是阿羅漢多致供養。其後
164a06 病死。諸弟子懼失供養故。夜盜出之。於其
164a07 臥處安施被枕。令如師在其[1]狀如臥。人
164a08 來問疾師在何許。諸弟子言。汝不見床上
164a09 被枕耶。愚者不審察之。謂師病臥大送
164a10 供養而去。如是非一。復有智人來而問
164a11 之。諸弟子亦如是答。智人言。我不問被枕
164a12 床褥。我自求人發被求之竟無人可得。除
164a13 六事相更無我人。知者見者亦復如是。復
164a14 次若眾生於五眾因緣有者。五眾無常眾生
164a15 亦[2]應無常。何以故。因果相似故。若眾生無
164a16 常則不[3]至後世。復次若如汝言。眾生從本
164a17 [*]已來常有。若爾者眾生應生五眾。五眾不
164a18 應生眾生。今五眾因緣生眾生名字。無智
164a19 之人逐名求實。

简体字

譬如一长老大德比丘，人谓是阿罗汉，多致供养。其后病死，诸弟子惧失供养故，夜盗出之；于其卧处安施被枕，令如师在，其状如卧。人来问疾："师在何许？"诸弟子言："汝不见床上被枕耶？"愚者不审察之，谓师病卧，大送供养而去，如是非一。复有智人来而问之，诸弟子亦如是答。智人言："我不问被枕、床褥，我自求人。"发被求之，竟无人可得。除六事相，更无我人；知者、见者，亦复如是。

复次，若众生于五众因缘有者，五众无常，众生亦无常。何以故？因果相似故；若众生无常，则不至后世。

复次，若如汝言，众生从本已来常有；若尔者，众生应生五众，五众不应生众生；今五众因缘生众生名字，无智之人，逐名求实。

b) A Deceased Guru Disguised (Illustrative Story)

This is analogous to the case of an old, senior, and very venerable bhikshu. People were of the opinion that he had become an arhat and so brought forth many offerings. Later on, he became ill and died. Because the disciples were alarmed that they would lose the offerings, they surreptitiously removed him during the night and in that place where he had been lying down, they arranged blankets and pillows, causing it to appear as if their master was still present, but merely lying down. People came and asked about his illness, inquiring "Where is the Master?"

The disciples replied, "Don't you see the blankets and pillows on the bed?" The gullible ones did not investigate into it. They believed this master was lying down there stricken with illness, went ahead and presented large offerings, and then left. This happened more than once.

Next, a wise man came along and asked after the Master. The disciples replied in the same way. That wise man then said, "I did not ask about blankets, pillows, beds, or cushions. I'm looking instead for a 'person.'" He then threw back the covers, looking for that master. In the end, there was no 'person' to be found there at all.

Apart from the characteristic features of the six [sense-based] phenomena, there is no additional "self" or "person" at all. As for a "knower" or a "perceiver," they are identical in this respect.

6) Refutation Based on Consequence of Beings' Impermanence

Moreover, if it were the case that a "being" existed somewhere in the causes and conditions of the five aggregates, since the five aggregates are impermanent, beings, too, ought to be impermanent. Why? This is on account of the similitude in the causes and conditions. If beings were impermanent, then it would be impossible for them to extend on to any subsequent lifetime.

7) Refutation Based on Later Arising of Aggregates

Furthermore, if it is as you say, then beings must have existed eternally from the very beginning on forward through time to the present. If that were so, then it should be that beings are what produce the five aggregates. It should not be the case that the five aggregates produce beings. Now, however, it is actually the causes and conditions associated with the five aggregates that give rise to the application of this name: "being." People who have no wisdom then proceed to chase after these names in search of something real.

正體字

以是故眾生實無。若無眾
164a20 | 生亦無殺罪。無殺罪故亦無持戒。復次是
164a21 | 五眾深入觀之。分別知空如夢所見如
164a22 | 鏡中像。若殺夢中所見及鏡中像無有殺
164a23 | 罪。殺五陰空相眾生亦復如是。復次若人
164a24 | 不[4]樂罪貪著無罪。是人見破戒罪人則
164a25 | 輕慢。見持戒善人則愛敬。如是持戒則是
164a26 | 起罪因緣。以是故言於罪不罪不可得故。
164a27 | 應具足尸羅波羅蜜

简体字

以是故，众生实无。若无众生，亦无杀罪，无杀罪故，亦无持戒。

复次，是五众，深入观之，分别知空，如梦所见，如镜中像；若杀梦中所见，及镜中像，无有杀罪。杀五阴空相众生，亦复如是。

复次，若人不乐杀罪，贪著无罪，是人见破戒罪人则轻慢，见持戒善人则爱敬；如是持戒，则是起罪因缘。以是故，言于罪不罪不可得故，应具足尸罗波罗蜜。

3. Concluding Discussion of Unfindability and Its Import

For all of these reasons, beings are in fact nonexistent. If beings are nonexistent, then the karmic offense of killing is nonexistent as well. Because the karmic offense of killing is nonexistent, then the observance of moral precepts is also nonexistent.

Also, when one enters deeply into the contemplation of these five aggregates, one analyzes them and consequently realizes that they are empty of inherent existence, are like something seen in a dream, and are like images appearing in a mirror. If one kills something only seen in a dream or kills what is only an image in a mirror, then there is no karmic offense of "killing" that is actually committed. One merely engages in killing the empty marks of the five aggregates.[33] Beings, too, are [unfindable] in this same way.

Additionally, if a person is displeased by karmic offenses and thus is covetously attached to being free of karmic offenses, if he observes someone with karmic offenses which have arisen from breaking moral precepts, he will act in a slighting and arrogant manner. If he observes a good, precept-observing person, he will behave toward them in an affectionate and respectful fashion. If one's upholding of moral precepts is carried out in this manner, then this itself generates causal bases for the commission of karmic offenses. It is for this reason that [the Sutra] states, "It is based on the unfindability of offense and non-offense that one should engage in perfecting *śīla pāramitā*."

Part Two Endnotes

1. These reduced-font parenthetical notes are all integral to the received Chinese text preserved in the Taisho Tripiṭaka. They may or may not originate with Kumārajīva's explanations to his translation scribes.
2. This "divisive speech" includes not only the milder evils such as mindless rumor-mongering, but also the more clearly evil forms of deceit such as back-stabbing, character assassination, and slander into which the afflicted mind may stray even while still not having the direct intention to impart those deliberately formulated lies which are the primary concern of the "false speech" precept.
3. Frivolous speech" refers primarily to lewd speech, but also secondarily includes all of the forms of useless, time-wasting, and distracting chatter which pull the mind away from focus on the Path, involving it instead in any of a host of sensual and worldly concerns.
4. The *eraṇḍa* tree has red blossoms which, although beautiful in appearance, stink horribly even when miles away.
5. These statements refer to the future retributions due for the respective actions.
6. The five heinous transgressions (五逆罪) are patricide, matricide, killing an arhat, spilling the blood of a buddha, and causing a schism in the harmoniously-united monastic Saṃgha. The Sanskrit term (*pañcānantarya*) connotes immediacy, unavoidability, and relentlessness of hell-bound retribution. These transgressions are discussed in Chapter Four of *The Abhidharma-kośa-bhāṣyam*.
7. Kātyāyanīputra lived about 200 BCE.
8. At the very conclusion of primary expository sections in this work, Nāgārjuna's text sometimes supplements those expositions with recitation of standard *abhidharma* analytic data, often in very cryptic, highly-condensed, and barely decipherable format. My translation of this and other such brief sections is necessarily only tentative.
9. This may refer not only to those who denounce the killer, but also to the ghosts of the killer's victims.
10. "Both eras" refers to both present and future lives.
11. The rationale of this statement takes for granted that we realize that, based on the retributive power of karmic actions, killing brings about the karmic effect of having a short lifespan.
12. A *srota-āpanna* is a "stream-enterer," one who has reached the first of four stages in the individual-liberation path culminating in arhatship.
13. One should understand that taking one's own life is a matter not to be taken lightly. For most of us, it would involve psychically depressed

circumstances attended by deeply-afflicted and intensely emotional influences. These are conditions that tend to conduce to less fortunate rebirth circumstances. The situation of this *srota-āpanna* was quite different: Because he was a "stream-enterer," he had already reached a level of realization in which his eventual complete liberation was guaranteed. He had already moved beyond being affected significantly by the afflictions and he was no longer subject to falling into lower states of rebirth. Because most of us do not enjoy such spiritually advanced circumstances, it would be better for us to forego taking our own lives while also refusing to kill the sheep.

14. The Vinaya is one of the three primary divisions of the Buddhist canon. It contains all of the authoritative pronouncements on moral ethics in general and in particular articulates the various sets of moral codes for the different categories of Buddhist disciples among the monks, the nuns, and the laity.

15. The reference here is to karmic retribution arising from stealing.

16. "Unforeseen events" probably refers to being recognized as the perpetrator by accidentally encountering a witness after the fact. One may care to note that in alternate editions there is a variant reading involving transposition of characters (substituting 時行 for 行時). That reading would translate as: "Bad timing leads to unforeseen circumstances." This could be interpreted as a reference to the common circumstance wherein the robber ends up committing other crimes to cover up his actions or else ends up being injured or killed by either the victim or authorities who happen on the scene.

17. According to all standard provisional-level dispensations of the Buddha's teachings, an *anāgāmin,* otherwise known as a "never-returner," is not bound to take up future human or lower-realm rebirths. Rather, all remaining births are taken in celestial realms.

18. Explanations of the Sanskrit names for these and most of the other hells may be found toward the end of Nāgārjuna's extensive explanation of the perfection of vigor in Part Four of "Nāgārjuna on the Six Perfections," Subchapter 27, pages 515–537. (See Bibliography.) The characteristic sufferings endured in each hell are described in considerable detail there as well.

19. The other three offenses in addition to false speech are divisive speech, harsh speech, and frivolous (i.e. lewd or useless) speech).

20. Again, "two eras" is a reference to the present and the future.

21. In this analogy of an entire human life to the life of a single flower, the six seasons most likely refer to the major life-phases such as: birth, youth, the prime of life, old age, sickness, and death. In a story

illustrating the shortness of a human life compared to that in the heavens, a heavenly maiden suffered accidental death one morning, subsequently lived a long life among humans during which she constantly made offerings to her former heavenly lord, and then was reborn again in the same heaven, arriving back there even before that single day in the heaves had come to an end.

22. "Guitar, bass, harp, and lute" are approximate Western correlates for Kumārajīva's *qin, si, zheng,* and *konghou,* four ancient Chinese instruments.

23. The Pārijātaka tree is in the Trāyastriṃśa heaven. It is said to be one hundred *yojanas* tall, fifty *yojanas* wide, to have roots going down fifty *yojanas,* and is supposed to be a place in which one avails oneself of the most excellent sensual pleasures.

24. Nāgārjuna devotes Subchapter Thirty-six of the *Exegesis* to the "eight recollections," among which is "recollection of the heavens," wherein this same question about an apparent contradiction regarding rewards of the Path comes up. We find there supplementary arguments and a fine analogy.

25. *Asuras* are demigods renowned for their lack of merit, their jealousy of the gods, and their combative nature which provokes them to make repeated attacks on the domains of the gods.

26. "Six days" refers to the eighth, fourteenth, fifteenth, twenty-third, twenty-ninth, and thirtieth of each lunar month whereas "spiritual" months refers to the first, fifth and ninth lunar months and most specifically to the first through fifteenth days of those three months.

27. I have preferred the "five" signs of deterioration which accords with four other editions instead of the "three" appearing through scribal error in Taisho. The most common version of this list includes dirtiness of the heavenly garments, wilting of the floral chaplet, armpit perspiration, body odor, and unhappiness at remaining in one's seat. For a god, these indicate imminent death.

28. "Great mind" is almost certainly a reference to the bodhisattva vow to defer final nirvāṇa indefinitely in favor of striving endlessly for the spiritual liberation of all beings.

29. The "original" Subchapter 23 title as recorded in Taisho appears to be incorrectly placed here at page T25n1509_p0160c17–18 when in fact it should really be placed at the top of Taisho page 162. As it stands, it reads, "In Explanation of the Meaning of Chapter One's Praise of Śīla Pāramitā" (釋初品中讚尸羅波羅蜜義), this even though the text is simply continuing on at this point with an ongoing discussion of particular aspects of moral precept observance not directly

associated with the explanation and praise of *śīla pāramitā* explored later in this chapter. As a consequence, while still adhering to the Taisho text's placement of the chapter break, I have felt compelled to divide this Subchapter 23 into two parts with "Part One" noting the continued discussion of these additional precept specifics and "Part Two" marking the commencement of the actual explanation and praise of *śīla pāramitā*.

30. There is no new-subchapter break *per se* at this point in the text as preserved in Taisho. Rather Taisho only records a new-fascicle break titled: "The Continued Explanation of Chapter One's Śīla Pāramitā," this even though this point in the text is where Nāgārjuna begins his focused discussion of *śīla pāramitā*. As a consequence, I have introduced a "Subchapter 23, Part 2" title here reflecting the actual pivot point in the discussion.

31. Lest the reader be mystified by Nāgārjuna's assertion that offenses don't exist, one should understand that he is referring solely to the ultimate reality of the matter. He in no way means to infer that they do not exist on the level of conventional reality. Nor does he mean to infer that karmic consequences are ever somehow suspended by virtue of cognizing the ultimate reality of which he speaks.

32. This is the *reductio ad absurdum* consequence of eternally-existing beings never dying.

33. Again, the author is speaking in terms of ultimate truth, but does not intend to infer that understanding this truth provides immunity from karmic accountability. In other words, even if one directly perceives the absence of inherent existence in all phenomena and in all beings, if he nonetheless deliberately sets up and carries through the conditions resulting in the death of someone only perceptible as a "being" on the level of conventional reality, he still engenders the offense of killing and still produces the causes for future retribution. He will then be bound to undergo that retribution at some point later in his own karmic continuum—this in spite of the fact that he all-the-while directly perceives the complete absence of inherent existence in all phenomena and in all beings.

    A failure to understand this concept may constitute a karmically disastrous misinterpretation of emptiness and may bring on what is referred to in the tradition as "grasping the snake of emptiness by the tail." (One thus becomes subject to the karmically-fatal snake bite inflicted by erroneous interpretation of emptiness.) Those new to the doctrine of emptiness should take heed, realizing that the "unfindability" of offense and non-offense confers no license to ignore cause-and-effect and the inevitable karmic consequences.

Part Two Bibliography

Conze, E., & Suzuki Gakujutsu Zaidan. (1967). Materials for a Dictionary of the Prajñāpāramitā Literature. Tokyo: Suzuki Research Foundation.Dharmamitra. (2009) Nāgārjuna on the Six Perfections: An Ārya Bodhisattva Explains the Heart of the Bodhisattva Path. A translation of chapters 17-30 of Ārya Nāgārjuna's Exegesis on the Great Perfection of Wisdom Sutra. Seattle: Kalavinka Press.

Dharmamitra. (2009) Nāgārjuna on the Six Perfections. A translation of Chapter One, Subchapters 17–30 of Ārya Nāgārjuna's *Mahāprajñāpāramitā Upadeśa* (大智度論 / T25, No. 1509). Seattle: Kalavinka Press.

Edgerton, F. (1953). Buddhist Hybrid Sanskrit grammar and dictionary. (William Dwight Whitney linguistic series). New Haven: Yale University Press.

Hirakawa, A. (1997). Buddhist Chinese-Sanskrit Dictionary / Bukkyō Kan-Bon daijiten. Tokyo]; [Tokyo] :: Reiyūkai : Hatsubaimoto Innātorippusha; 霊友会 : 発売元いんなあとりっぷ社.

Kumārajīva (c. 405). Dazhidulun, *Mahāprājnāpāramitopedeśa (大智度論). T25, no. 1509).

Ruegg, D. (1981). The Literature of the Madhyamaka school of Philosophy in India (History of Indian literature ; v. 7, fasc. 1). Wiesbaden: Harrassowitz.

Takakusu, J., & Watanabe, Kaigyoku. (1924). Taishō shinshū Daizōkyō. Tōkyō; 東京 :: Taishō Issaikyō Kankōkai; 大正一切經刊行會.

Williams, M. Monier, Sir. (n.d.). A Sanskrit-English Dictionary. Delhi: Sri Satguru.

Zhonghua dian zi fo dian xie hui. (2004). CBETA dian zi fo dian ji cheng = CBETA Chinese electronic Tripitaka collection (Version 2004. ed.). Taibei; 台北 :: Zhonghua dian zi fo dian xie hui; 中華電子佛典協會.

Part Two Glossary

A

Abhidharma: A category of Buddhist texts devoted to detailed scholastic analyses of the teachings contained in the sutras.

afflictions: Otherwise known as "the three poisons" (*triviṣa*) these are: 1) greed (including lust and desire in general); 2) hatred (including all of the permutations of aversion such as irritation, anger, and rage); and 3) delusion or ignorance. There are many subcategories of afflictions (*kleśa*) listed in the various dharma schemas. For example, in the Sarvāstivāda school, there are six root afflictions and ten subsidiary afflictions.

aggregates: See "five aggregates."

arhat: An arhat is one who, having put an end to all of the afflictions, fetters, and contaminants and having put an end to rebirth, has gained the fourth and final fruit on the individual-liberation path of the śrāvaka disciple.

ārya: One who has realized one of the fruits of the path from which they can never fall away. This includes any one of the eight fruits of the path to arhatship, or any of the irreversible stations on the bodhisattva path to buddhahood.

asura: As one of the paths of rebirth, this refers to a demi-god or titan. More loosely, this refers to beings much characterized by anger, hatred, jealousy, and contentiousness who may also appear as humans, animals, hungry ghosts (*pretas*), or hell-dwellers.

B

Bhagavat: "Bhagavat" is one of the titles of a Buddha. It may be translated as "Blessed One," "Lord," or, as rendered in Chinese Buddhist texts, "World Honored One," *shizun* (世尊).

bhikshu: A fully ordained celibate Buddhist monk within one of the traditional schools of Buddhism.

bhikshuni: A fully ordained celibate Buddhist nun within one of the traditional schools of Buddhism.

bodhi: "Enlightenment" or "awakening." In its most exalted form this refers exclusively to the utmost, right, and perfect enlightenment (*anuttarasamyaksaṃbodhi*) of a buddha.

bodhisattva: A bodhisattva is a being who, in his pursuit of the utmost, right, and perfect enlightenment of buddhahood, is equally dedicated to achieving buddhahood for himself while also facilitating all other beings' achievement of buddhahood. His primary practice is classically described as focusing on the six (or ten) "perfections" (*pāramitā*): giving, moral virtue, patience, vigor, meditative skill (*dhyāna*), and world-transcending wisdom (*prajñā*).

bodhi tree: The tree in Bodhgaya in the Indian state of Bihar under which the Buddha reached enlightenment approximately 2600 years ago.

Brahmā: Per PDB: "An Indian divinity who was adopted into the Buddhist pantheon as a protector of the teachings and king of the Brahmaloka ['Brahma world'] (in the narrow sense of that term)." "Brahmaloka" here refers to the first three heavens of the form realm. In this text, he is also referred to as "the Brahmā Heaven King."

brahmacārin: Per MW, "A young Brahman who is a student of the veda (under a preceptor) or who practises chastity, a young Brahman before marriage (in the first period of his life)."

brahmacarya: *Brahmacarya* refers to celibacy in particular and the religious renunciant's way of life in general.

brahman: Someone who belongs to the highest caste in Hinduism; a member of the Hindu priestly caste.

buddha: Anyone who has achieved the utmost, right, and perfect enlightenment (*anuttarasamyaksaṃbodhi*), whether we speak of the Buddha of the present era in this world, Śākyamuni Buddha, any of the seven buddhas of antiquity, or, in Mahāyāna cosmology, any of the countless buddhas of the ten directions and three periods of time.

C

contaminants: "Contaminants" (*āsrava*) are usually defined as either threefold or fourfold: 1) sensual desire (*kāma*); 2) [craving for] becoming (*bhāva*), i.e. the craving for continued existence; 3) ignorance (*avidyā*), i.e. delusion; 4) views (*dṛṣṭi*) This fourth type is not included in the very earliest Theravāda Buddhist listings. Often-encountered alternate translations include "taints" and "outflows" and, less commonly "influxes" and "fluxes."

D

dāna pāramitā: The perfection of giving

desire realm: The lowest of the three realms of existence, the desire realm is the realm inhabited by the beings in the hells, among hungry ghosts, among humans, and among the devas or gods inhabiting the six lowest levels of heavens known as "the six desire realm heavens."

deva: Devas or, more loosely, "gods," are divinities residing in the heavens that collectively constitute the highest of the six rebirth destinies within the realm of *saṃsāra*. There are 27 categories of devas and their heavens in the desire realm, form realm, and formless realm. Although the lifespans of the devas in these various heavens may be immensely long, when their karmic merit runs out, they are all still destined to eventually fall back into the other five paths of rebirth wherein they are reborn in accordance with their residual karma from previous lifetimes.

Dharma: The teachings of the Buddha

dharmas: 1) Fundamental constituent aspects, elements, or factors of mental and physical existence, as for instance, "the 100 dharmas" with which Vasubandhu analytically catalogued all that exists. In this sense, dharmas are somewhat analogous to the elements of the periodic table in chemistry; 2) Any individual teaching, as for instance in "the dharma of conditioned origination."

Dharma wheel: The "wheel of Dharma" or "Dharma wheel" (*dharmacakra*) refers to the eight-spoked wheel emblematic of the Buddha's teaching of the eight-fold path of the Āryas or "Noble Ones" consisting of right views, right volition or intentional thought, right speech, right physical action, right livelihood, right effort, right mindfulness, and right meditative concentration. This term is also synonymous with the three turnings of the four truths as initially taught by the Buddha to his original five disciples.

dhyāna: "*Dhyāna*" is a general term broadly corresponding to all forms of Buddhist meditative skill. The Chinese "*ch'an*" or "*chan*" (禪) and the Japanese term "*zen*" are transliterations of the same Sanskrit word "*dhyāna*." All forms of Buddhist "calming" and "insight" meditation are subcategories of "*dhyāna*." "*Dhyāna*" also refers to the four or eight levels of meditative attainment referred to as "the four *dhyānas* or eight *dhyānas*.

dhyāna pāramitā: The perfection of meditative skill.

E

eightfold right path: right views; right intention; right speech; right action; right livelihood; right effort; right mindfulness; and right concentration.

eight precepts: Eight vows involving abstaining from: 1) killing; 2) taking what is not given; 3) sexual misconduct; 4) false speech; 5) intoxicants; 6) use of perfumes, jewelry, other personal adornments, dancing, singing, or watching such performances; 7) sleeping on high or wide beds; and 8) eating after midday.

eraṇḍa tree: An *eraṇḍa* tree has red blossoms which, although beautiful in appearance, stink horribly even when miles away.

F

fetters: The fetters (*saṃyojana*) are ten mental characteristics of unenlightened existence that bind beings to uncontrolled rebirths in the six destinies of rebirth. They are: 1) "Truly existent self view," the wrong view that believes in the existence of an eternally existent self in association with the five aggregates; 2) "Skeptical doubt" about the truth of the Dharma and the path to enlightenment; 3) "Clinging to [the observance of] rules and rituals" in and of themselves as constituting the essence of the path to spiritual liberation; 4) Sensual desire; 5) Ill will; 6) Desire for rebirth in the form realm [heavens]; 7) Desire for rebirth in the formless realm [heavens]; 8) "Conceit," i.e. the belief that "I" exist; 9) "Agitation" or "restlessness" that prevents deep concentration; and 10) "Ignorance."

five aggregates: 1) form; 2) feelings (i.e. sensations as received through eye, ear, nose, tongue, body, or mind); 3) perceptions; 4) karmic formative factors (such as volitions); and 5) consciousness (visual, auditory, olfactory, gustatory, tactile, and mental).

five desires: Wealth, sex, fame, flavors, and leisure or, alternatively, the objects of the five basic sense faculties (visual forms, sounds, smells, tastes, and touchables).

five faculties: faith; vigor; mindfulness; concentration; wisdom.

five heinous transgressions: The five heinous transgressions (五逆罪) refer to: patricide; matricide; killing an arhat; drawing the blood of a buddha; or causing a schism in the harmonious saṃgha.

five powers: When the five above-listed "five faculties" are perfected they become the five powers of faith, vigor, mindfulness, concentration, and wisdom.

five precepts: Five vows involving abstaining from killing, stealing, sexual misconduct, false speech, and intoxicants.

five sense faculties: The five sense faculties are those of the eyes, ears, nose, tongue, body, and mind.

four great elements: earth, water, fire, wind.

four right efforts: Causing already arisen evil to cease; causing not yet arisen evil to not arise; causing already arisen goodness to increase; causing not yet arisen goodness to arise.

four stations of mindfulness: Mindfulness of the body; mindfulness of feelings or sensations (experienced via the eye, ear, nose, tongue, body, and mind consciousnesses); mindfulness of thoughts or mind states; mindfulness of dharmas.

four truths / four truths of the Āryas: Suffering; its origination; its cessation; the path to its cessation.

G

gandharva: *Gandharvas* are a type of celestial music spirit that is said to rely on fragrances as their means of survival.

garuḍa: *Garuḍas* are a type of spirit that manifests as an immense golden-winged bird that feeds on young dragons.

ground, grounds: These are levels or planes of spiritual development through which a practitioner proceeds on the way to complete enlightenment.

H

hindrances: "Hindrances" usually refers to "the five hindrances" which are desire, ill will, lethargy-and-sleepiness, excitedness-and-regretfulness, and afflicted doubtfulness. These five hindrances must be overcome in order to successfully enter deep states of meditation.

I

inverted views: The four inverted views (*viparyāsa-catuṣka*) consist of imputing permanence to the impermanent, pleasure to what cannot deliver it, self to what is devoid of any inherently existent self, and purity to what does not actually possess that quality. Standard objects of such upside-down perception are: thought, or mind states, the six categories of "feeling" manifesting in association with the six sense faculties, dharmas (as components of the falsely imputed "self"), and the body.

K

kalpa: The Sanskrit "*kalpa*" roughly corresponds to the English term "eon" with the primary distinction being that, in Buddhist and Hindu cosmology, kalpas occur in various relatively precisely designated immensely long durations.

kāṣāya robe: The ochre-colored robe of a fully ordained bhikshu or bhikshuni.

koṭī: A *koṭī* is a number that is defined in the Flower Adornment Sutra Chapter Thirty as the product of multiplying a *lakṣa* (100,000) by a *lakṣa*. Hence it equals 10,000,000, i.e. ten million.

kṣaṇa: A *kṣaṇa,* corresponds to a micro-moment. This is variously defined, one traditional definition being "a ninetieth of a finger-snap." Elsewhere in the text, this may be referred to as "a single thought," "a mind-moment," or "a thought-moment" as approximate translations of the term.

kṣānti pāramitā: The perfection of patience.

M

mahāsattva: A *mahāsattva* is a great bodhisattva, one who has cultivated the bodhisattva path for countless kalpas.

Māra, *māras*: In Buddhism, Māra is generally regarded as the personification of evil and death who is also a particular deity dwelling in one of the desire realm heavens who delights in interfering with a practitioner's quest to gain spiritual liberation from perpetual rebirths in *saṃsāra*. More specifically, there are said to be four kinds of *māras*: 1) the *māra* of the five mental and physical aggregates in association with which all beings wander endlessly in *saṃsāra*; 2) the *māra* of the afflictions consisting of the three poisons of greed, hatred, and delusion and all of their subcategories; 3) the *māra* of death; and, as mentioned above, 3) the deity known as Māra as well as all of his *devaputra* minions. Additionally, there are also "ghost and spirit" *māras* who may manifest in countless ways to interfere with a practitioner's cultivation of the path.

mind-moment: See *kṣaṇa*.

mahorāga: *Mahorāgas* are a type of serpent spirit often portrayed as having the upper body of a human and the lower body of a snake.

moral precepts: the various sets of moral standards established by the Buddha as rules to be followed in a practitioner's cultivation of the path to spiritual awakening including the five precepts, the eight precepts, and the monastic precepts.

N

nayuta: A very large number, usually defined as a one hundred billion.

nirvāṇa: Nirvāṇa is the ultimate goal of the path of Buddhist spiritual cultivation that corresponds to the elimination of the three poisons (covetousness, aversion, delusion) and the ending of compulsory and random rebirth in *saṃsāra,* the cycle of existences in the deva realm, the demigod realm, the human realm, the animal realm, the hungry ghost realm, and the hell realms.

In the case of the individual liberation path practitioner exemplified by arhats and *pratyekabuddhas,* all future existence ends for them with the acquisition of nirvāṇa.

In the case of the universal liberation practitioners exemplified by bodhisattvas and buddhas, they achieve the direct cognition of the emptiness of all beings and phenomena and realize an ongoing realization of a nirvana-like state even as, by force of vow, they continue to take on intentional rebirths within *saṃsāra* in order to facilitate the spiritual liberation of all beings.

nirvāṇa without residue: The final nirvāṇa realized at death by fully awakened beings whether they be arhats, *pratyekabuddhas,* or buddhas.

P

pāramitā: One of the six (or ten) "perfections" cultivated and perfected by the bodhisattva on the path to buddhahood.

prajñā: *Prajnā* is the world-transcending wisdom that cognizes and understands all phenomena associated with "self," others, and the world as they truly are and in accordance with ultimate reality.

prajñā pāramitā: The perfection of wisdom.

pratyekabuddha: One who, in the absence of a buddha or his Dharma, achieves a level of enlightenment comparable to that of an arhat, doing so on his own through the contemplation of the cycle of dependent origination (*pratītyasamutpāda*). Mahāyāna literature attributes this ability to awaken in the absence of a buddha or his Dharma to direct exposure to the Dharma in previous lives, the seeds of which enable enlightenment in the present life.

R

rākṣasa: A swift flying malignant flesh-eating demon which changes its form to seduce humans and eat them.

rishi: (Sanskrit: *ṛṣi*; Chinese: 仙人) According to various definitions in Monier Williams Sanskrit-English Dictionary, the meaning of *rishi* connotes: "a saint or sanctified sage in general, an ascetic, anchorite (this is a later sense; sometimes three orders of these are enumerated, viz. Devarṣis, Brahmarṣis, and Rājarṣis; sometimes seven, four others being added, viz. Maharṣis, Paramarṣis, Śrutarṣis, and Kāṇḍarṣis).

S

samādhi: Samādhi refers both to any single instance of one-pointed concentration and also, more usually, to enduring states of persistently maintained one-pointed concentration.

saṃghāṭī robe: The *saṃghāṭī* is the monastic's outer robe.

saṃsāra: *Saṃsāra,* for which the usual Sino-Buddhist rendering is "births-and-deaths," *shengsi* (生死), refers to the endless cycle of rebirths in the six realms of rebirth: devas (gods), *asuras* ("demigods" or "titans"), humans, animals, hungry ghosts (*preta*), and hell-dwellers.

Saṃgha – The Sanskrit spelling of the Pali word "Sangha." In the context of the Three Refuges, "the Saṃgha" refers to "the *ārya* Saṃgha" consisting exclusively of those who have awakened to one of the stages of the path. Otherwise, in common parlance, it may refer simply to "the common Saṃgha" consisting of monks and nuns.

As a group, a "saṃgha" is a community of at least ten fully ordained bhikshus in Buddhist countries or at least five fully ordained bhikshus in countries where Buddhism is only just being established for the first time. As noted above, the third object of refuge in "the Three Refuges" or "the Three Jewels," refers exclusively to those persons who have already acquired one of the fruits of the path from which they can never fall away, whether on the individual-liberation paths of the arhats or *pratyekabuddhas*, or on the universal-liberation path of the bodhisattva.

seven enlightenment factors: assessment or skillful selection of dharmas; vigor; joy; mental pliancy; concentration; equanimity with respect to the saṃskāra (karmic formative factors) aggregate.

śikṣamāṇā: A *śikṣamāṇā* is a novice nun during an initial two-year probationary period.

śīla: *Śīla* refers to moral virtue in general and the moral precepts in particular.

śīla pāramitā: The perfection of moral virtue.

six rebirth destinies: gods (*deva*), demi-gods or titans (*asura*), humans, hungry ghosts (*pretas*), animals, and hell-dwellers.

six sense faculties: The "six sense faculties" refer to the sense faculties of eye, ear, nose, tongue, body, and mind.

skandha: See "aggregates."

skillful means: "Skillful means" (*upāya*) are individually tailored skillful techniques adopted by the bodhisattva in teaching the various kinds of beings. These various techniques are adopted precisely because all beings are possessed of different capacities, karmic obstacles and predilections due to which they respond best to individually tailored teachings.

spiritual superknowledges: The usual Sanskrit antecedent for "spiritual superknowledges" is *abhijñā* ("superknowledges") or *ṛddhi* ("supernatural powers"). This includes such abilities as "the six superknowledges" (the spiritual powers, the heavenly eye, the heavenly ear, the cognition of others' thoughts, past life recall for both self and others, and complete elimination of all "defiling contaminants" or "taints" [*āsrava*]).

śramaṇera: A *śramaṇera* is a novice monk.

śramaṇerikā: A *śramaṇerikā* is a novice nun.

śramaṇa: More generally, a *śramaṇa* is a mendicant, one who has left the home life and relies on alms for sustenance. In the Buddhist context, this refers specifically to a bhikshu, i.e. a Buddhist monk.

śrāvaka, śrāvaka disciple: A follower of the individual-liberation path to arhatship.

stream enterer: The stream enterer (*srota-āpanna*) is one who has gained the first of the four fruits of the path to arhatship.

sutra: A scripture attributed to the Buddha.

T

Tathāgata: "*Tathāgata*" ("Thus Come One") is one of the ten primary titles by which all buddhas are known.

Ten directions: North, south, east, west, the four midpoints, the zenith, and the nadir.

Three Jewels: The Buddha, the Dharma, and the Ārya Sangha.

Three periods of time: Past, present, and future.

Three Realms: Also referred to as "the three realms of existence," this refers to the desire realm, the form realm (a.k.a. "the subtle form realm"), and the formless realm. All beings, from the those in the lowest hells to those in the highest heavens, reside within these three realms of existence.

Three Refuges: The Buddha, the Dharma, and the Ārya Sangha, the Three Jewels in which one "takes the refuges" to become a Buddhist disciple and upon which one must rely to advance on the Buddhist path.

Three Vehicles: The Śrāvaka-disciple Vehicle, the Pratyekabuddha Vehicle, and the Great Vehicle (Mahāyāna) the endpoints of which are arhatship, *pratyekabuddhahood*, and buddhahood.

three wretched destinies: The three wretched destinies (*trayo durgatayaḥ*) consist of rebirth as either an animal, a hungry ghost (*preta*), or a hell dweller.

trichiliocosm: A world system consisting of countless worlds.

tripiṭaka: The three divisions of the three-fold Buddhist canon, otherwise known as "the Tripiṭaka": the sutras (scriptures attributed to the Buddha or disciples authorized by the Buddha), the commentarial treatises (śāstra), and the moral codes (*vinaya*).

tripiṭaka master: A "*tripiṭaka* master" is someone who has completely mastered the three divisions of the three-fold Buddhist canon.

twelve sense bases: the six sense faculties (eye, ear, nose, tongue, body, and mind) and their respective sense objects (visual forms, sounds, smells, tastes, touchables, and ideas, etc. as objects of mind).

Two Vehicles: The two individual liberation vehicles taught by the Buddha, the Śrāvaka-disciple Vehicle leading to arhatship and the Pratyekabuddha Vehicle leading to pratyekabuddhahood.

U

upāsaka: An *upāsaka* is a Buddhist layman who has taken the three refuges and who observes the five precepts.

upāsikā: An upāsikā is a Buddhist laywoman who has taken the three refuges and who observes the five precepts.

V

vajra: An indestructible substance equated with the diamond. A symbol of indestructibility. Also, a pestle shaped sceptre or "thunderbolt" weapon held by Dharma protectors and deities.

vinaya: The Vinaya is one of the three primary divisions of the Buddhist canon. It contains all of the authoritative pronouncements on moral ethics in general and in particular articulates the various sets of moral codes for the different categories of Buddhist disciples among the monks, the nuns, and the laity.

vīrya pāramitā: The perfection of vigor.

W

wheel-turning king: In Buddhism, a "wheel-turning king" (*cakravartin*) is a universal monarch.

worthy: In Mahāyāna literature, a "worthy" (*bhadra*) is a bodhisattva practitioner who has brought forth the bodhisattva vow but who is still cultivating the preparatory stages and thus has not yet reached the ten bodhisattva grounds and has not yet become an ārya.

wretched destinies: The three wretched destinies consist of rebirth among animals, among hungry ghosts (*pretas*), or in the hells.

Y

yakṣa: *Yakṣas* are a kind of either good or evil spirit possessed of supernatural powers that may either serve as a guardian or a demon.

yojana: A measure of distance in ancient India usually defined as being the distance that an ox cart would travel in a day without unharnessing (somewhat less than ten miles).

Part Two Variant Readings in Other Chinese Editions

Fascicle Thirteen Variant Readings

【經文資訊】大正新脩大藏經第 25 冊 No. 1509 大智度論
【版本記錄】CBETA 電子佛典 Rev. 1.18 (Big5)，完成日期：2004/03/16
【編輯說明】本資料庫由中華電子佛典協會（CBETA）依大正新脩大藏經所編輯
【原始資料】維習安大德提供，佛教電腦資訊庫功德會提供，眾生出版社提供，厚觀法師提供，北美某大德提供，其他
【其他事項】本資料庫可自由免費流通，詳細內容請參閱【中華電子佛典協會資料庫版權說明】

[0153006]〔中〕－【宋】【元】【宮】
[0153007] 義第二十一＝上第二十二【宋】，＝上【元】，
　　　　＝上第十七【宮】，＝上第六【石】，〔義第二十一〕－【明】
[0153008]〔【經】〕－【宋】【宮】【石】
[0153009]〔【論】〕－【宋】【宮】【石】
[0153010] 秦＝此【明】
[0153011]〔相〕－【宋】【元】【明】【宮】【石】
[0153012] 天＋（天）【石】
[0153013] 猗＝倚【元】
[0153014]〔持戒〕－【宋】【宮】【石】
[0153015]〔將來〕－【宋】【宮】【石】
[0153016]〔令人〕－【元】【明】
[0153017] 欲＝求【宋】【宮】【石】
[0153018] 得＝求【宋】【宮】【石】
[0153019] 苦＝共【石】
[0153020] 祀＝禮【石】
[0153021]〔能〕－【宋】【宮】【石】
[0153022] 政＝正【宋】【元】【明】【宮】＊［＊1］
[0153023] 考＝拷【宋】【元】【明】【宮】＊［＊1］
[0154001] 所＝何【宮】
[0154002] 自＝亦【宮】
[0154003] 物＝利【宋】【元】【明】【宮】【石】
[0154004]〔周滿〕－【宋】【宮】【石】
[0154005] 行禪＝禪定【宋】【元】【明】【宮】【石】
[0154006]〔以是…戒〕八字－【宋】【元】【明】【宮】【石】
[0154007] 苽＝瓜【元】【明】
[0154008] 大＝火【宋】【元】【明】【宮】
[0154009] 群＋（中）【宋】【元】【明】【宮】【石】

[0154010] 儜＝[病-丙+(心/皿/丁)]【宋】【宮】
[0154011] 林＋（中）【宋】【元】【明】【宮】
[0154012] 鍱＝葉【宮】
[0154013] 鬼＝卒【宋】【元】【明】【宮】【石】
[0154014] 惡＝便【宮】
[0154015] 〔大智度論釋初品中戒相義第二十二之一〕－【宮】【石】，〔大智度論〕－【明】＊
[0154016] 第二十二之一＝第二十三【宋】，－【元】【明】
[0154017] 〔名〕－【宋】【宮】【石】
[0154018] 〔相〕－【宋】【宮】【石】＊［＊ 1]
[0154019] 作＋（是名為戒）【元】【明】
[0154020] 〔名〕－【宋】【元】【明】【宮】【石】
[0154021] 故＝殺【宮】
[0154022] 生＋（惡）【元】【明】
[0154023] 罪＋（相）【元】【明】
[0154024] 〔果〕－【宋】【元】【明】【宮】
[0155001] 隨＝限【宋】
[0155002] 無＋（量）【石】
[0155003] 無漏＝不繫【宋】【元】【明】【宮】【石】
[0155004] 〔法〕－【宋】【宮】【石】
[0155005] 〔時〕－【宋】【元】【明】【宮】【石】
[0155006] 〔丹注…戒〕十五字－【宋】【元】【明】【宮】【石】
[0155007] 〔丹注…證〕七字－【宋】【元】【明】【宮】【石】
[0155008] 〔丹注…上〕八字－【宋】【元】【明】【宮】【石】
[0155009] 〔法〕－【宋】【元】【明】【宮】【石】
[0155010] 〔戒〕－【宋】【元】【明】【宮】【石】
[0155011] 〔非心相應法〕－【宋】【元】【明】【宮】【石】
[0155012] 〔皆〕－【宋】【石】
[0155013] 〔丹注…也〕十一字－【宋】【元】【明】【宮】【石】
[0155014] 令＝今【元】【明】【石】
[0155015] 行獨遊＝獨遊行【宋】【元】【明】【宮】【石】
[0155016] 〔人〕－【宋】【元】【明】【宮】【石】
[0155017] 兩＝後【宮】【石】
[0155018] 入＋（汝）【石】
[0155019] 〔罪〕－【宋】【元】【明】【宮】【石】
[0155020] 刑＝形【石】
[0155021] 生＋（口言）【宋】【元】【明】
[0155022] 〔已〕－【宋】【元】【明】【宮】

[0155023] 中＝申【石】
[0155024] 泥梨＝泥犁【宋】【元】【明】【宮】下同
[0155025] 昆＝蜫【宋】【元】【明】【宮】
[0155026] 全＝令【石】＊［＊ 1 2 3 4 5］
[0156001] 倍＝億【宮】
[0156002] 可＝以【宋】【宮】【石】
[0156003] 計挍＝校計【宋】【元】【明】【宮】【石】
[0156004] 者＋（是）【宋】【元】【明】【宮】【石】
[0156005] 〔為〕－【宋】【元】【明】【宮】【石】
[0156006] 〔有〕－【宋】【宮】
[0156007] 被＝[月*皮]【宮】
[0156008] 〔等〕－【宮】【石】
[0156009] 偈說＝說偈【石】
[0156010] 穿踰＝穿窬【宋】【元】【明】【宮】，
＝[穴/身]踰【石】
[0156011] 〔故〕－【宋】【宮】
[0156012] 罪重＝重罪【元】【明】，＝罪【宮】
[0156013] 劇＝處【宋】【元】【明】【宮】
[0156014] 懊＝淚【石】
[0156015] 〔若〕－【宋】【元】【明】【宮】
[0156016] 不作＝放捨【宋】【元】【明】【宮】【石】
[0156017] 而＋（偷）【宋】【元】【明】【宮】，〔而〕－【石】
[0156018] 強＝健【宮】【石】
[0156019] 禍＝福【石】
[0156020] 〔丹注云重罪人疑〕－【宋】【石】，〔丹注云〕
－【元】【明】
[0156021] 行時＝時行【宋】【元】【明】【宮】【石】
[0156022] 朋＝多【宮】
[0156023] 〔若〕－【宮】
[0156024] 誑誘＝誘誑【宋】【元】【明】【宮】
[0156025] 娠＝身【宋】【元】【明】【宮】【石】＊［＊ 1 2］
[0156026] 〔如是…種〕十二字－【宋】【元】【明】【宮】【石】
[0156027] 〔丹注…罪〕十五字－【宋】【元】【明】【宮】【石】
[0156028] 妷＝泆【宋】【元】【明】【宮】
[0156029] 態＝能【石】
[0157001] 恚我若＝毒若我【宋】【元】【明】【宮】【石】
[0157002] 〔所〕－【宋】【元】【明】【宮】
[0157003] 〔賊〕－【石】

[0157004] 解生＝生解【石】
[0157005] 人＋（為）【石】
[0157006] 力＝為【宮】
[0157007] 洗＝浴【宋】【元】【明】【宮】
[0157008] 祇洹＝祇桓【宋】【元】【宮】【石】
[0157009] 故＝欲【宮】
[0157010] 野人＝人為【宮】＊ [＊ 1]
[0157011] 此＝是【宋】【元】【明】【宮】
[0157012] 事＝意【宋】【元】【明】【宮】【石】
[0157013] 奈＝奈【宋】【元】【明】，＝柰【宮】
[0157014] 嗥哭＝號咷【宋】【元】【明】【宮】
[0157015] 獄＋（地獄）【石】
[0157016] 天＝王【石】
[0157017] 阿＝呵【宋】【元】【明】【宮】【石】＊ [＊ 1 2 3]
[0157018] （五）＋百【宋】【元】【明】【宮】【石】
[0158001] 夫士之生＝夫世之士【宮】
[0158002] 毒苦＝苦毒【宋】【元】【明】【宮】
[0158003] 十＝千【石】
[0158004] 五＝三【宮】
[0158005] 形＝刑【石】
[0158006] 槃＝盤【宋】【元】【明】【宮】＊ [＊ 1]
[0158007] 語＝謀【宋】【元】【明】【宮】【石】
[0158008] 蒱桃＝蒲萄【宋】【元】【明】【宮】，＝蒲陶【石】
[0158009] 麴＝麯【宋】【元】【明】【宮】
[0158010] 蹄＝跡【宮】
[0158011] 以＋（故）【宋】【元】【明】【宮】
[0158012] 現＋（在）【宋】【元】【明】【宮】
[0158013] 病＝疾【宋】【元】【明】【宮】
[0158014] 怳＝恍【宋】【元】【明】【宮】
[0158015] 色＝已【元】【明】
[0158016] 語＝言【宋】【元】【明】【宮】
[0158017] 事重＝重事【宋】【元】【明】【宮】【石】
[0158018] 〔自〕－【宋】【元】【明】【宮】
[0159001] 聾＝瓏【宋】【宮】
[0159002] 映繡＝照文繡【元】【明】
[0159003] 愛＝服【宋】【元】【明】【宮】【石】
[0159004] 鬚＝飾【宮】【石】
[0159005] 妊＝任【石】
[0159006] 嬉＝熙【元】【明】

[0159007] 〔故〕－【宋】【元】【明】【宮】【石】
[0159008] 富＝福【宋】【元】【明】【宮】
[0159009] 〔能〕－【宋】【元】【明】【宮】
[0159010] 甚＝最【宋】【元】【明】【宮】
[0159011] 過＝失【宋】【元】【明】【宮】【石】
[0159012] 秦＝此【明】
[0159013] 共住＝善宿【宋】【元】【明】【宮】【石】
[0159014] 〔如〕－【宋】【元】【明】【宮】
[0159015] 〔亦〕－【宋】【元】【明】【宮】
[0159016] 〔願〕－【宋】【元】【明】【宮】
[0159017] 〔得〕－【宋】【元】【明】【宮】【石】
[0159018] 掌＝手【宮】【石】
[0159019] 二＝一【宮】
[0159020] 〔我〕－【宋】【元】【明】【宮】【石】
[0159021] 〔是〕－【宋】【元】【明】【宮】【石】
[0160001] 業＝德【宋】【元】【明】【宮】【石】
[0160002] 〔一〕－【石】
[0160003] 悅＋（說）【宋】【元】【明】【宮】【石】
[0160004] （諸）＋天【宋】【元】【明】【宮】【石】
[0160005] 〔見諸天歡喜〕－【宮】【石】
[0160006] 三＝五【宋】【元】【明】【宮】
[0160007] 〔行〕－【宋】【元】【明】【宮】
[0160008] 〔神〕－【宋】【元】【明】【宮】
[0160009] 〔神父〕－【石】
[0160010] 〔八〕－【宋】【元】【明】【宮】
[0160011] 將＝持【宋】【元】【明】【宮】【石】
[0160012] 役＝伎【宮】
[0160013] 危＝厄【宋】【元】【明】【宮】
[0160014] 剋＝克【宋】【元】【明】【宮】
[0160015] 〔得〕－【石】
[0160016] 〔大智…三〕十九字－【宮】【石】
[0160017] 〔羅〕－【宋】【元】【明】【宮】
[0160018] 〔第二十三〕－【元】【明】
[0160019] 三＝四【宋】
[0161001] 業＝生【石】
[0161002] 紛＝忿【宋】【元】【明】【宮】
[0161003] 〔當〕－【宋】【元】【明】【宮】【石】
[0161004] 〔具足〕－【宋】【元】【明】【宮】【石】
[0161005] 〔有〕－【宋】【元】【明】【宮】【石】

[0161006] 愁＝疑【宋】【元】【明】【宮】【石】
[0161007] 戒＝形【元】【明】
[0161008] 優＝欝【宋】【元】【明】【宮】【石】
[0161009] 女＋（皆）【宋】【元】【明】【宮】
[0161010] 祇洹＝祇桓【宋】【元】【宮】【石】
[0161011] 〔後〕－【宋】【元】【明】【宮】【石】
[0161012] 那＝尼【宋】【元】【宮】
[0161013] 和上＝和尚【宋】【元】【明】【宮】下同
[0161014] 阿闍梨＝阿闍黎【明】下同
[0161015] 裟＋（衣）【宋】【元】【明】【宮】【石】
[0161016] 剃＝涕【宮】
[0161017] 手＋（急）【宋】【元】【明】【宮】
[0161018] 〔何〕－【石】
[0161019] 歲＝年【宋】【元】【明】【宮】
[0161020] 〔戒〕－【宋】【元】【明】【宮】【石】
[0161021] 〔是名…法〕九字－【石】
[0161022] 〔名〕－【宋】【元】【明】【宮】
[0161023] 〔受六法是式叉摩那〕八字－【宋】【元】【明】【宮】，〔受六法〕－【石】
[0161024] 〔欲〕－【宋】【元】【明】【宮】【石】
[0161025] 〔用〕－【宮】【石】
[0161026] 盂＝杅【石】＊［＊ 1］
[0161027] 〔百〕－【石】
[0161028] 羯磨＝羯摩【宋】【元】【宮】
[0161029] 訖＝說【元】

Fascicle Fourteen Variant Readings

【經文資訊】大正新脩大藏經第 25 冊 No. 1509 大智度論
【版本記錄】CBETA 電子佛典 Rev. 1.18 (Big5)，完成日期：2004/03/16
【編輯說明】本資料庫由中華電子佛典協會（CBETA）依大正新脩大藏經所編輯
【原始資料】維習安大德提供，佛教電腦資訊庫功德會提供，眾生出版社提供，厚觀法師提供，北美某大德提供，其他
【其他事項】本資料庫可自由免費流通，詳細內容請參閱【中華電子佛典協會資料庫版權說明】

[0162001] 義之餘＝下第二十三之餘【宋】，＝下【元】，＝之餘【明】，＝下第十八【宮】，＝下第十八羼提波羅蜜上【石】
[0162002] 上＝是【石】
[0162003] 全＝令【石】
[0162004] 往＝住【宮】
[0162005] 服＝莊【宮】
[0162006] 按＝桉【宮】，＝案【石】
[0162007] 眠＝眼【宋】【元】【明】
[0162008] 絕＝終【宋】【元】【明】【宮】
[0162009] 是＝也【宋】【元】【明】【宮】【石】
[0162010] 虛＝稱【元】【明】
[0162011] 智慧＝善智【宋】【元】【明】【宮】【石】＊ [＊1]
[0162012] 〔得〕－【宋】【元】【明】【宮】【石】
[0162013] （清）＋淨【宋】【元】【明】【宮】
[0162014] 熏＝動【石】
[0162015] 至＝生【宋】【宮】【石】
[0162016] 律儀戒＝戒律儀【宋】【元】【明】【宮】＊ [＊1]
[0162017] 名＝則【宋】【元】【明】【宮】
[0162018] 持＝治【宋】【元】【明】【宮】【石】
[0162019] 明註曰間南藏作門
[0162020] 走＝赴【宋】【宮】【石】
[0162021] 蹶＝蹸【宮】
[0162022] 求自＝自求【宋】【元】【明】【宮】
[0162023] 有時＝時間【宋】【元】【明】【宮】【石】
[0162024] 屏＝避【宋】【宮】【石】，＝并【元】
[0163001] 干＝千【宮】
[0163002] 明註曰間關南藏作門開
[0163003] 差＝瘥【宋】【元】【明】【宮】
[0163004] 畢＝得【宋】【元】【明】【宋】【石】
[0163005] 持＝於【宋】【元】【明】【宮】【石】

[0163006] 諸＋（不）【宋】【宮】【石】
[0163007] 結使＝使結【石】
[0163008] 逸＝實【宋】【元】【明】【宮】【石】
[0163009] 人＝下【宋】【宮】【石】
[0163010] 上＝下【石】
[0163011] 〔若〕－【宋】【元】【明】【宮】【石】
[0163012] 衆＋（生）【石】
[0163013] 污＝淤【元】【明】
[0163014] 〔者〕－【宋】【元】【明】【宮】【石】
[0163015] 〔慧〕－【宋】【元】【明】【宮】
[0163016] 如是名＝如是等名【宋】【元】【明】【宮】，＝如是等【石】
[0163017] 惑＝戒盜【宋】【元】【明】，＝戒【宮】，＝惑盜【石】
[0163018] 於＝持【石】
[0163019] 〔故〕－【宋】【元】【明】【宮】【石】
[0163020] 若＋（人）【宋】【元】【明】【宮】【石】
[0163021] 謂＝為【宋】【元】【明】【宮】
[0163022] 〔也若〕－【宋】【元】【明】【宮】
[0163023] 無戒＝戒無【石】
[0163024] （不）＋可【元】【明】＊
[0163025] 不＋（可）【元】【明】＊［＊ 1］
[0163026] 有＝出【宋】【宮】【石】
[0163027] 〔滿〕－【宋】【元】【明】【宮】
[0163028] 已＝以【石】＊［＊ 1］
[0163029] 拳＝捲【石】＊［＊ 1］
[0164001] 狀＝床【宋】【宮】
[0164002] 〔應〕－【宋】【元】【明】【宮】【石】
[0164003] 至＝生【石】
[0164004] 樂＋（殺）【元】【明】

About the Translator

Bhikshu Dharmamitra (ordination name "Heng Shou" – 釋恆授) is a Chinese-tradition translator-monk and one of the earliest American disciples (since 1968) of the late Guiyang Ch'an patriarch, Dharma teacher, and pioneer of Buddhism in the West, the Venerable Master Hsuan Hua (宣化上人). He has a total of 42 years in robes during two periods as a monastic (1969–1975 & 1991 to the present).

Dharmamitra's principal educational foundations as a translator of Sino-Buddhist Classical Chinese lie in four years of intensive monastic training and Chinese-language study of classic Mahāyāna texts in a small-group setting under Master Hsuan Hua (1968–1972), undergraduate Chinese language study at Portland State University, a year of intensive one-on-one Classical Chinese study at the Fu Jen University Language Center near Taipei (1987–1988), two years of course work in Classical Chinese at the University of Washington's Department of Asian Languages and Literature (1988–90), and an additional three years of auditing graduate courses and seminars in Classical Chinese readings, again at UW's Department of Asian Languages and Literature (2016–2018).

Since taking robes again under Master Hua in 1991, Dharmamitra has devoted his energies primarily to study and translation of classic Mahāyāna texts with a special interest in works by Ārya Nāgārjuna and related authors. To date, he has translated more than fifteen important texts comprising approximately 150 fascicles, including most recently the 80-fascicle *Avataṃsaka Sūtra* (the "Flower Adornment Sutra"), Nāgārjuna's 17-fascicle *Daśabhūmika Vibhāṣa* ("Treatise on the Ten Grounds"), and the *Daśabhūmika Sūtra* (the "Ten Grounds Sutra"), all of which are current Kalavinka Press publications.

Kalavinka Buddhist Classics

(http: www.kalavinka.org)

Spring, 2024 Title List

Meditation Instruction Texts

The Essentials of Buddhist Meditation

A marvelously complete classic *śamathā-vipaśyanā* (calming-and-insight) meditation manual. By Tiantai Śramaṇa Zhiyi (538–597).

Six Gates to the Sublime

The early Indian Buddhist meditation method involving six practices used in calming-and-insight meditation. By Śramaṇa Zhiyi

Bodhisattva Path Texts

The Flower Adornment Sutra (3 Volumes, 2490 pages)

Bhikshu Dharmamitra's English translation of *The Mahāvaipulya Buddha Avataṃsaka Sūtra* edition translated from Sanskrit in 699 CE by Tripiṭaka Master Śikṣānanda (T0279: 大方廣佛華嚴經)

On Generating the Resolve to Become a Buddha

On the Resolve to Become a Buddha by Ārya Nāgārjuna
Exhortation to Resolve on Buddhahood by Patriarch Sheng'an Shixian
Exhortation to Resolve on Buddhahood by the Tang Literatus, Peixiu

Letter from a Friend - The Three Earliest Editions

The earliest extant editions of Ārya Nāgārjuna's *Suhṛlekkha*:
As Translated by Tripiṭaka Master Guṇavarman (*ca* 425 CE)
As Translated by Tripiṭaka Master Saṇghavarman (*ca* 450 CE)
As Translated by Tripiṭaka Master Yijing (*ca* 675 CE).

Marvelous Stories from the Perfection of Wisdom

130 Stories from Ārya Nāgārjuna's *Mahāprājñāpāramitā Upadeśa.*

Nāgārjuna's Guide to the Bodhisattva Path

The Bodhisaṃbhāra Treatise with abridged Vaśitva commentary.

The Bodhisaṃbhāra Treatise Commentary

The complete exegesis by the Indian Bhikshu Vaśitva (*ca* 300–500).

Nāgārjuna on Mindfulness of the Buddha

Ch. 9 and Chs. 20–25 of Nāgārjuna's *Daśabhūmika Vibhāṣā*
Ch. 1, Subchapter 36a of Nāgārjuna's *Mahāprājñāpāramitā Upadeśa.*

Nāgārjuna on the Six Perfections

Ch. 1, Subchapters 17–30 of Nāgārjuna's *Mahāprājñāpāramitā Upadeśa.*

A Strand of Dharma Jewels (Ārya Nāgārjuna's *Ratnāvalī*)
The earliest extant edition, translated by Paramārtha: *ca* 550 CE

The Ten Bodhisattva Grounds
Śikṣānanda's translation of The Flower Adornment Sutra, Ch. 26

Nāgārjuna's Treatise on the Ten Bodhisattva Grounds
Nāgārjuna's 35-chapter *Daśabhūmika Vibhāṣā*

The Ten Grounds Sutra
Kumārajīva's translation of the *Daśabhūmika Sūtra*

Vasubandhu's Treatise on the Bodhisattva Vow
By Vasubandhu Bodhisattva (*ca* 300 CE)

Bodhisattva Moral Virtue (*Śīla*) Texts

The Bodhisattva's Practice of Moral Virtue
Part One: The Brahmā's Net Sutra Bodhisattva Precepts
Part One Supplement: The Semimonthly Bodhisattva Precepts Recitation Ceremony
Part Two: Nāgārjuna on the Perfection of Moral Virtue (from Ārya Nāgārjuna's *Mahāprajñāpāramitā Upadeśa*)

www.ingramcontent.com/pod-product-compliance
Lightning Source LLC
Chambersburg PA
CBHW020741160426
43192CB00006B/234
* 9 7 8 1 9 3 5 4 1 3 3 8 7 *